Birnbaum's

Walt Disney World®

Stephen Birnbaum
Founding Editor

Tom Passavant
Editorial Director

Deanna Caron
Pamela S. Weiers
Senior Editors

Todd Sebastian Williams
Associate Art Director

Steve Ferazani
Alice Garrard
Contributing Editors

Miranda Spencer
Copy Editor

Alexandra Mayes Birnbaum
Consulting Editor

HYPERION AND HEARST BUSINESS PUBLISHING, INC.

Table of

7   Getting Ready to Go

Here is all the practical information you need to organize a Walt Disney World visit, down to the smallest detail: when to go; how to get there; how to save money; plus hints for parents, travelers with disabilities, singles, and older visitors.

See our exclusive guide to 25th anniversary happenings on page 15!

45   Transportation & Accommodations

The fundamental questions at Walt Disney World are where to stay and how to get around. Accommodations range from luxurious hotel suites to modest campsites, with thousands of hotel rooms, villas—even treehouses—in between. Our comprehensive guide describes fully all the resorts at Walt Disney World, along with some lodging options off the property. We also tell you how to use the World's extensive transportation system.

91   Magic Kingdom

The enchantment of Walt Disney World is most apparent in the host of attractions and amusements that fill this, the most famous entertainment oasis anywhere. Our land-by-land guide describes all there is to see and do, where to shop, and how to avoid the crowds, plus plenty of other insider tips.

125   Epcot

A gleaming silver geosphere introduces Walt Disney World's greatest adventure—an ambitious exploration of the world of the future as well as the present. Future World and World Showcase offer every visitor the opportunity to be a global and cerebral voyager, without ever setting foot outside Central Florida. Here's how to make the most of this uniquely fascinating destination.

Contents

For Steve, who merely made all this possible.

ISBN: 0-7868-8192-5

Printed in the United States of America

Other 1997 Birnbaum Travel Guides

Bahamas and Turks & Caicos
Bermuda
Canada
Cancun/Cozumel & Isla Mujeres
Caribbean
Country Inns & Back Roads
Disneyland
Hawaii
Mexico
Miami & Ft. Lauderdale
United States
Walt Disney World For Kids, By Kids
Walt Disney World Without Kids

A WORD FROM THE EDITORS

For some of us, our first Walt Disney World experience dates back to 1971, the year this "Disneyland in Florida" made its debut. At that time, there was only one theme park, the Magic Kingdom, and it could be explored easily in a few days. Early visitors will remember, too, that many attractions were still under construction. Nonetheless, for those who came, it was usually love at first sight, and we've returned again and again.

But can it really be *25 years*—a full quarter century since that initial encounter? Well, the calendar doesn't lie, and just as Walt Disney World has prepared one amazing celebration, so have we buffed and polished this guide and added an exclusive section providing all the incredible details about the grandest party the World has ever seen. And, as the Official Guide, we couldn't help but sprinkle a little pixie dust of our own. We hope you'll follow this star-spangled trail to your best Walt Disney World vacation yet.

When Steve Birnbaum launched this guide back in 1981, he made it very clear what was expected of anyone who worked on it. The book would be meticulously revised each year, leaving no attraction untested, no snack or meal untasted, no hotel untried. When Steve became curious as to how efficiently the bus system ran at Walt Disney World, he dispatched an editor to spend an entire day riding buses around the resort and report her findings. (The buses did, by the way, run on schedule.)

It is experiences like these, accumulated over the past 16 years, that make this book the most authoritative guide to the World. That expertise, however, has been achieved not by our being escorted through back doors of attractions or bypassing lines, but rather by waiting with all the other visitors in hopes of uncovering strategies that would allow readers to avoid the pitfalls many first-timers encounter. In one typical case, an editor waited more than an hour to take a backstage tour at the Studios. Standing in line with notebook and tape recorder in hand, she was asked by the man behind her if there was a quiz at the end. When she explained what she was doing, he expressed surprise to learn that she was waiting with the rest of the hordes. How better, she replied, to help people like you?

After a full quarter century, the World—and the number of visitors passing through it—have expanded enormously. On some occasions, we've encountered sweltering weather and swelling crowds, times when even the happiest of families or best of friends turn into arch-enemies for the day. At times the lines seemed endless and, in a triumph of bad planning, we managed to take in just a few attractions before dinnertime. Had we known then what we know now, we could have spared ourselves some trying experiences.

What we've endeavored to do in this book is keep you from making the same mistakes. This marks the 16th annual edition of this guide, and we've learned a lot about Walt Disney World over the years. More important, we now know that even the most meticulous vacation planner needs detailed, accurate, and objective information to prepare an intelligent itinerary.

Anyone who takes the time to read even the outlines of the pages that follow will find an emerging pattern that fits his or her special needs and tastes; for those unwilling to exert even that much effort, we've compiled specific day-by-day itineraries for visits of varying length—in order to protect you from yourself.

This guidebook owes an enormous debt to the special people who manage and run Walt Disney World. Despite the designation "Official Guide," we want to stress that *the Walt Disney World staff members have exercised no veto power whatsoever over the contents of this book.* What they *have* done is opened their files and explained operations to us in the most generous way, so that we could prepare the comprehensive appraisals, charts, and schedules that are necessary to help visitors understand the very complex workings of a very complex enterprise.

We daresay there have been times when the Disney folks are less than delighted with some of our opinions, yet these statements all remain in the guide. Furthermore, we've been flattered again and again by Disney staff who've commented about how much they've learned from the material presented here.

As for our readers, we firmly believe that the combination of our years of experience and independent voice, together with our access to accurate, up-to-date inside information from the Disney staff, makes this book uniquely useful. We even like to think it's indispensable, but we'll let you be the judge of that a couple of hundred pages from now.

The fact remains that this guide would never have become as useful as it is without the extremely forthcoming cooperation of Walt Disney World personnel at every level. Both in the park and behind the scenes, they've been the source of the most critical factual data. We hope we're not omitting any names in specifically thanking Kim Carlson (Information Management); Robin Domigan (Resorts); Jack Holland (Product Development); Dwight Dorr (Transportation); Greg Albrecht and Rick Sylvain (Publicity); and Gene Duncan and Robbie Pallard (Photography). To Tom Elrod, Bo Boyd, Marty Sklar, Charlie Ridgway, Linda Warren, Julie Woodward, Laura Simpson, Diane Hancock, Mariella Ure, and Richard Gregorie, who do so much to make our job easier (and often possible), more thanks for their extraordinary help.

We'd also like to thank our favorite off-site Disney expert, Wendy Lefkon, who edited these guides for many years and is still instrumental in their publication as executive editor at Hyperion. Hats off to Shari Hartford, who kept our own cast of characters on schedule; Susan Hohl, who provided valuable artistic input; and Laura Vitale, for her wondrously uncompromising sense of style.

Of course, no list of acknowledgments would be complete without mentioning our founding editor, Steve Birnbaum, whose spirit, wisdom, and humor still infuse these pages, as well as Alexandra Mayes Birnbaum, who continues to be a guiding light—to say nothing of a careful reader of every word.

Finally, it's important to remember that every worthwhile travel guide is a living enterprise; while the book that you hold in your hands may be our best effort at explaining how to enjoy Walt Disney World at this moment, its text is in no way cast in bronze. Walt Disney World is constantly changing and growing, and in each annual revision we expect to refine and expand our material to serve our readers' needs even better. For this year's edition, though, this must be the final word.

Have a great visit!

The Editors

Don't Forget to Write...

No contribution is of greater value to us in preparing the next edition of this book than your comments on what we have written and on your own experiences at Walt Disney World. Please share your insights with us by writing to:

The Editors, Official Disney Guides
1790 Broadway, Sixth Floor
New York, NY 10019

Getting Ready to Go

The key to a fabulous vacation at Walt Disney World is advance planning, especially during this 25th anniversary year. This remarkably varied complex is just too vast and diverse to allow a spontaneous visit to be undertaken with much success—especially when you consider the rapid rate at which it is expanding. That doesn't mean that even the most casual visitors can't have some significant fun, but they're bound to have regrets later about things they didn't get to see because of time pressures or a simple lack of information. The primary purpose of this guide is to eliminate that potential frustration.

What follows, then, is intended to provide a sensible scheme for planning a satisfying visit to Walt Disney World, one that will offer the most fun and the least disappointment. But where do you start? One of the very best ways to judge which of the countless activities in the World most appeal to you and your family is to have a clear idea of all that is available well before arriving in the Orlando area.

 Unless otherwise noted, all phone numbers are in area code 407.

WHEN TO GO

When talk finally turns to the best time to make a trip to Walt Disney World, Christmas and Easter are often mentioned, as well as the weeks that comprise the traditional summer vacation period—especially if there are children in the family. But there is also good reason to avoid these periods, namely the hordes they inevitably attract. And when Walt Disney World is crowded, it can be very crowded indeed. On the busiest days, visitors may wait more than an hour to see some particularly popular attractions—that's at least twice as long as during less crowded times of year.

Considering the seasonal hours, and the weather and crowd patterns described in the charts that follow, optimal times to visit Walt Disney World are late February through early March, late April through early June, September, October, early November, and most of December (except Christmas week).

Note that during some of the less crowded times of the year—particularly during January and February—some attractions are typically closed for renovations. In addition, the water parks are often closed for refurbishment during the cooler months.

The period between the end of the Thanksgiving weekend and the week before Christmas stands out as the best timing for a visit. This is the most festive season at Walt Disney World, and savvy travelers who make their pilgrimage during this time are rewarded with special events including holiday parades and fireworks displays, special stage shows, holiday parties, themed dinners, and some of the most spectacular holiday decorations to be found anywhere. And, most importantly, all these extras can be savored at Walt Disney World during one of its least crowded times of the year.

The Magic Kingdom, Epcot, and Disney-MGM Studios are decorated to the nines for the holiday season, complete with nightly tree-lighting ceremonies. Many special events are held during this period, including Mickey's Very Merry Christmas Party in the Magic Kingdom (separate admission ticket required). The party brings a dusting of snow to Main Street from 8 P.M. to 1 A.M. for several days during the first two weeks of December. It also features holiday shows around the park, including Mickey's Very Merry Christmas Parade, plus a special finale of Fantasy in the Sky fireworks. Select performances from Mickey's Very Merry Christmas Party are also staged in the park during regular hours throughout the holiday season.

Epcot celebrates the season with Holidays Around the World, including nightly performances of the Candlelight Processional, complete with a 450-voice choir, a 50-piece orchestra, and a reading of the Christmas story by a celebrity narrator. Dinner packages are available for selected World Showcase restaurants and the night ends with a holiday version of IllumiNations. The Disney-MGM Studios features the largest family-owned collection of Christmas lights, in a display of more than two million lights depicting holiday scenes and a 65-foot "wall of angels" that together illuminate Residential Street.

The best way to take advantage of all there is to see and do at Walt Disney World during this time of year is to book a Jolly Holidays package, offered from late November through late December. The packages are available for two to ten nights and include admission to the Jolly Holidays Dinner Show held at the Contemporary resort. This festive show, available only as part of a package, features an all-you-can-eat, old-fashioned holiday feast and a lively performance by a cast of more than 100 singers and dancers. A steady stream of Disney and Christmas characters enchants kids as traditional carols sate adults.

There are holiday receptions at WDW hotels as well, including a turn-of-the-century Christmas at the Grand Floridian, a seaside party at the Yacht Club and Beach Club, a Southwestern Christmas at the Contemporary, and a Cajun holiday at Dixie Landings. Transportation is provided to each of the receptions as part of the packages, most of which also include unlimited admission to the theme parks and Pleasure Island. For reservations, contact your travel agent, or call W-DISNEY (934-7639), or the Walt Disney Travel Company at 800-828-0228.

Keeping WDW Hours

Because operating hours often fluctuate, we advise calling 824-4321 for up-to-the-minute schedules for the time of your visit.

THEME PARKS: Hours of operation at the Magic Kingdom, Epcot, and the Disney-MGM Studios vary from season to season. For more than a third of the year—in May, September, October, parts of November and December, and all of January—the Magic Kingdom is usually open from 9 A.M. to 7 P.M.; Epcot is generally open from 9 A.M. to 9 P.M.; and the Disney-MGM Studios is open from 9 A.M. to 7 P.M. Note that in Epcot, hours are staggered: In Future World they're from 9 A.M. to 7 P.M., in World Showcase, from 11 A.M. to 9 P.M.

The Magic Kingdom keeps later hours through the end of 1997 to honor Walt Disney World's 25th anniversary. Epcot and the Disney-MGM Studios stay open till 10 P.M. during Presidents' week and during spring school breaks; and till midnight during the summer and certain holiday periods (Thanksgiving, Christmas, and Easter). On New Year's Eve, the theme parks stay open until 1 A.M. or 2 A.M.

Each day, WDW resort guests can enter one of the three theme parks 1½ hours before its official opening time. Note that only some pavilions and attractions in the given park open early. For details about early-entry days, see "Park Primer" at the beginning of each theme park chapter (pages 94, 128, and 166).

DISNEY VILLAGE MARKETPLACE: Marketplace shops are open from 9:30 A.M. to 11 P.M. daily. Restaurant hours vary.

PLEASURE ISLAND: Clubs on the island are open from about 7 P.M. to 2 A.M. daily; shops, from 11 A.M. to 2 A.M.; and restaurants, from about 11:30 A.M. to midnight. At the AMC Theatres cineplex, movies are shown throughout the day, beginning at about 1 P.M.

WATER PARKS: Hours vary, with extended hours in effect during summer months.

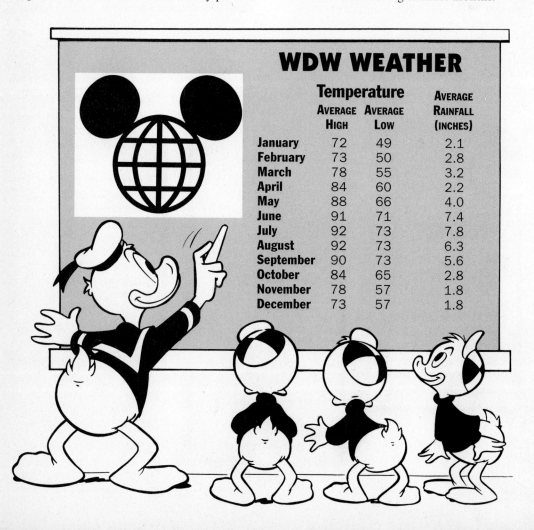

WDW WEATHER

| | Temperature | | Average Rainfall (Inches) |
	Average High	Average Low	
January	72	49	2.1
February	73	50	2.8
March	78	55	3.2
April	84	60	2.2
May	88	66	4.0
June	91	71	7.4
July	92	73	7.8
August	92	73	6.3
September	90	73	5.6
October	84	65	2.8
November	78	57	1.8
December	73	57	1.8

Crowd Patterns

Day-to-Day Trends

Most visitors to Walt Disney World assume that weekends are by far the busiest days in the parks. But barring holidays and special events, Sunday morning is perhaps the most peaceful time to visit the Magic Kingdom. With the exception of certain holiday periods, Monday, Thursday, and Saturday tend to be the most crowded days at the Magic Kingdom; Tuesday and Friday generally net the biggest throngs at Epcot; and Wednesday and Sunday draw larger crowds at the Disney-MGM Studios. Keep in mind that this year's 25th anniversary celebration might bring in more visitors than usual, especially to the Magic Kingdom.

When the time comes to plot an itinerary, it's helpful to know about crowd patterns beyond the three theme parks as well. As a rule, Pleasure Island, the Disney Village Marketplace, and Disney's water parks host their largest throngs on weekends; this is partly due to a greater influx of locals. Of course, in these circles, a bigger crowd can often mean a better time. Golfers should note that weekend tee times are typically in highest demand, while Monday and Tuesday times are easiest to come by.

Seasonal Shifts

The chart below indicates the density of crowds in the theme parks throughout the year. Though it's tough to generalize about a property as vast and ever-changing as Walt Disney World—special events and package deals can swell park attendance during a period typically marked by smaller crowds—the chart highlights historic trends. Again, the 25th anniversary celebration could bring thicker crowds year-round.

Least crowded means that there may be some lines, but by and large most attractions can be visited without much waiting; average attendance refers to times when there are lots of people around but lines are still manageable; and most crowded reflects times when lines at the most popular attractions can mean a wait of an hour or more.

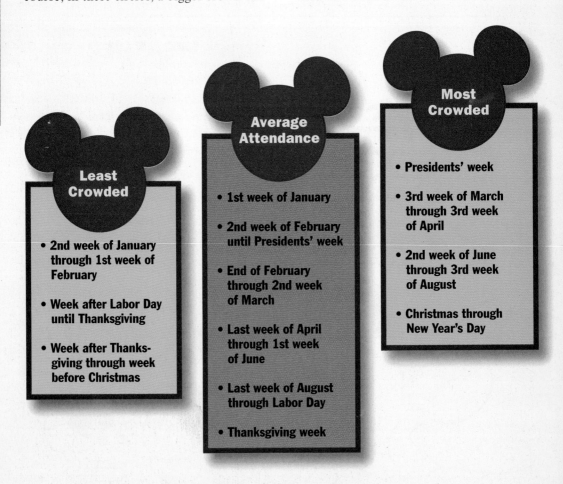

Least Crowded

- 2nd week of January through 1st week of February

- Week after Labor Day until Thanksgiving

- Week after Thanksgiving through week before Christmas

Average Attendance

- 1st week of January

- 2nd week of February until Presidents' week

- End of February through 2nd week of March

- Last week of April through 1st week of June

- Last week of August through Labor Day

- Thanksgiving week

Most Crowded

- Presidents' week

- 3rd week of March through 3rd week of April

- 2nd week of June through 3rd week of August

- Christmas through New Year's Day

Disney Cruise Line Countdown

When the Disney Cruise Line's first ship, the *Disney Magic*, makes its debut in February 1998, vacationers will be able to combine a Walt Disney World stay and a cruise without ever formally saying bon voyage to Mickey. The weeklong vacations will reinvent the cruise experience in distinctly Disney fashion. From the innovative ship design to the entertainment options, families, teens, and adults traveling without kids all will have their own comfort zones afloat.

Vacations will begin with a three- or four-day stay at a WDW resort. After transferring to Port Canaveral, guests will board the 1,760-passenger *Disney Magic* for a three- or four-day cruise. The itinerary includes a stop at Nassau in the Bahamas, plus a day-long stay on Disney's private Bahamian island, Castaway Cay, which will accommodate recreation interests from biking to snorkeling. Back at Port Canaveral, guests will be transported to the Orlando airport. Luggage is taken care of during all transfers, and there is no second check-in on the ship, ensuring a seamless land-sea vacation.

The ship's classic exterior will hark back to the early ocean liners. Guests will enter the ship to a three-story atrium, where traditional definitions of elegance expand to include a demure bronze statue of Mickey as helmsman and subtle cut-out Disney character silhouettes along the grand staircase. Disney's touch is evident throughout the ship, as even the elevators have entertainment value (guests see different scenes as they travel).

Among the *Disney Magic*'s assets are some of the most spacious staterooms afloat; 73% will be outside staterooms, and nearly half will feature private verandas. Family suites accommodate five people and include two-room bathrooms.

The cleverly themed restaurants (and picturesque adults-only alternative dining room) are sure to be a hit. French food, chandeliers, and *Beauty and the Beast* trompe l'oeil effects characterize Lumière's. A second is colorfully Caribbean, complete with Sebastian wall sconces. But the most extraordinary, perhaps, is Animator's Palate, a technological marvel in which the entire environs change from strictly black and white to vivid Technicolor during the course of the meal.

The pools, lounges, and recreational areas are strategically located to attract families, teens, and adults to different parts of the ship. There's a themed family pool, a sports-activity pool, even an adults-only pool. Teens have their own club and arcade. Children's recreation areas garner unprecedented space, with computer stations, interactive games, and state-of-the-art activity zones sure to compete with the pools for kids' attention. And of course, Disney characters will be on hand for greetings.

Evening options include stage shows; lounges with cabaret, live jazz, and comedy; movies in the ship's two-story cinema; and lectures. There's even an entertainment lounge especially for families.

While rates were not formally set at press time, the cost, including air, is expected to be about $4,300 for a family of four. Bookings for the *Disney Magic* are handled through travel agents and are already being accepted. The *Disney Wonder* won't follow in its sister's wake until December 1998.

Holidays & Special Events

Inside Walt Disney World

Special affairs are staged often throughout the year, not only to mark holidays, but also to celebrate other interests. The Magic Kingdom, Epcot, Disney-MGM Studios, and Disney Village Marketplace host numerous happenings, from sporting events to festivals geared toward jazz, gardens, animation, or even soap operas. But the biggest event of all is Walt Disney World's 25th anniversary celebration, which extends from October 1, 1996 through the end of 1997. Refer to the special section on page 15 for all the details about the festivities. Call 824-4321 for more information about any of the listed events.

JANUARY

Walt Disney World Marathon (January 5). Some 6,000 entrants run through all three theme parks and other scenic areas of the resort during this 26.2-mile race. Call 939-7810 for further information.

World Festival of Kites (January 11–February 9). Epcot hosts the largest kite festival in North America. Highlights include choreographed kite flying on World Showcase Lagoon, stunt shows, kite-making workshops, and indoor kite-flying demonstrations.

LPGA HealthSouth Inaugural (January 16–19). Top women pros mark the dawn of a new season with this three-day tournament on the Lake Buena Vista course.

Indy 200 (January 25). Indy race cars burn rubber in this annual event, held on a one-mile track just south of the Magic Kingdom.

FEBRUARY

Pleasure Island Mardi Gras (February 8–11). Jazz bands, Creole food, and street performers toast New Orleans' biggest party.

MARCH

Easter (March 30). A nationally televised, promenade-style parade in the Magic Kingdom makes this holiday celebration special. The Magic Kingdom, Epcot, and the Disney-MGM Studios stay open late during the two weeks straddling the Easter holiday. This is an extremely busy time to visit.

APRIL–MAY

U.S. First (April). Radio-controlled robots, built by teams of high school students and professional engineers, compete in elimination matches at Epcot.

Epcot International Flower and Garden Festival (April 19–June 2). Epcot is blooming with elaborate gardens (30 million blossoms) and topiary displays, behind-the-scenes tours, gardening workshops, and guest speakers. Learn from the experts how to create a beautiful garden at home. Call 827-7200 for package information.

Grad Nites (April 25–26, May 2–3, 9). The Magic Kingdom is taken over from 11 P.M. to 5 A.M. by graduating high school students in this special-ticket event. Top rock entertainers perform in the park throughout the night. For more information, call 800-472-3648.

JUNE

Discover Awards & Technology Expo. Inventors from around the world will converge on Epcot for the "Academy Awards of Science," *Discover* magazine's Awards for Technological Innovention. The finalists will demonstrate their inventions at the Technology Expo.

JULY

Fourth of July Celebration. Double-size fireworks over the Magic Kingdom, the Disney-MGM Studios' spectacular Sorcery in the Sky fireworks show, and Epcot's IllumiNations make for a colorful night. This is a very busy time to visit.

AUGUST

Animation Celebration (August–September). The Disney-MGM Studios honors Disney's animated classics with exhibits, interactive workshops, film screenings, and entertainment focusing on the past, present, and future of animation. Guests get to talk with Disney artists, and kids have extra opportunities to meet and take photos with the stars of the animated films.

SEPTEMBER

Disneyana. A veritable heaven for Disney collectors. The 1997 event will be held at Disneyland in California; Walt Disney World hosts the following year.

Night of Joy (September 5–6, 12). Three nights of musical celebration highlight the best in contemporary Christian music.

Epcot International Food and Wine Festival (September–October). World Showcase celebrates food, beverages, and cultures from around the world (even those not represented around the lagoon). Guests experience the flavor of a variety of countries through free tastings, chef cooking demonstrations, guest lectures, wine and cooking seminars, and special entertainment.

OCTOBER

Pleasure Island Jazz Fest. The greatest jazz from today and yesterday is performed live throughout the island.

Soap Opera Festival. A weekend-long celebration of the ABC daytime dramas is held at the Disney-MGM Studios. Guests can meet favorite soap stars, learn how dramas are made, talk to the producers and writers, see the sets, props and costumes from the shows, and even have a shot at an audition.

Walt Disney World/Oldsmobile Golf Classic (October 16–19). Top PGA Tour players compete alongside amateurs in this big tourney, played on the Palm, Magnolia, and Lake Buena Vista courses.

Mickey's Not-So-Scary Halloween Party (October 31). All the lands of the Magic Kingdom get dressed up for the occasion in festive Halloween decor. Activities include a costume contest and parade, special appearances by Disney villains, trick-or-treating, plus fireworks and SpectroMagic.

Especially for Kids

During four weekends a year, Epcot's World Showcase supplements its usual multicultural offerings with kids' activity zones with a playful twist. Past activities have included piñata decorating (in Mexico), macaroni art (in Italy), and watercolor painting (in France). The United Kingdom hosts the popular Alice's Tea Party. All events are free to Epcot guests.

The Disney Village Marketplace has its fun Kidsummer Nights from June through August, featuring jugglers, balloonists, stilt walkers, and face painters. For exact dates for either event, call 824-4321.

NOVEMBER–DECEMBER

Festival of the Masters (November). This three-day fine art show, one of the South's best, draws over 200 top artists to the Disney Village Marketplace to showcase their work.

Teddy Bear & Doll Convention (November). Both long-time collectors and newcomers descend on the Contemporary resort and Epcot to see world-renowned craftspeople's creations. Packages include seminars and workshops, a limited-edition private sale, an auction, parties, and an awards ceremony.

Disney's Magical Holidays (November 22–December 31). Decorations and special festivities abound in Walt Disney World's parks and resorts. The Magic Kingdom hosts Mickey's Very Merry Christmas Party on several nights during the first two weeks of December, complete with snow on Main Street and hot cocoa. Entertainment for the special-ticket party includes Mickey's Very Merry Christmas Parade and a holiday edition of Fantasy in the Sky fireworks; select performances are also staged during regular hours throughout the holiday season. Epcot's nightly Holidays Around the World show features a special edition of IllumiNations, and a Candlelight Processional with choral concert. Lights, Camera, Christmas! brightens the Disney-MGM Studios with over two million sparkling lights on Residential Street. A variety of packages include admission to special-ticket holiday shows and parties, including the Jolly Holidays Dinner Show at the Contemporary resort, a feast and musical extravaganza. For information on these events and the Jolly Holidays packages offered during this period, call 934-7639, or call the Walt Disney Travel Company at 800-828-0228.

Walt Disney World New Year's Eve Celebration (December 31). There are extra-large fireworks displays over the theme parks, which are open until 2 A.M. (the Disney-MGM Studios, 1 A.M.) for the occasion. Pleasure Island hosts a grand special-ticket bash.

Outside Walt Disney World

The communities around Walt Disney World offer a diverse array of seasonal events capable of inspiring a short detour.

JANUARY

Orlando; Citrus Bowl. Two leading college football teams square off in this post-season game, held January 1; 423-2476.

Casselberry; Scottish Highland Games. The sizeable Scottish population of the area turns out in force for Highland dancing and bagpipe competitions, sponsored by the Scottish American Society of Central Florida; 422-8226.

Eatonville; Zora Neale Hurston Festival of the Arts and Humanities. A celebration of the acclaimed local writer, it focuses on African-American culture and arts, and on Eatonville itself, the oldest incorporated black municipality in the United States; 647-3307.

FEBRUARY

Apopka; The Battle of Townsend's Plantation. Held the first weekend of the month, it brings the Civil War and plantation era back to life, with cane grinding, butter churning, and blacksmithing demonstrations and Civil War battle enactments; 880-1313.

Daytona; Speed Weeks. Top names in stock-car racing gather at the Daytona International Speedway for a week of competition, culminating in the Daytona 500; 904-253-7223.

Kissimmee; Silver Spurs Rodeo. This three-day event, also held in July, draws professional cowboys from all over the United States, who compete in bull and bronco riding, steer-wrestling, and more; 677-6336.

MARCH

Orlando; Bay Hill Invitational. Held annually in mid-March; Arnold Palmer hosts this major PGA Tour event, one of five in Florida, at the Bay Hill Club; 876-2888.

Winter Park; Winter Park Sidewalk Art Festival. On the third weekend of the month, more than 250 artists display their pottery, photography, sculpture, and crafts in Central Park and along Park Avenue in this rather arts-oriented community; 644-8281.

Davenport; Kansas City Royals Spring Training. Baseball enthusiasts can watch the Royals train at the Baseball City Complex; 813-424-2500.

Kissimmee; Kissimmee Bluegrass Festival. Crafts, food, and children's activities complement live bluegrass and gospel music performances; 847-5000 or 800-472-7773.

APRIL

Orlando; Minor League Baseball. A Tampa Bay Devil Rays farm team plays at Tinker Field from early April through early September. Tinker Field; 287 Tampa Ave. S.; Orlando, FL 32805; 872-7593.

Orlando; Orlando Shakespeare Festival. The month-long event features two professional Shakespearean productions at the Walt Disney World Amphitheater at Lake Eola; 245-0985 or 841-9787.

Lakeland; Sun 'N Fun Fly In. Aircraft exhibits and aerial acrobatic demonstrations are highlights of the country's second-largest air show (after Oshkosh), scheduled in 1997 for April 6–12; 813-644-2431.

JULY

Orlando; Lake Eola Picnic in the Park. Special activities, games, entertainment, and fireworks complete this Fourth of July celebration on the banks of Lake Eola; 649-3152.

Kissimmee; Silver Spurs Rodeo. (See February listing for details.)

OCTOBER

Orlando Magic Basketball. One of the NBA's top franchises plays some 45 home games from October through April at the Orlando Arena; 896-2442.

DECEMBER

Winter Park; Christmas in the Park. Tiffany windows from the large Charles Hosmer Morse Museum of American Art collection are displayed in Central Park as the backdrop for the Bach Festival Choir and Children's Choir, held on the Thursday following the first Saturday in the month; 644-8281.

WDW 25th Anniversary

It would be easy to sum up Walt Disney World's first 25 years simply by citing its astonishing growth, but such a portrayal would tell only half the story. The place that welcomed its very first guests on October 1, 1971, has come quite a long way from those early days when Walt Disney World encompassed nothing more than the Magic Kingdom (and its 23 attractions), two hotels, three golf courses, a small fleet of rental boats, and a campground. In the process of expanding—adding Epcot, the Disney-MGM Studios, and Pleasure Island, among many other enticements—the World acquired a greater legacy.

This legacy is less tangible, but it's something that all WDW vacationers take away with them—something that has rippled through generations of past guests. It's what the first folks ever to visit the Magic Kingdom share with the family now passing through the turnstiles, more than half a million guests later. By now, past guests are smiling knowingly, remembering vacations awash in pixie dust. They know we're referring to the World's cherished gift of magic.

During Walt Disney World's silver anniversary year, Disney invites visitors to join the loyal legions as guests of honor at the biggest party the World has ever seen. Celebrations began October 1, 1996, and run through December 31, 1997.

Disney has pulled out all the stops to make this celebration an unforgettable experience that will knock the socks off of even the most diehard Disney fans. As if it weren't enough to launch a new parade and transform Cinderella Castle into a giant birthday cake, Disney has put up decorations propertywide, pumped up its entertainment schedule, and created lots of new attractions. In the pages that follow, we provide complete details on the exciting entertainment and festivities on tap. There may never be a better time to remember, to discover, and to share with friends and younger generations the incomparable magic of Walt Disney World. So join us in toasting the World's success and then start planning that 25th anniversary getaway.

A TIME TO CELEBRATE

In the years since its October 1, 1971 opening, Walt Disney World has marked many milestones, but no event has even approached the magnitude of the 25th anniversary celebrations overtaking the World from October 1, 1996, through December 31, 1997. While an incredible transformation of Cinderella Castle is certainly the most elaborate tribute, the entire property is resplendent in decorations befitting the occasion. At the center of the excitement is the Magic Kingdom, where all manner of special happenings are afoot. Hallmarks of the silver anniversary shindig—spectacular new entertainment, lengthened Magic Kingdom hours, and a host of grand openings—are ongoing through the end of 1997, so the festive spirit will continue into the party's latest hours. Proof that Disney's thought of everything: There are even commemorative Disney Dollars and theme park tickets.

While we've also commemorated Walt Disney World's 25 years with nostalgic tidbits throughout the book, this concise guide provides complete details on all the anniversary goings-on. Specifics are subject to change, so we recommend calling 824-4321 to confirm events happening during your visit. Enjoy!

Cinderella Castle Cake

It makes sense that the grandest, most conspicuous salute of all should come from the Magic Kingdom's most famous and beloved feature. Disney wouldn't toy with the likes of Cinderella Castle for just any occasion, but it couldn't resist the notion of turning the castle into an oversize birthday cake for the duration of the 25th anniversary celebration.

After contemplating some 150 schemes, Disney Imagineers settled on a cake with bright pink icing and lots of candy decorations. The requisite 25 birthday candles are perched atop the freshly iced spires and placed along adjacent walkways. These candles are lighted each night in a glowing tribute that makes Cinderella Castle Cake something truly special to behold.

25th Anniversary Parade

This 25-minute dazzler is a demonstration of Disney's parade panache, with an interactive twist: cameo appearances by about 1,400 pre-selected Magic Kingdom visitors. A hit with kids and adults alike, the commemorative 3 P.M. parade winds from Frontierland to Main Street, stopping eight times en route for special participatory sequences called "magical moments." These interactive segments climax with the floats launching theme-keyed surprises into the air: confetti, white doves, even fireworks.

The parade has six floats, all inspired by Disney films, serenaded by the official 25th anniversary song as well as familiar Disney tunes, and overflowing with characters. The first float reprises the music and magic of *Cinderella*, complete with coach and crystal castle, Mickey and pals in formal wear, and

not a few waltzing theme park–goers. Next, a manse straight from *Beauty and the Beast* makes its stunning appearance, with Belle and the rest leading another magical round of dancing. *The Little Mermaid* float is as entertaining as they come, with water-spewing clams and fish that form conga lines. Then, Aladdin and Jasmine ride by on Abu the elephant, watching as guests play "Genie Says" amid dancing carpets and piles of treasure. The fifth float, themed to *The Lion King*, revives the film's "Hakuna Matata" spirit with a little help from guests recruited as drummers. The spectacular finale float—Disney's Enchanted Forest—hosts almost every other character imaginable, from Snow White and the dwarfs to Sleeping Beauty, Winnie the Pooh, Alice in Wonderland, and Pocahontas and John Smith. Unsuspecting onlookers are always surprised when *Fantasia* character topiaries hop off the float and dance. At the climactic moment, fireworks are shot right off of the float, bursting over the delightful forest's very own castle.

Guests are tapped for participation by cast members walking along the parade route, beginning about 45 minutes before starting time.

Nightly SpectroMagic & Fireworks

The Magic Kingdom is staying open at least until dark for the duration of the celebration, and for good reason. It's breaking away from entertainment as usual to make nightly events of its best and brightest shows: the SpectroMagic parade and the Fantasy in the Sky fireworks. This is a big treat because both the parade and the fireworks (described on pages 120 to 122) are usually performed only during holidays and busy seasons.

Returning Guest Tribute

In appreciation for their loyalty to Walt Disney World over the years, Disney is taking time during this auspicious occasion to recognize returning guests. Every day in front of Cinderella Castle, WDW alums will be honored in a rousing fashion. The daily tribute invites returnees of all ages to hop up on stage and show their Disney spirit with cheers.

The Party Starts Here

Folks visiting the Magic Kingdom during WDW's silver anniversary should make the Welcome Center (next to Disneyana Collectibles in Town Square) their first stop. In addition to being chief headquarters for information about events, it is the main point for guest registration. Both first-time and returning visitors are encouraged to stop in and say hello. They're also asked to complete a card—with their name, address, and the years of past WDW visits—so they can be officially recognized as special guests of honor. Upon registering, guests receive a commemorative lithograph.

The center also contains an exhibit that chronicles the World's evolution, provides a glimpse of its future, and offers insight to Disney fans young and old.

Returning visitors are also encouraged to check in at the Welcome Center to receive a warm greeting and register as an alum (see "The Party Starts Here," above, for specifics).

IllumiNations 25

Lest the Magic Kingdom have all the fun, Epcot is celebrating WDW's momentous anniversary in high style, as well. The park's signature nighttime entertainment, IllumiNations, has a new spin that goes well beyond the usual eye-popping display of lasers, fireworks, and dancing fountains set to music. IllumiNations 25 features traditional celebratory music from around the world. For the finale, bursting fireworks create a rhythmic prelude to the closing song, "Circle of Life," then linger over World Showcase Lagoon for about ten seconds in the form of a spectacular birthday cake. IllumiNations 25 is performed nightly and is visible from any point on the World Showcase Promenade. For further details, see page 161.

Magical Milestones

The timeline below captures just a few of the defining moments in Walt Disney World's illustrious history.

1964—Disney secretly begins buying land in Central Florida with a mind to building a new theme park, dubbed Project X.

1965—The word has leaked out that Disney is the land buyer, so Walt Disney calls a press conference on November 15 to announce plans to build a theme park.

1971—On October 1, the Magic Kingdom welcomes its first guests.

1973—Steve Birnbaum and Alexandra Mayes Birnbaum visit Walt Disney World for the very first time.

1974—A year after the arrival of Pirates of the Caribbean, Space Mountain debuts.

1976—River Country opens. The water park's popularity leads Disney to create encores.

1982—The park that Walt Disney called his "greatest gift to mankind" comes to fruition, with the grand opening of EPCOT Center.

1985—WDW greets its 200 millionth guest.

1989—The Disney-MGM Studios and Pleasure Island debut.

1991—Jim Henson's Muppet*Vision 3-D premieres and SpectroMagic replaces the Electric Light Parade.

1992—The Magic Kingdom gets its third major thrill attraction, Splash Mountain.

1994—The Twilight Zone Tower of Terror drops into the Disney-MGM Studios.

1995—Friday, October 13th yields WDW's 500 millionth guest.

1996—Mickey's Starland makes way for an all-new land, Mickey's Toontown Fair. WDW hits the big 25.

1997—Disney's Coronado Springs resort opens, raising WDW's room count to more than 23,000.

1998—Disney Cruise Line sets sail. Disney's Animal Kingdom roars into the picture.

2021—Walt Disney World turns 50.

A Year for Grand Entrances

The icing on Walt Disney World's anniversary cake is surely the wealth of permanent attractions making their formal debut during this celebratory period. Each of the newcomers mentioned below is described fully in the appropriate chapter. To spotlight these auspicious openings, listings are specially marked with our 25th anniversary symbol, shown below. Look for this symbol throughout the book to ensure you don't miss a word of our 25th anniversary coverage.

MAGIC KINGDOM
- Mickey's Toontown Fair

EPCOT
- Test Track
- Universe of Energy

DISNEY-MGM STUDIOS
- Backstage Pass to 101 Dalmatians
- The Hunchback of Notre Dame— A Musical Adventure

RESORTS
- BoardWalk
- Disney's Coronado Springs

SPECIAL EVENTS
- Animation Celebration
- Epcot International Food & Wine Festival

EVERYTHING ELSE
- Disney's Sports Complex
- Fantasia Gardens
- World of Disney superstore
- Disney's Entertainment District

PLANNING AHEAD
Logistics

Organizing a trip properly takes time, but most travelers find that the increased enjoyment is well worth the effort. The fact is, planning can become a pleasant sort of "armchair" exercise, and kids will enjoy their visit to Walt Disney World all the more if they, too, are involved in the planning process. To aid in that effort, we immodestly recommend our guide, *Birnbaum's Walt Disney World For Kids, By Kids* ($9.95), a comprehensive look at the World from a young person's perspective, written for kids 7 to 14. For adults traveling sans children, our newest guide, *Birnbaum's Walt Disney World Without Kids* ($10.95), is the definitive source.

Information Sources

For information about Walt Disney World, call WDW Information at 824-4321 or write to the Walt Disney World Co.; Box 10,000; Lake Buena Vista, FL 32830-1000. For details about other things to see and do in Central Florida, contact the Florida Department of Commerce Division of Tourism; 126 W. Van Buren St.; Tallahassee, FL 32399-2000; 904-487-1462. To find out about Orlando-area attractions, contact the Official Visitor Information Center; 8445 International Dr.; Orlando, FL 32819; 363-5871 or 800-551-0181.

WDW on-line: Internet users can tap into updates about the World's latest offerings. Simply enter *http://www.disneyworld.com* to gain access. Travelers can confirm park hours, check ticket prices, and make WDW resort reservations. Repeat visitors should check the "What's New" feature to find out what has opened since their last trip.

Disney/AAA Travel Center: It's best to arrive on site with a confirmed hotel reservation. Those driving to Walt Disney World from points north can arrange that assurance easily at this full-service visitors center located at the intersection of I-75 and S.R. 200 in Ocala, Florida, about 90 miles north of Orlando. The facility is equipped to help WDW-bound vacationers plan their time, purchase theme park tickets, and make (or confirm) hotel reservations. For departing guests who didn't buy enough pairs of mouse ears, it also stocks character merchandise.

On-site resources: Upon arrival, a variety of other information sources is available. Those staying at WDW resorts should consider their hotel's Guest Services desk the primary resource. WDW resort guests can also turn their room TV to Channel 5 for a preview of attractions (a good orientation for first-time visitors). Fort Wilderness campers are advised to stop at the Pioneer Hall Information and Ticket Window, call extension 2788, or touch 11 on a phone at any comfort station.

Guests at Disney Village Hotel Plaza establishments can access a tourist-information program of their own on Channel 7. Some other area hotels also show a version of the orientation, usually aiming to provide an overview of all Central Florida attractions.

For day visitors: All day visitors—that is, those staying off the property or living in the Orlando area—receive a handout at the Auto Plazas detailing useful information. When purchasing one-day admission to a given theme park, guests receive a guidemap to that park. Multi-day pass holders may receive all three park guides upon request. Extra guides are available at City Hall (in the Magic Kingdom) and at Guest Relations (in Epcot and the Disney-MGM Studios).

What to Pack

While there is hardly a dress code at Walt Disney World, casual clothing is the rule, with few exceptions. Most notably, jackets are required for men at Victoria & Albert's restaurant in the Grand Floridian resort.

More generally, T-shirts and shorts are acceptable during the day. For evening, slacks, jeans, or Bermuda shorts are appropriate most anywhere on property. Bathing suits are a must, as are the right togs for any other sport you want to pursue. On the tennis courts, tennis whites are appropriate, though not required.

Lightweight sweaters are necessary even in summer—to wear indoors when the air-conditioning gets frigid. From November through March, warmer clothing is a must for evening. Pack for weather extremes so you'll be comfy should it become unseasonably warm or cool. Always bring plenty of sunscreen, since even the winter sun here can be brutal. In summer, don't forget to pack lightweight raingear and a compact umbrella.

The most important item of all? Comfortable, broken-in walking shoes.

Package Pointers

The sheer number and diversity of packages offering vacations in Central Florida are enough to bewilder even the savviest traveler. Still, such plans are worth exploring. They offer the convenience of a vacation that's completely organized in advance, and that will generally cost less than the sum of the same transportation, accommodations, and admission elements purchased separately.

The main difference among packages, cost aside, is the matter of lodging (on-site hotels versus off-property accommodations). Delta Air Lines (800-872-7786), American Express Vacation Travel (800-937-2639), and the Walt Disney Travel Company (800-828-0228) offer packages featuring WDW's own on-site hotels. Other major operators offering Walt Disney World tours include Kiwi Vacations, Adventure Tours, Carlson Travel, Go Go Tours, Funjet, Carnival Cruise Lines, and Premier Cruise Lines. Delta and Kiwi airlines packages include the added attraction of low-cost air transportation. AAA members should inquire at the nearest club office about AAA Disney Driveaway Vacation packages, which offer perks for travelers driving to the World.

Generally, the Walt Disney Travel Company's offerings run the gamut from value to deluxe lodging, with airfare, theme park admission, or meals sometimes incorporated. Some WDW vacation plans are available year-round, such as the special 25th anniversary packages offered this year; others, such as Jolly Holidays, Sunshine Getaway, and Fall Fantasy, are tied to seasonal WDW events. Still others are designed around a specific type of vacation—a golf getaway, a honeymoon—and include special elements such as unlimited tee times or champagne upon arrival. Finally, add-on escapes allow guests to combine a WDW vacation with a short cruise or a stay at the new Disney Vacation Club resort at Vero Beach.

The value of a given package depends entirely on your specific needs. Before considering your options, use the descriptions in this book to help determine which of the plethora of accommodations, activities, and attractions at Walt Disney World most appeal to you. There's real value in some package elements such as airport transfers and meal discounts. Some packages also include meals with the Disney characters, tennis lessons, golf greens fees, tennis court fees, boat rentals, and the like. But don't

Disney's Animal Kingdom

A live-action adventure park five times the size of the Magic Kingdom is due to open in spring 1998. The new theme park, west of the Disney-MGM Studios, will present thrilling animal encounters while imparting important lessons in wildlife conservation and respect for the natural world. Although specifics are likely to change, the following descriptions offer an idea of what's in store.

Oasis Gardens: Guests will enter the park through a setting filled with waterfalls, rushing streams, and lush vegetation. Visitors will see all kinds of wildlife, from deer to flamingos. Discreet barriers will create the illusion that guests are walking among the animals.

Safari Village: The park's central land will be defined by bright colors, jungle surroundings, and exotic architecture reminiscent of Africa and the islands of the Caribbean and South Pacific. Safari Village is also important as the departure point for a boat ride on Discovery River, which offers a great orientation to the lands of the Animal Kingdom.

Tree of Life: The park's central icon—a banyan-like tree constructed by Disney Imagineers—will be 14 stories tall, with a 50-foot-wide trunk, hand-carved by Disney artists in

an intricate wildlife tapestry. Inside the trunk, guests will see an ecologically themed show with characters from *The Lion King*.

Africa: At more than 100 acres, this land is by itself bigger than the Magic Kingdom. On the Serengeti Safari, open-air vehicles will travel along dirt roads as passengers observe free-roaming herds of African creatures. Some animals will venture close, while others, like lions and cheetahs, will be separated from guests via invisible barriers. Vehicles cross a rickety bridge that dangles precariously over real crocodiles. In an exciting twist, safari-goers embark on a mad pursuit of poachers through a water-filled canyon. Guests exit via the Gorilla Valley sanctuary.

Conservation Station: A train here will journey behind the scenes, revealing the park's veterinary facilities. The area will feature interactive stations related to zoology and environmental issues.

Dinoland: A towering brontosaurus presides over this land, themed as an archaeological dig site. A thrill ride called Countdown to Extinction will take guests on a time-travel journey fraught with frightening run-ins with a 30-foot-long carnataurus.

The Rental Car Dilemma

A car is a must strictly for those planning to visit Orlando-area restaurants and any attractions outside Walt Disney World. If you plan to spend all of your time on WDW turf, you can spare yourself the expense. Shuttle service from the airport to all area hotels is available around the clock, and taxis are in good supply. Within the World, an exhaustive network of bus, monorail, and boat transportation efficiently brings guests from point to point. Visitors lodging off-property can usually get to and from Walt Disney World theme parks via their hotel's own bus service (inquire in advance about schedules and costs). See "From the Airport" on page 31 for airport shuttle information and the *Transportation & Accommodations* chapter for details on WDW internal transportation.

pick a package that includes elements you don't want or won't have time to enjoy. Remember that while extras such as welcoming cocktails sound attractive, their cash value is negligible. Also beware of packages that announce as selling points certain services available to every WDW guest.

Cost-Cutting Tips

Lodging: When it comes to saving money on accommodations, timing is almost everything. While off-season dates vary depending on the hotel, value season for Disney resorts generally means January through early February and mid-August through mid-December.

Also consider how much time you will be spending at your hotel, and don't pay for a place packed with perks you won't have time to enjoy. If swimming pools and other amenities matter, consider the non-budget chain establishments that have them—but remember that cutoff ages (above which there is a charge for children sharing their parents' room) do vary. Budget chains such as Days Inn, Econo Lodge, and Holiday Inn Express can prove economical but usually do not offer many frills. A good source of information is the *State by State Guide to Budget Motels* by Loris G. Bree, revised annually and available in bookstores for $12.95, or for $15.95 from Marlor Press; 4304 Brigadoon Dr.; St. Paul, MN 55126; 612-484-4600.

When considering the cost-effectiveness of off-property lodging, factor in the time, money, and inconvenience of commuting to and from attractions. Realize, too, that the advantages of staying on property (including access to WDW transportation) also apply to those staying in the least expensive rooms in Disney's brood of hotels. The most important addresses for budget-watching Disney fans, the All-Star Sports and All-Star Music resorts, offer the lowest rates on WDW property. Rooms at Caribbean Beach, Dixie Landings, Port Orleans, and Coronado Springs are slightly higher priced. See the *Transportation & Accommodations* chapter for details.

Food: Eat fast-food meals instead of going to full-service restaurants. Visit fancier establishments (if you must) at lunchtime rather than at dinner (the same entrées usually cost less then). Carry sandwich fixings and have lunches alfresco when possible. Look for lodging with kitchen facilities: The savings on food, especially for families at breakfast time, may be more than the extra accommodations expense.

Transportation: Comparison shopping is vital. See "How to Get There" in this chapter to weigh your travel options. If you decide to fly, don't neglect to factor in the cost of getting to and from the airport. To avoid rental car costs, stay on Disney property.

Discounts: Membership in the Magic Kingdom Club means discounts on: Disney vacation packages, park admission, accommodations (based on availability), car rentals, select theme park restaurant meals, select merchandise at the Disney Village Marketplace and in The Disney Store and The Disney Catalog, and more. Many companies offer free membership in the club as an employee benefit. For others, The Gold Card costs $65 for a two-year family membership ($50 for seniors 55 and over). The cost outside the United States is $85. For more information or to join the club, call 800-893-4763. Allow at least two weeks to receive membership materials.

Discounts are also available to Florida residents, and other seasonal promotions occur. Call 824-4321 for up-to-the-minute details.

At-a-Glance Reservations Guide

Walt Disney World vacations go more smoothly when details are planned ahead of time. Procrastinators may find no room at the inn, or no space left for a show that they wanted to see, particularly during busy seasons. Golf starting times, tennis courts, restaurant priority seating, and other special affairs should also be reserved in advance.

Accommodations: It is important to book a room in advance to get your first choice, although most requests can be satisfied. Stays during popular summer and holiday periods must be booked well in advance. Guests should call their travel agent or Central Reservations Operations; the phone number is W-DISNEY (934-7639). The office is open Monday through Friday from 8 A.M. to 10 P.M.; Saturday and Sunday from 9 A.M. to 6 P.M. Most calls are answered within one minute. Have pen and paper (and your credit card) close at hand when calling, to jot down dates and the number of your reservation. (Parties needing ten or more rooms should call 828-3318.)

Packages: A great option for the convenience of having all your vacation arrangements made with one phone call. For Walt Disney Travel Company package reservations, call 800-828-0228. For more details about WDW packages, see "Package Pointers" on page 20.

Dining: Priority seating has replaced reservations at almost all WDW restaurants except for dinner shows (see page 246 of the *Good Meals, Great Times* chapter for details about the new policy). Most dinner show reservations and restaurant priority seating arrangements are handled by one phone number—WDW-DINE (939-3463).

Sports: Reservations for sporting activities are handled by the individual resorts and sporting facilities. It's always wise to make your plans and reserve your place as far in advance as WDW policy will allow. (See chart below.)

ACTIVITY	Phone for reservations (area code 407)	Advisability of reservations	How far in advance can reservations be made?
SPORTS			
Golf starting times—all courses	WDW-GOLF (939-4653)	Necessary from January through April; suggested at other times	60 days for guests staying at WDW resorts or Hotel Plaza properties 30 days for others (if reserved with credit card; 7 days if not)
Golf lessons Palm and Magnolia courses	WDW-GOLF (939-4653)	Necessary	...................1 year..................
Tennis Contemporary	824-3578	Suggested	...................30 days ....
Grand Floridian	824-2694	Necessary	...................30 days ....
Swan and Dolphin	934-4396	Suggested	...................no limit..............
Tennis lessons Contemporary	824-3578	Necessary	...................1 year..................
Grand Floridian	824-2694	Necessary	...................1 year..................
Trail rides Fort Wilderness	824-2621	Necessary	...................14 days ....
Fishing trips Fort Wilderness	824-2621	Necessary	...................14 days ....
Dixie Landings	934-5409	Necessary	...................14 days ....
Disney Village Marketplace	828-2204	Necessary	...................30 days ....
Yacht and Beach	934-3256	Necessary	...................30 days ....
Waterskiing	824-2621	Necessary	...................14 days ....
Parasailing	824-1000, ext. 3586	Necessary	...................no limit..............

ACTIVITY	Phone number (area code 407)	Advisability of priority seating or reservations	How far in advance can arrangements be made?
GOOD MEALS			
Polynesian resort	WDW-DINE		...............60 days...............
'Ohana		Suggested	
Coral Isle Café		Available	
Grand Floridian resort	WDW-DINE		...............60 days...............
Victoria & Albert's		Necessary	
Narcoossee's		Suggested	
Flagler's		Suggested	
1900 Park Fare		Suggested	
Grand Floridian Café		Available	
Contemporary resort	WDW-DINE		...............60 days...............
California Grill		Suggested	
Concourse Steakhouse		Suggested	
Chef Mickey's		Suggested	
Wilderness Lodge resort	WDW-DINE		...............60 days...............
Artist Point		Suggested	
Whispering Canyon Café		Suggested	
Beach Club resort	WDW-DINE		...............60 days...............
Ariel's		Suggested	
Cape May Café		Available	
Yacht Club resort	WDW-DINE		...............60 days...............
Yachtsman Steakhouse		Suggested	
Yacht Club Galley		Suggested	
Dixie Landings resort	WDW-DINE		...............60 days...............
Boatwright's Dining Hall		Suggested	
Port Orleans resort	WDW-DINE		...............60 days...............
Bonfamille's Café		Suggested	
Old Key West resort	WDW-DINE		...............60 days...............
Olivia's Café		Suggested	
Disney Institute	WDW-DINE		...............60 days...............
Seasons Dining Room		Suggested	
Swan resort	934-1609		...............60 days...............
Garden Grove Café		Suggested	
Kimono's		Suggested	
Palio		Suggested	
Dolphin resort	934-4858		...............60 days...............
Sum Chows		Suggested	
Harry's Safari Bar & Grille		Suggested	
Juan & Only's		Suggested	
Fulton's Crab House	WDW-DINE	Suggested	...............60 days...............
Fireworks Factory	934-8989	Suggested	...............60 days...............
In the theme parks	WDW-DINE	Suggested	...............60 days...............
GREAT TIMES			
Hoop-Dee-Doo Musical Revue Fort Wilderness	WDW-DINE	Necessary	...............2 years...............
Polynesian Luau Polynesian resort	WDW-DINE	Necessary	...............2 years...............
Mickey's Tropical Luau Polynesian resort	WDW-DINE	Necessary	...............2 years...............
WDW Character Meals (see page 244 for locations)	WDW-DINE	Suggested	...............60 days...............

All About
Theme Park Tickets

The Disney organization defines a ticket as admission for one day only; admission media valid for longer periods are called passes. All passes are nontransferable. Special commemorative passes are available at The Disney Store and other ticket locations during WDW's 25th anniversary year.

Deciding factors: One-day tickets are valid for admission to one park only—the Magic Kingdom, Epcot, or the Disney-MGM Studios. Four-Day Value Passes may be used for one day in each park, plus one optional day in the park of your choice, but not at more than one park on the same day. Four-Day Park Hopper Passes and Five-Day World Hopper Passes can be used at all three parks on the same day. The Five-Day World Hopper Pass also allows admission to Disney's water parks and Pleasure Island for a seven-day period beginning with the first use of the pass.

Guests staying at WDW resorts can purchase a multi-day pass geared to the length of their visit. The Length of Stay Pass offers savings over other passes, and includes unlimited admission to all three theme parks, the Disney water parks, and Pleasure Island for the duration of a guest's stay.

Unlike one-day tickets, all multi-day passes include unlimited use of WDW transportation. Multi-day passes need not be used on consecutive days. Unused days on any multi-day pass—with the exception of Length of Stay passes—may be used for a future visit. Guests who have at least one day left on a Four-Day Value Pass or Four-Day Park Hopper Pass can upgrade to a Five-Day World Hopper Pass by paying the difference.

Purchasing tickets and passes: Admission media are sold at the theme park entrances, and at WDW resorts, Disney Village Hotel Plaza properties, the Orlando International Airport, the Transportation and Ticket Center (TTC), and The Disney Store. Cash, traveler's checks, personal checks (with proper ID), American Express, Visa, MasterCard, and The Disney Credit Card are accepted as payment.

Passes by phone: Multi-day passes can be purchased in advance by calling 824-4321. There is a $2 handling fee. Allow two to three weeks for delivery.

Passes by mail: Allow three to four weeks for requests to be processed, and be sure to include a return address. Send a check or money order (for the exact amount plus $2 for handling), payable to Walt Disney World Company, to:

Walt Disney World
Box 10,030
Lake Buena Vista, FL 32930-0030
Attention: Ticket Mail Order

Admission Prices

ONE-DAY TICKET
(Restricted to use in one park only.)
Adult $40.81
Child* $32.86

FOUR-DAY VALUE PASS
(Valid for one day in each park, plus one optional day in the park of your choice. Includes use of WDW transportation system.)
Adult $136.74
Child* $109.18

FOUR-DAY PARK HOPPER PASS
(Valid in all three parks for four days and includes use of WDW transportation system.)
Adult $152.64
Child* $121.90

FIVE-DAY WORLD HOPPER PASS
(Valid in all three parks for five days; includes use of WDW transportation system, and allows admission to Typhoon Lagoon, Blizzard Beach, River Country, and Pleasure Island for up to seven days from the first use of the pass.)
Adult $207.76
Child* $166.42

LENGTH OF STAY PASS
(Available to WDW resort guests only. Valid in all three parks, Typhoon Lagoon, Blizzard Beach, River Country, and Pleasure Island for the duration of stay; includes use of WDW transportation system.)

Length of Stay	Adult	Child*
4 days	$175.96	$140.98
5 days	$204.58	$164.30
6 days	$231.08	$185.50
7 days	$255.46	$204.58
8 days	$277.72	$222.18
9 days	$297.86	$238.29
10 days	$315.88	$252.71

The cost of a **THEME PARK ANNUAL PASS** is $250.16 for adults and $217.30 for children; renewals are $227.90 for adults and $195.04 for children. The cost of a **PREMIUM ANNUAL PASS** is $348.74 for adults and $306.34 for children; renewals are $315.88 and $278.78 for children; in addition to the three theme parks, it includes admission to Pleasure Island, Typhoon Lagoon, Blizzard Beach, and River Country.

Prices quoted include sales tax and were correct at press time, but may change during 1997.

*3 through 9 years of age; children under 3 free

Step-by-Step Sample Schedules

It's no exaggeration to say that a visitor could spend three weeks in Central Florida and still not have time to see everything that's worthwhile. Walt Disney World alone requires every bit of four days just to cover the major attractions, and even that doesn't really allow enough time to take in everything. The basic inventory of attractions—namely, the Magic Kingdom, Epcot, the Disney-MGM Studios, Pleasure Island, Disney Village Marketplace, Typhoon Lagoon, Blizzard Beach, River Country, and Fort Wilderness—only begins to suggest the nearly endless and irresistible entertainment opportunities available. And we haven't even mentioned the beaches, the 99 holes of golf, and all the other tempting sports facilities. This year, with all of the 25th anniversary celebration happenings and special entertainment, there's even more reason to make sure to allow plenty of time during your vacation to see and experience the best of Walt Disney World.

The schedules suggested here should help put you on the right track—and maybe even keep you there. Deviations from the programs we describe should be based on our "Hot Tips" (pages 124, 162, and 178). In general, good sense and normal human stamina dictate that a first-time visitor should count on spending at least two days at the Magic Kingdom, two days at Epcot, and one full day at the Disney-MGM Studios. That allows time for shopping, the inevitable lines at certain attractions, and unhurried meals. **Note:** These schedules are for periods when extended park hours are in effect. A bonus: The Magic Kingdom has extended hours year-round for 1997.

Remember, too, that it's crucial to begin days in the theme parks promptly at park opening. (It's wise to recognize that Epcot and the Disney-MGM Studios frequently open a half-hour or more before the officially posted time.) Guests staying at WDW resorts might consider taking advantage of early-bird admission (1½ hours before the park opens to the public) to get an early crack at selected attractions in the designated park. (Keep in mind that others are apt to have the same idea.) See "Park Primer" at the beginning of each theme park chapter (pages 94, 128, and 166) for details about the program.

One to Three Days

There's so much to see and do at Walt Disney World that we don't really recommend a visit this frustratingly brief. But if that's all the time you've got, first decide which of the three theme parks (the Magic Kingdom, Epcot, or the Disney-MGM Studios) you want to see, and then study all available material in advance so that you're as familiar as possible with the park's layout and offerings. Be sure to arrive early and move quickly while there. For optimal results, follow our schedules to the letter.

MAGIC KINGDOM

• Arrive in the parking lot at least 45 minutes before the scheduled park opening, so as to be at the Central Plaza end of Main Street at the official opening time. Go to City Hall to pick up a guidemap and make priority seating arrangements (if you haven't made advance plans) for an early dinner at a Magic Kingdom restaurant. Try a character meal at Crystal Palace or Liberty Tree Tavern.

• Move rapidly and purposefully from one attraction to the next—first to Space Mountain and Alien Encounter, then to Splash Mountain, Big Thunder Mountain Railroad, The Haunted Mansion, Pirates of the Caribbean, and Jungle Cruise.

• If you're traveling with young children, your best bet is to begin by taking the Walt Disney World Railroad directly to Mickey's Toontown Fair (formerly Mickey's Starland) and then visiting the Fantasyland attractions.

• Plan on lunching at around 11 A.M. to avoid mealtime lines. After visiting the most popular attractions, see Tom Sawyer Island and the Swiss Family Treehouse before or after lunch, as time allows.

• Make a second trip around the park, stopping at The Timekeeper, Legend of The Lion King, It's A Small World, Peter Pan's Flight, The Hall of Presidents, the shops and entertainment en route, and anything else that catches your eye.

• Eat an early dinner at a Magic Kingdom restaurant. It's also easy to take the monorail to the Contemporary, Polynesian, or Grand Floridian resorts, each of which offers a variety of dining options (see the *Good Meals, Great Times* chapter for recommendations).

• An alternative plan is to leave the Magic Kingdom about 4 P.M. for the Hoop-Dee-Doo Musical Revue at Fort Wilderness. (Call to make these reservations long before leaving home, since they can be very hard to come by. Even when you call early, there may not be any seats available.)

• Another option for a change of pace is to have dinner at Planet Hollywood or another Pleasure Island restaurant and spend the evening exploring the clubs, or shop at the Disney Village Marketplace next door. Or head to the BoardWalk resort for dinner and a nostalgic walk on the boards.

• Since attractions are open late throughout 1997, we definitely recommend spending the time after dinner at the Magic Kingdom, where fireworks and the late installment of SpectroMagic combine to make an evening especially memorable. This is also a great time to visit favorite attractions again, since lines are usually shorter during the parades and before closing.

EPCOT

• Arrive at least a half hour before the park's official opening. Go immediately to Guest Relations to arrange for dinner priority seating around 7:30 P.M. (if you haven't made advance plans) at one of the international restaurants in World Showcase. Pick up a guidemap while you're there.

• When Test Track opens this spring, it will be extremely popular, so stop here first. Then see as much as you can of Wonders of Life and The Land in Future World. When World Showcase opens, head there and see *O Canada!* in the Canada pavilion and *Impressions de France* in the France pavilion.

• Pausing to grab a bite at one of the international fast-food spots, travel from country to country, making sure to catch the show at The American Adventure and the boat ride in Norway. Check out the street entertainment and any shops that catch your eye.

• Try to return to Future World by mid- to late-afternoon. See Journey Into Imagination and Spaceship Earth first. If there is time, stop in at Universe of Energy for the renovated show there. Then spend the remaining time at Innoventions before heading back to World Showcase for dinner.

• Keep an eye on the time so that you can secure a good spot around World Showcase Lagoon (we like the little island between Italy and The American Adventure) to watch IllumiNations 25, a special 25th anniversary edition of Epcot's evening entertainment.

DISNEY-MGM STUDIOS

• Arrive at the park at least a half hour before the scheduled opening time. Note that some attractions open later in the morning; pick up a guidemap, and consult it for exact times. If you'd like to try one of the sit-down restaurants for lunch or dinner, and you haven't made advance plans, stop at the corner of Hollywood and Sunset boulevards or at the individual eatery to arrange for priority seating. Try the 50's Prime Time Café for some old-time television nostalgia or the Brown Derby for a touch more elegance.

• If you're up for a 13-story drop (or two), head directly to the Tower of Terror. Then see Voyage of the Little Mermaid or The Hunchback of Notre Dame show. Afterwards, head for Muppet*Vision 3-D and Star Tours, since these attractions are very crowded later in the day.

• Plan on grabbing a quick lunch at one of the fast-food eateries around 11 A.M. to avoid mealtime crowds.

• See The Magic of Disney Animation and The Great Movie Ride. Slot in times to see Indiana Jones Epic Stunt Spectacular, SuperStar Television, and the Monster Sound Show (be sure to volunteer to participate). If small children are along, spend some time at the Honey, I Shrunk the Kids Movie Set Adventure. Browse through the shops along Hollywood Boulevard and Sunset Boulevard, taking time to notice all the Studios' interesting details.

• At about 5 P.M., head for the Studio Backlot Tour and the Backstage Pass to 101 Dalmatians tour. Also see *The Making of...* for a behind-the-scenes perspective on the latest Disney release.

• After a leisurely dinner at your chosen spot, catch the Beauty and the Beast show (it's particularly wonderful at night), any attractions you missed, and the scheduled nighttime entertainment.

Four Days

This plan is recommended only for the highly energetic, since all the new attractions at Walt Disney World make it barely possible to see even the high points in such a time frame. During peak seasons, nothing less than four full days will do the trick. On each day, the idea is to make a quick tour of the premises, visiting the major attractions during the least crowded hours of the early morning, then repeating the circuit of the park once again later in the day.

On the day of your arrival at Walt Disney World, check in as close as possible to 3 P.M. Then spend time by the pool at your resort, have a leisurely dinner in one of the resort's restaurants, and plan to make it an early night. Of course, you may prefer to head straight to the Magic Kingdom for an evening of fireworks and the SpectroMagic parade.

DAY 1

- Spend your first full day at Epcot. Arrive at least a half hour before the posted opening time. If you haven't had breakfast, grab a quick bite at the Sunshine Season Food Fair in The Land pavilion.
- First ride Test Track (opening in spring 1997). Then see as much of The Land and Wonders of Life as possible before 11 A.M.
- When it opens, head immediately for World Showcase and see the movies in the Canada and France pavilions. Backtrack and fully explore France, United Kingdom, and Canada. Perhaps have lunch at Le Cellier.
- Then return to Future World, where you'll spend the remainder of the day. Check the Tip Board in Innoventions Plaza before proceeding to The Living Seas, Universe of Energy, Journey Into Imagination, and any other attractions you have not yet seen.
- Save Spaceship Earth until the rest of Future World closes at 7 P.M. Spend the next hour or so exploring Innoventions, where you can pass quite a bit of time.
- Plan to be around World Showcase Lagoon for the evening's presentation of IllumiNations 25.

DAY 2

- On your second full day, have breakfast as early as possible. Plan to arrive at the Magic Kingdom turnstiles at least a half hour before scheduled opening—and to be at the Central Plaza end of Main Street at the official opening time. Follow our outline for a one-day visit to the Magic Kingdom.

DAY 3

- On the third full day of your visit, arrive at the Disney-MGM Studios at least a half hour before the scheduled opening. Then follow the schedule outlined in our one-day visit to the Disney-MGM Studios.

DAY 4

- On your fourth full day, arrive at Epcot about half an hour before the park's official opening. If you were unable to make advance plans, go directly to Guest Relations to make priority seating arrangements for lunch and dinner in World Showcase. Secure a 1:30 P.M. seating for lunch and an 8:30 P.M. seating for dinner. (See *Good Meals, Great Times* for additional guidance and our dining suggestions).
- That done, take in any major attractions in Future World that you missed on your first day. Spend the remaining time before 11 A.M. at Innoventions.
- Next, head for World Showcase as close to its 11 A.M. opening time as possible. Start your route around the promenade with Mexico, making sure to catch the boat ride in Norway and the movie in China before heading to your lunch spot.
- Slot in a time to see the show at The American Adventure pavilion. Even if you hate shopping, browse through Germany's collectibles and toy shops and Morocco's brass and jewelry bazaars. Check your guidemap for the best times to look in on the entertainers who perform daily along World Showcase Promenade.
- Stop at one of the many snack stands for a late-afternoon international treat. The hours between 6 P.M. and your scheduled dinner time should be spent seeing any attractions that were missed on your previous circuits.
- Remember to allot enough time to walk to your dining spot. Skip dessert at the restaurant and instead head for the Boulangerie Pâtisserie in the France pavilion for pastry and espresso.
- If you couldn't get priority seating in the Epcot restaurant of your choice, or you need a change of pace, head for Pleasure Island, the Disney Village Marketplace, or the BoardWalk, where there are plenty of restaurants from which to choose (see *Good Meals, Great Times*).

Five Days

A stay of this length, while not exactly leisurely, is still the shortest time that can be conscientiously recommended for families with young children, older visitors, or anyone else who wants to visit all the best of Walt Disney World at a less than breakneck clip. Although the pace of this five-day plan is slower than that required during a four-day visit, it's still important not to waste time in order to cover all the high points. Before leaving home, try to make a 5 P.M. reservation for the Hoop-Dee-Doo Musical Revue for the fifth full day of your visit.

On the day of your arrival at Walt Disney World, check in as close as possible to 3 P.M. Then spend time by the pool at your resort, have a leisurely dinner in one of the resort's restaurants, and plan to make it an early night. Of course, you may prefer to head straight to the Magic Kingdom for an evening of fireworks and the SpectroMagic parade.

DAY 1

● Spend the first full day of your visit at Epcot. Proceed as for Day 1 of the four-day visit described on page 27.

DAY 2

● On the second full day of your visit, arrive at the Magic Kingdom parking lot at least 45 minutes before the official park opening. Have breakfast at one of the restaurants on Main Street that begin serving early and be at the Central Plaza end of Main Street at the park's official opening time. Then begin circumnavigating the park, taking in just the major attractions described for the first morning of a one-day visit.

● At about noon, leave the park and head for Typhoon Lagoon, Blizzard Beach, or River Country. Have lunch and enjoy the water park's various swimming areas, water slides, and recreational activities. Golfers may want to reserve ahead to sample one of the World's first-rate golf courses instead.

● Return to the Magic Kingdom at about 5 P.M. and grab a quick dinner. Then take another ride on Space Mountain and Splash Mountain. By 8 P.M. head for Main Street to stake a claim to a segment of curb for the 9 P.M. showing of the SpectroMagic parade. Watch the Fantasy in the Sky fireworks after the parade.

DAY 3

● On the third full day of your visit, head for the Disney-MGM Studios (arriving at least a half hour before the posted opening time). Follow the schedule outlined in the one-day visit described on page 26.

DAY 4

● Devote the fourth full day of your visit to another tour of Epcot. Proceed as for Day 4 of the four-day visit described on page 27.

DAY 5

● On the fifth full day of your visit, try one of the character breakfasts (described in *Good Meals, Great Times*).

● Head over to the Magic Kingdom and spend the rest of the day following our guidelines for the afternoon of a one-day visit, taking time for any other attractions that catch your eye.

● If you'd like to see the 25th Anniversary Parade, stake out a good spot on Main Street no later than 2:30 P.M. If you would like to participate, be in that spot at least 45 minutes before the 3 P.M. start; volunteers are chosen randomly from along the parade route.

● At about 4 P.M. head over to Fort Wilderness for the 5 P.M. Hoop-Dee-Doo Musical Revue.

● After the show (if you still have the energy), go to Pleasure Island for some dancing, comedy, or music. If tired feet prohibit such activity, take in a movie at the multiplex cinema next door. Or, since Magic Kingdom attractions are open late throughout 1997 for the 25th anniversary, return for another round of your favorites in the cooler evening hours.

Longer Visits

In addition to our program for five days, an even longer stay allows a chance to sample some of the World's other offerings. Spend another day in the one park you most enjoyed. Lounge by the pool, play tennis or golf, or bike. Go shopping at the Disney Village Marketplace. Cool off at one of Disney's innovative water parks. Have lunch at a WDW resort and try a special dinner at Victoria & Albert's at the Grand Floridian, or at Pleasure Island's Portobello Yacht Club. Check out the clubs at Pleasure Island or spend the evening at the new Board-Walk. Take golf or tennis lessons. Go fishing or waterskiing. Visit the spa at the Grand Floridian or the Disney Institute. Participate in a behind-the-scenes program. Play miniature golf at Fantasia Gardens. Enroll for a stay (or a day) at the Disney Institute. For more ideas, see our *Sports*, *Everything Else in the World*, and *Good Meals, Great Times* chapters.

HOW TO GET THERE

By Car

Here are some suggested routes to Walt Disney World from the downtown sections of several metropolitan areas. Figure on driving 350 to 400 miles a day—a reasonable distance that won't wear you down so much that you can't enjoy your stay.

Atlanta: I-75 south, I-475 south around Macon, I-75 south, Florida's Turnpike south, U.S. 27 south, U.S. 192 east to entrance. Total mileage: 428 miles.

Baltimore: I-95 south, I-495 east and south around Washington, I-95 south, I-295 around Jacksonville, I-95 south, I-4 west, U.S. 192 west to entrance. Total mileage: 948 miles.

Boston: I-90 west, I-84 west, I-91 south, I-95 south, I-287 west, Garden State Parkway south, New Jersey Turnpike south to Delaware Memorial Bridge, I-95 south (through Fort McHenry Tunnel in Baltimore), I-495 west and south around Washington, D.C., I-95 south, I-295 around Jacksonville, I-95 south, I-4 west, U.S. 192 west to entrance. Total mileage: 1,366 miles.

Buffalo: I-90 west, I-79 south, U.S. 19 south, West Virginia Turnpike south, I-77 south, I-26 east, I-95 south, I-295 around Jacksonville, I-95 south, I-4 west, U.S. 192 west to entrance. Total mileage: 1,250 miles.

Chicago: I-94 south, I-80 east, I-65 south, I-465 south around Indianapolis, I-65 south to Nashville, I-24 east to Chattanooga, I-75 south, I-285 west and south around Atlanta, I-75 south, I-475 south around Macon, I-75 south, Florida's Turnpike south, U.S. 27

south, U.S. 192 east to entrance. Total mileage: 1,172 miles.

Cincinnati: I-75 south, I-285 west and south around Atlanta, I-475 south around Macon, I-75 south, Florida's Turnpike south, U.S. 27 south, U.S. 192 east to entrance. Total mileage: 885 miles.

Cleveland: I-77 south, West Virginia Turnpike south, I-77 south, I-26 east, I-95 south, I-295 around Jacksonville, I-95 south, I-4 west, U.S. 192 west to entrance. Total mileage: 1,101 miles.

Dallas: I-20 east to Shreveport, S. R. 3132 south, I-49 south, S. R. 1/U.S. 71 south through Alexandria, I-49 south, I-10 east, I-12 east around New Orleans, I-10 east, I-75 south, Florida's Turnpike south, U.S. 27 south, U.S. 192 east to entrance. Total mileage: 1,174 miles.

Detroit: I-75 south, I-285 west and south around Atlanta, I-75 south, I-475 south around Macon, I-75 south, Florida's Turnpike south, U.S. 27 south, U.S. 192 east to entrance. Total mileage: 1,158 miles.

Indianapolis: I-65 south to Nashville, I-24 east to Chattanooga, I-75 south, I-285 west and south around Atlanta, I-75 south, I-475 south around Macon, I-75 south, Florida's Turnpike south, U.S. 27 south, U.S. 192 east to entrance. Total mileage: 977 miles.

Louisville: I-65 south to Nashville, I-24 east to Chattanooga, I-75 south, I-285 west and south around Atlanta, I-75 south, I-475 south around Macon, I-75 south, Florida's Turnpike south, U.S. 27 south, U.S. 192 east to entrance. Total mileage: 877 miles.

Minneapolis: I-94 east to Madison (WI), I-90 east, I-294 south around Chicago, I-90 east, I-65 south, 465 south around Indianapolis, I-65 south to Nashville, I-24 east to Chattanooga, I-75 south, I-285 west and south around Atlanta, I-75 south, Florida's Turnpike south, U.S. 27 south, U.S. 192 east to entrance. Total mileage: 1,581 miles.

New York City: Lincoln Tunnel west, S.R. 495 west, New Jersey Turnpike south to Delaware Memorial Bridge, I-95 south (through Fort McHenry Tunnel in Baltimore), I-495 west and south around Washington, D.C., I-95 south, I-295 around Jacksonville, I-95 south, I-4 west, U.S. 192 west to entrance. Total mileage: 1,164 miles.

Philadelphia: I-95 south (through Fort McHenry Tunnel in Baltimore), I-495 east and south around Washington, D.C., I-95 south, I-295 around Jacksonville, I-95 south, I-4 west, U.S. 192 west to entrance. Total mileage: 1,015 miles.

Pittsburgh: I-279 south, I-79 south, U.S. 19 south, West Virginia Turnpike south, I-77 south, I-26 east, I-95 south, I-295 around Jacksonville, I-95 south, I-4 west, U.S. 192 west to entrance. Total mileage: 1,072 miles.

Richmond: I-95 south, I-295 around Jacksonville, I-95 south, I-4 west, U.S. 192 west to entrance. Total mileage: 757 miles.

Toronto: Queen Elizabeth Way south, I-190 east, I-90 west, I-79 south, U.S. 19 south, West Virginia Turnpike south, I-77 south, I-26 east, I-95 south, I-295 around Jacksonville, I-95 south, I-4 west, U.S. 192 west to entrance. Total mileage: 1,359 miles.

By Bus

Relatively few vacationers come to Walt Disney World by bus. But it makes sense to consider this means of transportation if you don't drive, if you're traveling only a short distance, if you have plenty of time, or if you don't like to fly. Bus travel can be economical, although the greater the distance involved, the more likely the lowest available airfare will be competitive.

Greyhound provides frequent direct service into Orlando and Kissimmee (the latter is closer to Walt Disney World). From either destination, you can hire a taxi to take you to your hotel, but first check to see if your hotel offers shuttle service.

Consider these sample travel times by bus to Orlando: from Jacksonville, Florida, it's about 4 hours; from Tallahassee, Florida, about 7 hours; from Atlanta, Georgia, about 12 hours; and from Mobile or Montgomery, Alabama, also about 12 hours.

For further information, call Greyhound at 800-231-2222.

Resources for Road Trippers

AUTOMOBILE CLUBS: Reputable national automobile clubs can offer help with breakdowns en route; emergency towing; insurance that covers personal injury, accidents, arrest, bail bond, and lawyers' fees for defense of contested traffic cases; and travel-planning services, including free maps and route mapping. Programs vary from one club to the next, and membership fees range from $25 to $80 a year.

Among the leading clubs:

Allstate Motor Club; 1500 W. Shure Dr.; Arlington Heights, IL 60004; 800-347-8880

American Automobile Association; 1000 AAA Dr.; Heathrow, FL 32746; 800-564-6222

Amoco Motor Club; Box 9046; Des Moines, IA 50368; 800-334-3300

Ford Auto Club; Box 224,688; Dallas, TX 75222; 800-348-5220 (free membership to owners of new Fords)

Gulf Motor Club; 6001 N. Clark St.; Chicago, IL 60660; 800-633-3224

Montgomery Ward Auto Club; 200 N. Martingale Rd.; 3rd Floor–Enrollment; Schaumburg, IL 60173; 800-227-6459

Motor Club of America; 95 Rte. 17 South; Paramus, NJ 07653; 800-833-3207

ROAD MAPS: Those who don't belong to a club can check with state tourist boards about the availability of free maps. Other excellent sources for maps are the AAA Road Atlas ($8.95) and the Rand McNally Road Atlas ($9.95), both sold in bookstores.

From the Airport

By car: For the most direct route, take the North Exit to Route 528 (Beeline Expressway), going west toward Tampa. Pick up I-4 west, and follow it until you reach the appropriate WDW exit. The distance is 22 miles, the trip takes about half an hour, and the tolls add up to $1.25. If this route is congested, an alternative (via the South Exit) is to take the Central Florida Greeneway (Route 417) to Route 536, which leads directly to Walt Disney World. The tolls total $2.

Shuttles: It's also possible, and easy, to get to WDW resorts from the Orlando Airport without a car. Mears Motor Shuttles offers vans about every 15 to 20 minutes around the clock, serving Disney resorts, Disney Village Hotel Plaza accommodations, and Lake Buena Vista–area hotels. The cost to most hotels is $14 one way, $25 round-trip per adult; $10 one way, $17 round-trip per child age 4 to 11; free for children under four. Fares to International Drive properties are $2 to $3 lower. Call 423-5566 for reservations.

By Train

Amtrak serves the Orlando area twice daily from New York City. The trip takes about 22 hours and costs anywhere from $146 to $320 round-trip. The train stops along the way to pick up additional passengers in Philadelphia and Washington, D.C., as well as various cities in Virginia, North Carolina, South Carolina, and Georgia. (Book early for lower fares; special discounts are often available, so check when booking.)

Amtrak also offers Auto Train service daily in both directions from Lorton, Virginia, which is 17 miles south of Washington, D.C., direct to Sanford, Florida, just 25 miles northeast of Orlando. Accommodation charges for cars and passengers for the 17½-hour trip vary depending on the time of year and the direction traveled (going south in winter, or north in summer, is pricier). The fare includes two meals and some entertainment.

For reservations and current schedule information on these and other routes, send a self-addressed, stamped envelope to Amtrak Distribution Center; 1549 W. Glenlake Ave.; Box 7717; Itasca, IL 60143; or call 800-USA-RAIL (800-872-7245).

By Air

Modernistic Orlando International Airport is continually upgrading to keep up with the millions of visitors who flock to Central Florida each year. Monorails transport passengers efficiently to and from the central terminal, where a well-stocked shop supplies arriving and departing travelers with T-shirts, watches, and other Disney paraphernalia.

Finding the Lowest Airfare: If there's a trick to unearthing the most economical fares, it's this: Shop around. Keep these tips in mind, as well.

• Find out which airlines fly from your point of departure (check out the list of nonstop flights to Orlando on the next page) and call them all. Or let your travel agent do this for you, at no charge.

• Watch the newspapers for ads announcing short-term promotional fares.

• The more flexible you can be in your dates and duration of stay, the more money you're likely to save. Fares tend to be lowest on competitive, heavily traveled routes.

• Fly when most other people don't: at night, on weekends on routes that usually serve business travelers, or midweek to and from vacation destinations.

• When it's necessary to change planes en route, it's best to stick with one airline; the airline agent will know his or her own company's routing—and its discounted fares—better than those offered by other carriers.

• Plan ahead so you can take advantage of advance-purchase fares (lower rates that apply if a ticket is bought two to three weeks prior to the date of departure).

• Keep in mind that the lowest airfares usually carry a penalty if you want to revise your flight schedule, and that certain discount fare tickets are nonrefundable.

• When you call to make a reservation, ask about any applicable fare restrictions, including obligatory Saturday night stayover.

• Most carriers guarantee their fares. This means that you won't have to pay more if fares go up after you buy your ticket. On the other hand, if fares come down, you can request a refund.

You can fly nonstop to Orlando from about 70 different cities, on more than two dozen airlines. Schedules change often, and flights may be dropped or new ones added. This was the operative nonstop service at press time:

Akron, OH ....FL
Albany, NY ....FL, US
Allentown, PA ....FL
Atlanta, GA ....DL, KP
Atlantic City, NJ ....NK
Baltimore, MD......................US, WN
Birmingham, AL......DL*, US*, FL, WN
Boston, MA ....DL, US, TZ
Buffalo, NY.............................US, FL
Charlotte, NC ....US
Chicago, IL............DL, AA, KP, TZ, UA
Cincinnati, OH ....DL, DL*, FL
Cleveland, OH ....CO
Columbus, OH ....WN, HP
Dallas/Ft. Worth, TX ....DL, AA, FL
Dayton, OH ....FL
Denver, CO.....................................UA
Detroit, MI ....SY, NK, NW
Ft. Lauderdale, FL........DL, DL*, UA*, WN, TZ, 3M
Ft. Myers, FL......................US*, DL*
Greensboro/Winston-Salem, NC ....CO
Greenville/Spartanburg, SC ....FL
Hartford, CT....................DL, FL, US
Houston, TX....................................CO
Indianapolis, IN ....US, TZ, WN
Jacksonville, FL ....DL*, US*
Kansas City, MO............................FL
Key West, FL ....DL*
Knoxville, TN..................................FL
Las Vegas, NV ....DL
Long Island Macarthur, NY .....US, KW
Los Angeles, CA ....DL, UA
Louisville, KY ....WN
Manchester, NH ....US
Melbourne, FL ....DL*
Memphis, TN...............................NW
Mexico City, Mexico..............DL, AM*
Miami, FL..............DL, DL*, UA, UA*, AA, US*, 3M, AA*
Milwaukee, WI ....TZ
Minneapolis/St. Paul, MN ....NW
Montego Bay, Jamaica ....JM
Montreal, Canada ....AC
Naples, FL ....DL*
Nashville, TN.................DL*, FL, WN
Nassau, Bahamas ....DL, DL*, UP
Newburgh, NY ....FL

New Orleans, LA ....DL*, WN
New York, NY/Newark, NJ ......DL, CO, US, TW, KP, US*, AA, LF, NW
Norfolk/Virginia Beach/ Williamsburg, VA ....FL
Omaha, NE ....FL
Panama City, FL ....US*
Pensacola, FL ....DL*, US*
Philadelphia, PA ....DL, US, NK
Phoenix, AZ....................................HP
Pittsburgh, PA ....US
Providence, RI ....FL, US
Raleigh/Durham, NC ....JI
Richmond/Williamsburg, VA ....FL
Rochester, NY..........................FL, US
St. Louis, MO.......................TW, WN
Salt Lake City, UT ....DL
San Antonio, TX ....FL
San Francisco, CA ....UA
San Juan, Puerto Rico ....DL, AA, TZ
Sarasota/ Bradenton, FL ....DL*, US*, TZ
Syracuse, NY ....FL, US
Tallahassee, FL ....DL*, US*
Tampa/St. Petersburg, FL ....DL*, HP, US*
Toronto, Canada ....CP, AC
Washington, DC................US*, DL, US, UA, WN
West Palm Beach, FL ....DL, DL*, US*, TZ

ABBREVIATIONS—AA: American. AA*: American Eagle. AC: Air Canada. AM*: Aeromexico. CO: Continental. CP: Canadian Airlines International. DL: Delta. DL*: The Delta Connection. FL: Airtran Airways. HP: America West. JI: Midway. JM: Air Jamaica. KP: Kiwi. KW: Carnival. LF: Jettrain. NK: Spirit. NW: Northwest. SY: Sun Country. 3M: Gulfstream International. TW: Trans World. TZ: American Trans Air. UA: United. UA*: United Express. UP: Bahamasair. US: USAir. US*: USAir Express. WN: Southwest.

Source: *Official Airline Guides*

CUSTOMIZED TRAVEL TIPS

Traveling with Children

Tell youngsters that a Walt Disney World vacation is in the works and the response is apt to be overwhelming. Try to get children involved in planning the trip so they know what to expect. Before leaving home, pick up a copy of our guide, *Birnbaum's Walt Disney World For Kids, By Kids* ($9.95). It's filled with information about the World from a kid's perspective, written for kids ages 7 to 14.

EN ROUTE: The journey is likely to be fraught with "Are-we-there-yet?" Certain ploys can quiet this refrain, such as setting up a series of intermediate goals to which kids can look forward. Young children can anticipate discovering the contents of a pint-size suitcase packed with familiar games and toys, plus a few surprises. Also, take along snacks to keep things peaceful when stomachs start rumbling and food is miles away. Above all, and especially if the trip is by car, take it easy, and allow time for plenty of breaks.

Those who fly should schedule travel during off-peak hours, when empty seats might be available. During takeoff and landing, babies should be given bottles, pacifiers, or even thumbs to promote swallowing and clear ears. Newborn babies should not be taken aloft, since their lungs may not adjust easily to the altitude. For finicky young eaters, request special meals when reserving seats.

AT WALT DISNEY WORLD: This vacationland ranks among the easiest spots on earth for families traveling with children. Older kids don't need to be driven around, and the general supervision is such that kids are hard pressed to get into trouble. With teens, it's enough to establish a specific meeting place and time inside the Magic Kingdom, Epcot, or the Disney-MGM Studios.

Theme Park Favorites: Although kids are usually enchanted by all of Walt Disney World, there are some attractions that hold their interest more than others. If you're traveling with very young children, your best bet is the Magic Kingdom. Visit Mickey's Toontown Fair first and then spend time in Fantasyland, keeping in mind that some of the attractions here frighten kids who are afraid of the dark. For older kids, thrill rides get the highest rating. Be sure not to miss Space Mountain, Alien Encounter, Splash Mountain, and Big Thunder Mountain Railroad in the Magic Kingdom; Test Track (opening this spring in Epcot); and the Tower of Terror at the Disney-MGM Studios. Other favorites include The Haunted Mansion, Legend of The Lion King, Pirates of the Caribbean, and Peter Pan's Flight in the Magic Kingdom; Wonders of Life, Journey Into Imagination, Innoventions, and Norway in Epcot; and Muppet*Vision 3-D, Star Tours, the Indiana Jones Epic Stunt Spectacular, and the Monster Sound Show in the Studios.

Restaurant Picks: Fast-food, buffet, and food court meals generally win with most kids, but here are a few specifics in the theme parks. In the Magic Kingdom, Lumière's Kitchen in Fantasyland and Tony's Town Square on Main Street are favorable spots for lunch. Aunt Polly's on Tom Sawyer Island is

Timely Tip

Families with small children should know about the "kid switch" policy at the theme parks. At attractions with age or height restrictions, a parent who waits with a young child while the other parent rides the attraction can go right on when the first parent comes off. If lines are long this can save a lot of time, so be sure to ask the attendant.

a good bet for a snack; while adults are sipping lemonade, the kids can explore every nook and cranny on the island. At Epcot, kids prefer the Sunshine Season Food Fair in The Land and the Liberty Inn at The American Adventure. The Sci-Fi Dine-In and the 50's Prime Time Café at the Studios are good choices as well. Any of the character meals are hits with kids of all ages (see page 244 in *Good Meals, Great Times* for details).

Resort Fun: All the WDW resorts have at least a small room full of video games, much to the satisfaction of kids of all ages; the arcades at the Contemporary and All-Star resorts are positively vast. Most of the hotels have playgrounds; the ones at the Polynesian, Dixie Landings, Caribbean Beach, and All-Star resorts get high marks from children. The best pools for kids are at the Yacht Club and Beach Club, Port Orleans, Dixie Landings, Polynesian, Dolphin and Swan, and All-Star resorts.

Child Care: The Polynesian, Grand Floridian, Contemporary, Wilderness Lodge, Yacht Club, Beach Club, BoardWalk, Swan, and Dolphin have child-care facilities. In-room child care can be summoned to all WDW resort locations; contact the Guest Services desk. There is also a center known as Kinder-Care, which accepts kids ages one to four. For details and availability, phone 827-5444.

Strollers: Available for rent for $5 (plus a $1 deposit) at Strollers–Wheelchairs on the east side of Main Street at the entrance to the Magic Kingdom; in Epcot at the Stroller and Wheelchair Rentals Shop on the east side of the Entrance Plaza and at the International Gateway; and at Oscar's Super Service at the Disney-MGM Studios. The deposit is refundable. Be sure to hold on to your receipt. Present it when you return the stroller and you'll get a Disney Dollar back.

If the stroller disappears while you're inside an attraction, a replacement may be obtained at Merchant of Venus in Tomorrowland; at the Frontier Trading Post in Frontierland; at Tinker Bell's Treasures in Fantasyland; at the World Traveler Shop at Epcot's International Gateway and the Germany pavilion in World Showcase; and at Oscar's at the Disney-MGM Studios. Stroller renters should also be aware that guests have to pay only once a day for a stroller. If you rent one in the morning and plan to spend the afternoon at another park, just present the receipt for a stroller there.

Baby Services: Located at the Magic Kingdom (next to Crystal Palace restaurant on Main Street), Epcot (in the Odyssey Center between Future World and World Showcase), and the Disney-MGM Studios (in Guest Relations just inside the gate), these centers can be helpful to parents with young children. There are rooms with comfortable rocking chairs and love seats for nursing mothers, and cheery feeding rooms (with highchairs, bibs, and plastic spoons available). The baby centers have facilities for changing infants, preparing formulas, and warming bottles. Disposable diapers and nurser bags, pull-on rubber pants, baby bottles, formula (Similac, Isomil, and Enfamil), teethers, pacifiers, prepared cereal, juices, and strained and junior baby food in a limited selection are for sale. The decor is soothing; the atmosphere is such that it seems a million miles away from the parks. A stop for diaper changing makes a good break for child and parent alike. Changing areas are available in most women's and some men's restrooms as well. Hours at the baby centers vary; check at City Hall or Guest Relations.

Lost children: The security forces inside the theme parks are far more careful than the happy appearance of things indicates. This is a welcome thought on those rare instances when a child suddenly disappears or fails to show up on schedule. If this happens, check the lost children's logbooks at Baby Services or City Hall in the Magic Kingdom; at Guest Relations or Baby Services (behind the Odyssey Center) in Epcot; or at Guest Relations at the Disney-MGM Studios. Every Disney employee knows where these logbooks are—and what to do if a lost-looking child suddenly starts to call for his or her parents. There are no paging systems in the parks, but in serious emergencies an all-points bulletin can be put out among employees. The staff at the Guest Relations windows at the entrances to Epcot, the Magic Kingdom, and the Disney-MGM Studios can also assist.

If there are younger children along, it's not a bad idea to stop and pick up a special name tag to facilitate a reunion in case the family gets separated. These are available at City Hall and Baby Services at the Magic Kingdom, Guest Relations and Baby Services in Epcot, and Guest Relations at the Studios.

Older Travelers

Walt Disney World can overwhelm an elderly traveler not accustomed to unfamiliar places. Epcot encompasses significant distances, and the Magic Kingdom and the Disney-MGM Studios can be disorienting because of their profusion of sights, sounds, and crisscrossing pathways. And the heat, particularly in summer, can be hard to take. But with the proper planning and precautions, all of Walt Disney World can be just as delightful for older visitors as for kids. Here are a few suggestions:

• Join a tour. Surprisingly enough, not many companies offer tours to WDW specifically designed for older travelers. One that does is Eventures Unlimited Inc.; 7648 Southland Blvd., Suite 101; Orlando, FL 32809; 826-0055 or 800-356-7891.

• Schedule visits for off-peak seasons and hours when the crowds will not be overwhelming and discouraging. Also, note that special values are available to Florida residents during selected non-peak dates. Call 824-4321 for details.

• Read all WDW literature carefully before arrival so that things are familiar, and you are alert to the facilities and services available to you.

• In the parks, don't be timid about asking for directions or advice. Disney employees are extremely knowledgeable and always happy to help out.

• Always try to eat early or late to avoid the mealtime crowds. In the Magic Kingdom, select more sedate restaurants such as Tony's Town Square on Main Street or King Stefan's Banquet Hall in Cinderella Castle. Or take the monorail to the still calmer Polynesian, Contemporary, or Grand Floridian resort. It's a quick trip, and pleasant dining options (from casual to fancy) abound. In Epcot, the Coral Reef restaurant in Future World and Le Cellier in World Showcase are especially restful spots for lunch. At the Disney-MGM Studios, the Hollywood Brown Derby offers a relaxing sit-down meal.

• Don't try to save money by scrimping on food. Touring takes energy, and only a good meal can provide it.

• Protect yourself from the sun, which can be hot even through the winter. Always wear a hat, and don't skimp on the sunscreen. (And remember to cover your legs, which are easily sunburned by light rays reflected from pavements.)

• Don't become overheated. Take frequent rest stops in the shade, and get out of the mid-afternoon heat by stopping for a snack in an air-conditioned restaurant. Avoid standing in line at attractions where the queue is not wholly protected from the sun and can therefore be very hot, such as the Magic Kingdom's Big Thunder Mountain Railroad. In Epcot, spend afternoon hours in Innoventions, Wonders of Life, or the Sea Base Alpha exhibit at The Living Seas in Future World.

• Don't underestimate the distances at Epcot; you may need to walk as much as two miles in the course of a day. If taken slowly and in short increments, this is not too onerous. But if you don't think you can cover that distance, be sure to rent a wheelchair at the outset of your visit. The buses that circumnavigate World Showcase Lagoon and the launches that make regular crossings can help—but only when there are no long queues. It is better to walk between pavilions, resting frequently en route, than to wait 15 or 20 minutes in line for a ride in a bus or boat.

• Pace yourself. It's smart to head back to your hotel for a swim or a nap in the afternoon, and then return to the parks later on. This is easy enough to do via WDW transportation if you're staying at an on-property hotel; some off-property hotels also offer free shuttle service to and from the theme parks, but be sure to check the schedules.

• Above all, don't push yourself. Half the fun of Walt Disney World—the part that younger travelers often miss—is just sitting under a tree on a park bench, watching the people go by.

Travelers with Disabilities

Walt Disney World gets high marks among travelers with disabilities because of the attention paid to their special needs. Still, it's important to study the information provided here to become fully aware of the myriad services available.

GETTING AROUND: Special parking is available for guests visiting the Magic Kingdom, Epcot, and the Disney-MGM Studios; ask for directions at the Auto Plazas upon entering. From the Transportation and Ticket Center (TTC), the Magic Kingdom is accessible either by ferry or by monorail (for those using wheelchairs, the former is preferable, since the slant of the monorail ramp makes it a bit taxing to hold a wheelchair when there are lines). Note that all WDW monorail stations are accessible to guests in wheelchairs except the one at the Contemporary resort, which can be reached only by escalator. Valet parking is available at Pleasure Island and the Disney Village Marketplace and complimentary to guests with disabilities.

Wheelchairs: In each of the theme parks, wheelchairs are available for rent; they cost $5 per day, with a $1 refundable deposit. In the Magic Kingdom, wheelchairs are rented at Strollers–Wheelchairs on the right side of the souvenir area, just inside the turnstiles. Epcot's rental area is just inside the turnstiles on the left. Oscar's Super Service rents wheelchairs at the Disney-MGM Studios.

Electronic Convenience Vehicles (ECVs) are also available in each of the parks. The price to rent an ECV is $30 plus a $2 refundable deposit, per park per day. There is a limited number available, and they usually sell out within the first couple of hours that the parks are open.

Accessibility: It's easy to get around the theme parks by wheelchair. Most restrooms have extra-wide cubicles with wall bars for people in wheelchairs. Most attractions are accessible to guests who can be lifted to and from their chairs with assistance from a member of their party, and many can accommodate guests who must remain in their wheelchairs at all times. Consult the *Walt Disney World Guidebook for Guests with Disabilities* (see box on the next page) for details about attraction access, or check with the ride host or hostess. At the water parks, life jackets are available for travelers with disabilities.

All WDW hotels are easily explored by wheelchair and have accommodations for guests with disabilities. For assistance in selecting a WDW hotel whose rooms best serve your specific requirements, ask to speak to someone in the Special Requests Department when you call Central Reservations (934-7639). The representatives are extremely informed and helpful.

RESOURCES: For guests who are sight impaired, a tape recorder and a cassette that describes the Magic Kingdom, Epcot, and the Disney-MGM Studios are available. A $25 refundable deposit is required for recorder use. Service animals are permitted in the parks.

Assistive listening devices that amplify attraction sound tracks for guests who are hearing impaired are available at City Hall in the Magic Kingdom, and at Guest Relations in both Epcot and the Disney-MGM Studios. A $25 refundable deposit and presentation of a major credit card is required. Guests who use telecommunications devices for the deaf (TDDs) can call 827-5141 for WDW information. TDDs are available for guest use at City Hall in the Magic Kingdom, Guest Relations in Epcot and at the Disney-MGM Studios, Guest Services at the Disney Village Marketplace, and at all the resorts. There is no charge for use of the TDDs. Also, written scripts are available at each show and attraction for use by guests with hearing impairments.

Tours: The Society for the Advancement of Travel for the Handicapped (347 Fifth Ave., Suite 610; New York, NY 10016; 212-447-7284) has a number of member travel agents who are knowledgeable about tours for travelers with disabilities and experienced in arranging both individual and group tours. Send a self-addressed stamped envelope and $5 to receive a copy of their listings and other information. Flying Wheels Travel (143 W. Bridge St.; Owatonna, MN 55060; 800-535-6790) is another company that organizes trips to Walt Disney World for travelers with disabilities.

Theme Park Resource

The *Walt Disney World Guidebook for Guests with Disabilities*, which describes the accessibility of all WDW attractions, is essential reading that will prove beneficial throughout your visit. The guidebook may be obtained at wheelchair rental locations, City Hall in the Magic Kingdom, and Guest Relations in both Epcot and the Disney-MGM Studios. It is also available by mail. Write to: Walt Disney World Guest Communications; Box 10,000; Lake Buena Vista, FL 32830.

Local Assistance: Holiday Assistants (7798 Indian Ridge Trail North; Kissimmee, FL 39749; 397-4845 or 800-945-2045) is a valuable resource for travelers with disabilities visiting Central Florida because it provides free referrals for many needs, from medical care and barrier-free hotels to hourly helpers.

GETTING THERE: The most important thing to remember is to plan in advance. Allow extra time, and at each stage of the trip, inform air, bus, train, and hotel personnel of your special needs.

Traveling by car: Major car-rental companies in the Orlando area each have a limited quantity of hand-controlled cars; it's a good idea to call well in advance to reserve one.

Traveling by plane: Airlines are more helpful than in the past in assisting travelers with disabilities. Occasionally, a vacationer can enter the aircraft in his or her own chair—provided the chair is narrow and the plane's aisles are wide; more often, travelers transfer to a narrower airline chair at the door of the aircraft, while their own chair is sent down to the luggage compartment. Passengers in wheelchairs are usually pre-boarded and then deplaned after other passengers. If you're not taking your own wheelchair along and have a tight connection to make, be sure to advise the airline's attendants well in advance. If a passenger wishes to use an airline's wheelchair at a connecting point or destination, this wheelchair service should be ordered at the same time flight reservations are being made.

Policies on motorized wheelchairs vary, depending on the airline and the type of chair; check with carriers in advance. Service animals are always allowed aboard aircraft (though some carriers may require them to be muzzled), but arrangements should be handled at the same time reservations are made so that a bulkhead seat may be requested.

Traveling by train: Whether riding with or without reservations, it's smart to phone in advance to arrange for one of the seats that Amtrak maintains for travelers with disabilities. Wheelchairs are available at major Amtrak stations, including Orlando's. Cars have barrier-free seats, bathrooms, and sleeping compartments.

Battery-powered, standard-size wheelchairs are permitted in coaches. However, fuel-powered and oversize chairs must be stored in the baggage car for the duration of the trip. Always be sure to phone the train stations and reservations center well before your departure date to arrange for any specific facilities or services you may need.

Passengers who are visually impaired or have other disabilities get a 15% discount on the lowest available fare, though companions must pay full fare. Service animals may ride with passengers at no extra charge.

Traveling by bus: Greyhound allows vacationers with disabilities to travel with a companion (for help with boarding and disembarking) for the price of a single adult ticket. Greyhound transports motorized and nonmotorized wheelchairs at no additional charge.

Lost & Sought

Occasionally, traveling companions do get separated in the crush of the crowds, or someone may fail to show up at an appointed meeting spot. When this happens, it's good to know that messages can be left for fellow travelers at Guest Relations at City Hall in the Magic Kingdom, or at the Guest Relations buildings in Epcot and the Disney-MGM Studios.

Single Travelers

Walt Disney World does not exactly attract the young singles crowd, so those on the lookout for romantic encounters would probably do better elsewhere. But those who travel alone for the freedom and fun of it can have as enjoyable a time here as they would anywhere else.

WDW employees are generally a friendly and entertaining lot; chatting with a painter about the perpetual repainting of Main Street woodwork, or discussing life abroad with one of the World Showcase employees born and educated in the country a pavilion represents, a single traveler usually learns more about the ways of the World than any group member. Other visitors who might be encountered in the course of a day are away from their own home base as well, and are apt to be just that much less standoffish.

For singles on the lookout for company, Pleasure Island's clubs and restaurants can prove to be fertile meeting places. Likewise, the BoardWalk is a lively destination. In addition to WDW guests, lots of folks from the Orlando area also patronize these locales (especially on weekends).

Single women traveling alone will find the bars and lounges at WDW hotels welcoming. The same relaxed atmosphere prevails at the Catwalk Bar at the Disney-MGM Studios and at the Rose & Crown Pub (in the United Kingdom pavilion) and the Matsu No Ma lounge (Japan) in Epcot's World Showcase. The Biergarten in World Showcase's Germany pavilion and the Teppanyaki Dining Rooms in Japan's Mitsukoshi restaurant are especially convivial, as parties are seated together at large tables.

Another way to meet people is to sign up for a behind-the-scenes tour. The Disney Institute is the best place to meet folks with similar interests. River Country, Blizzard Beach, Typhoon Lagoon, and the hotel swimming pools and beaches are also good places for making friends.

A note for budget watchers: Rates at all WDW resorts, hotels at Disney Village Hotel Plaza, and most other area accommodations are the same whether one or two persons occupy a room. The Disney Institute, however, does offer single rates.

How to Get the Best Photos

There are so many wonderful images all over the World that just about any camera in working order can capture them for you. Here are some useful hints:

- Flash photography is not permitted inside any WDW attractions.

- Don't shoot closer than 4 feet from your subject, and don't try for a flash picture from more than 60 feet away.

- For more interesting photos, fill the frame with as much of the prime subject as possible.

- Don't shoot directly into the sun. Instead, stand so light falls directly on your subject—coming from behind you or from the side.

- To photograph fireworks, your camera must have a manually adjustable shutter speed and aperture. Use color negative film (ASA 400). Set the aperture at f8 and the shutter speed at B. Hold the lens open for three to five seconds at each burst; cover between explosions.

- Photo spots around the theme parks can help you capture the best photos.

- If your camera isn't functioning correctly, visit the Camera Center on the east side of Main Street near Town Square in the Magic Kingdom; the Camera Center near Spaceship Earth, or Cameras and Film at Journey Into Imagination at Epcot; or The Darkroom on Hollywood Boulevard at the Disney-MGM Studios.

- Film is available at many shops around the Magic Kingdom, Epcot, the Disney-MGM Studios, and the WDW resorts. The best selection can be found at the camera shops in each park.

Film processing: Two-hour processing is available at the Magic Kingdom, Epcot, the Disney-MGM Studios, WDW resorts, and the Disney Village Marketplace wherever a Photo Express sign is displayed. Film is processed right on the premises.

Rental cameras: Video cameras may be rented at the camera shops in all three theme parks. Cost is $25 per day with a $300 refundable deposit that can be charged to American Express, Visa, or MasterCard. While no 35mm cameras are available for rent, disposable cameras may be purchased.

WDW Weddings & Honeymoons

Walt Disney World is the most popular honeymoon destination in the country. The resorts offer romantic stretches of white-sand beaches for evening strolls, fine restaurants for candlelight dinners, and a host of activities to rival most any Caribbean or Hawaiian destination. Add to that the fantasy of the Magic Kingdom, the wonder of Epcot, and the glamour of the Disney-MGM Studios, plus Pleasure Island and BoardWalk nightlife, Disney Village Marketplace shopping, and water park thrills, and it's not very hard to see why Walt Disney World is number one with newlyweds. Because honeymooners have been flocking to the WDW resorts for many years, a variety of packages is now available catering specifically to newly married couples (call 800-828-0228 for information).

For many years, the folks at Walt Disney World received hundreds of requests from couples who wanted to get married at one of Walt Disney World's theme parks. Today, couples can tie the knot in evening ceremonies at any of them during seasons that the parks close early. The Yacht Club, Beach Club, Polynesian, Wilderness Lodge, and Contemporary resorts also host their share of weddings, with The Villas at the Disney Institute providing a more rustic option.

The Wedding Pavilion near the Grand Floridian offers a Victorian-style indoor setting with a prime view of Cinderella Castle. A combination of stained glass, sage green and soft pink florals, and benches with heart-shaped cutouts (seating around 260) creates the romantic ambience. Couples can fill their wedding album with photos taken at Picture Point, under a trellis of climbing white roses, with the faraway castle prominently in the background. Private ceremonies can also be performed at this scenic spot.

Weddings range from elegant affairs without a hint of Disneyana, to ceremonies in which the bride and groom arrive in Cinderella's coach and Mickey and Minnie are among the guests. At Franck's Studio, WDW wedding coordinators work with couples to customize each individual wedding. Among the services offered are gown design, formal-wear rentals, invitations, photography, hairstyling, manicures, flower arranging, and musical entertainment.

Wedding specialists also help to arrange accommodations for guests, rehearsal dinners, bachelor parties, and just about any other activities you might require. For additional information about a WDW wedding, call 363-6333. For information about honeymoon packages, call 800-828-0228.

FINGERTIP REFERENCE GUIDE

BARBERS AND SALONS

The most amusing place to get a haircut is the old-fashioned Harmony Barber Shop (824-6550) in the Magic Kingdom. It's tucked away at the end of the flower-filled cul-de-sac just off the west side of Main Street. This is also the place where the "Dapper Dans," the park's own barbershop quartet, are most likely to be heard throughout the day. Children can get special souvenir Mouseketeer hats, and mustache cups and other nostalgic shaving items are for sale.

Haircuts, coloring, manicures, pedicures, and other services are available at the following resort locations: the salon on the third floor of the Contemporary (824-3411), the Periwig Salon at the Yacht Club and Beach Club (934-3260), Ivy Trellis at the Grand Floridian (824-3000, ext. 2581), and the Niki Bryan shop at the Dolphin (934-4250).

CAR CARE

There are several Exxon gas stations with convenience stores on the property. The one on Buena Vista Drive across from Pleasure Island is open 24 hours a day. The one on Floridian Way near the Magic Kingdom

Auto Plaza is open daily from 7 A.M. till two hours after the Magic Kingdom closes. A third station opened recently near the BoardWalk resort and the Disney-MGM Studios entrance on Buena Vista Drive; it's open 24 hours and has a car wash. It's also reassuring to know that breakdowns don't mean disaster. All WDW roads are patrolled constantly by security vehicles equipped with radios that can be used to call for help. Riker's Wrecker Service provides 24-hour towing service; call 352-0842.

DISNEY DOLLARS

Commemorative 25th anniversary Disney Dollars bearing Mickey's, Goofy's, or Simba's image are available from City Hall (Magic Kingdom) and Guest Relations (Epcot and the Disney-MGM Studios) in $1, $5, and $10 denominations. They are accepted as cash anywhere at Walt Disney World.

DRINKING LAWS

In Florida, the legal drinking age is 21. There are many bars and lounges all over Walt Disney World; minors are permitted to accompany their parents, but are prohibited from sitting or standing at the bar. No alcohol is

served in the Magic Kingdom (where even the piña coladas are nonalcoholic), but alcoholic beverages are sold at restaurants and bars in Epcot, Disney-MGM Studios, Pleasure Island, and Disney Village Marketplace.

By the bottle: Alcoholic beverages are sold in at least one shop at most WDW resorts. The Gourmet Pantry at the Disney Village Marketplace has a broader selection. Liquor may be purchased from room service at the Polynesian, Contemporary, Grand Floridian, Yacht Club, Beach Club, BoardWalk, Dolphin, and Swan resorts; beer and wine are usually available for delivery at other resorts.

LOCKERS

Attended lockers can be found in the following theme park locations: underneath Main Street Railroad Station in the Magic Kingdom; on the west side of Spaceship Earth in Epcot; and next to Oscar's Super Service near the main entrance at the Disney-MGM Studios. Lockers are also available at two locations at the Transportation and Ticket Center (TTC): next to the Lost and Found on the west side and beside the bus parking lot on the east side. Cost is $3 per day (plus a $2 deposit) for unlimited use. Items too big to fit can be checked at the Guest Relations windows at the TTC, at City Hall in the Magic Kingdom, at the package pickup area in Epcot, and at Guest Relations at the Disney-MGM Studios.

LOST & FOUND

The extensive indexing system maintained by Walt Disney World's Lost and Found department is impressive, especially when a prized possession turns up missing, whether it's false teeth or a camera. (Both have been lost in the past; the dentures were never claimed.) If you lose (or find) something, report it at these Lost and Found locations: the Guest Relations window on the east end of the Transportation and Ticket Center (TTC); City Hall in the Magic Kingdom; the Gift Stop in the entrance plaza at Epcot; Oscar's Super Service just inside the Disney-MGM Studios; or the Guest Services desk in the lobby of any WDW resort. At Fort Wilderness, dial 7-2726 from a comfort station telephone; from outside the campground, phone 824-2726; and from the Disney Village Marketplace, phone 828-3058.

Items lost in one of the theme parks can be claimed on the day of the loss at the park's Lost and Found, and thereafter at the main Lost and Found station at the TTC. To report lost items after your visit, call 824-4245.

Articles not claimed by the owner may be claimed by the finder—providing an added incentive for visitors to turn over valuable items to the nearest Lost and Found.

MAIL

Postage stamps can be purchased at all WDW resorts, at City Hall in the Magic Kingdom, near the lockers in both Epcot and the Disney-MGM Studios, and at Guest Services in the Disney Village Marketplace.

The old-fashioned, olive-drab mailboxes that punctuate the thoroughfares in the three theme parks are not official U.S. post boxes, but letters can be mailed there. Postmarks read "Lake Buena Vista," not "Walt Disney World." The post office is located at the Shoppes at Lake Buena Vista shopping center (opposite Summerfield Suites); it's open from 9 A.M. to 4 P.M. weekdays and 9 A.M. to noon on Saturday (283-0223).

Mail may be addressed to guests in care of their hotel; the address for WDW resorts is Walt Disney World; Box 10,000; Lake Buena Vista, FL 32830-1000.

MEDICAL MATTERS

For travelers with chronic health problems, it's a good idea to carry copies of all prescriptions and to get names of local doctors from hometown physicians. However, Walt Disney World is equipped to deal with many types of medical emergencies. In the Magic Kingdom, next to the Crystal Palace, there's a First Aid Center staffed by a registered nurse; there is another at Epcot in the Odyssey Center complex. At the Disney-MGM Studios, the First Aid Center is in the Guest Relations building at the main entrance, accessible from both inside and outside the park.

Walt Disney World resort guests and those staying at other area hotels have access to services providing non-emergency medical care. HouseMed (239-1195) can have a physician dispatched directly to a guest's room 24 hours a day. The service also operates two walk-in medical treatment centers: MediClinic, just east of I-4 on U.S. 192, is

open 8 A.M. to 9 P.M. daily, and the recently expanded MediClinic Lake Buena Vista at the intersection of S.R. 535 and International Drive is open 8 A.M. to 8 P.M. daily. The Centra Care Walk-In Medical Care (239-6463) at 12,500 South Apopka-Vineland Road is open 8 A.M. to 8 P.M. weekdays (to 5 P.M. weekends). Round-trip shuttle service is available from most area hotels to all three clinics.

The most common malady? Not sensitive stomachs upset by rides, but simple sunburn. So be forewarned. Wear a hat, and slather on sufficient sunblock or sunscreen, especially during the spring and summer. Serious emergencies can be reported to the nearby Sandlake Hospital (351-8550).

For diabetics: Walt Disney World resorts provide refrigeration services for insulin. All villa accommodations have their own refrigerators, and small refrigerators are available at other resorts for a nominal per diem.

Prescriptions: For a referral to the closest pharmacy or to have medications delivered, call HouseMed at 239-1195.

MONEY

Cash, traveler's checks, personal checks, American Express, MasterCard, Visa, and The Disney Credit Card are accepted as payment for most charges at Walt Disney World. Checks must bear your name and address, be drawn on a U.S. bank, and be accompanied by proper identification—a valid driver's license and a major credit card. Note that some fast-food restaurants and all snack stands accept only cash. WDW resort guests who have left a credit card imprint at check-in may use their hotel IDs to cover purchases in shops, most lounge and restaurant charges, and recreational fees incurred inside Walt Disney World. These cards are not valid for charges made past check-out time on the last day of the guest's stay.

Automated Teller Machines: ATMs are now scattered throughout Walt Disney World. Theme park locations include three in the Magic Kingdom (in the SunTrust bank

next to City Hall, in Adventureland near Tropical Serenade, and in the Tomorrowland arcade), two in Epcot (near the main entrance and on the pathway between Future World and World Showcase), and one at the Disney-MGM Studios (at the entrance), plus one at the TTC. Most WDW resorts have ATMs in the lobby (except the Yacht Club, Grand Floridian, The Villas at the Disney Institute, and the Swan); the Fort Wilderness ATM is outside Pioneer Hall. Others can be found at Pleasure Island (near the entrance to the Rock 'n' Roll Beach Club) and at the Disney Village Marketplace (near Guest Services). Most bank cards and credit cards are accepted; there is a nominal fee for use.

Banking Services: SunTrust, which has an old-fashioned branch on Main Street inside the Magic Kingdom and one across from the Disney Village Marketplace, can:

• Give cash advances on MasterCard and Visa credit cards, with a $25 minimum.

• Cash and sell traveler's checks and provide refunds for lost American Express and Bank of America traveler's checks.

• Cash personal checks for up to $25 upon presentation of a driver's license and a major credit card. American Express cardholders can cash personal checks for up to $200 (green card) or $500 (gold card) upon presentation of their cards (part payable in cash and the rest in traveler's checks).

• Help with wire transfers of up to $5,000 from a guest's bank to the SunTrust branch.

The SunTrust branch in the Magic Kingdom is open from 9 A.M. to 4 P.M. daily (until 6 P.M. Thursday); 828-6102. The branch across from the Disney Village Marketplace is open from 9 A.M. to 4 P.M. weekdays (until 6 P.M. Thursday); drive-in teller windows are open from 8 A.M. to 6 P.M. weekdays; 828-6106.

Traveler's checks: Even the most careful of vacationers occasionally loses a wallet, and traveler's checks can take the sting out of that loss. Look for special promotions by banks at home in the months preceding a vacation to see if one of the five major brands—American Express, MasterCard, Visa, Citicorp, and Bank of America—is available free. Stash the receipt bearing the check numbers in a place separate from the

checks themselves, along with one piece of identification such as a duplicate driver's license or a spare credit card to speed the refund process should your checks get lost.

Foreign currency exchange: This can be done from 9 A.M. to 4 P.M. daily at Guest Relations in all three theme parks, and at the SunTrust bank inside the Magic Kingdom. Currency can be exchanged at WDW resorts or the Sun Trust across from the Disney Village Marketplace at other times.

PETS

No pets (other than service dogs) are allowed in the Magic Kingdom, Epcot, the Disney-MGM Studios, or the WDW resorts, except certain campsites at Fort Wilderness (request a pet site for $3 extra per day). Travelers who bring pets along can lodge them in one of four air-conditioned Pet Care Kennels: near the Transportation and Ticket Center (TTC); to the left of the Epcot Entrance Plaza; at the Disney-MGM Studios entrance; and at the Fort Wilderness campground entrance, next to a huge field where pet owners can take their animals out for a run. During busy seasons, it's best to arrive before the 9 A.M. morning rush hour. Be sure to note that the kennels close an hour after park closing.

Bears, cougars, and ocelots have all been accommodated by the kennels, and exotic pets may be accepted—if a bit reluctantly. However, owners themselves must put the more unusual animals into the kennel's cages; and snakes, rabbits, birds, turtles, hamsters, and other animals unsuited (because of size) to cat- and dog-size cages must have their own escape-proof accommodations.

Guests may board their pets overnight in any WDW kennel. Cost is $11, including dry food (WDW resort guests pay $9 per night to leave pets overnight); a day stay is $6, with one feeding. Guests who board pets overnight are encouraged to stop by to walk them at least twice a day, as the animals are not otherwise let out of their cages. Pets will be fed special food, if provided.

Be sure to bring along your pet's certificate of vaccination, since Florida law requires proof of immunization for animals involved in biting incidents. And never leave pets in your car. It is against the law in Florida.

For more information and reservations (accepted, not required), call 824-6568.

Outside Walt Disney World: A number of hotels in the Orlando area, notably the Holiday Inn in Kissimmee, permit pets. For further information, contact the Orlando/Orange County Convention and Visitors Bureau (363-5871).

POCKET PAGERS

Two types of devices are available to signal a telephone call or message. They can be rented at nearly all WDW hotels.

RELIGIOUS SERVICES

A number of services are held at Walt Disney World and in the surrounding area. For more information on nearby Catholic and Protestant services, call the Christian Service Center at 425-2523.

Protestant: 9 A.M. on Sunday at Luau Cove at the Polynesian resort.

Catholic: 8 A.M. and 10:15 A.M. on Sunday at Luau Cove at the Polynesian resort. For more information, check with Guest Services at any WDW hotel or call 239-6600. The closest Catholic church off the property is Mary, Queen of the Universe Shrine, 2½ miles north of Lake Buena Vista on the I-4 service road. This enormous church seats 3,000 people, and has beautiful gardens and fountains. Call 239-6600 for mass times.

Jewish: Conservative services are at 7:30 P.M. on Friday and 9:30 A.M. on Saturday at Temple Ohalei Rivka, also known as the Southwest Orlando Jewish Congregation (11,200 Apopka-Vineland Rd.; 239-5444), located about three miles from the Disney Village Marketplace. Reform services are at 10:30 A.M. on Saturday and Shabat services at 8:15 P.M. on Friday (except the first Friday of the month) at the Congregation of Liberal Judaism (928 Malone Dr., Orlando; 645-0444), near Winter Park about 20 miles from Walt Disney World.

SMOKING

Disney is committed to providing guests with a smoke-free environment. All buildings and attraction waiting areas are designated no-smoking areas. All Walt Disney World–owned restaurants are included, excepting outdoor seating areas. However, most clubs at Pleasure Island (except Adventurers Club and Comedy Warehouse), as well as many of the WDW resort lounges, allow smoking in certain areas.

SHOPPING FOR NECESSITIES

Almost any everyday item can be purchased right on the property. The following resort shops stock toiletries: Concourse Sundries & Spirits in the Contemporary, the Grog Hut at the Polynesian, Sandy Cove at the Grand Floridian, Calypso Trading Post at Caribbean Beach, Fittings & Fairings at the Yacht Club, Atlantic Wear and Wardrobe Emporium at the Beach Club, Dundy's Sundries at BoardWalk, Jackson Square Gifts & Desires at Port Orleans, Fulton's General Store at Dixie

Disney Village Marketplace is the best source for books. Other places to look include the Emporium in the Magic Kingdom, which has children's books. Books related to themes of Epcot's Future World pavilions are sold at Centorium. In World Showcase, the United Kingdom's Pooh Corner and Germany's Der Bücherwurm stock children's books. At the Disney-MGM Studios, adult and children's books are sold at Legends of Hollywood; Animation Gallery stocks books about animation; and Buy the Book has a far-reaching selection.

TELEPHONE NUMBERS

The folks at home can reach Walt Disney World resort guests at the following phone numbers (all are in area code 407):

All-Star Music:	939-6000
All-Star Sports:	939-5000
Beach Club:	934-8000
BoardWalk Inn:	939-5100
BoardWalk Villas:	939-6200
Caribbean Beach:	934-3400
Contemporary:	824-1000
Coronado Springs:	939-1000
Dixie Landings:	934-6000
Dolphin:	934-4000
Fort Wilderness:	824-2900
Grand Floridian:	824-3000
Old Key West:	827-7700
Polynesian:	824-2000
Port Orleans:	934-5000
Swan:	934-3000
Villas at the Disney Institute:	827-1100
Wilderness Lodge:	824-3200
Yacht Club:	934-7000

Weather: Call Walt Disney World Weather Information at 824-4104.

Landings, Conch Flats General Store at Old Key West, Wilderness Lodge Mercantile at the Wilderness Lodge, Maestro Mickey's at the All-Star Music, Sport Goofy's Gifts and Sundries at the All-Star Sports, Panchito's Gifts & Sundries at Coronado Springs, Daisy's Garden at the Dolphin, Disney Cabana at the Swan, and the Meadow and Settlement Trading Posts at Fort Wilderness.

In addition, a number of over-the-counter health aids, plus many other useful items, can be purchased at the Emporium on Main Street in the Magic Kingdom; they're kept behind the counter, so ask for the supplies you want. Aspirin and sunscreen are also available at Mickey's Star Traders in Tomorrowland. In Epcot, sundries are available in at least one shop in each of the World Showcase pavilions and at all the retail outlets in Future World. At the Disney-MGM Studios, stop by the Crossroads of the World and Movieland Memorabilia shops.

Gooding's supermarket, found at the Crossroads of Lake Buena Vista shopping center near Hotel Plaza, has a large pharmacy.

Reading matter: Newspapers, magazines, best-sellers, and paperbacks are available at the resort shops mentioned above, with one exception: at the Polynesian, News from Civilization is the place to go. Most of these shops carry the daily papers from Orlando and Miami, *The Wall Street Journal*, and, on Sunday, *The New York Times* and *The Chicago Tribune*.

By far, 2R's Reading and Riting at the

TIPPING

Walt Disney World is not one of those places where bellmen stick out their hands even before they put down your luggage. Instead, they seem genuinely glad to help out. Oddly enough, this pleasant attitude seems to discourage tipping at the same time it arouses the sentiments that make most travelers reach for their wallets.

Tips are no less valued at WDW resorts than they would be at any other good hotel—the standard $1 per bag is appropriate for lugging luggage. Gratuities of 15% to 18% are also customary at full-service restaurants at Walt Disney World.

Gratuities are not required in fast-food restaurants, but in the salons, it's customary to leave a tip of about 15% of the total bill.

Cab drivers in the Orlando area expect a 15% tip. Baggage handlers at the train station and airport expect about $1 per bag.

Transportation& Accommodations

The popularity of Walt Disney World has made the region around Orlando one of the world's major tourism and commercial centers, and transportation facilities from a state-of-the-art airport to an efficient network of highways bring visitors to the area by the millions. There's no doubt that getting to and around the Walt Disney World region can be very confusing. The only more perplexing dilemma may be choosing the best accommodations for your family from among the huge assortment of hotels and motels.

The accommodations operated by Walt Disney World itself range from futuristic high-rise towers to treehouses buried deep in piney woods. In between are resorts that evoke striking images of the South Pacific, old Florida, the Pacific Northwest, the Caribbean, New England, early Atlantic City, Louisiana, northern Mexico, and the sports and music worlds, plus efficient trailer-type facilities in a sprawling, beautifully maintained campground. And that list doesn't include the many villas that provide extraordinary space and luxury at surprisingly affordable prices, or the studios and homes with one, two, and three bedrooms that can be purchased through a unique vacation-ownership system. What follows should help travelers sort out all the lodging options on Walt Disney World property, as well as shed light on the broad range of possibilities that exist outside the WDW gates.

☎ **Unless otherwise noted, all phone numbers are in area code 407.**

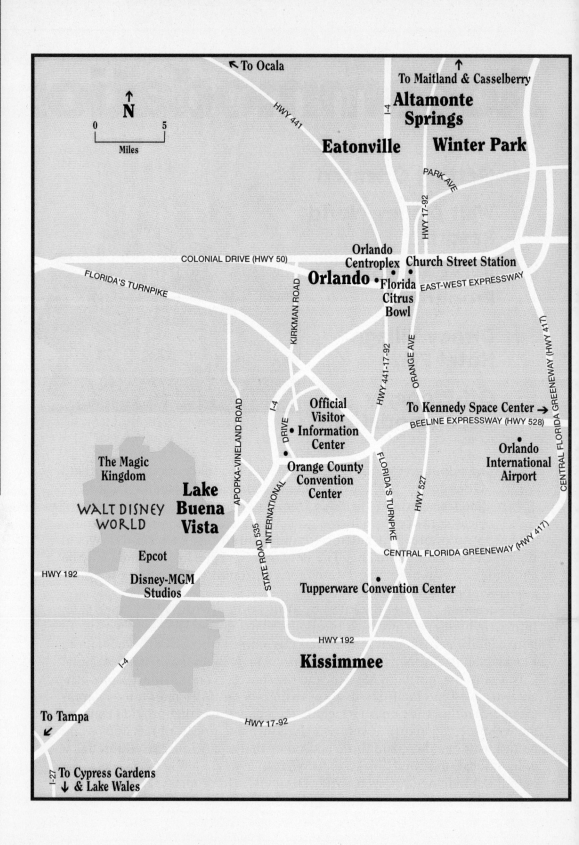

To Ocala

To Maitland & Casselberry

Altamonte Springs

N
0   5
Miles

HWY 441

I-4

Eatonville   **Winter Park**

PARK AVE

HWY 17-92

COLONIAL DRIVE (HWY 50)

Orlando
Centroplex   Church Street Station

Orlando   Florida
Citrus
Bowl

EAST-WEST EXPRESSWAY

FLORIDA'S TURNPIKE

KIRKMAN ROAD

HWY 441-17-92

ORANGE AVE

CENTRAL FLORIDA GREENEWAY (HWY 417)

Official
Visitor
Information
Center

To Kennedy Space Center

BEELINE EXPRESSWAY (HWY 528)

APOPKA-VINELAND ROAD

I-4

DRIVE

Orange County
Convention
Center

FLORIDA'S TURNPIKE

HWY 527

**Orlando
International
Airport**

The Magic
Kingdom

**Lake
Buena
Vista**

WALT DISNEY
WORLD

INTERNATIONAL

STATE ROAD 535

CENTRAL FLORIDA GREENEWAY (HWY 417)

HWY 192

Epcot

Disney-MGM
Studios

Tupperware Convention Center

HWY 192

Kissimmee

I-4

To Tampa

HWY 17-92

I-27   To Cypress Gardens
& Lake Wales

GETTING ORIENTED

Orlando, the Central Florida city of nearly 170,000 residents, is the municipality with which Walt Disney World is most closely associated. Walt Disney World, however, is actually in a far smaller community called Lake Buena Vista, 15 miles away. Many hotels and restaurants are located here, though there are far more in Orlando proper, to the north. Among the more compelling adjacent communities are Winter Park (on Orlando's northeastern extremity), Maitland (just northwest of Winter Park), and Altamonte Springs (north of Maitland).

ORLANDO-AREA HIGHWAYS: The most important Orlando traffic artery is I-4, which runs diagonally through the area from southwest to northeast, cutting through the southern half of Walt Disney World. It then angles on toward Orlando and Winter Park, ending near Daytona Beach at I-95, which runs north and south along the coast.

All the city's other important highways intersect I-4. From south to north, these include U.S. 192 (a.k.a. Irlo Bronson Memorial Highway), which takes an east-west course that crosses the WDW entrance road and leads into downtown Kissimmee on the east; S.R. 528 (a.k.a. the Beeline Expressway), which shoots eastward from I-4; S.R. 435, also known as Kirkman Road, which runs north and south and intersects International Drive, where many motels catering to WDW visitors are located; U.S. 17-92-441 (a.k.a. Orange Blossom Trail), which runs due north and south, paralleling Kirkman Road on the east; and S.R. 50 (a.k.a. Colonial Drive), which runs due east and west.

WALT DISNEY WORLD EXITS: The 45-square-mile tract that is Walt Disney World is roughly rectangular. I-4 runs through its southern half from southwest to northeast. The major WDW destinations are most efficiently reached by taking the I-4 exits suggested below; off the highway, clear signage makes it easy for visitors to get anywhere in the World. Keep in mind that special events will often require rerouting of traffic patterns, so it's best to follow signs as directed.

• **Exit 27**, marked "S.R. 535/Lake Buena Vista," is the route taken to Pleasure Island, the Disney Village Marketplace, Disney Village Hotel Plaza, the Disney Institute, Lake Buena Vista golf course, or the Crossroads shopping center.

• **Exit 26B**, marked "Epcot/Disney Village," leads to Epcot, Typhoon Lagoon, Bonnet Creek Golf Club, and the BoardWalk, Caribbean Beach, Swan, Dolphin, Yacht

Club, Beach Club, Port Orleans, Dixie Landings, and Old Key West resorts. It is also a good alternate route to the Disney-MGM Studios and Disney Village Marketplace.

• **Exit 25**, marked "192/Magic Kingdom," leads to the Magic Kingdom, Disney-MGM Studios, Blizzard Beach, Fort Wilderness, River Country, Palm and Magnolia golf courses, and the All-Star Music, All-Star Sports, Coronado Springs, Contemporary, Polynesian, Grand Floridian, and Wilderness Lodge resorts.

WDW TRANSPORTATION: The internal transportation system at Walt Disney World is quite extensive, with boats, buses, and the famed monorail all doing their part to shuttle guests around property. The system is always being revised to serve the ever-increasing number of attractions and accommodations. Visitors staying at WDW hotels receive detailed information about transportation options upon checking in. For up-to-the-minute information about WDW transportation, call 824-4321.

The system's central link is a hub called the Transportation and Ticket Center (TTC), located at the northernmost end of Walt Disney World near the Magic Kingdom. Monorail, bus, and ferry service connect the TTC to points throughout the World. Day visitors must park here before taking a monorail or ferry to the Magic Kingdom. (Disney resort guests can bypass the TTC via direct buses.)

WDW's elevated monorail train operates along a circular route near the Magic Kingdom, making stops at the TTC, the Polynesian, the Grand Floridian, the Contemporary, and the Magic Kingdom. A separate extension of the monorail system connects the TTC to Epcot. Monorails run from 7 A.M. until about two hours after park closing.

Bus service, offered between most points, is considered the cornerstone of the WDW transportation system. With a few exceptions, buses circulate every 15 to 20 minutes, from one hour prior to park opening until just after closing; bus stops are clearly marked. Travel time varies, depending on the route.

From several Walt Disney World locales, water launches usher guests to the Magic Kingdom, Epcot, the Disney-MGM Studios, or between resorts. Boats generally depart every 20 to 30 minutes. Travel time varies depending on the point of departure.

Transportation ID Requirements

Guests wishing to use the Walt Disney World transportation system must be prepared to present proof of their riding privileges, usually a park ticket or WDW resort ID card. The various accepted IDs afford different degrees of access. Specific requirements and limitations are noted below.

• WDW resort ID cards allow guests unlimited use of any WDW buses, monorails, and boats.

• Four-Day Value Passes, Four-Day Park Hopper Passes, Five-Day World Hopper Passes, Length of Stay Passes, and Annual Passes allow guests use of any WDW transportation.

• Valid one-day theme park tickets permit guests to use all monorails and the ferries running between the TTC and the Magic Kingdom. They do not allow use of WDW buses.

• River Country and Hoop-Dee-Doo Musical Revue dinner show tickets allow guests use of buses from the TTC, water launches from the Contemporary resort, and water launches from the Magic Kingdom to River Country and Pioneer Hall in Fort Wilderness.

ACCOMMODATIONS

Orlando and its environs contain tens of thousands of hotel and motel rooms. Few of these, however, whether inside or outside the World, are of a design much beyond the predictable Anywhere, USA, motel-modern decor, usually with two standard double beds, plush carpeting, simulated-wood paneling, a color television set, and a private bathroom.

The biggest differences among accommodations seem to be in the dimensions of the rooms and bathrooms, the attention to decor, the level of service, the variety of dining options, the recreational facilities, the landscaping of the surrounding grounds, and the location.

Basically, Walt Disney World area accommodations fall into two main categories: those located within the boundaries of Walt Disney World and those outside the property. Rates are generally higher at WDW addresses than at most other motels in the area, with the exception of the All-Star Sports and All-Star Music resorts, but the convenience is so much greater that the extra expense is not at all unreasonable. There are additional benefits available to on-property guests, such as guaranteed theme park admission even when parks are full, use of the WDW transportation system, closed-circuit TV announcing WDW events, early admission to the three theme parks on designated days, free delivery of purchases back to your resort, and the best possible access to Guest Services personnel. Resort guests can also reserve tee-off times on the golf courses up to 60 days in advance. Considering all of the advantages, you should be wary of anyone who encourages you to stay elsewhere for reasons other than a major difference in price.

It's helpful to think of accommodations on the WDW grounds in terms of their location. Therefore, the Walt Disney World Resorts part of this chapter is divided into several sections, describing resorts in the Magic Kingdom Area, Epcot Area, Disney-MGM Studios Area, and Village Area, plus those accommodations at Fort Wilderness and Disney Village Hotel Plaza.

Off-property options are described in the latter part of the chapter. Locations of the off-site properties are quite scattered. Those closest to Walt Disney World are located on or just off S.R. 535 in Lake Buena Vista. Others are located in Kissimmee, along U.S. 192 (which runs east and west) intersecting the WDW entrance road, and along International Drive (off S.R. 435 at the Orlando city limits). Note that the U.S. 192 establishments are closer to the WDW main

entrance—many only a few miles away—while those on International Drive are some ten miles from the WDW theme park gates. The latter area, however, presents an extensive array of accommodations, restaurants, and other attractions. Its proximity to still more of the same in Orlando, just a few miles north, constitutes an additional lure.

In choosing a place to stay, first decide just how much you can afford to spend. If your budget permits, try to get a reservation at one of the on-site properties. (Remember that there are Disney accommodations in varying price ranges, starting as low as $69 per night.) If not, select accommodations outside the World based on your budget and the guidelines given in this section.

Remember, when examining rate sheets for the best buy for your family, check the cutoff age at which children accompanying you (and staying in the same room) will be billed as extra adults. Those with large families should note that the Disney villa-type accommodations, which may seem more expensive at first glance, actually can prove less costly in the long run—by eliminating the necessity of securing an additional hotel room, and by providing cooking facilities that can mean big savings on meals.

Walt Disney World Resorts

With the addition of moderately priced rooms at Caribbean Beach, Port Orleans, Dixie Landings, and Coronado Springs (opening mid-1997) and the even more economical rooms at the All-Star Sports and All-Star Music resorts, we find it difficult to recommend staying off the property. And reservations are generally easy to obtain, since there are now more than 21,000 rooms available.

In general, rooms at the Contemporary, Polynesian, Grand Floridian, Yacht Club and Beach Club, BoardWalk Inn, and the Swan and Dolphin are quite large and can accommodate up to five guests in a single room without difficulty. Rooms at the Wilderness Lodge, Caribbean Beach, Port Orleans, Dixie Landings, Coronado Springs, All-Star Sports, and All-Star Music resorts accommodate up to four people. Many rooms have patios or balconies. And considering the incredibly high occupancy rate, it's astonishing that things look so fresh. Even the rooms without dramatic views often have pleasant vistas, if only across gardens.

The Villas at the Disney Institute, which can accommodate larger groups, makes particularly good sense for families, especially those who want to cook some of their own meals "at home." The vacation villas at the Old Key West resort are also popular with families. At Fort Wilderness there are both campsites and fully equipped Wilderness Homes set on 700 acres of quiet woods. With the recent opening of the BoardWalk Villas, larger groups have 532 new vacation villas from which to choose.

The WDW hotels in this section are broken into five geographic groups: Magic Kingdom Area, Epcot Area, Village Area, Disney-MGM Studios Area, and Fort Wilderness. The hotels, rooms, and facilities are described in detail. All WDW resorts offer laundry facilities and dry-cleaning services, and rooms feature clock radios and voice-mail messaging. Restaurants listed here are described at length in the *Good Meals, Great Times* chapter. Note that all restaurants at WDW resorts are nonsmoking, as are all public spaces with the exception of lounges.

Disney Rates the Resorts

The Walt Disney World rating system helps you choose the resort, hotel, villa, or campsite that best suits your needs. Here's a breakdown of the core amenities, room rates, and resorts in each category. For specific pricing, see the chart on pages 78 and 79.

Deluxe ($165 to $390)
- Full-service restaurants
- Room service
- Bellman luggage service, valet parking
- Swimming pools, beach access
- On-site recreation such as boat rental
- Most rooms sleep five
- On-site child-care programs
- Monorail, boat, or bus transportation to all theme parks

Resorts
- Beach Club (page 61)
- BoardWalk Inn (page 65)
- Contemporary (page 52)
- Dolphin (page 64)
- Grand Floridian (page 55)
- Polynesian (page 53)
- Swan (page 63)
- Wilderness Lodge (page 57)
- Yacht Club (page 61)

Home Away From Home ($185 to $1,185)
- Kitchen facilities, pizza delivery
- Luggage service
- Swimming pools
- Front-door parking for your vehicle
- Flexible room arrangements accommodating 4 to 12 guests
- Privacy; wooded or golf course environment
- Bus transportation to all theme parks

Resorts
- Disney's BoardWalk Villas Resort (page 65)
- Fort Wilderness Homes (page 75)
- Disney's Old Key West Resort (page 71)
- The Villas at the Disney Institute (page 69)

Moderate ($114 to $149)
- Full-service restaurants, food courts, pizza delivery
- Bellman luggage service
- Swimming pools with slides
- On-site recreation such as playgrounds and bike rental
- Rooms sleep four
- Bus transportation to all theme parks

Resorts
- Caribbean Beach (page 59)
- Disney's Coronado Springs (page 74)
- Dixie Landings (page 68)
- Port Orleans (page 67)

Value ($69 to $89)
- Food courts, pizza delivery
- Hourly luggage service
- Swimming pools
- Bus transportation to all theme parks

Resorts
- All-Star Music (page 73)
- All-Star Sports (page 73)

Campground ($35 to $64)
- Received perfect ratings from *Trailer Life* magazine and from Woodall's

- Fort Wilderness Campground (page 75)

Magic Kingdom Area

Contemporary

Watching the monorail trains disappear into this hotel's enormous 15-story, A-frame tower never fails to amaze first-timers. The sleek trains look like long spaceships docking as they slide inside, or the sight may bring to mind the story of Jonah being swallowed by the whale. (Note that guests who use a wheelchair cannot board the monorail here, but they can at the Polynesian and Grand Floridian, whose platforms are fully accessible.)

Passengers, for their part, are impressed by the cavernous lobby, with its tiers of balconies and, at its center, designer Mary Blair's huge 90-foot-high, floor-to-ceiling tile mural depicting Native American children, stylized flowers, birds, trees, and other scenes from the Southwest. (Look carefully and you may be able to spot the five-legged goat.)

This imposing structure has 1,041 rooms in its tower and the wings that flank it on either side. There are seven shops, three restaurants, two snack bars, two lounges, a marina, a beach, a health club, and more. The renovated pool area incorporates two whirlpools, a water slide, and water jets. The lively Food and Fun Center—a vast area with an arcade and snack bar—is open until midnight. A large convention center offers access to business services.

A concierge package is available for guests who stay in the hotel's 14th-floor suites. Amenities include express check-in and check-out, complimentary continental breakfast, hors d'oeuvres and refreshments at night, and nightly turndown service. The telephone number for the Contemporary resort is 824-1000.

ROOMS: Modern-art designs accented by bold colors drive the decor of rooms evenly apportioned among the tower and two wings. Rooms in the tower boast private balconies and fantastic views of Bay Lake or the Magic Kingdom. Most rooms can accommodate five guests (plus one additional child under three). Typical units have two queen-size beds and a daybed; some rooms have a king-size bed and a daybed. Adjoining and/or connecting rooms may be requested. Rooms equipped for guests with disabilities and nonsmoking rooms are available. Bathrooms in the Contemporary resort are large and well laid out. A variety of elegant suites, consisting of a parlor and one or two bedrooms, can accommodate 7 to 12 people.

WHERE TO EAT: In addition to the many restaurants and snack spots, 24-hour room service provides a wide range of offerings.

California Grill: On the 15th floor. The specialty is California fare, including pizza baked in wood-burning ovens, grilled meats, seafood, and market vegetables. An added treat: the spectacular view of the Magic Kingdom fireworks, and sensational sunsets.

Concourse Steakhouse: On the fourth-floor concourse. A full breakfast; individual pizzas, burgers, salads, and sandwiches for lunch; and steaks and prime rib for dinner are offered on the menu here.

Chef Mickey's: On the fourth-floor concourse. Chef Mickey and his friends cook up daily buffets. Breakfast features Mickey waffles, as well as more traditional items. Dinner offers two carved meats and a variety of entrées, plus a sundae and dessert bar.

Food and Fun Center: On the first floor. Serves light fare from 6 A.M. to midnight.

WHERE TO DRINK: The Magic Kingdom's no-alcohol policy doesn't trickle over to its nearest neighbor.

California Grill Lounge: On the 15th floor adjoining the California Grill. Prime views provide a backdrop for sampling California wines and other drinks, plus appetizers.

Outer Rim: On the fourth-floor concourse, overlooking Bay Lake. Serves appetizers, cocktails, and specialty drinks.

Sand Bar: This poolside spot offers drinks and light snacks seasonally.

WHAT TO DO: The Contemporary boasts more activities and recreational facilities than many large resorts. Volleyball nets are set up on the beach. Waterskiing, fishing, and parasailing excursions are available (see *Sports* for details).

Boating: Sailboats (including catamarans), pontoon and canopy boats, as well as Water Sprites and Seariders, are available for rent at the marina, near the beach.

Children's Program: The Mouseketeer Clubhouse is open from 4:30 P.M. to midnight for children ages 4 to 12 (four-hour maximum stay). Cost is $4 per hour per child. Reservations are necessary; call 824-3892.

Health Club: The Olympiad health club has Nautilus equipment, stair climbers, rowing machines, bicycles, sauna, lockers, and massage (by appointment).

Salon: Contemporary Resort Salon on the third floor of the tower provides haircuts, facials, manicures, and other services.

Shopping: The fourth-floor concourse is home to several first-class shops. The Fantasia Shop sells an array of Disney character merchandise including plush animals, and clothing, for both children and adults. The Contemporary Woman offers a range of good-quality women's clothing (and plenty of bathing suits) in all price ranges, and the adjoining Contemporary Man stocks casual clothes and beachwear. The adjacent Kingdom Jewels Ltd. specializes in jewelry, including Disney character jewelry. Bayview Gifts carries souvenirs, gifts, and fresh flowers. Concourse Sundries & Spirits has a selection of newspapers, magazines, books, snack foods, and liquor—just what's needed for a cocktail party on the terrace.

Swimming: In addition to a round quiet pool, the newly designed free-form pool features a 17-foot-high curving slide. Two large whirlpools have been added, one on a peninsula protruding into the pool. Water jets shoot unexpectedly while smaller fountains spout randomly, delighting older and younger kids alike. A toddler's wading pool is located near the hotel's north wing. Swimming is also permitted in the roped-off area of Bay Lake beside the beach.

Tennis: Disney's Racquet Club, WDW's premier tennis center, is located near the north wing. Recently renovated, it features six state-of-the-art hydrogrid clay courts. Private lessons are available (see *Sports* for details). The shop here has tennis equipment, fashions, and shoes. Racquet restringing is also available.

Video Arcade: On the first floor, the Food and Fun Center boasts everything from Skee-Ball to air hockey, and all the favorites of the pinball-and-electronic-games-playing set. A much smaller arcade is near the pool.

TRANSPORTATION: The resort is connected to the TTC and the Magic Kingdom by monorail. Board just above the fourth-floor concourse, inside the atrium area of the tower. From the TTC, Epcot can be reached via another monorail, and Typhoon Lagoon, Pleasure Island, and the Disney Village Marketplace can be reached by bus. Direct buses go to the Disney-MGM Studios and Blizzard Beach. Watercraft travel from the marina to Fort Wilderness.

Polynesian

The Polynesian resort is as close an approximation of the real thing as Walt Disney World's designers could create. The vegetation is as lush as anywhere in the World and the architecture summons the tropics.

The mood is set by a three-story garden that occupies most of the lobby. To call the construction at the center a fountain is to do it a grave injustice; it's more like a waterfall. The water cascades over craggy volcanic rocks. Coconut palms tower over about 75 different species of tropical and subtropical plants—anthuriums, banana trees, gardenias, orchids, ferns, and other greens. The climatic conditions are nearly perfect, so that everything blooms year-round.

The structure that contains this mass of greenery, the Great Ceremonial House, is the central building in the resort complex. The front desk, the shops, and most of the restaurants are located here. Flanking the Great Ceremonial House on either side are 11 two- and three-story village "longhouses" named for various Pacific islands. These structures house the Polynesian resort's 853 guestrooms. The monorail stops at this hotel, making it an especially convenient place to stay; in fact, it's just a few minutes' ride to the Magic Kingdom. But because accommodations are scattered around the property, things seldom feel as hectic as at some other resorts.

The Polynesian offers a concierge service called King Kamehameha. Special amenities with the service include express check-in and check-out, continental breakfast each morning, soft drinks and hors d'oeuvres every afternoon, and access to a peaceful lounge with a prime fireworks view. A concierge is on duty from 7 A.M. to 11 P.M. Concierge rooms and suites are located in the Tonga and Bali Hai buildings, and are the most expensive in the hotel. The telephone number for the Polynesian resort is 824-2000.

ROOMS: Many rooms have balconies, and most have a view of the gardens, Seven Seas Lagoon, or one of the resort's swimming

pools; rooms in the Oahu, Moorea, and Pago Pago buildings are the largest. All rooms have two queen-size beds and a daybed, and can accommodate five guests (plus a sixth under age three). Connecting or adjoining rooms may be requested. The Oahu and Pago Pago buildings have rooms specially equipped for guests with disabilities. Non-smoking rooms are available.

The resort's suites—located exclusively in the Bali Hai building—can accommodate four to six guests. Some have a king-size bed in the bedroom and two queen-size beds in the parlor.

WHERE TO EAT: A variety of specialties is available from room service between 6:30 A.M. and midnight. Also, some interesting eating spots are located here.

Captain Cook's Snack & Ice Cream Company: On the lobby level of the Great Ceremonial House. This is a good spot for continental breakfast. Sandwiches, snacks, and (of course) ice cream are available 24 hours a day.

Coral Isle Café: On the second floor of the Great Ceremonial House. This restaurant with South Seas decor serves the usual assortment of breakfast items, plus a WDW specialty, banana-stuffed french toast; it also does a booming business in steaks and seafood at lunch and dinner. A good bet for a no-fuss meal.

'Ohana: On the second floor of the Great Ceremonial House. 'Ohana serves family-style dinners roasted in the World's largest fire pit. Minnie's Menehune character breakfast is held daily. The room is large and open, and offers fine views across Seven Seas Lagoon to Cinderella Castle.

WHERE TO DRINK: The Polynesian theme has inspired a whole raft of deceptively potent potables. As might be expected, both the drink offerings and the settings in which they are served are decidedly tropical.

Barefoot Bar: Adjoining the Swimming Pool Lagoon, and open seasonally.

Tambu: There's a tropical air about this lounge adjoining 'Ohana. The bar serves appetizers and exotic specialty drinks while guests wait to be seated.

WHAT TO DO: A wide range of activities is available at the Polynesian resort. Water-skiing and fishing excursions can also be arranged (see *Sports* for details).

Boating: Several types of sailboats (including catamarans), speedy little Water Sprites, and pontoon boats are available for rent at the marina.

Children's Program: The Never Land Club is a supervised evening activity program for children ages 4 to 12. The program operates between 5 P.M. and midnight, with a kids' buffet from 6 P.M. to 8 P.M. The cost is $8 per hour and there is a three-hour minimum. Reservations are necessary and can be made by calling 939-3463.

Playground: The playground next to the Swimming Pool Lagoon features an assortment of apparatuses for climbing, swinging, and sliding.

Shopping: News from Civilization, on the first floor of the Great Ceremonial House, is the locale for hotel and Florida logo items, as well as newspapers, magazines, film, sun-care products, and gifts. Robinson Crusoe, Esq., sells casual sportswear and swimwear for men; the Polynesian Princess stocks brightly colored resort fashions, bathing suits, and accessories for women. Upstairs, Trader Jack's sells souvenirs, toys, fashions, and miscellaneous items; the Grog Hut has food, liquor, wine, beer, soft drinks, and other fixings for an impromptu party.

Swimming: There are two main pools here: the elliptical East Pool, in the shadow of the Oahu, Tonga, Hawaii, Bora Bora, and Moorea buildings, and the larger free-form Swimming Pool Lagoon, found closer to the marina and main beach. The latter is framed by a large cluster of boulders that forms a water slide much beloved by youngsters; to get to the ladder they must duck underneath a waterfall. Toddlers have their own shallow wading pool. Swimming is also permitted in the roped-off areas of Seven Seas Lagoon.

Video Arcade: Moana Mickey's Arcade has a small assortment of video games. It is located on the eastern edge of the property near the Oahu guest building.

TRANSPORTATION: The resort is on the monorail line to the Magic Kingdom and the TTC; the platform is on the second floor of the Great Ceremonial House. From the TTC, Epcot is accessible by another monorail, and Typhoon Lagoon, Pleasure Island, and the Disney Village Marketplace can be reached by bus. Direct buses go to the Disney-MGM Studios and Blizzard Beach. Launches leave from the Polynesian dock for the Magic Kingdom and the Grand Floridian.

Shades of Green

This resort (formerly The Disney Inn) is a recreational retreat for active and retired military personnel and their families, members of the reserves and the National Guard, and Department of Defense employees. The 288-room resort features two tennis courts, two pools, a small health club, restaurant, bar and lounge, gift shop, arcade, laundry facilities, and free transportation around Walt Disney World. Very attractive room rates based on military or civilian grade range from $49 to $92 per day. Discounted Length of Stay Passes are also available. The property's three golf courses—the Palm, the Magnolia, and Oak Trail—are open to all WDW guests (See *Sports* for details). All other activities are for hotel guests and their families only. The telephone number for Shades of Green is 824-3400.

Grand Floridian

At the turn of the century, Standard Oil magnate Henry M. Flagler saw the realization of his dream: The railroad he had built to "civilize" Florida had spawned along its right-of-way an empire of grand hotels, lavish estates, prominent families, and opulent lifestyles. High society blossomed in winter, as the likes of John D. Rockefeller and Teddy Roosevelt checked into the Royal Poinciana in Palm Beach, enjoying the sea breezes from the oceanside suites.

The hotel later burned to the ground, and Florida's golden era faded with the Depression. But nearly a century after Flagler first made Florida a fashionable resort destination, Walt Disney World opened a grand hotel—a 900-room Victorian structure with gabled roofs and carved moldings—on 40 acres of Seven Seas Lagoon shorefront, between the Magic Kingdom and the Polynesian resort.

Like its late-19th-century predecessors, the Grand Floridian boasts abundant verandas, ceiling fans, intricate latticework and balustrades, turrets, towers, and red-shingle roofs. White-sand beaches hold the promise of clambakes. And yet, it offers all the advantages of 21st-century living—including monorail service. With five restaurants, two lounges, five shops, and an arcade, plus a child-care facility, a convention center offering access to business services, a swimming pool, marina, and new health club and spa, the Grand Floridian is not only a grand hotel but a complete resort.

The main building houses a 14,800-square-foot Grand Lobby, a palatial space soaring five stories to a ceiling of stained-glass domes and glittering chandeliers. Potted palms and an aviary decorate the sitting area; an open-cage elevator carries guests to the shops and restaurants on the second floor. The turn-of-the-century theme is apparent everywhere, from the Edwardian costumes worn by the staff to the shop displays, from the restaurants to the room decor. The telephone number for the Grand Floridian resort is 824-3000.

ROOMS: The accommodations are quite luxurious, with rooms decorated as they might have been a century ago—in soft colors, with printed wall coverings, armoires and light-wood furnishings, marble-topped sinks, ceiling fans, and Victorian woodwork. The resort's main building houses 65 concierge rooms and 9 suites; five lodge buildings, each four and five stories high, contain 623 standard rooms, 161 slightly smaller "attic" chambers, and 16 suites. Most rooms measure about 400 square feet and include two queen-size beds, plus a daybed, to accommodate five people. Many rooms have terraces. Suites include a parlor, plus one, two, or three bedrooms; there are king-size or queen-size beds in the bedrooms. Most of the 15 honeymoon rooms, located on the second, third, fourth, and fifth floors, enjoy wonderful views. In the main building, access to the upper three concierge-suite levels is restricted by private elevator only to guests occupying rooms on those floors. On the third floor, the concierge desks offer such personalized services as reservations and information. The fourth floor features a quiet seating area where continental breakfast and evening refreshments are served. Rooms equipped for guests with disabilities and nonsmoking rooms are available.

WHERE TO EAT: Most of the restaurants and lounges are located on the first two floors of the main building. In addition, room service offers a wide assortment of items 24 hours a day.

1900 Park Fare: A buffet restaurant on the Windsor Level (first floor), festively decorated with carousel horses, plenty of plants, and Big Bertha—the carnival organ. Breakfast and dinner with the characters are served daily.

Flagler's: On the Alcazar Level (second floor). The largest of the hotel's restaurants, seating 285, features Italian cuisine complete with strolling musicians. Open for dinner.

Gasparilla Grill & Games: This 24-hour snack bar on the first floor offers light items for all-day dining, plus video games.

Grand Floridian Café: Located on the first floor. Its peaches-and-cream color scheme and veranda-like feel make this the best place to get a quick, sit-down breakfast. Lunch and dinner are also available.

Narcoossee's: This octagonal restaurant and bar has a romantic shoreline location. Steaks, seafood, and chicken cooked in an open kitchen characterize the lunch and dinner menu. Beer is served in yard-tall glasses.

Victoria & Albert's: On the second floor. The hotel's finest dining establishment, it is named after the former queen and prince consort of England. Elegant meals are served to no more than 90 guests; service is refined and diligent. Jackets are required for men and priority seating is a must.

WHERE TO DRINK: Guests will find the refined lounges here to be nice escapes.

Garden View: This pleasant spot on the first floor offers a view of the hotel's lush, landscaped garden and pool area. Afternoon tea is served.

Mizner's: Named after the eccentric, wildly prolific architect who defined much of the flavor of Palm Beach County, this bar is on the second floor.

Summerhouse: The only bar serving the pool and beach, this spot features a variety of snacks and beverages.

WHAT TO DO: The Grand Floridian offers all the recreational facilities of a typical beachside resort—and much more. Water-skiing and fishing excursions can be arranged (see *Sports* for details). Volleyball equipment is available.

Boating: Sailboats (including catamarans), canopy boats, pedal boats, and Water Sprites are rented at Captain's Shipyard Marina.

Children's Program: The Mousekeeter Club is a supervised program for kids ages 4 to 12. It's open from 4:30 P.M. to midnight; the cost is $4 per hour for each child. There is a four-hour maximum. Reservations are required; phone 824-2985.

Health Club: The spa within the new 9,000-square-foot Grand Floridian Spa & Health Club offers 17 treatment rooms for massage, herbal wraps, and aromatherapy. The health club has exercise equipment and an area for aerobics, plus separate men's and women's saunas, whirlpools, and steamrooms.

Playground: Adjacent to the Mouseketeer Clubhouse, the play area includes swings and a climbing apparatus.

Salon: The Ivy Trellis salon offers a full line of services for hair and nails.

Shopping: On the first floor (Windsor Level) of the main building is Summer Lace, a women's apparel shop, and Sandy Cove, where guests may purchase gifts and sundries. One floor up at the Alcazar Level is the M. Mouse Mercantile character shop, the Balley leather-goods store, and Commander Porter's, a men's shop.

Swimming: In addition to the 275,000-gallon swimming pool just outside the main building, the hotel has its own white-sand beach along Seven Seas Lagoon.

Tennis: There are two clay courts for play. Reservations are required; phone 824-2694. Private lessons are available.

Video Arcade: Gasparilla Grill and Games, located on the first floor of the main building, features video games.

TRANSPORTATION: The Grand Floridian is connected to the TTC and the Magic Kingdom by monorail. The platform is located outside the hotel under an awning on the second floor. From the TTC, Epcot is accessible by another monorail, and Typhoon Lagoon, Pleasure Island, and the Disney Village Marketplace can be reached by bus. Direct buses go to the Disney-MGM Studios and Blizzard Beach. Launches leave from the dock for the Magic Kingdom and the Polynesian.

Wilderness Lodge

This resort recalls both the spirit of the early American West and the feeling of the National Park Service lodges built in the early 1900s. These grand structures architecturally unified the elements of the unspoiled wilderness parks, kept harmony with nature, and incorporated the culture of Native Americans. The Wilderness Lodge artfully recaptures this rustic charm.

The resort is situated between the Contemporary resort and Fort Wilderness on Bay Lake. Guests arrive along a winding road shaded by pines. The lobby is in an impressive eight-story, log-structured building. Massive bundled log columns support a series of trusses. Four large chandeliers with torch-cut iron bands featuring silhouettes of Indians and buffalo are topped with glowing tepees. Two authentic Pacific Northwest totem poles soar 55 feet on each side of the lobby. Both the grand stone fireplace and the intricately

detailed, multicolored floor recall Northwest Indian designs. Four levels of corridors surround the lobby, providing access to guestrooms, sitting nooks, and terraces. There are 38 rooms equipped for guests with disabilities, and nonsmoking rooms are available. The telephone number for the Wilderness Lodge is 824-3200.

ROOMS: The 728 guestrooms are located in a U-shaped building. Most rooms have two queen-size beds, a table and chairs, and a balcony. Some rooms have one queen-size bed and a bunk bed. The bathroom has a separate vanity area with double sinks; the fixtures resemble pewter. The wallpaper has a Native American–motif border, and the colorful bedspreads and traditional plaid curtains add to the decor. Images of wildlife complete the theme.

WHERE TO EAT: The American West theme is carried out with flair in the hotel's eateries. Breakfast room service is served from 7 A.M. to 11 A.M.; dinner selections are available through room service from 4 P.M. to midnight.

Artist Point: Decorated with artwork representing the painters who first chronicled the Northwest landscape, this fine dining spot features wild salmon, game, steaks, seafood, and wines from the Pacific Northwest. Pocahontas hosts breakfast here daily.

Lobby Coffee Bar: Continental breakfast is served here, and evenings bring coffee and hot chocolate to this fireside spot.

Roaring Fork: Light snacks are available here, in the hotel's arcade, 24 hours a day.

Whispering Canyon Café: A casual, family-style restaurant with all-day dining. The cowboy silhouette cutouts are great for picture taking.

WHERE TO DRINK: Two spots are available for a relaxing break.

Territory: Located between the Whispering Canyon Café and Artist Point, this spot honors the survey parties who led the move westward. In addition to light appetizers, specialty drinks, microbrewed beer, and espresso are served. A lunch menu of salads and sandwiches is served until 4:30 P.M.

Trout Pass: The poolside bar features a variety of specialty drinks and snacks.

WHAT TO DO: A resort unto itself, it offers a plethora of activities. Teton Boat & Bike Rental is located in the Colonels's Cabin by the lake. Waterskiing excursions on Bay Lake may also be arranged (see *Sports* for details). Or consider taking one of the two daily guided tours of the lodge.

Biking: Bicycles can be rented for a ride around the resort. A three-quarter-mile path leads to Fort Wilderness and River Country.

Boating: A variety of watercraft, including Water Sprites, canopy boats, sailboats, and pontoon boats can be rented for a trip around Bay Lake.

Children's program: The Cubs Den is a supervised dining and entertainment club for kids ages 4 to 12. Supervised activities, including Disney movies and western themed arts and crafts, occupy kids from 5 P.M. to midnight. Cost is $6 per hour per child, including dinner. Call 939-3463 for reservations, which are required.

Shopping: Wilderness Lodge Mercantile stocks necessities and sundries as well as a line of clothing with the Wilderness Lodge logo. A selection of Disney character merchandise is featured as well.

Swimming: The themed pool actually begins as a hot spring in the hotel lobby. From there, water flows out of the building into Silver Creek, a quiet setting in the upper courtyard. The creek widens as it develops first into a roaring waterfall and then into a swimming area that looks as if it were carved from the rockscape. A beach, a kiddie pool, two whirlpools, and an Old Faithful–style geyser complete the design. Fire Rock Geyser erupts on the hour from early morning until 10 P.M.; those nearby should be prepared for a splash.

Video Arcade: The Roaring Fork Arcade features about 30 of the latest games to keep kids occupied for hours.

TRANSPORTATION: Boats go to the Magic Kingdom from the dock behind the hotel. Direct buses go to Epcot, the Disney-MGM Studios, Blizzard Beach, and the TTC. From the TTC, transfer for buses that make the trip to Typhoon Lagoon, Pleasure Island, and the Disney Village Marketplace. It's also possible to ride a bicycle to Fort Wilderness and River Country.

Epcot Area

Caribbean Beach

This colorful hotel is set on 200 acres southeast of Epcot and near the Disney-MGM Studios. It is composed of five brightly colored "villages" surrounding a 45-acre lake called Barefoot Bay. Each village is identified with a different Caribbean island—Martinique, Barbados, Trinidad, Aruba, and Jamaica—and features cool pastel walls, white railings, and vividly colored metal roofs. There are 2,112 rooms in all, making the Caribbean Beach resort one of the largest hotels in the United States.

The villages consist of a cluster of two-story buildings, a swimming pool, a guest laundry, and a lakefront stretch of white-sand beach. Guests check in at the Custom House, a reception building that immediately projects the feeling of a tropical resort.

Decor, furnishings, and staff costumes all reflect the Caribbean theme. Old Port Royale, a complex located near the center of the property, evokes images of an island market. Stone walls, pirates' cannons, and tropical birds and flowers add to the atmosphere. The area houses the resort's food court, restaurant and lounge, two shops, and an arcade. The port opens onto a lakeside recreation area that includes a pool with waterfalls and a slide; the main beach; the Barefoot Bay Boat Yard and Bike Works, where boats and bicycles may be rented; a 1.4-mile promenade around the lake that's perfect for biking, walking, or jogging; and Parrot Cay Island, an area in the middle of Barefoot Bay with a playground and wildlife trail. The telephone number for the Caribbean Beach resort is 934-3400.

ROOMS: Rooms are located in two-story buildings in each island village. A typical 340-square-foot room has two double beds and can sleep up to four. The rooms here are a bit larger than the standard rooms at Disney's other moderately priced resorts, and the bathrooms are amply sized. The rooms are decorated in tones softer than the colors found on the exterior, with furniture made of white oak. Each room has a minibar and coffeemaker. Rooms equipped for travelers with disabilities and nonsmoking rooms are available.

One note for the budget-conscious: All the rooms here are identical in terms of size and comfort, and the only difference between the most and least expensive is the view.

WHERE TO EAT: A full-service eatery called Captain's Tavern and a food court with six counter-service restaurants are located in Old Port Royale. Pizza delivery is available from 4 P.M. to midnight.

Captain's Tavern: The menu at this 200-seat restaurant at Old Port Royale includes prime rib, baked chicken, and a catch of the day. Tropical drinks, wine, beer, and traditional cocktails are also served.

Bridgetown Broiler: Spit-roasted chicken and home-style meals are menu highlights.

Cinnamon Bay Bakery: Freshly baked rolls, croissants, and pastries are available in addition to ice cream and other treats.

Kingston Pasta Shop: A variety of pasta dishes is served.

Montego's Deli: Soups, salads, and cold sandwiches are offered.

Port Royale Hamburger Shop: Hot sandwiches and burgers are on the menu.

Royale Pizza Shop: Very good pizza is available by the slice or the pie, along with a variety of hot and cold pasta dishes.

WHERE TO DRINK: The tropical, Caribbean theme is carried out in the specialty drinks found at **Banana Cabana**. Snacks are also available at this poolside spot.

WHAT TO DO: There are many recreational opportunities. The 1.4-mile promenade around the lake is perfect for walking, biking, or a morning jog. Nature walks are conducted at Parrot Cay Island.

 Biking: Bikes can be rented at the Barefoot Bay Boat Yard and Bike Works.

 Boating: Sailboats, Water Sprites, canopy boats, canoes, and pedal boats are available for rent at the Barefoot Bay Boat Yard and Bike Works for use on the resort's scenic 45-acre lake.

 Playground: A lovely playground is on Parrot Cay Island, across the footbridge from the Barefoot Bay Boat Yard and Bike Works. Playgrounds are also located on the Barbados, Jamaica, and Trinidad beaches.

 Shopping: At Old Port Royale, the Calypso Straw Market carries items with the Caribbean Beach resort logo and a variety of island-themed goods. Calypso Trading Post stocks a large selection of character merchandise and sundries.

 Swimming: Each village has its own pool, and the main pool features waterfalls and a slide in a Caribbean-themed setting.

 Video Arcade: Goombay Games at Old Port Royale offers a selection of games.

TRANSPORTATION: Buses go directly to the Magic Kingdom, Epcot, the Disney-MGM Studios, and Blizzard Beach. Other routes lead to the Disney Village Marketplace, Pleasure Island, and Typhoon Lagoon.

Meetings & Conventions

With the mid-1997 opening of Coronado Springs, convention-goers will have yet another resort to choose from within the ranks of WDW hotels. Coronado Springs, the first moderately priced Disney resort to offer convention facilities, boasts the largest ballroom in the Southeast.

 Convention centers at Walt Disney World range in size from 20,000 to over 200,000 square feet. The Dolphin's center, featuring an exhibit hall and an executive board room, is the largest; the Swan provides additional space. The Contemporary has three ballrooms and a spacious pre-function area with lots of natural light. The convention center at the Yacht Club and Beach Club is reminiscent of a grand turn-of-the-century New England town meeting hall. The Grand Floridian has a lavish center with silk brocade walls. The BoardWalk offers a smaller convention area with a lakeside gazebo for outdoor events.

 Among the unique services available to Disney conventioneers is the use of Disney characters and performers for their events. Resort business centers offer clerical staffs and computers, in addition to faxing and photocopying. Business travelers should note that these services are available to all resort guests.

 Those interested in scheduling a convention should call 828-3200 for reservations or information. Organizers are advised to book their events six months in advance, especially for large groups. Keep in mind that the busiest seasons are February through May, and early fall.

Yacht Club & Beach Club

The New England seaside exists at Walt Disney World in the form of the Yacht Club and its sister next door, the Beach Club. Situated just west of Epcot, the hotels, designed by noted architect Robert A. M. Stern, are set around a 25-acre lake. (The rooms and restaurants in each hotel differ, and we describe them separately. But because the two adjacent properties share most facilities—including a convention center offering access to business services—and transportation options, we've combined the "What to Do" and "Transportation" sections.)

YACHT CLUB

The Yacht Club's design evokes images of the New England seashore hotels of the 1880s. Guests enter the five-story, oyster-gray clapboard building along a wooden-planked bridge. Hardwood floors, millwork, and brass enhance the nautical theme. A lighthouse on the pier serves as a beacon to welcome guests back to the hotel from WDW attractions. The telephone number for the Yacht Club resort is 934-7000.

ROOMS: The 630 rooms are spacious and decorated in a nautical motif. Concierge rooms are available. The furniture in each room is white, and the headboard design on the one king-size bed or two queen-size beds incorporates small ship's wheels. Some rooms also have daybeds. Most of the suites have a king-size bed as well as two sleeper sofas. The carpeting is blue, and the drapes and bedspreads are blue and dusty rose. The large bathrooms have a separate vanity with double sinks, and silver mirrors trimmed

with brass. Each room has a ceiling fan, minibar, table (complete with checkerboard top), and two chairs. Chess and checker sets are provided. There are rooms equipped for guests with disabilities, and nonsmoking rooms are available.

WHERE TO EAT: The yachting theme also dominates the hotel's restaurants. A wide variety of menu items is available from room service 24 hours a day.

Yacht Club Galley: The buffet breakfast is bountiful. Breakfast, lunch, and dinner are available from an à la carte menu.

Yachtsman Steakhouse: Select cuts of aged beef are the specialty of the house. Fresh seafood and poultry are also offered.

WHERE TO DRINK: The lounges here offer a variety of specialty drinks in settings with a nautical feel.

Ale and Compass: This lobby lounge features specialty coffees and drinks, a nice respite after a long day in the parks.

Crew's Cup: The place to try a wide assortment of beers shipped in from the world's seaports before dining at Yachtsman Steakhouse next door.

BEACH CLUB

Distance from the ocean is irrelevant at this sand- and surf-focused resort, approached along an entrance drive flanked by palm trees. A patterned walkway leads past a croquet court to beachside cabanas on the white-sand shore. Guests are met by hosts and hostesses dressed in colorful beach resort costumes of the 1870s. The telephone number for the Beach Club resort is 934-8000.

ROOMS: The 583 rooms are spacious and, naturally, reflect a beach motif. The wallpaper is seafoam green, and the curtains and bedspreads are white and seafoam green with a border of mauve beach umbrellas. The room layouts are similar to those at the Yacht Club; each unit features a ceiling fan, two queen-size beds (some rooms have a

king-size bed and a daybed), double sinks, and a wall-mounted makeup mirror. There are rooms equipped for guests with disabilities, and nonsmoking rooms are available.

WHERE TO EAT: The sea plays an important role in the restaurants here. In addition, a variety of options is available from room service 24 hours a day.

Ariel's: Named for the heroine of *The Little Mermaid*, this restaurant specializes in fresh contemporary American seafood, but also serves a few dishes for landlubbers.

Cape May Café: An indoor clambake is held here each night. The varied buffet features several types of clams and mussels, plus pasta and chicken. Lobster is available for an extra charge. A character breakfast is served daily.

WHERE TO DRINK: The two lounges provide a relaxing respite.

Martha's Vineyard: Selections from American and international vineyards are served in sample sizes and by the glass or bottle at this lounge adjacent to Ariel's.

Rip Tide: The lobby lounge features a variety of California wines, wine coolers, and frosty concoctions.

AT THE YACHT CLUB & BEACH CLUB

WHERE TO EAT: These two spots are shared by the Yacht Club and Beach Club resorts.

Beaches & Cream Soda Shop: A classic American soda fountain where shakes, malts, and oversize sundaes are the prime lures. The other specialty is the Fenway Park Burger, served as a single, double, triple, or home run.

Hurricane Hanna's Grill: Burgers, hot dogs, sausages, and other snacks are served at this spot at Stormalong Bay. A full bar is also located here, and poolside beverage service is available.

WHAT TO DO: There is enough to do right at this resort to fill an entire vacation. A sand volleyball court and a croquet court may be found on the Beach Club side of the property. Equipment for both pursuits is available at no cost at the Ship Shape health club. The Fantasia Gardens miniature golf complex is close at hand, and guided fishing excursions can be arranged (see *Sports* for details).

Boating: Pedal boats, canopy boats, sailboats, and Water Sprites are available for rent at the Bayside Marina.

Children's Program: The Sandcastle Club, for children 4 to 12, is available from 4:30 P.M. to midnight. Cost is $4 per hour for each child. Reservations are required; call 939-3463. A variety of toys, videos, games, and Apple computers are on hand to keep children entertained. Milk and snacks are also served.

Health Club: The Ship Shape health club is located in the area between the two resorts, and features Nautilus and cardiovascular machines, sauna, whirlpool, steamroom, personal trainers, and massage (by appointment). The health club is open only to Yacht Club and Beach Club guests, who must be over 13 to use the facilities.

Playground: A small play area with a slide and climbing apparatus is located by the pool.

Salon: The Periwig salon for men and women is located in the central area.

Shopping: At the Yacht Club, Fittings & Fairings Clothes and Notions is an all-purpose shop offering nautical fashions, character merchandise, and sundries. At the Beach Club, Atlantic Wear and Wardrobe Emporium features a similar selection of goods (albeit with a beach theme).

Swimming: Between the marina and the beach is the centerpiece of the dual resort—Stormalong Bay, a 750,000-gallon pool that's really a mini water park. There is a lagoon expressly for relaxed bathing, and another "active" lagoon with currents, jets, and sand-bottomed areas. Several whirlpools are scattered throughout the area. Adjacent to the main pool is a shipwreck where guests can enjoy a variety of unique water slides. There is also a quiet pool and a whirlpool at the far end of each hotel.

Tennis: There are two lighted tennis courts on the Beach Club side of the property. Rental equipment is available at the Ship Shape health club.

Video Arcade: Lafferty Place Arcade, located in the central area, has about 60 video games and pinball machines.

TRANSPORTATION: Guests ride boats or walk to the nearby Epcot entrance (beside the France pavilion). Watercraft go to the Disney-MGM Studios. Buses go to the Magic Kingdom, Pleasure Island, the Disney Village Marketplace, Typhoon Lagoon, Blizzard Beach, and the TTC.

Swan

The exterior of this 758-room waterfront hotel, operated by Westin, is painted a sun-washed coral beneath rolling waves of turquoise. The guestrooms are encased in a striking 12-story main building and two 7-story wings. And just in case the shape and color of the buildings weren't distinctive enough, two 46-foot swan statues, each weighing about 56,000 pounds, sit atop the resort at either end of the main building. The Swan sits next to its sister property, the Dolphin, on the shore of Crescent Lake. Both hotels were designed by noted architect Michael Graves as prime examples of what has come to be known as "entertainment architecture." The Swan's convention center offers access to business services. The telephone number for the Swan is 934-3000. Room reservations can be made by calling 800-248-7926.

ROOMS: The corridors outside the guestrooms feature patterned carpets and murals on the walls that extend the wave theme from the exterior design. Inside, the rooms are decorated in shades of coral and turquoise, and feature such whimsical touches as lamps in the shape of birds and pineapples painted on the dressers. Each has one king-size or two queen-size beds; safes and minibars are among the amenities. There are 45 concierge rooms on the 11th and 12th floors, and 64 suites. Rooms equipped for guests with disabilities and nonsmoking rooms are available.

WHERE TO EAT: In addition to several restaurant choices, 24-hour room service provides an extensive all-day dining menu.

Garden Grove Café: This eatery features a greenhouse atmosphere, and serves breakfast and lunch daily. At dinner, the restaurant transforms into Gulliver's Grill. The theme is played out with exaggerated serving utensils, and steak and seafood entrées with imaginative names like Blushklooshen (red snapper). A buffet breakfast with the characters is held on Saturday, while a character dinner takes place three nights a week.

Kimono's: The Asian decor helps make this spot an inviting place for sushi and other Japanese specialties.

Palio: A pleasant Italian bistro featuring veal specialties, homemade pasta, and brick-oven pizza. There are tasty daily specials and live entertainment.

Splash Grill: A poolside café serving breakfast, lunch, dinner, and snacks. A full-service bar is also located here.

WHERE TO DRINK: The **Lobby Court** offers a respite from the hubbub. Enjoy gourmet coffees with fresh pastries in the morning and wine and specialty drinks at night in a European-style bistro setting. Also, don't overlook Kimono's as an option.

WHAT TO DO: Many activities are available at the Swan, which shares some of its facilities with the Dolphin. Volleyball nets and a few hammocks are set up on the beach. The new Fantasia Gardens mini golf complex and BoardWalk entertainment district are nearby.

Boating: Pedal boats, Hydro Bikes, and CraigCats (motorized lounge chairs), are available for rent on the white-sand beach between the Swan and Dolphin.

Children's program: Camp Swan, open to children 3 to 12, offers supervised activities from 4 P.M. to midnight. The cost is $5 per hour for the first child and $3 per hour for each additional child. Dinner, ordered through room service, is extra.

Health Club: A small health club with basic exercise equipment is near Splash Grill.

Playground: A large play area for the Swan and Dolphin is located near the grotto pool.

Special Room Requests

Central Reservations accepts requests for rooms with particular views or in certain locations. Agents will do their best to accommodate such requests, but cannot guarantee they will be able to fulfill every wish. Call W-DISNEY (934-7639).

Shopping: Located in the lobby. Disney Cabanas features men's and women's fashions, character merchandise, and sundries.

Swimming: A small rectangular pool and a whirlpool are right near the Swan. There is also a themed grotto pool and several whirlpools nearby between the two resorts.

Tennis: Four hard-surface courts, lighted for night play, are open 24 hours a day; the courts are located behind the pool area of the Dolphin but are shared with Swan guests.

Video Arcade: A small room with video games is located near the pool.

TRANSPORTATION: Guests ride boats or walk to Epcot's entrance near the France pavilion. Boats make the trip to the Disney-MGM Studios. Buses go to the Magic Kingdom, Pleasure Island, Disney Village Marketplace, Typhoon Lagoon, and Blizzard Beach.

Dolphin

The hotel's 27-story turquoise triangular tower was honored by *Progressive Architecture* magazine. It is flanked by four coral-colored guestroom wings, nine stories each, that stretch out to the shores of Crescent Lake. The exterior of the Dolphin complements the Swan in color scheme, though its exterior walls feature a mural of banana leaves. And not to be outdone by its neighbor, it is topped by two 56-foot-tall dolphin statues. A lush, tropical setting has been created, and a lovely waterfall cascades down the face of the triangle into a series of seashells, then into a large shell-shaped pool supported by smaller dolphin statues. The hotel's vast convention center offers access to business services. The telephone number for the Dolphin, which is operated by Sheraton, is 934-4000. Reservations can be made by calling 800-227-1500.

ROOMS: The 1,509 rooms, including 136 suites, are decorated in a lighthearted fashion, with lamps in the shape of palm trees and colorful bedspreads and curtains. All feature two double beds or a king-size bed, as well as minibars, vanity dressing areas, irons and ironing boards, and coffeemakers. Concierge rooms are located in the main building. There are rooms equipped for guests with disabilities, and nonsmoking rooms are available.

WHERE TO EAT: There are many restaurants from which to choose, plus room service, which is available 24 hours.

Cabana Bar & Grill: This full-service poolside spot serves burgers, sandwiches, yogurt, and fruit for a nice break from the sun. The full bar serves specialty drinks.

Coral Café: Bountiful buffets, as well as à la carte selections, are served for breakfast, lunch, and dinner in a casual setting.

Dolphin Fountain: Homemade ice cream is the specialty here. Huge sundaes, burgers, shakes, and malts are also offered.

Harry's Safari Bar & Grille: Grilled beef, poultry, and seafood are served here; a character brunch takes place on Sundays.

Juan & Only's: This eatery features authentic Mexican food amid a festive atmosphere of warm hues and rich fabrics of old Mexico.

Sum Chows: A blend of Asian dishes is served in an elegant atmosphere (usually closed Tuesday and Wednesday).

Tubbi's: A cafeteria with a little flair. The checkerboard design makes this a pleasant place for a quick meal. The 24-hour convenience store here sells snacks and sundries.

WHERE TO DRINK: It's not too tough to find an interesting spot for a drink here.

Copa Banana: The tabletops are shaped like slices of fruit, and the tropical atmosphere make this a lively place for a drink. Deejay music, a dance floor, karaoke, and eight large screen televisions provide the entertainment.

Harry's Safari Bar: Pull up a stool and enjoy the jungle-like atmosphere and frosty drinks.

Only's Bar & Jail: Patrons at the companion lounge to Juan & Only's restaurant can enjoy the warm atmosphere here while sampling margaritas, sangria, rare tequilas, and beers from every region of Mexico.

WHAT TO DO: There are many activities at this resort. The beach offers two volleyball nets and several hammocks. The nearby BoardWalk and Fantasia Gardens mini golf complex add to the options.

Boating: Pedal boats, Hydro Bikes, and CraigCats (motorized lounge chairs) are available for rent on the beach.

Children's Program: Camp Dolphin offers a dinner club for kids from 6 P.M. to 11 P.M. Cost is $40 for the first child, $30 for the second child, and $20 for each additional child. Counselors provide themed evenings filled with arts and crafts, dinner, activities, and a movie.

Health Club: A branch of Body by Jake (run by television fitness guru Jake Steinfeld) is near the pool area. State-of-the-art equipment is available, as are personal trainers. There are aerobics classes (including water aerobics), a sauna, a steam room, a large whirlpool, and massage.

Playground: Dolphin and Swan guests have use of an extensive play area with swings, slide, wooden chain bridge, sandpit, and three climbing apparatuses, located next to the grotto pool.

Salon: The Niki Bryan shop here provides a full line of services, including haircuts, manicures, and pedicures.

Shopping: At Brittany Jewels, a large selection of Cartier and other name-brand jewels is available. Indulgences allows chocolate lovers a chance to sample some tasty concoctions. Statements of Fashion offers resortwear for men and women. Daisy's Garden is the place to find character merchandise and sundries.

Swimming: There is a large rectangular pool perfect for laps. A themed grotto pool with slide lies just beyond, and a few whirlpools are scattered around the area.

Tennis: Four hard-surface courts, lighted for night play, are open 24 hours a day; the courts are shared with Swan guests.

Video Arcade: A room full of games is located near Tubbi's.

TRANSPORTATION: Guests may take a boat or walk to Epcot's entrance near the France pavilion. Watercraft make the trip to the Disney-MGM Studios. Buses go to the Magic Kingdom, Pleasure Island, the Disney Village Marketplace, Typhoon Lagoon, and Blizzard Beach.

BoardWalk

The enchantment of a bygone era is recaptured in the recently opened BoardWalk. The resort combines a waterside entertainment complex with deluxe hotel accommodations and vacation villas. Dining, recreation, shopping, and entertainment venues line the boardwalk, and twinkling lights trim the buildings. It's all designed to recall the boardwalks of yesteryear, where a stroll along the boards was the ticket to excitement, day or night. The boardwalk ambience continues throughout, with intricately detailed architecture featuring sherbet-colored facades, deep colonnades, flagged turrets, and striped awnings, all reminiscent of the turn of the century. The BoardWalk resort is adjacent to Epcot's International Gateway and connected via walkway. The telephone number for the BoardWalk Inn is 939-5100; the number for Disney's Board-Walk Villas Resort is 939-6200.

ROOMS: Accommodations evoke the charm of early Eastern Seaboard inns. All have private balconies. The BoardWalk Inn has 378 deluxe hotel rooms decorated with cherry wood furniture, boardwalk postcard–print curtains, and light-green accents. Guestrooms at the Inn sleep up to five, and feature two queen-size beds (or one king-size bed) and a child's daybed. Romantic two-story garden suites each have a private rose garden enclosed by a white picket fence. They sleep four and feature a living room on the first floor and a king-size bed in the bedroom loft. The Inn also has one-story concierge suites.

The 532 vacation villas are collectively called Disney's BoardWalk Villas Resort. These are Disney Vacation Club villas, available when not occupied by members. Each studio features a queen-size bed and double sleeper sofa, plus a wet bar with microwave, coffeemaker, and small refrigerator. Larger (one-, two-, and three-bedroom) villas sleep 4 to 12 people, and feature dining rooms, fully equipped kitchens, laundry facilities, master baths with whirlpool tubs, and VCRs. They also include king-size beds in the master bedroom, living rooms with queen sleeper sofas, and two queen-size beds (or one plus a double sleeper sofa) in any additional bedrooms.

WHERE TO EAT: By virtue of its entertainment district status, the resort's boardwalk has a wealth of dining and snacking options. An assortment of vendors along the boardwalk tempt with hot dogs, popcorn, pizza by the slice, and cotton candy. For those looking to eat in, 24-hour room service is available.

BoardWalk Bakery: This popular stop offers baked goods, ice cream, espresso, and cappuccino. Huge display windows allow passerby to watch bakers at work. Bun rises are held here every morning.

Flying Fish Café: This restaurant has a show kitchen and its menu emphasizes seafood, steak, and fresh seasonal items.

Seashore Sweets': An old-fashioned sweet shop serves cookies, candies, taffy, hand-dipped gelato, and specialty coffees.

Spoodles: Mediterranean cuisine is the focus of this establishment geared toward families. Outdoor dining is available.

WHERE TO DRINK: Guests of this resort have a multitude of options right in their backyard, with the BoardWalk's clubs and lounges on hand. The variety ensures that even the undecided needn't wander far.

Atlantic Dance: Dance or sip champagne while listening to the ten-piece band play music from the 1940s through the '90s. Enjoy hors d'oeuvres and a drink from the bar.

Belle Vue Room: Listen to old-time tunes on antique radios in this relaxing cocktail lounge in the lobby.

Big River Grille & Brewing Works: This working brew pub serves pub grub and beer breads, complemented with fresh specialty ales. View the on-site brewmaster through floor-to-ceiling glass walls. Indoor and outdoor seating is available.

ESPN Club: A serious sports bar for serious sports fans, it provides interactive sports video entertainment and all-day dining. To ensure that guests don't miss a minute of whatever game they're watching, there are even televisions in the restrooms.

Jellyrolls: Dueling pianos provide nonstop live entertainment in a casual warehouse atmosphere. Snacks are also served.

Leaping Horse Libations: The carousel-themed pool bar located at Luna Park serves burgers, hot dogs, ice cream, and a variety of cocktails.

WHAT TO DO: The 2½-mile pathway encircling Crescent Lake (en route to Epcot) provides a ready venue for walkers and joggers. BoardWalk guests may rent boats from a neighboring resort's marina. The Fantasia Gardens miniature golf complex is easily reached via walkway. At the resort itself, Ferris W. Eahlers Community Hall rents equipment for just about any recreational pursuit, including croquet, shuffleboard, table tennis, Frisbee, badminton, in-line skating—even book and video rentals.

Biking: Community Hall offers a variety of bicycles for rental.

Children's Program: Little Toot's provides supervised activities for children 4 to 12 from 4 P.M. to midnight. Cost is $4 per child per hour; dinner is available for an additional charge. Call 939-3463 for necessary reservations.

Fishing: Two-hour guided excursions can be arranged through Community Hall, and poles can be rented for fishing off the dock.

Health Club: Muscles & Bustles health club offers steam rooms, Nautilus machines, and circuit-training equipment, as well as massages (by appointment).

Midway Games: This area on the Board-Walk's Wildwood Landing features games of luck and skill similar to those found along traditional boardwalks.

Playground: Luna Park Crazy House and an elephant-studded play area offers kids water pranks and other fun activities.

Rolling Chair Ride: A trip along the boardwalk in a unique "rolling chair" is available for a small fee.

Shopping: Dundy's Sundries in the lobby is the source for film and basic necessities. Character Carnival on the BoardWalk features children's apparel as well as a large selection of Disney character merchandise. Screen Door General Store stocks groceries, dry goods, snacks, and beverages. Thimbles & Threads, located on the BoardWalk, carries resortwear, swimwear, and accessories for men and women.

Swimming: The BoardWalk's amusement park–themed swimming area, Luna Park, features a large pool with a 200-foot water slide, "Keister Coaster," patterned after a wooden roller coaster. A family of elephants is found posed throughout the area; their trunks act as a shower for adults on the pool deck or children in the wading pool. The resort's two quiet pools are heated; one is located within the Inn's courtyard, the other, adjacent to Community Hall in the Villas area. Tubes may be rented.

Tennis: Two lighted soft-surface tennis courts are available for play.

Video Arcades: Side Show Games has poolside video games, and a sports-themed arcade called The Yard entertains at the ESPN Club.

TRANSPORTATION: Guests get to Epcot via boats or walkways, and to the Disney-MGM Studios via boats or buses. Buses go to the Magic Kingdom, Typhoon Lagoon, Blizzard Beach, Pleasure Island, and the Disney Village Marketplace.

Village Area

Port Orleans

This 1,008-room resort invites comparisons to the historic French Quarter of New Orleans. Starting at the entrance gate, with its wrought-iron portal and overgrown landscape, the appeal of the Delta City surrounds arriving guests. The entry drive leads to the heart of the city, which is Port Orleans Square. The central building, The Mint, was based on an original turn-of-the-century mint where farmers would go to trade their harvest for "dixes." A dix was a ten-dollar bill, and when the farmers said they were going to get their dixes, they probably didn't know they had coined a phrase. The Mint houses the hotel's check-in facilities, the Guest Services desk, a shop, the food court, an arcade, and the restaurant. It has a vaulted ceiling, and the check-in desks are designed as old-fashioned bank-teller windows. The mural behind the check-in counter, featuring a Mardi Gras street scene, was painted by an artist in three parts; each piece was shipped here separately. The musical notes in the mural are the notes to "When the Saints Come Marching In." The telephone number for Port Orleans is 934-5000.

ROOMS: The guestrooms are located in seven 3-story buildings (with elevators), and each can accommodate four people. Each room has two double beds and some king-size beds are available. The rooms are a bit smaller than the standard rooms at the more expensive Disney hotels, but they are comfortable for a family of four. The photographs on the walls were donated by Disney cast members, and the captions explain their history. The buildings are painted cream, pink, blue, purple, and yellow, and feature wrought-iron railings of varying designs. About half the rooms have doors connecting to a neighboring room. Connecting rooms can be requested, but they cannot be guaranteed. The rates are based on the room's view. The least expensive rooms overlook parking areas, the mid-range units overlook gardens, and the most expensive room options offer water views. Rooms equipped for guests with disabilities and nonsmoking rooms are available.

WHERE TO EAT: Options here include one restaurant with waitress service and a food court with counter-service stands. Also, Sassagoula Pizza Express delivers hand-tossed pizza, salads, desserts, and soft drinks directly to guestrooms from 4 P.M. to midnight.

Bonfamilles Café: The name of this waitress-service eatery comes from the Disney movie *The Aristocats*. Steaks, seafood, and Creole cooking highlight the dinner menu. Breakfast is also served.

Sassagoula Floatworks & Food Factory: This food court has a 300-seat dining area. A variety of specialty foods is available, including gumbo, spit-roasted chicken with red beans and rice, fresh beignets, and other traditional Creole dishes. Burgers, pizza, ice cream, and baked goods are also served.

WHERE TO DRINK: The New Orleans theme is carried through in the hotel's watering holes.

Mardi Grogs: The poolside bar serves specialty drinks, popcorn, hot dogs, and ice cream during pool hours.

Scat Cat's Club: A traditional bar featuring nightly entertainment and a light menu of hors d'oeuvres.

WHAT TO DO: A special pool is the highlight of the recreational opportunities here.

Biking: Bicycles are available for rent at Port Orleans Landing.

Boating: Pedal boats, canoes, rowboats, canopy boats, and pontoon boats are available for rent at Port Orleans Landing.

Playground: A small play area with slides is located across from the food court.

Shopping: Jackson Square Gifts & Desires, located at Port Orleans Square, features Disney character merchandise, clothing featuring the Port Orleans logo, and sundries.

Swimming: Doubloon Lagoon is a pool built around a sea serpent that, as the legend goes, is still lingering underground. His tail can be seen jutting up in spots along the walkways, and the water slide is actually the serpent's tongue. The shower at the pool has an alligator's head, and there is a large clam shell where an alligator band serves as the centerpiece of a fountain. A whirlpool is located nearby. Port Orleans guests may also swim at Dixie Landings' Ol' Man Island.

Video Arcade: South Quarter Games is located at Port Orleans Square. It features state-of-the-art video and arcade games.

TRANSPORTATION: Buses go to the Magic Kingdom, TTC, Epcot, the Disney-MGM Studios, Typhoon Lagoon, Blizzard Beach, Pleasure Island, and the Disney Village Marketplace. The Sassagoula River Cruise makes the trip to Dixie Landings, Pleasure Island, and the Disney Village Marketplace.

Dixie Landings

The city feel of Port Orleans gives way to the rural South upriver at Dixie Landings. The resort is divided into "parishes." Closest to the "city," guestrooms are found in Mansion homes; further upriver are the Bayou rooms with a more rustic feel. The guest registration area is located in a building designed to resemble a steamship. When guests check in, they are booking passage on the steamboat. The food court, restaurant, lounge, and Fultons General Store all are located in the same building. The telephone number for Dixie Landings is 934-6000.

ROOMS: The 2,048 Mansion and Bayou guestrooms are of the same size, and each room features two double beds (some king-size beds are available); 963 of the Bayou rooms have trundle beds as well. The Magnolia Bend Mansion rooms are situated in sprawling, elegant manor homes with stately columns and grand staircases. The Alligator Bayou rooms are in rustic, weathered-wood tin-roofed buildings that are tucked among trees and bushes native to the area. These rooms surround Ol' Man Island, a 3½-acre recreational area with a pool, playground, and fishing hole. Decorative touches in the rooms include wood and tin armoires and pedestal sinks with brass fittings. The beds have hickory bedposts. The rooms are a bit smaller than the standard rooms at the more expensive Disney hotels, but they are comfortable for a family of four. Rooms equipped for guests with disabilities and nonsmoking rooms are available.

WHERE TO EAT: In addition to its full-service restaurant and themed food court, the hotel offers limited room service via Sassagoula Pizza Express, which delivers salads, hand-tossed pizza, desserts, and soft drinks to guestrooms from 4 P.M. to midnight.

Boatwright's Dining Hall: This 200-seat, waitress-service eatery next to Colonel's Cotton Mill serves Cajun specialties and traditional American specialties for dinner. The restaurant is modeled after a boatmaking warehouse. Breakfast is also served.

Colonel's Cotton Mill: The hotel's food court is designed to resemble an old-fashioned cotton mill with a 30-foot working water wheel that powers a real cotton press inside. The five counter-service stands here offer all sorts of choices. Basic selections are available for breakfast also. Acadian Pizza 'n' Pasta has pasta dishes, fresh pizza with a variety of toppings, and calzones. Bleu Bayou Burgers and Chicken offers fried and grilled chicken and an assortment of burgers. Cajun Broiler serves spit-roasted chicken and barbecued ribs. Riverside Market and Deli is a convenience store that stocks snack foods, soda, salads, sandwiches, beer, and wine. Southern Trace Bakery specializes in pastries, freshly baked pies, and sticky buns.

WHERE TO DRINK: The two lounges both possess a certain degree of charm.

Cotton Co-Op: Situated in a room designed as a cotton exchange, this lounge features specialty drinks, some light hors d'oeuvres, and live entertainment.

Muddy Rivers: The poolside bar serves specialty and traditional drinks plus hot dogs, popcorn, and ice cream during pool hours.

WHAT TO DO: Many of the resort activities are found at Ol' Man Island, a 3½-acre recreation center featuring a themed pool, whirlpool, children's wading pool, playground, and fishing hole stocked with a variety of fish for catch and release.

Biking: Bicycles of all types can be rented at the Dixie Levee.

Boating: Pedal boats, canoes, rowboats, canopy boats, and pontoon boats are available for rent at Dixie Levee.

Fishing: Two-hour guided fishing excursions are available, and guests may fish on their own at the Ol' Fishin' Hole.

Playground: A fun play area is located on Ol' Man Island next to the pool.

Shopping: Fulton's General Store in the Dixie Landings building stocks Disney character merchandise, clothing with the Dixie Landings logo, and sundries.

Swimming: In addition to the themed pool and children's wading pool at Ol' Man Island, there are five pools set among the parishes of the resort. Dixie Landings guests may also swim at Port Orleans' Doubloon Lagoon next door.

Video Arcade: The Medicine Show Arcade, located in the Dixie Landings building, features a small selection of games.

TRANSPORTATION: Buses go to the Magic Kingdom, Epcot, the Disney-MGM Studios, Typhoon Lagoon, Blizzard Beach, Pleasure Island, and the Disney Village Marketplace. Port Orleans, the Disney Village Marketplace, and Pleasure Island can also be reached aboard the Sassagoula River Cruise.

The Villas at the Disney Institute

The area near the Disney Village Marketplace and the Lake Buena Vista golf course is dotted with villa-type accommodations (formerly known as Disney's Village Resort), many fitted out with fully equipped kitchens and other extras and amenities. Some may cost more than individual guestrooms at the conventional Disney hotels, but they accommodate more people as well. For families of more than five (who might otherwise need to rent an extra hotel room), this is the most economical way to stay hereabouts. Smaller families can often break even by cooking some of their own meals (especially breakfast) in their villa. Accommodations for guests with disabilities are available in the Fairway Villas. Nonsmoking accommodations are available in the Bungalows and selected villas.

The resort serves as headquarters for the Disney Institute (see the *Everything Else in the World* chapter for details). Guests participating in the Institute's enrichment programs are housed in the Bungalows and Town Houses. Recreational facilities are available to all guests when not in use for Institute programming (additional charges apply for use of the Sports & Fitness Center and The Spa).

The villas are exceptionally spacious, quiet, and secluded—albeit decorated on the dull side, at least as Disney accommodations go. The resort's pace is relaxed and the atmosphere is low-key (except at the Town Houses near Pleasure Island, which can be lively until late in the evening). The Villas are conveniently located with respect to Epcot, the Disney-MGM Studios, Pleasure Island, Disney Village Marketplace, and Typhoon Lagoon, although a few are a bit of a walk from the Institute campus. The telephone number for The Villas at the Disney Institute is 827-1100.

TYPES OF ACCOMMODATIONS: There are five major types of villas. All have either full kitchens or wet bars with small refrigerators. Check-in and check-out for all guests takes place at the Welcome Center near the Bungalows and the Fairway Villas.

One-bedroom Bungalows: The 316 Bungalows are slightly northeast of the Town Houses. Each of the smallest one-bedroom units is roughly L-shaped, with a sitting area (equipped with a daybed, wet bar, refrigerator, microwave, and coffeemaker) that's pleasantly removed from the sleeping area, with its two queen-size beds. The layout provides families with a bit more privacy and space than they would get in the standard rooms at the WDW hotels. (The single disadvantage for families: small bathrooms.) All have a balcony or a patio.

One- and two-bedroom Town Houses: These accommodations are located about a five minutes' walk from the Disney Village Marketplace. They are simple in feeling and decor; living rooms have cathedral ceilings. A one-bedroom unit can accommodate four; there's a queen-size bed in the bedroom and a queen-size sleeper sofa in the living room. A two-bedroom unit, which can accommodate six, features a queen-size bed in the master bedroom, two twin-size beds in the loft bedroom, and a queen-size sleeper sofa in the living room.

Fairway Villas: These cedar-sided, slant-roofed units, located near the first, second, eighth, and ninth fairways of the Lake Buena Vista golf course, are among the World's most spacious and attractive accommodations, with cathedral ceilings, rough-hewn walls, large windows, contemporary-styled furniture, and an overall feeling that there's lots of elbow room. There is a queen-size bed in one bedroom, two double beds in the other, and either a sico bed or a double sleeper sofa in the living room. Each villa can sleep eight, plus there's room for a crib.

Treehouse Villas: Guests who lodge in one of these octagonal houses-on-stilts, scattered along a barbell-shaped roadway, go to sleep to a cacophony of crickets and wake up to a chorus of birds. You're literally in the woods, alongside some of the winding WDW canals, and you feel a million miles from the rest of the World. Upstairs lie the small (but modern) kitchen, the living room (where the television set is located), two bedrooms (each with a queen-size bed), and two bathrooms; the entire floor is surrounded by a deck. Downstairs, there's a bedroom with a double bed, and a utility room equipped with a washer and dryer. The canals offer some of the World's best fishing, mainly for bass, and the roadways—shady, flat, and generally untrafficked—are terrific for jogging.

Grand Vista Homes: Four ultraluxurious homes—each with two or three bedrooms and a fully equipped kitchen—are available for rent. Each features a master bedroom with a king-size bed, and most of the other bedrooms have two queen-size beds (some have two twins). Bed-turndown service and daily newspaper delivery are provided, refrigerators are stocked with staples, and furnishings are all first class. Use of golf carts and bicycles is included in the price. (For complete price information, see the chart "Rates at Walt Disney World Properties" on page 78.)

WHERE TO EAT: The **Seasons Dining Room** features four dining areas, each with a different seasonal decor. A limited selection of breakfast and lunch items can be boxed to go; full-service meals are served in the dining room. Dinner, available family-style, highlights a different regional theme and cuisine each night of the week. There are also many options at the nearby Disney Village Marketplace and Disney Village Hotel Plaza. (See *Good Meals, Great Times* for more details.)

Groceries: In these parts, many guests cook their own meals. Dabblers, located in the Welcome Center, has a limited selection of groceries. The Gourmet Pantry at the Disney Village Marketplace stocks staples of all sorts. Purchases can be delivered to your villa; if you won't be there to receive them, arrangements may be made for the delivery person to be let in so that perishables can be stashed in the refrigerator. It's also possible to order by phone; call 828-3886 for the Gourmet Pantry, or 827-4453 for Dabblers. A Gooding's supermarket is located at the Crossroads of Lake Buena Vista shopping center.

WHERE TO DRINK: For liquid refreshment, head for the **Seasons Lounge**, located in the lobby of the restaurant. At the Disney Village Marketplace, nearby, you'll find Cap'n Jack's Oyster Bar, or try one of Pleasure Island's clubs. (For details, see *Everything Else in the World*.)

WHAT TO DO: In addition to boating, fishing, and shopping at the Disney Village Marketplace (discussed in more detail in *Sports* and *Everything Else in the World*), you can also enjoy a variety of activities around the villas themselves. Two sand volleyball courts are situated among the villas. The Disney Institute Recreation Center is located near the Bungalows and the North Studios on Willow Lake, and offers a pool, a whirlpool, a coffee shop, and canoe and bike rentals.

Biking: The rustic pathways and meandering roads around the villas can make for an enjoyable hour of pedaling. Bicycles are rented at the Recreation Center.

Boating: Canoes are available for hourly and daily rental from the Recreation Center.

Golf: Fairways of the Lake Buena Vista course based here nudge right up to the Fairway and Treehouse villas. Practice greens and a driving range are available, along with top-quality rental clubs and shoes. (For fees and starting information, see *Sports*.)

Health Club: The large Sports & Fitness Center features aerobics, a gymnasium, and Cybex equipment (complimentary to guests participating in Institute programs; available to any WDW resort guest for a fee). A full-service spa is within the center (use of facilities included with purchase of treatments).

Playground: A play area is located near the main pool.

Shopping: Dabblers in the Welcome Center offers a mix of merchandise related to Institute programs. Browse through books, gardening and cooking accessories, spa-at-home inspirations, plus logo items.

Swimming: There are six pools and several whirlpools dotted about the grounds.

Tennis: The four lighted clay courts are often given over to Institute programs, but are available to any guest (with a fitness center pass) at other times.

Video Arcade: A small arcade with electronic games and pinball machines is located near the Town Houses.

TRANSPORTATION: Buses go to the Magic Kingdom, Epcot, the Disney-MGM Studios, Blizzard Beach, Typhoon Lagoon, Pleasure Island, and the Disney Village Marketplace. These circulate through the villa areas, making pickups at bus stops located at regular intervals along the roadways.

Another option: transport to the Marketplace via an electric golf cart or bike. Both are rented at the Recreation Center.

Disney's Old Key West Resort

Escape to the spirit of the Florida Keys. Disney's Old Key West Resort is the flagship Disney Vacation Club property (see the box on the next page for details), but villas not occupied by members are available for nightly rental. It has the laid-back feel of a resort community and all the amenities that go with resort life. Conch Flats Community Hall provides a wide range of activities, from board games and movie rentals to basketball and table tennis, plus an activities director to schedule events. The homey accommodations have lots of space and the convenience of kitchen facilities, making the resort especially comfortable for longer stays. The villas are designed in a Key West theme with soothing color schemes of seafoam green and mauve. The telephone number for Disney's Old Key West Resort is 827-7700.

VILLAS: There are studios and villas with one, two, and three bedrooms. Each studio consists of a large bedroom with two queen-size beds, a table and chairs, and a kitchenette with a small refrigerator, coffeemaker, microwave, and sink. The bathrooms are spacious. Each one-bedroom villa has a king-size bed in the master bedroom and a queen-size sleeper sofa in the living room; the master bath has a whirlpool tub, sink, and shower.

Disney Vacation Club

Imagine a club that gives members the convenience of ready-made vacations from year to year, with the flexibility of choosing when and where to visit, how long to stay, and the type of accommodations. It starts with the purchase of a real estate interest in a Disney Vacation Club property. For a one-time price and annual dues, members garner vacation stays that can be enjoyed at any of four destinations: Disney's Old Key West Resort and Disney's BoardWalk Villas Resort at Walt Disney World, Disney's Vero Beach Resort, and Disney's Hilton Head Island Resort in South Carolina.

Disney's Vero Beach Resort is a two-hour drive from Walt Disney World. It has villa-type accommodations comparable to those at Disney's Old Key West Resort—with lush surroundings, an endless uncrowded beach, and lots of local sights. The proximity makes it easy to tack a beach vacation onto a WDW visit (for the vacation needed *after* the vacation). Members can also elect to stay at their choice of more than 100 other resorts worldwide. Accommodations are subject to availability.

The two-bedroom villa features a king-size bed in the master bedroom, two queen-size beds in the second bedroom, a large living room with a queen-size sleeper sofa and a VCR, a full dining room with a table and chairs, and a spacious kitchen equipped with a full-size refrigerator, dishwasher, toaster, and coffeemaker, plus dishes, silverware, glasses, cooking utensils, and more. The master bathroom is split into two separate rooms with an extra-large whirlpool tub and a sink in one and an oversize shower, sink and vanity, and toilet in the other. There's a terrace off the living room and bedroom, and ceiling fans grace each room. The configuration of the three-bedroom Grand Villas is similar to that of the two-bedroom models, but adds a third bedroom with two double beds. As for capacity, the studios and one-bedroom villas sleep 4 people, the two-bedroom villas sleep 8, and three-bedroom villas accommodate 12. Some units are equipped for guests with disabilities. Nonsmoking villas are available.

WHERE TO EAT: In addition to the restaurant and snack bar here, there are grills and picnic tables available for meals outdoors.

Guests can also make a short boat journey to the Disney Village Marketplace. Pizza delivery is available from Dixie Landings from 5 P.M. to midnight.

Good's Food to Go: Pick up continental breakfast or burgers, conch fritters, and snacks at this casual spot by the main pool.

Olivia's Café: This casual full-service restaurant serves an assortment of Key West favorites plus more traditional items for breakfast, lunch, and dinner. Menus change seasonally. A Winnie the Pooh character breakfast is held on Wednesday and Sunday.

WHERE TO DRINK: The watering holes at Old Key West are as laid-back as they come.

Gurgling Suitcase: Near the main pool area, this bar serves specialty drinks, cocktails, wine, beer, and soft drinks. Sit at outdoor tables or on stools inside.

Turtle Shack: In the recreation area off Turtle Pond Road, a poolside spot serves pizza, salads, sandwiches, and snacks (seasonal).

WHAT TO DO: An activities director is on hand to schedule events for guests and members alike. At Conch Flats Community Hall, table tennis, board games, playing cards, a large-screen television set, video rentals, and planned activities all are on hand. Basketball, shuffleboard, and volleyball courts are located throughout the resort, and equipment is available from Hank's Rent 'N Return.

Biking: A variety of bicycles may be rented from Hank's.

Boating: Pedal boats, rowboats, and pontoon boats are available for rent at Hank's.

Health Club: The R.E.S.T. health club features Nautilus and cardiovascular machines, a sauna, and massage (by appointment).

Playground: The kids' play area is located between the main swimming pool and the tennis courts.

Shopping: Conch Flats General Store stocks groceries, books, magazines, sun-care products, and Disney character merchandise.

Swimming: The sprawling main pool, with a large whirlpool nearby, is located behind the Hospitality House. The children's pool and play area resembles a giant sand castle. Additional pools are found around the resort.

Tennis: There are two lighted courts located near the main pool. A third court, located in a more removed area, is not equipped for night play.

Video Arcade: The Electric Eel Arcade is located in the Hospitality House.

TRANSPORTATION: Buses go to the Magic Kingdom, Epcot, the Disney-MGM Studios, Blizzard Beach, Typhoon Lagoon, Pleasure Island, and the Disney Village Marketplace. Water launches also make the trip to Pleasure Island and the Marketplace.

Studios Area

All-Star Sports & All-Star Music

The first Disney entries into the value-priced hotel market, the All-Star Sports and All-Star Music resorts are the most startlingly themed at Walt Disney World. Each resort has 1,920 rooms housed in ten buildings, devoted to five sports and five types of music, respectively.

Sports fans will find themselves in a world of baseball, football, tennis, surfing, or basketball at the All-Star Sports resort. Brightly colored, larger-than-life football helmets, surfboards, tennis balls, basketball hoops, and baseball bats adorn the buildings. Stairwells in the shape of three-story soda cups, lifeguard shacks, and tennis ball cans lead guests to the second and third floors.

At the All-Star Music resort, Broadway, country, jazz, rock, and calypso are the five themes. A walk-through, neon-lit jukebox, a three-story pair of cowboy boots, and a Broadway theater marquee are among the giant icons.

Guests check in at Stadium Hall for All-Star Sports or at Melody Hall for All-Star Music. These central buildings each house a food court, large arcade, shop, and Guest Services. The telephone number for the All-Star Sports resort is 939-5000; the telephone number for the All-Star Music resort is 939-6000.

ROOMS: The guestrooms, measuring 260 square feet, are rather small compared with the rooms at Port Orleans and Dixie Landings, which are 314 square feet. Each room has two double beds (with the exception of rooms designed for travelers with disabilities, which have one king-size bed and a small refrigerator), a vanity area with a single sink, a separate bathroom, a closet bar and shelf, a small dresser, and a small table with two chairs. Nonsmoking rooms are available.

WHERE TO EAT: The **End Zone** food court in Stadium Hall and the **Intermission** food court in Melody Hall each features a bakery, convenience market, and several stands geared to barbecue, pizza and pasta, and burgers. Each food court has a common seating area with a central beverage bar. For entertainment, the End Zone offers children's movies during the day and showcases big games on its large-screen TV; Intermission features Tuesday night karaoke. Both All-Star Sports and All-Star Music deliver pizza, salads, beer, and wine to rooms from 5 P.M. to midnight.

WHERE TO DRINK: There are no lounges at the All-Star resorts; however, the **Team Spirits** pool bar and the **Singing Spirits** pool bar serve drinks throughout the day and evening. These bars are located at the main pool areas.

All-Star Trivia

- It would take all the water at Typhoon Lagoon's wave pool to fill one of the Coca-Cola cups at the baseball-themed Home Run hotel.
- The tennis racquet at Centre Court would almost cover an entire regulation tennis court.
- It would take 9,474,609 tennis balls to fill one of Centre Court's tennis ball cans.
- The gold star in front of Melody Hall, one of 727 stars there, is one-fourth the size of Epcot's Spaceship Earth.
- The jukeboxes at Rock Inn could hold 4,000 compact discs, enough to supply music for 135 days straight.
- The boots doing the two-step at Country Fair would fit a size 270 foot.

WHAT TO DO: Swimming takes first priority. Guests may pay one fee for unlimited boat rentals at the nearby Caribbean Beach resort.

Playground: A playground is located in each hotel's courtyard area.

Shopping: Sport Goofy Gifts and Sundries in Stadium Hall and Maestro Mickey's in Melody Hall feature magazines, books, sun-care products, character merchandise, and sundries.

Swimming: Each hotel has two pools and one kiddie pool. At the All-Star Sports resort, Surfboard Bay has an ocean motif. The smaller Grand Slam Pool is shaped like a baseball diamond. At the All-Star Music resort, the Calypso Pool is in the form of a giant guitar, while the Piano Pool is designed to look like—you guessed it.

Video Arcade: The Game Point Arcade in Stadium Hall offers 100 games, and Note'able Games in Melody Hall has 90 games.

TRANSPORTATION: Buses make pickups at Stadium Hall and Melody Hall for trips to the Magic Kingdom, Epcot, the Disney-MGM Studios, Blizzard Beach, Typhoon Lagoon, the Disney Village Marketplace, and Pleasure Island.

Disney's Coronado Springs

This resort, slated to open in late summer 1997, has the mystical feel of a lost kingdom of riches that's only recently been unearthed. Inspired by explorer Francisco de Coronado's unsuccessful search for the fabled realm of Cibola, it reveals its theme in such elements as an intricately tiled stucco lobby with a fountain, and a stepped pyramid with water tumbling down from it that appears to have created the pool. The hotel's 1,967 rooms are found in three distinct guest areas that stretch around a 15-acre lake, reflecting urban, rural, and coastal regions from the American Southwest to northern Mexico. The food court, restaurant, lounge, and health club are centrally located near the rotunda lobby. A convention center offers access to business services. The telephone number for Coronado Springs is 939-1000.

ROOMS: Standard guestrooms are smaller than those at Disney's deluxe hotels, but perfectly adequate for a family of four; each features two double beds (some king-size beds are available). In-room amenities include a coffeemaker, safe, and extra phone jack. Decor varies in each section, but is characterized by vibrant yellow, blue, and scarlet accents, and Mexican and Southwestern touches. In the Casitas area, where most of the hotel's 46 suites are located, terra-cotta guest buildings occupy a citylike landscape interspersed with colorful plazas and palm-shaded courtyards; rooms are awash in autumnal tones. In the pueblo-style Ranchos, scattered along a dry stream bed amid cacti, rooms have a more rustic feel. Cabanas, located along the rocky palm-lined beach, reflect the fun, casual feel of their namesake both inside and out; over half have water views. Walkways link guest areas with the recreational area. Rooms equipped for guests with disabilities and nonsmoking rooms are available.

WHERE TO EAT: A full-service restaurant features a show grill and cooking with southwestern flavor. The **Pepper Market** food court offers lots of stands in a casual setting akin to an indoor marketplace. Room service is available.

WHERE TO DRINK: Options include a colorful lounge providing cocktails and evening entertainment, and a pool bar.

WHAT TO DO: The recreation area's hallmark is a stepped pyramid with a water slide that spills into a large pool. A children's wading pool, a huge whirlpool, an archaeological dig–themed playground, and a sand volleyball court are nearby. Bikes and pedal boats may be rented. There is a quiet pool at each guest area. Other facilities include a health club, salon, and gift shop. The hotel boasts two arcades.

TRANSPORTATION: Buses take guests to the Magic Kingdom, Epcot, the Disney-MGM Studios, Typhoon Lagoon, Blizzard Beach, Pleasure Island, and the Disney Village Marketplace.

Fort Wilderness Resort & Campground

The very existence of this canal-crossed expanse—more than 700 acres of cypress and pine laced with pleasant blacktop roadways—always surprises visitors who come to Walt Disney World expecting to find the theme parks and nothing more. If they've heard about Fort Wilderness at all, they often confuse it with the Magic Kingdom's Frontierland section.

But the Fort Wilderness atmosphere is relaxed and not at all frenetic. In one corner, a group of kids may be battling it out at tetherball, and on the playing fields there are often a couple of energetic touch football games in progress. In the morning, the campground smells sweetly of dew-dampened pines, then of frying bacon. In the evening, the warmth and stillness of the afternoon give way to dinnertime bustle, and fish and steaks are tossed onto grills as next-door neighbors organize get-togethers. Later on, groups of kids gather alongside the trading posts or at the arcade at Pioneer Hall.

The recreational possibilities make Fort Wilderness one of the livelier places to be at Walt Disney World. There's a marina and a beach, a nature trail, and a number of waterways where fishing, canoeing, and pedal boating are popular. The Meadow Recreation Complex, located behind the Meadow Trading Post, features two lighted tennis courts, a swimming pool, an arcade, and a snack bar.

You can enjoy the Fort Wilderness experience even if you don't have your own camping gear. Among the 1,192 campsites there are 408 air-conditioned Wilderness Homes available for rent, complete with kitchen utensils, dishes, linens, a color television wired for cable, daily maid service, and enough other amenities that the woods all around are the only reminders of the fact that you're camping out. The cost is comparable to that of some of the more expensive rooms at the hotels. (But those don't have kitchens and so don't offer the money-saving option of cooking some of your vacation meals "at home.") The telephone number for the Fort Wilderness resort is 824-2900.

CAMPSITES: Fort Wilderness has 784 traditional campsites, ranging in length from 25 to 65 feet, spaced throughout 20 camping loops. All types of camping can be accommodated—RV, travel trailer, and tent. Preferred campsites feature cable-TV connections as well as electricity hookups (100 volt–20 amp, 110 volt–30 amp, or 200 volt–50 amp), water, and sanitary disposal. Partial-hookup campsites supply electricity and water hookups only. All campsites are bordered by lush wilderness and feature a paved driveway pad, picnic table, and charcoal grill. All loops have at least one air-conditioned comfort station equipped with restrooms, private showers, an ice machine, telephones, and a laundry room. A site allows for occupancy by up to ten people. Each site has room for parking one car (in addition to the camping vehicle). Additional cars can be parked in the main parking lot.

The various campground areas are designated by numbers. The 100, 200, 300, 400, and 500 loops are closest to the beach, the Settlement Trading Post, and Pioneer Hall. The 1500, 1600, 1700, 1800, 1900, and 2000 loops are farthest away from the beach and many other Fort Wilderness activities, but they are quieter and more private. Pets are welcome at certain campsites for an additional nightly charge of $3.

WILDERNESS HOMES: The 408 Wilderness Homes here provide all the advantages of villa accommodations—with woodsy surroundings to boot. There are two types of homes. One model sleeps four adults and two children; it has a bedroom with a double bed, a bunk bed, plus a separate vanity area and a spacious living room with a pull-down double bed and a ceiling fan. The other trailers sleep four, with a double bed in the bedroom and a pull-down double bed in the living room. Both types come equipped with pots and pans, dishes, and all basic kitchen equipment, plus a color TV set and a complete bathroom. The bathroom is not the sort of makeshift setup you might expect; in fact, it's comparable to a bathroom in a standard hotel room. There are Wilderness Homes equipped for travelers with disabilities, and nonsmoking trailers are available. **Note:** No extra camping equipment is permitted on the

site; all guests must be accommodated in the Wilderness Home. (For complete price information, see the chart "Rates at Walt Disney World Properties" on page 78.)

WHERE TO EAT: There are a couple of options here, but most people cook their own meals. Groceries and supplies are available at the Meadow Trading Post and the Settlement Trading Post (open from 8 A.M. to 10 P.M. in winter, to 11 P.M. in summer). Sandwiches, fruit, ice cream, and chips are available there for takeout. Also, Gooding's supermarket is located at the Crossroads of Lake Buena Vista shopping center across from the Disney Village Hotel Plaza.

Trail's End Buffet: An informal, log-walled, beam-ceilinged cafeteria inside Pioneer Hall, where home-style fare is served for breakfast, lunch, and dinner. Pizza is an option from 9:30 P.M. to 11 P.M. nightly. Beer and wine are also available.

Crockett's Tavern: Also inside Pioneer Hall, this restaurant serves cocktails, unique appetizers, steaks, ribs, and chicken in the evening. A children's menu is available.

WHERE TO DRINK: Beer, wine, and cocktails are served at Crockett's Tavern in Pioneer Hall. It's also a short ride to Pleasure Island and its many clubs, or to Cap'n Jack's at the Disney Village Marketplace.

FAMILY ENTERTAINMENT AFTER DARK: The Hoop-Dee-Doo Musical Revue is presented three times nightly at 5 P.M., 7:15 P.M., and 9:30 P.M.; reservations are required and are so hard to come by that they need to be made well in advance by calling WDW-DINE (939-3463). Cancellations do occur, however. WDW resort guests who can't get a reservation can go to the Pioneer Hall Ticket Window 45 minutes before showtime and place their names on the waiting list.

There's also a nightly campfire program held at the center of the campground, near the Meadow Trading Post. A sing-along (featuring Chip 'n' Dale) and free screenings of Disney movies and cartoons are the main goings-on. At 9:45 P.M., catch the Electrical Water Pageant—a procession of waterborne floats, during which an assortment of sea creatures is outlined in tiny colored lights. This can be viewed from the Fort Wilderness beach. (For more details, see *Everything Else in the World* and *Good Meals, Great Times*.)

WHAT TO DO: More on-site activities are available at Fort Wilderness than at almost any other area in the World. There are two tennis courts in the campground, and the Osprey Ridge and Eagle Pines golf courses play from the nearby Bonnet Creek Golf Club.

There are two heated swimming pools and an ample beach for swimming in Bay Lake.

You can rent tandems and other bicycles at the Bike Barn for afternoon excursions or as transportation around the campground. Visits to the Petting Farm and the horse barn near Fort Wilderness are amusing. Boating is popular; rentals are available at the marina. Canoes and pedal boats can be hired at the Bike Barn. Pony rides are available from 9 A.M. to 5 P.M. Basketball, checkers, electric cart rentals, fishing (on your own in the canals or on organized morning or afternoon angling excursions), horseback riding (on guided trail outings), horseshoes, tetherball, volleyball, and waterskiing are also available. Or you can just stroll along the three-quarter-mile trail leading to the Wilderness Lodge. All of these activities are described in detail in the *Everything Else in the World* and *Sports* chapters. Video-game fans have two hangouts: Davy Crockett's Arcade in Pioneer Hall and Daniel Boone's Arcade at the Meadow Trading Post.

River Country, an attraction in its own right with a separate admission charge, is also located at Fort Wilderness. The features of this watery playground are discussed in detail in *Everything Else in the World*.

TRANSPORTATION: Buses circulating at 20-minute intervals provide transportation within the campground, while buses and watercraft connect Fort Wilderness to the rest of the World. The Magic Kingdom and the Contemporary resort are most efficiently reached via watercraft that depart regularly from the marina. Buses make the trip from the Settlement Depot to Blizzard Beach. To get to other WDW points, take a bus from the Fort Wilderness visitor parking lot to the TTC. Here, change to a monorail for Epcot or take another bus for the Disney-MGM Studios, Typhoon Lagoon, Pleasure Island, and Disney Village Marketplace.

Electric golf carts can be rented at the Bike Barn as an alternative means of getting around within the campground. Call 824-2742 for reservations.

WDW Resort Primer

The Walt Disney World hotels and villas have some important operating procedures that first-time guests don't always take seriously—much to their later dismay.

Deposit requirements: Deposits equal to one night's lodging (or campsite rental) are required within 21 days of the time that a reservation is made. Personal checks, traveler's checks, cashier's checks, and money orders are acceptable forms of payment. To have deposit charges billed to an American Express, Visa, MasterCard, or The Disney Credit Card account, you'll need to provide the reservation agent with your credit card number and its expiration date. Deposits will be fully refunded if you cancel your reservation at least 48 hours before your scheduled arrival. Reservations are canceled if deposits are not received by the 21-day deadline. (Reservations booked less than 30 days prior to arrival will receive special instructions for deposits.)

Check-in and check-out times: While not unique to the Orlando area, the early check-out time (11 A.M. at all WDW lodging places) and the late check-in times (1 P.M. at the campsites, 3 P.M. in the resort hotels, 4 P.M. in the villas) often surprise. They needn't be an inconvenience, however. When checking in, guests should pre-register, purchase passes, and head for the parks. Luggage can be stored at the resorts.

Payment methods: Hotel bills may be paid with credit cards (American Express, Visa, MasterCard, or The Disney Credit Card), traveler's checks, cash, or personal checks. Checks must bear the guest's name and address, be drawn on a U.S. bank, and be accompanied by proper identification—that is, a valid driver's license or a government-issued passport.

Additional per-person charges: Certain charges apply when more than two adults (over 17 years of age) occupy a standard room. The fee is $5 per extra adult per day at Fort Wilderness homes; $2 per extra adult per day at Fort Wilderness campsites; $8 per extra adult per day at the All-Star resorts; $12 per extra adult per day at Caribbean Beach, Port Orleans, Dixie Landings, and Coronado Springs; and $15 per extra adult per day at all other WDW resorts, with the exception of the Swan, where the applicable fee is $25.

WDW ID cards: Issued on arrival at WDW-owned resorts, these cards are among resort guests' most valuable possessions while in Walt Disney World. They entitle you to:

• Theme park admission if you've purchased a Length of Stay Pass.

• Unlimited transportation by bus, monorail, and watercraft.

• Use of many of the roadways within Walt Disney World.

• Charge privileges: If you've left a credit card imprint with your hotel, the ID cards may be used (up to certain account limits) to cover purchases in shops, lounges, and restaurants, and recreational fees incurred anywhere in the World. At the Magic Kingdom, Epcot, and the Disney-MGM Studios, guests may use their IDs to charge meals at full-service restaurants, shops, and many fast-food locations, but not all food carts.

Note: ID cards are valid for use of transportation facilities through the end of the last day of your stay, but are not valid for charging past your check-out time. Also note that guests at the Swan and Dolphin hotels may not charge meals at restaurants outside their hotel to their rooms. Other restrictions may apply. Read the information on the cards carefully when checking in.

Rates at Walt Disney World Properties

	Charge for single or double occupancy		
	Value	Standard	Holiday
DELUXE			
BoardWalk Inn			
Rooms–Standard (5)	$229–$295	$244–$315	$259–$330
Rooms–Concierge (4)	$390–$440	$410–$460	$425–$475
Suites (6)		Call 934-7639 for prices	
Contemporary			
Rooms–Wings (5)	$199–$260	$219–$280	$234–$295
Rooms–Tower (5)	$280–$350	$299–$379	$315–$395
Suites (7 to 12)		Call 934-7639 for prices	
Dolphin			
Rooms–Standard (5)	$245–$305	$285–$365	
Rooms–Club Level (5)	$365	$395	
Suites (5 to 10)	$450–$2,400	$525–$2,400	
Grand Floridian			
Rooms–Standard (5)	$284–$350	$309–$375	$324–$390
Rooms–Concierge (5)	$375–$495	$395–$515	$410–$530
Suites (4 to 10)		Call 934-7639 for prices	
Polynesian			
Rooms–Standard (5)	$249–$305	$264–$320	$279–$335
Rooms–Concierge (5)	$305–$380	$325–$395	$340–$410
Suites (4 to 6)		Call 934-7639 for prices	
Swan			
Rooms–Standard (5)	$250–$290	$280–$320	
Rooms–Concierge (5)	$340	$370	
Suites (5 to 10)	$290–$1,750	$320–$1,750	
Wilderness Lodge			
Rooms (4)	$165–$280	$180–$299	$195–$315
Suites (4 to 6)		Call 934-7639 for prices	
Yacht Club and Beach Club			
Rooms–Standard (5)	$229–$295	$244–$315	$259–$330
Rooms–Concierge* (5)	$380–$395	$399–$415	$415–$430
Suites (5 to 10)		Call 934-7639 for prices	
*Yacht Club only			
HOME AWAY FROM HOME			
Disney's BoardWalk Villas Resort			
Studios (4)	$229–$260	$244–$280	$259–$295
1-BR villas (4)	$295–$340	$315–$360	$330–$375
2-BR villas (8)	$395–$445	$415–$465	$430–$480
Grand Villas (12)	$985	$995	$1,045
Disney's Old Key West Resort			
Studios (4)	$209	$229	$244
1-BR villas (4)	$285	$305	$320
2-BR villas (8)	$390	$410	$425
Grand Villas (12)	$825	$845	$860

| | Charge for single or double occupancy | | |
	Value	Standard	Holiday
Fort Wilderness Homes (6)	$185	$215	$230
The Villas at the Disney Institute			
Bungalows (4)	$195	$215	$230
1-BR Town Houses (4)	$285	$305	$320
2-BR Town Houses (6)	$320	$340	$355
Treehouse Villas (6)	$355	$375	$390
Fairway Villas (6 to 8)	$375	$400	$415
Grand Vista Homes (6 to 8)	$975–$1,150	$975–$1,150	$995–$1,185

MODERATE

	Value	Standard	Holiday
Caribbean Beach			
Rooms (4)	$114–$129	$124–$139	$134–$149
Disney's Coronado Springs			
Rooms (4)	$114–$129	$124–$139	$134–$149
Suites (4 to 6)	Call 934-7639 for prices		
Dixie Landings			
Rooms (4)	$114–$129	$124–$139	$134–$149
Port Orleans			
Rooms (4)	$114–$129	$124–$139	$134–$149

VALUE

	Value	Standard	Holiday
All-Star Sports and All-Star Music			
Rooms (4)	$69–$74	$79–$84	$84–$89

CAMPGROUND

	Value	Standard	Holiday
Fort Wilderness Campsites			
Sites w/partial hookup (10)	$35	$44	$49
Sites w/full hookup (10)	$43	$52	$59
Preferred Sites (10)	$49	$58	$64

Check-in time: 3 P.M. except at The Villas at the Disney Institute and Old Key West, where check-in time is 4 P.M. and at Fort Wilderness, where it's 1 P.M. **Check-out time:** 11 A.M. for Fort Wilderness and all hotels.

Value rates apply: January 1, 1997 through February 6, 1997, and August 24, 1997 through December 17, 1997 for all properties except the Swan and Dolphin; they further extend July 7, 1997 through August 23, 1997 for all Home Away From Home and Deluxe properties except the Swan and Dolphin. Value seasons at the Swan and Dolphin are mainly January and late April through mid-December. **Standard rates apply:** February 7, 1997 through March 20, 1997, and April 3, 1997 through July 6, 1997 for all properties except the Swan and Dolphin; they further extend July 7, 1997 through August 23, 1997 for all Moderate and Value resorts. Standard seasons at the Swan and Dolphin are mainly February through mid-April, and late December. **Holiday rates apply:** March 21, 1997 through April 2, 1997, and December 18, 1997 through December 31, 1997. These designations in no way reflect park attendance.

Note: The prices provided here were correct at press time, but the rates do change, so be sure to double-check with the hotels before setting your final vacation budget.

Room capacity: Numbers provided in parentheses after accommodations reflect maximum occupancy based on existing beds. Cots and cribs usually may be requested.

CALL W-DISNEY (934-7639) FOR RESERVATIONS

Disney Village Hotel Plaza

The seven hotels here—the Hilton, Buena Vista Palace, Travelodge, Grosvenor, Doubletree Guest Suites, Royal Plaza, and Courtyard by Marriott—occupy a unique position among Orlando-area accommodations not owned by Disney: They are located inside the boundaries of Walt Disney World, within walking distance of the Disney Village Marketplace, Pleasure Island, and Planet Hollywood. Hotel Plaza guests receive preferred access to the five Disney golf courses, guaranteed admission to the theme parks during busy seasons, and preferred admission at Planet Hollywood before 5 P.M. Three of the properties offer meals with Disney characters.

All the hotels offer complimentary bus service to the Magic Kingdom, Epcot, and the Disney-MGM Studios, with limited service to the Disney Village Marketplace, Pleasure Island, and the WDW water parks. All sell park tickets, have Disney gift shops, and offer car rental and meeting facilities. The Hilton, Buena Vista Palace, and Grosvenor are directly across the street from the Marketplace, and the other properties are within a half mile. All are near a 24-hour grocery.

You can book through the individual hotel or through WDW Central Reservations at W-DISNEY (934-7639). Disney Village Hotel Plaza properties are included in several Walt Disney Travel Company packages.

The following listings are arranged according to standard room rates, from highest to lowest starting price.

HILTON: This hotel, with a splashy new beige, salmon, and aqua facade, is a good choice for its 23 well-groomed acres, its laid-back resort ambience, its impressive pool area, and its upscale shops. The 814 rooms are tastefully decorated and feature mini-bars and telephone systems with voice mail and computer hookups.

Among the hotel's seven restaurants and lounges, Finn's Grill offers dinners of seafood and steaks in an old Key West atmosphere; County Fair serves breakfast (with characters in attendance on Sunday), lunch, and dinner; and the Rum Largo Pool Bar & Café offers hamburgers, salads, sandwiches, and tropical drinks. The menu runs the gamut from ice cream to pizza at the Old-Fashioned Soda Shoppe; you can eat outside at the County Fair Terrace. A Benihana Japanese steak house, complete with sushi bar, is also on the premises. For light meals, snacks, or cocktails, drop by John T's Plantation Bar in the lobby.

Recreational facilities include two whirlpools and heated swimming pools, a children's pool with a fountain at the center, and a spa and health club with Nautilus equipment. The Vacation Station Kid's Hotel, designed for children 4 to 12 years old, has a video room, play area, and scheduled recreational activities supervised by a trained staff. The cost is $4 for the first child, with a $1 discount for each additional child. There are rooms for travelers with disabilities. Nonsmoking rooms are available. Rates range

from $195 to $255; suites are $459 to $759. Hilton at Walt Disney World Village; 1751 Hotel Plaza Blvd.; Lake Buena Vista, FL 32830; 827-4000 or 800-782-4414.

BUENA VISTA PALACE: The largest of the Disney Village Hotel Plaza properties (and a good choice for its nightlife), it is actually a cluster of towers, one of them 27 stories high, set on 27 acres beside Lake Buena Vista. The lobby has several intimate nooks with overstuffed chairs and couches; the staff is helpful; and all guest requests are handled efficiently with just one touch of the telephone. Each of the 1,014 contemporary rooms has a ceiling fan, air conditioning, and two telephones (one with voice mail), and most have a balcony or patio. The concierge rooms offer special amenities. The hotel's European-style spa (the first luxury hotel in Central Florida to have one) opened in 1996 with 14 treatment rooms, a full-service salon, a fitness center with personal trainers, and a lap pool. Recreation Island features three swimming pools, a kiddie pool, a whirlpool, three lighted tennis courts, a sand volleyball court, bike and boat rentals, and a children's play area. Kids' Stuff is a recreational program for children 4 to 12.

The hotel also provides 24-hour room service, a Disney-run gift shop, a guest laundry, and the Family Calling Center (a large booth with a speakerphone). Eating spots include the lakeside Watercress Café, which serves breakfast, lunch, and dinner, with a buffet available for breakfast and dinner (characters are in attendance on Sunday morning); the adjacent Watercress Pastry Shop, open 24 hours for counter-service baked goods and sandwiches; Arthur's 27, with an international menu and a gorgeous view; the Outback restaurant, which serves hefty portions of fresh seafood and Black Angus steaks; and the Courtyard Café for relaxed snacking around a fountain.

The Laughing Kookaburra Good Time Bar, nicknamed "The Kook," has live bands, dancing, and 99 brands of beer on the wall. Noise from the restaurants can flow through the atriums and penetrate the solid oak doors, so if silence matters, choose accommodations in the poolside Island Resort building (also good for families) or the 27-story tower. The Top of the Palace lounge provides the perfect perch to gaze at the sunset or fireworks and sip fine wines. There are 12 rooms equipped for guests with disabilities. Nonsmoking rooms are available, and for the allergy prone, there are 20 EverGreen Rooms with filtered air and water. Rooms are from $145 to $250 per night (no charge for children under 18); suites are $240 to $455. Buena Vista Palace Resort & Spa; 1900 Buena Vista Dr.; Lake Buena Vista, FL 32830; 827-2727 or 800-327-2990.

DOUBLETREE GUEST SUITES: Striking outside and in, this 229-unit property has a low-slung, futuristic facade, public areas with bright colors and whimsical patterns, and an aviary in the lobby, where a child's check-in desk stands next to the "grownup" one. Young guests receive a bag of gifts, and adults get an oversize cookie when they register. The only all-suite hotel at Walt Disney World, it features 640-square-foot units, each with a living room (and sleeper sofa), a large dressing area, and a separate bedroom. Each can sleep up to six persons; there are some two-bedroom suites, as well. Most bedrooms have two double beds, though some kings are available. Room amenities include two remote-control televisions, a small TV in the bathroom, a wet bar, a refrigerator, a coffeemaker with daily coffee and tea refills, a microwave oven, and a hair dryer.

Recreational facilities include a heated pool, whirlpool, arcade, children's play area, sand volleyball court, and two lighted tennis courts (with pro instruction available). The children's playroom has a big-screen television, toys, games, and seasonal children's activities. The menu at festive Streamers restaurant features American classics. Streamers Market sells snacks items and groceries. There are suites for guest with disabilities. Nonsmoking suites are available. Rates range from $129 to $239. Doubletree Guest Suites; 2305 Hotel Plaza Blvd.; Lake Buena Vista, FL 32830; 934-1000 or 800-222-8733.

GROSVENOR: The 629 rooms are located in a mauve 19-story tower and two wings on formal grounds. Each room has a VCR, minibar, coffeemaker, and movie rental. An exercise room, two lighted tennis courts, handball and shuffleboard courts, a basketball court, a volleyball court, two heated pools, a children's pool, a large play area, and an arcade are available. Baskervilles, the hotel's main restaurant, incorporates a

Sherlock Holmes museum, and serves breakfast and dinner buffets; characters are in attendance for breakfast on Tuesday, Thursday, and Saturday, and for dinner on Wednesday. Baskervilles is also the scene, during dinner on Saturday, for the Murder Watch Mystery Theatre. Continental breakfast, snacks, and lighter fare are available 24 hours a day at Crumpets Café. Crickets lounge offers occasional entertainment. The Grosvenor (pronounced GROVE-nor) is affiliated with Best Western. There are several rooms accessible to guests with disabilities. Nonsmoking rooms are available. Rates range from $115 to $175 for two, year-round; suites are $195 to $495. Grosvenor; 1850 Hotel Plaza Blvd.; Lake Buena Vista, FL 32830; 828-4444 or 800-624-4109.

TRAVELODGE: This 18-story tower surrounded by pines and located just minutes from the Crossroads of Lake Buena Vista shopping center, has 325 spacious rooms and suites. All rooms have either one king-size or two queen-size beds, phones with voice mail, minibars, coffeemakers, safes, hair dryers, and private balconies (floors 7 through 16 provide a WDW view). The four suites on the 18th floor offer a fine view of Disney Village Hotel Plaza and the fireworks at the theme parks. The hotel also has an arcade, small pool, kiddie pool, landscaped playground with new equipment, and a coin-operated laundry. Traders restaurant serves breakfast and dinner. The Parakeet Café offers light entrées for breakfast, lunch, and dinner, as well as snacks and made-to-order pizza. Besides views of Pleasure Island and Epcot, Toppers lounge, on the 18th floor, has dart machines, pool tables, music videos, and a small dance floor. Flamingo Cove is the cocktail lounge. There are two rooms for travelers with disabilities. Nonsmoking rooms are available, as are EverGreen Rooms with filtered air and water. Rates range from $99 to $169 for guestrooms; $199 to $299 for suites. Travelodge; 2000 Hotel Plaza Blvd.; Box 22205; Lake Buena Vista, FL 32830; 828-2424 or 800-348-3765.

ROYAL PLAZA: The 394 guest units here are divided between a 17-story high-rise and two-story lanai wings with gated patios or small balconies. Each tower room has a sitting area, desk, dresser, double armoire with closet space, safe, and honor bar. The baths have marble counters and corner tubs (whirlpools on the concierge level). All rooms have VCRs, hair dryers, and coffeemakers. There are also 22 suites. Recreation facilities include a heated pool, a spa, two saunas, an arcade, and four lighted tennis courts. The Plaza Diner serves à la carte or buffet meals. There's also a delicatessen and a large bar with an Indiana Jones theme. Rooms specially equipped for travelers with disabilities and nonsmoking rooms are available. Depending on the season and the view, room rates range from $99 to $159 for up to five in a room; suites are $139 to $189. Royal Plaza; Box 22203; 1905 Hotel Plaza Blvd.; Lake Buena Vista, FL 32830; 828-2828 or 800-248-7890.

COURTYARD BY MARRIOTT: This pleasant 323-room hotel, the country's second-largest Courtyard, has some of the most spacious guestrooms in Hotel Plaza. Situated in a 14-story tower and a 6-story annex, rooms feature sitting areas, computer-data ports, clock radios, marble vanities, voice mail, coffeemakers with china mugs, irons and ironing boards. The bathrooms tend to be small. A breakfast bar, tables topped with colorful umbrellas, and the Tipsy Parrot lounge fill the atrium lobby. The Courtyard Café & Grille is a full-service restaurant with a breakfast buffet, and the Village Deli serves snacks, muffins, fruit, sandwiches, TCBY yogurt and Pizza Hut pizza. There are three heated pools, including one for children; a whirlpool; playground; arcade; and exercise room. A pool bar is open seasonally. There are rooms for guests with disabilities. Nonsmoking rooms are available. Rates range from $79 to $169 year-round. Courtyard by Marriott; Box 22,204; 1805 Hotel Plaza Blvd.; Lake Buena Vista, FL 32830; 828-8888 or 800-223-9930.

Off-Property Accommodations
In Lake Buena Vista

A full lineup of accommodations, from laid-back to luxurious, abuts the crossroads at I-4 and S.R. 535 in the heart of Lake Buena Vista. Most offer free transportation to the three main Disney parks. Prices are highly competitive, so shop around before making a reservation. The following listings are arranged according to standard room rates, from highest to lowest starting price.

HYATT REGENCY GRAND CYPRESS: Adjacent to Disney Village Hotel Plaza and just three miles from Epcot, this 1,500-acre resort has a dramatic 200-foot atrium lobby and 750 Florida-inspired guestrooms and suites with wicker furniture, ceiling fans, and shutters, The hotel has four bars and five restaurants, including the ever-popular Hemingway's, which serves game, seafood, and steaks. Four concierges are kept very busy.

The secluded Villas of Grand Cypress house the resort's exquisite Mediterranean-style accommodations. Each club suite consists of a spacious bedroom with a separate sitting area, a large luxury bath with a separate shower, a sundeck, and a patio or a veranda. The villas proper each contain a large living room, a dining room, and a fully equipped kitchen. The Villas area has three dining possibilities, including the sophisticated Black Swan restaurant. Fairways is a casual eatery.

The Hyatt Regency Grand Cypress and the

Villas of Grand Cypress share a half-acre free-form swimming pool with 12 waterfalls, 2 water slides, and 3 whirlpools (the Villas also has its own pool and whirlpool); a 21-acre lake with rental boats; and a tennis complex with 12 courts. Also offered are racquetball and volleyball courts, a playground, bicycling, a 4.7-mile jogging trail, a 45-acre nature area, and a health club. Forty-five holes of Jack Nicklaus–designed golf separate the Hyatt Regency from the Villas (which are actually 1½ miles apart; a 24-hour shuttle connects the two). The superb original course features two Scottish-style shared greens, grassy dunes, elevated tees, and a greens fee that will set you back $125 ($85 in the summer). Sports buffs may sign up for activities at the Grand Cypress Academy of Golf, Equestrian Center, or Racquet Club.

Shuttle service to the three Disney theme parks costs $5 round-trip. The resort has accommodations for guests with disabilities. Nonsmoking rooms and villas are available. Rates at the Hyatt Regency range from $185 to $370; suites start at $650. Rates at the Villas range from $190 to $350 for a club suite, $265 to $425 for a one-bedroom villa, and $380 to $700 for a two-bedroom villa. Hyatt Regency Grand Cypress; One Grand Cypress Blvd.; Orlando, FL 32836; 239-1234 or 800-233-1234; Villas of Grand Cypress; One N. Jacaranda; Orlando, FL 32836; 239-4700 or 800-835-7377.

SUMMERFIELD SUITES LAKE BUENA VISTA: A bit off the beaten track but still close to everything, this popular all-suite hotel has 150 units, most of which feature two separate bedrooms with a king-size bed in the master bedroom, each with a private bath, three televisions, VCR, living room, and good-size, fully equipped kitchen with full-size refrigerator. A guest laundry and a deli-convenience store are on the property. The staff will even do your grocery shopping for you if you provide a list early in the day. Nearby restaurants offer takeout. Complimentary shuttle service to the Disney theme parks is provided. There are suites for guests with disabilities. Nonsmoking suites are available. Rates range from $169 to $209 for a one-bedroom unit (for up to four guests), and $199 to $219 for a two-bedroom trio unit (for up to eight guests). Prices include a breakfast buffet. Summerfield Suites Lake Buena Vista; 8751 Suiteside Dr.; Orlando, FL 32836; 238-0777 or 800-833-4253.

VISTANA: This sprawling complex of more than 1,100 two bedroom, two bath units is only a mile from the Disney Village Marketplace, near the intersection of I-4 and S.R. 535. One of the area's earliest time-share resorts—it still is one—it also operates as a luxury resort behind its controlled-entry gate. Each of the stylishly decorated 1,200-square-foot villas sleeps six to eight people and has a living room with a queen-size sleeper sofa and VCR, and a fully equipped kitchen, complete with a clothes washer and dryer. The housekeepers do the dishes daily. Facilities include 13 lighted tennis courts with instruction available, 6 outdoor swimming pools, 5 children's pools, volleyball, a miniature golf course, and a video library. There are three recreational centers with steam rooms, saunas, exercise rooms, and arcades. A number of adult and children's activity programs are available for a nominal charge. Two restaurants are on the property, along with a general store and a Pizza Hut. Complimentary bus service to the three Disney theme parks is provided. There are villas for guests with disabilities. Nonsmoking villas are not available. Rates range from $159 to $275 per villa per night. Vistana; 8800 Vistana Centre Dr.; Orlando, FL 32821; 239-3100 or 800-877-8787.

MARRIOTT'S ORLANDO WORLD CENTER: The 27-story, Y-shaped tower dominates the landscape from the non-Disney side of the I-4 and S.R. 535 interchange—so much so that someone unfamiliar with the area might think it's the Orlando skyline. Sabal palms, banana trees, and jade plants fill the atrium lobby, and museum-quality 16th- and 17th-century Chinese artifacts grace the grounds. The 1,503 guestrooms make it one of the largest hotels in Florida, and a big convention draw. However, the property, set amid 200 manicured acres, is so vast that leisure guests often are unaware of that fact. The guestrooms have tropical decor, a single-sleeper sofa, and either two double beds or one king-size bed.

Extensive recreational facilities include an 18-hole Joe Lee–designed golf course, four heated swimming pools (one indoors), eight lighted tennis courts, volleyball courts, a miniature golf course, a health club (free to guests), five whirlpools, an arcade, and several shops. The Lollipop Lounge, a program for kids 3 to 12, operates from 8 A.M. to 11 P.M. There are six restaurants, including Mikado's, a Japanese steak house, and Tuscany's Ristorante, which features northern Italian dishes, homemade pastas and sauces, and Italian wines. The hotel has three lounges. There are rooms for travelers with disabilities. Nonsmoking rooms are available. Rates range from $139 to $229, depending on the season; $250 to $2,000 for suites. Marriott's Orlando World Center; One World Center Dr.; Orlando, FL 32821; 239-4200 or 800-228-9290.

BEST WESTERN BUENA VISTA SUITES: This 279-suite hotel, located where S.R. 535 meets International Drive, about 1½ miles from Walt Disney World, is well situated for those who plan to tour Central Florida. Each of the standard two-room suites has stylish modern decor, a separate bedroom and a living room with a queen-size sofa bed. Each unit has a coffeemaker, refrigerator, wet bar, two televisions, a VCR, a safe, two telephones, and a microwave. The phones are

equipped with voice mail and data ports. Each of the deluxe suites features a king-size bed, a huge living room, and a whirlpool.

Other hotel facilities include an exercise room, small heated pool, whirlpool, arcade, movie rentals, guest laundry, gift shop, and small market. Limited complimentary transportation to the three Disney theme parks is provided. Sandwiches and snacks are served at the Patio Grille. The Citrus Lounge is a poolside setting for lunch and evening cocktails. There are rooms for guests with disabilities. Nonsmoking rooms are available. Rates include a full American breakfast and range from $109 to $149 for standard suites and $129 to $169 for deluxe suites. Best Western Buena Vista Suites; 14450 International Dr.; Orlando, FL 32830; 239-8588 or 800-537-7737.

HOLIDAY INN SUNSPREE–LAKE BUENA VISTA: Pretty and pink, this 507-unit property about 1½ miles from the Disney Village Marketplace has an innovative children's program and a most obliging staff. Its unique Kidsuites provide privacy for adults and kids, who get a soundproof, themed room-within-a-room. Among the options are Sesame Street, Noah's Ark, an igloo, a circus tent, or a space capsule—complete with three beds, TV, VCR, Nintendo, and cassette player. Kids' Corner rooms are similar, only semi-private. Each standard guestroom has a refrigerator, microwave, coffeemaker (with free coffee packet daily), hair dryer, electronic safe, and VCR. Most of the rooms have two queen-size beds, although some have king-size beds and sleeper sofas.

Camp Holiday is a licensed child care and activity program for children 2 to 12. The hours are 8 A.M. to midnight and it costs less than $1 per hour for each child—a bargain compared with the prices elsewhere and unusual for the long hours. Parents can rent a beeper for $5 so they can be reached at any time. Children receive a surprise when they register at the Kids' Check-In Desk, and a free bedtime tuck-in from Max, the hotel's mascot, on request. A child under 12 eats breakfast, lunch, and dinner free when accompanied by a paying adult.

Recreational facilities include a heated pool, two whirlpools, a basketball court, a playground, and a fitness center. Maxine's, a family restaurant, serves a buffet breakfast and dinner, as well as an à la carte menu. Pinky's Convenience Court, self-service for eating in or taking out, also carries baby supplies and diapers. Free transportation to the three Disney theme parks is provided. There are rooms for guests with disabilities. Nonsmoking rooms are available. Rates run $79 to $129, depending on the season; add an additional $39 for Kidsuites or $25 for Kids' Corner rooms. Anyone who's 100 years old (or older) stays free. Holiday Inn SunSpree–Lake Buena Vista; 13351 S.R. 535; Lake Buena Vista, FL 32821; 239-4500 or 800-366-6299.

HOWARD JOHNSON PARK SQUARE INN & SUITES: A top-rated property within the chain, it works hard to maintain that status. Located in the Vista Centre shopping and dining complex off S.R. 535, it is only

about a five-minute drive from the Disney Village Marketplace, and is popular with families. The 222 guestrooms and 86 suites all offer lake or courtyard settings. The rooms have two double beds, and the bathrooms are a decent size for the price. Each suite has a microwave oven–refrigerator unit and a coffeemaker, as well as a sleeper sofa. Recreational facilities include two large heated pools, a whirlpool, a children's pool, a small playground, and an arcade. The Courtyard Café serves a buffet breakfast and an à la carte dinner. A child under 18 eats free with a paying adult. The comfortable lobby lounge has a big-screen television. Complimentary shuttles carry guests to the three Disney theme parks. There are rooms for guests with disabilities. Nonsmoking rooms are available. Room rates range from $65 to $120; suites are $80 to $140, depending on the season. Howard Johnson Park Square Inn & Suites; 8501 Palm Pkwy.; Box 22,818; Lake Buena Vista, FL 32830; 239-6900 or 800-635-8684.

COMFORT INN: This 650-room property, also in Vista Centre, is one of the area's best-known bargains. The rooms are basic but clean; each offers two double beds, a phone with voice mail messaging, a safe, and a small bathroom. Tropical landscaping surrounds the two swimming pools (one of which is heated). Other on-site facilities include an arcade, a gift shop, a lounge, and a guest laundry. The property offers 24-hour security. The Boardwalk Buffet restaurant serves breakfast and dinner; up to three children under 11 eat free when accompanied by two adults. Free transportation to the three Disney theme parks is provided. Several rooms are designed for guests with disabilities, and nonsmoking rooms are available. Pets weighing up to 50 pounds are welcome. Rates range from $39 to $69, depending on the season. Comfort Inn; 8442 Palm Pkwy.; Lake Buena Vista, FL 32836; 239-7300 or 800-999-7300.

Along U.S. 192

The properties along this multilane highway (also known as Irlo Bronson Memorial Highway), which intersects I-4 in the community of Kissimmee, are closer to Disney's theme parks than those accommodations along Orlando's International Drive. The area itself is less attractive and tends to be cluttered, but the motels west of I-4, near the so-called main gate to Walt Disney World, are well maintained. (The term "main gate," by the way, is now fairly meaningless, since it originated when there was just one park, the Magic Kingdom.) Most of the hostelries described here are within two miles of Walt Disney World and just minutes from a shopping center with a 24-hour grocery, a large drugstore, a one-hour dry cleaner, numerous eateries, and a tourist information kiosk. All are recommended for their value and convenience.

The following hotel listings are arranged by standard room rates, from highest to lowest starting price.

HOLIDAY INN HOTEL & SUITES: Like its sister property, the Holiday Inn SunSpree in Lake Buena Vista, this 614-unit property, three miles from the World, was designed with families in mind. Each guestroom has a refrigerator, microwave, coffeemaker, ironing board, safe, and VCR. Kids have free use of sleeping bags. The whimsical Kidsuites give kids and their parents plenty of privacy, while the suites with a Murphy bed, sofa bed, and roomy kitchen and bar are also impressive. There are two large swimming pools, a kiddie pool, two playgrounds, two lighted tennis courts, and an arcade, as well as a P.A.W. (Pets are Welcome) Program and even a Paw Park.

Camp Holiday, a supervised activity program for children 3 to 12, is a bargain at $1 per hour for each child. It runs from 2 P.M. to 10 P.M. daily. For $5, parents can rent a beeper so they can always be reached. Kids receive free gifts and can be tucked into bed by the property's Holiday Hound mascots. Children under 12 eat free when with a paying adult. The Vineyard Café serves a breakfast buffet; snacks and light fare are available in the People's Choice Food Court; and the General Store sells groceries and snacks. Pizza delivery is available until midnight. Free scheduled transportation to the three Disney theme parks is provided. There are rooms equipped for guests with disabilities, and nonsmoking rooms are available. Rooms are $65 to $130, depending on the season; add an additional $39 for Kidsuites or $75 for standard suites. Holiday Inn Hotel & Suites; 5678 Irlo Bronson Memorial Hwy.; Kissimmee, FL 34746; 396-4488 or 800-366-5437.

HILTON GATEWAY ORLANDO/ KISSIMMEE: This well-appointed 500-unit hotel does a brisk meetings business, but it has not forgotten its leisure visitors. Each room has a small refrigerator, and the 147 luxury high-rise rooms feature microwaves. There are two outdoor pools (one heated), an exercise room, a guest laundry, an 18-hole putting green, and an arcade, as well as basketball courts and shuffleboard courts. The Palms restaurant is open for breakfast and dinner (buffets are offered seasonally). Children under 13 eat free when accompanied by a paying adult. A self-service deli–snack bar

Room Service

In this country's largest hotel market, with more than 82,000 rooms, rarely is is there no room at the inn. Almost every type of accommodation, from the all-suite hotel to the bed-and-breakfast inn to the budget motel, is represented in the area—and almost every major U.S. chain. But these categories (and even the number of rooms) do not include the profusion of rental condominiums, apartments, and single-family houses that are also available. By shopping around, you can find just what you need.

For more information, contact the Orlando/Orange County Convention & Visitors Bureau at 7208 Sand Lake Rd., Suite 300; Orlando, FL 32819; or call 363-5871. If you arrive in the area without secured lodging, go in person to the Official Visitor Information Center in the Mercado Mediterranean Shopping Village at 8445 International Drive (look for the red, white, and blue awning near the entrance), and ask a staffer to check the "black book" for the day's best rates on available rooms. You have to show up in person for this service, but it can save you time and money.

For information about the properties along U.S. 192, you can also contact the Kissimmee–St. Cloud Convention and Visitors Bureau, Box 422,007; Kissimmee, FL 34742-2007; 800-327-9159.

offers a good variety of items for eating in or taking out, and free coffee and tea from 6 A.M. to 10 A.M. Entertainment takes place nightly in the Ficus Lounge. The hotel boasts 24-hour security and is entered through a staffed gate. Complimentary shuttle service is provided to Walt Disney World. There are rooms specially equipped for guests with disabilities. Nonsmoking rooms are available. Rates range from $60 to $125 a night; suites start at $300. Hilton Gateway Orlando/Kissimmee; 7470 W. Irlo Bronson Memorial Hwy.; Kissimmee, FL 34747; 396-4400 or 800-327-9170.

COURTYARD BY MARRIOTT MAIN-GATE: A major renovation in 1994 turned this 198-room motel into a sleek hostelry with an Art Deco–style lobby. Rooms feature electronic locks, safes, clock radios, and in-room coffee and tea (supplies are replenished daily). Rooms with a king-size bed also have a small refrigerator and microwave. An outdoor pool, kiddie pool, small exercise room, arcade, gift shop, and guest laundry are available. The property's restaurant serves only breakfast, but the Tiki Bar at the pool offers sandwiches and light fare for lunch and dinner (children under 12 eat free). In-room pizza delivery is also available. Free shuttle service is provided to the three Disney theme parks. There are rooms equipped for guests with disabilities. Nonsmoking room are available. Rates run $59 to $109. Courtyard by

Marriott Maingate; 7675 W. Irlo Bronson Memorial Hwy.; Kissimmee, FL 34747; 396-4000 or 800-568-3352.

KNIGHTS INN MAINGATE: This revamped 121-room property is one of the best bargains along the U.S. 192 strip. The refurbished rooms, all on the ground floor, are spartan but functional, and the facilities include a heated pool, guest laundry, an attraction ticket sales counter, and an arcade. Complimentary shuttle service is provided to the three Disney theme parks. There are rooms for guests with disabilities; nonsmoking rooms are available. Rates are $23 to $47. Knights Inn Maingate; 7475 W. Irlo Bronson Memorial Hwy.; Kissimmee, FL 34746; 396-4200 or 800-944-0062.

ORLANDO/KISSIMMEE HOSTEL: The area's newest hostel opened in 1995 in a renovated motel on 2½ acres beside Lake Cecile, five miles from Walt Disney World. Besides dormitory rooms, it has rooms for families and couples, each with a private bath. The hostel also has a kitchen, laundry, common room, outdoor pool, tiled fountain, picnic area, and free boat rentals. There are rooms for guests with disabilities. Dorm rates are $13 to $16; private rooms are $29 to $49. Orlando/Kissimmee Resort Hostel; 4840 W. Irlo Bronson Memorial Hwy.; Kissimmee, FL 34746; 396-8282 or 800-444-6111.

Gone Camping

The lush, cypress-hung woods of WDW's Fort Wilderness are unrivaled by any other Orlando-area campground. But not everyone can get a reservation or afford to stay there. As an alternative, consider the Kissimmee/Orlando KOA campground; 4771 W. Irlo Bronson Memorial Hwy. (U.S. 192 west); Kissimmee, FL 34746; 396-2400 or 800-562-7791. Only five miles east of I-4 and convenient to Walt Disney World, it has a heated pool, tennis court, miniature golf, shuffleboard, playground, arcade, laundry, hot showers, and a convenience store. Some good, inexpensive eateries are nearby. Besides tent and RV sites, there are 33 air-conditioned cabins that sleep four or six people. Free shuttle service to the Magic Kingdom is provided. Rates are $18 for tent sites; $28 to $33.50 for RV hookups. Rates are for two adults and any children under 18; $5 more for each additional adult.

On International Drive

Many well-known hotel, motel, and restaurant chains—and one of Orlando's finest hotels—are located on International Drive, or I-Drive, as it is known locally. Many more are clustered nearby on Sand Lake and Kirkman roads close to where they intersect I-Drive. This famous thoroughfare has two distinct sectors: The more orderly south end, which stretches from Sea World to the Orange County Convention Center and beyond it to Sand Lake Road, and the more cluttered north end, jammed with restaurants, T-shirt shops, and outlet stores.

Convenient I-Ride buses traverse I-Drive, stopping at most of the properties listed here. The fare is only 75 cents, with exact change required; children under 12 ride free.

The following listings are arranged by standard room rates, from highest to lowest starting price. Hotels tend to book up and rates tend to rise when conventions are in town.

PEABODY ORLANDO: The only sister property to the famed Peabody in Memphis, this imposing 27-story, 891-room hotel is International Drive's most luxurious establishment. And, of course, there are the famous Peabody ducks, which every day at 11 A.M. waddle from a private elevator into the enormous lobby, down a red carpet, then settle into a marble fountain—a spectacle that continues to attract visitors and locals. They waddle back at about 5 P.M. Each of

the Peabody's guestrooms has a hair dryer, two telephones, two televisions (including a small one in the bathroom), and nightly turndown service. Facilities include an Olympic-size heated pool, four lighted tennis courts (tennis lessons available), a pro shop, an arcade, and a health club with aerobics

Worth Noting

Driving to the WDW theme parks from International Drive properties can take 15 to 30 minutes, depending on traffic conditions and the location of your hotel. Traffic tends to be heavier at rush hour and when large conventions are in town, adding an extra 15 minutes to any schedule. The I-Drive hotel stretch is convenient to downtown Orlando (10 to 15 minutes away), as well as to Winter Park (30 to 40 minutes away). An appealing town, Winter Park has outstanding museums, some good restaurants, and upscale shopping. Parking here is at a premium, so be prepared to search for a spot. Public parking is plentiful in downtown Orlando.

and personal trainers. Baby-sitting services by professional staff can be arranged.

Dux (where no duck is served) is the hotel's signature restaurant. Capriccio showcases northern Italian cuisine and mesquite-grilled specialties in an exhibition kitchen, and offers a champagne brunch on Sunday; and the B-Line Diner, the perfect re-creation of a fifties-style diner, serves entrées, sandwiches, and homemade confections 24 hours a day. Afternoon tea is served Monday through Friday in the Dux foyer. There are also four bars. The Peabody hosts many of the groups attending meetings at the Orange County Convention Center, which is right across the street. The hotel's whimsical Double-Ducker bus provides unlimited shuttle service to the three Disney theme parks (for guests and the general public) for $6 a day. There are rooms equipped for guests with disabilities. Nonsmoking rooms are available. Rates range from $230 to $290 for standard rooms; $425 to $1,350 for suites. Peabody Orlando; 9801 International Dr.; Orlando, FL 32819; 352-4000 or 800-732-2639.

RENAISSANCE ORLANDO: This luxury convention hotel at the south end of International Drive has an impressive atrium filled with more than 292 tons of marble and containing seven glass-enclosed elevators. The 780 guestrooms are built around the atrium, many with balconies overlooking it. The standard rooms are spacious, and many have pull-out sofas. Each suite has a large, separate sitting area. Complimentary coffee and a newspaper are provided with a wake-up call. The concierge floor has special amenities. Recreational facilities include an Olympic-size swimming pool, an oversize whirlpool, a children's pool, five lighted tennis courts, an arcade, a supervised children's center, and a health club. One of four restaurants on the property, Haifeng serves cuisine from all four regions of China, as well as Chinese wines and beers. The hotel also has a 24-hour deli and three lounges. A popular, elaborate brunch is held in the atrium on Sunday. There are rooms equipped for guests with disabilities. Nonsmoking rooms are available. Room rates range from $229 to $299. Renaissance Orlando; 6677 Sea Harbor Dr.; Orlando, FL 32821; 351-5555 or 800-468-3571.

SUMMERFIELD SUITES INTERNA-TIONAL DRIVE: This 146-unit property at the south end of I-Drive (with a sister property in Lake Buena Vista) requires plenty of advance notice during peak periods, when it tends to book up. It's so popular because most of its units contain two bedrooms separated by a living room, making them roomy enough for large families and private enough for two couples traveling together. In addition to a fully outfitted kitchen, all units have VCRs, irons and ironing boards, desks in each bedroom, computer hookups, and two telephones (three in the two-bedroom units) equipped with voice mail.

Other facilities include a lobby bar, a 24-hour convenience store with microwave entrées and movie rentals, plus a guest laundry, exercise room, heated pool, and whirlpool. To have grocery items delivered to their suite by 6:30 P.M., guests leave a completed form with the front desk early in the morning. Shuttle service is provided to Walt Disney World for $7 round-trip. Nonsmoking suites are available. There are no suites equipped for guests with disabilities. Rates

include a continental breakfast buffet and range from $159 to $199 for a one-bedroom unit (sleeps four), $179 to $219 for a two-bedroom unit (sleeps six), and $199 to $239 for a two-bedroom trio unit (sleeps eight). Summerfield Suites International Drive; 8480 International Dr.; Orlando, FL 32819; 352-2400 or 800-833-4353.

CLARION PLAZA: A good choice for its lively ambience, large outdoor heated pool, spacious rooms, and proximity to the Mercado Mediterranean Shopping Center and Orlando's Official Tourist Information Center, this 810-unit hotel is adjacent to the Orange County Convention Center. The guestrooms are decorated in vibrant colors, and each room has in-room movies, a separate vanity area, a safe, and in-room check-out. The property also has a whirlpool with a waterfall, an arcade, a guest laundry on every other floor, two restaurants, a babysitting service, and a business center. Jack's Place, with caricature sketches à la New York's legendary Sardi's, serves seafood, steaks, and memorable desserts. Café Matisse provides buffet and à la carte meals, and Lite Bite is a convenient (24-hour) bakery-deli. Backstage, a 400-person capacity nightclub, stays open until 2 A.M. and features a deejay and a generously long happy hour daily. Shuttle service to Walt Disney World costs $11 round-trip. There are rooms equipped for guests with disabilities. Nonsmoking rooms are available. Rates for up to four people range from $135 to $155 for doubles, although special-value rates as low as $79 are usually available during select periods of the spring and fall; suites are $310 to $680. There's no charge for children under 18. Clarion Plaza; 9700 International Dr.; Orlando, FL 32819; 352-9700 or 800-627-8258.

EMBASSY SUITES INTERNATIONAL DRIVE SOUTH: The lobby is lined with gleaming marble, and waterfalls and a wishing pond highlight the tropical atrium. The eight-floor hotel contains 144 king suites, 95 suites with two double beds, and 6 conference suites. Each suite offers a separate living room, as well as a wet bar, coffeemaker, microwave, refrigerator, and sleeper sofa. For families, the property offers a children's program, free use of strollers and booster seats, and emergency delivery of infant supplies. Facilities include indoor and outdoor swimming pools, and a whirlpool, sauna, steam room, health club, arcade, and laundry. There is a children's program. The hotel has a restaurant and lounge; guests receive a daily cooked-to-order breakfast and are invited to a cocktail reception. Free shuttle service to the three Disney theme parks is provided. Suites equipped for guests with disabilities are available. Nonsmoking rooms are available. Rates range from $109 to $169. Embassy Suites International Drive South; 8978 International Dr.; Orlando, FL 32819; 352-1400 or 800-433-7275.

HOLIDAY INN INTERNATIONAL DRIVE: This 650-room property's 13 tropically landscaped acres at the north end of International Drive are occupied by five buildings, including a 14-story tower. Each guestroom has a clock radio, safe, and hair dryer, as well as a small kitchenette with a microwave oven, refrigerator, and coffeemaker. Recreational opportunities include a huge free-form heated pool, a tropical courtyard and large sundeck, aquatic gardens, and shuffleboard and volleyball courts. You'll also find a playground, a large arcade, a fitness center, and a family fun center with scheduled activities for children. Up to four kids under 13 eat free when accompanied by an adult in three restaurants, including the pleasant Key Bar & Grille. The Comedy Zone nightclub features comedians nightly (for a cover charge). There are rooms equipped for guests with disabilities. Nonsmoking rooms are available. Rates run from $89 to $145. Holiday Inn International Drive; 6515 International Dr.; Orlando, FL 32819; 351-3500 or 800-465-4329.

WESTGATE LAKES: This small resort near International Drive has 320 beautifully decorated one- and two-bedroom villas. Each villa features a living room, a dining room, one or two bathrooms, and a fully equipped kitchenette. The complex is set on 97 acres facing 300-acre Sand Lake, which is used for water sports. The hotel has two tennis courts, 11 whirlpool spas, a swimming pool, a health club, three playgrounds, an arcade, and a free supervised children's program for kids 4 to 15. Fisherman's Cove restaurant specializes in fresh seafood, and serves breakfast, lunch, and dinner. Other facilities include a lounge and a seasonally operated pool bar and grill. There's full maid service daily. There are villas equipped for guests with disabilities. Nonsmoking villas are available. Depending on the season, rates for a one-bedroom villa (sleeps six) run $70 to $145; rates for a two-bedroom unit (sleeps eight), $115 to $235. Westgate Lakes; 10,000 Turkey Lake Rd.; Orlando, FL 32819; 354-0000 or 800-424-0708.

COUNTRY HEARTH INN: The rocking chairs on the porch make this the closest thing to a quaint inn you'll find on International Drive. The beautifully maintained property across the street from the convention center (though you'd hardly know it) *does* attract conventioneers, but it also maintains a loyal following among vacationers and wedding parties. A patterned tin ceiling,

hardwood floors, and half a dozen chandeliers grace the lobby. The 150 renovated guestrooms have French doors, polished cherry furniture, colorful drapes and bedspreads, verandas, and cable television. Most have two double beds, although a few rooms have king-size beds. Deluxe rooms feature refrigerators, microwaves, and coffeemakers. Movie rental is available. A good-size heated pool is nestled in a lush, landscaped courtyard, complete with gazebo (ask them how they got it). The Country Parlor restaurant serves a buffet and an à la carte breakfast, a Sunday champagne brunch, and an à la carte dinner. The inn also has room service and a popular cocktail lounge, the Front Porch. Some rooms are equipped for guests with disabilities. Nonsmoking rooms are available. Rates range from $49 to $109. Country Hearth Inn; 9861 International Dr.; Orlando, FL 32819; 352-0008 or 800-447-1890.

WYNFIELD INN WESTWOOD: Weatherbeaten shutters give this three-story motel, which is right off International Drive, the look of an inn, and the landscaped grounds make it even more appealing. Each of the 300 rooms is pleasantly decorated and features two double beds, phones with voice mail messaging, a separate vanity, and an in-room safe (for a nominal fee). Request a poolside room to avoid expressway noise. Guest laundry facilities are located throughout the property. An arcade is situated off the lobby, and guests also enjoy a heated swimming pool and a wading pool. The pool bar serves beer, wine, soft drinks, and snacks. Although there is no restaurant on the premises, nearby restaurants offer guests a 10% discount. Complimentary shuttle service to the three Disney theme parks is provided. There are rooms specially equipped for travelers with disabilities. Nonsmoking rooms are available. Rates run from $29 to $82 and include coffee, tea, and fruit in the lobby each morning. Wynfield Inn Westwood; 6263 Westwood Blvd.; Orlando, FL 32821; 345-8000 or 800-346-1551.

Magic Kingdom

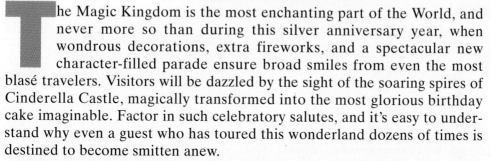

The Magic Kingdom is the most enchanting part of the World, and never more so than during this silver anniversary year, when wondrous decorations, extra fireworks, and a spectacular new character-filled parade ensure broad smiles from even the most blasé travelers. Visitors will be dazzled by the sight of the soaring spires of Cinderella Castle, magically transformed into the most glorious birthday cake imaginable. Factor in such celebratory salutes, and it's easy to understand why even a guest who has toured this wonderland dozens of times is destined to become smitten anew.

What makes the Magic Kingdom timeless is its combination of the classic and the futuristic. Both childhood favorites and space-age creatures have a home here. Every land has a theme, carried through from the costumes worn by the hosts and hostesses and the food served in the restaurants to the merchandise sold in the shops, and even the design of the trash bins. Thousands of details contribute to the overall effect, and recognizing these touches makes any visit more enjoyable.

But the delight most guests experience upon first glimpse of the Magic Kingdom can disappear when disorientation sets in. There are so many bends to every pathway, so many sights and sounds clamoring for attention, it's too easy to wander aimlessly and miss the best the Magic Kingdom has to offer. So we earnestly suggest that you study this chapter before your visit.

MAGIC KINGDOM

 Unless otherwise noted, all phone numbers are in area code 407.

91

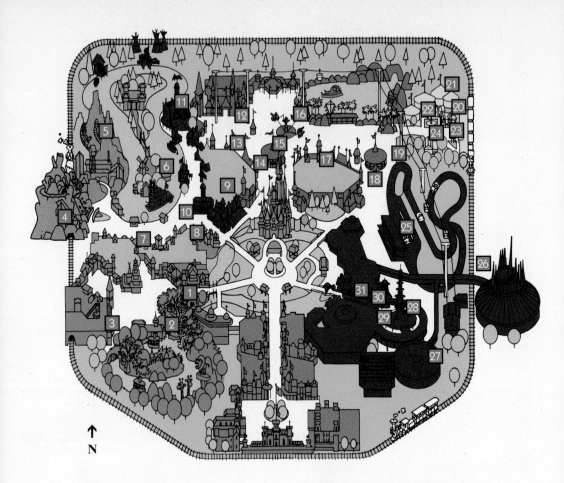

N

ADVENTURELAND

1 Swiss Family Treehouse

2 Jungle Cruise

3 Pirates of the Caribbean

FRONTIERLAND

4 Splash Mountain

5 Big Thunder Mountain Railroad

6 Tom Sawyer Island

7 Country Bear Jamboree

8 Diamond Horseshoe Saloon Revue

LIBERTY SQUARE

9 The Hall of Presidents

10 Liberty Square Riverboat

11 The Haunted Mansion

FANTASYLAND

12 It's A Small World

13 Peter Pan's Flight

14 Legend of The Lion King

15 Cinderella's Golden Carrousel

16 Dumbo, the Flying Elephant

17 Snow White's Adventures

18 Mr. Toad's Wild Ride

19 Mad Tea Party

MICKEY'S TOONTOWN FAIR

20 Mickey's Country House

21 Mickey's Toontown Fair Hall of Fame

22 Minnie's Country House

23 Donald's Boat

24 The Barnstormer at Goofy's Wiseacres Farm

TOMORROWLAND

25 Tomorrowland Speedway

26 Space Mountain

27 Walt Disney's Carousel of Progress

28 Astro Orbiter

29 Take Flight

30 The Timekeeper

31 Alien Encounter

GETTING ORIENTED

When visiting Walt Disney World's original theme park, it's vital to know the lay of the lands. The Magic Kingdom has seven sections, or "lands"—Main Street, U.S.A.; Adventureland; Frontierland; Liberty Square; Fantasyland; Mickey's Toontown Fair (formerly Mickey's Starland); and Tomorrowland. Main Street begins at Town Square, located just inside the park gates, and runs directly to Cinderella Castle. The area in front of the Castle is known as the Central Plaza, or, more aptly, the Hub. Bridges over the several narrow waterways here serve as passages to each of the lands.

As you enter the park, the first bridge to your left goes to Adventureland; the next, to Liberty Square and Frontierland. On your right, the first bridge heads to Tomorrowland, the second to Fantasyland and Mickey's Toontown Fair. The end points of the pathways leading to the individual lands are linked by an avenue that is roughly circular, so that the layout of the Magic Kingdom resembles a wheel. All of the park's attractions, restaurants, and shops are found along the rim and spokes of this wheel.

A note on north, south, east, and west: When you stand at the Magic Kingdom entrance and face Cinderella Castle, you're looking north. Main Street is straight ahead, with Fantasyland and Mickey's Toontown Fair beyond the Castle. Adventureland, Liberty Square, and Frontierland are to the west. Tomorrowland flanks the Hub on the east.

HOW TO GET THERE

Take Exit 25 off I-4. Continue about four miles to the Auto Plaza and park; walk or take a tram to the main entrance complex, known as the Transportation and Ticket Center (TTC). Choose either a five-minute ferry ride or a slightly shorter trip by monorail for the last leg of what is traditionally an anticipation-filled journey.

By WDW Transportation: From the Grand Floridian, Contemporary, and Polynesian: monorail (the Contemporary also has a walkway). From Epcot: monorail to the TTC, then transfer to the TTC–Magic Kingdom monorail or ferry. From the Disney-MGM Studios, the Disney Village Marketplace, and the Disney Village Hotel Plaza: buses to the TTC, then transfer to ferry or monorail. From Fort Wilderness and the Wilderness Lodge: boats. From all other WDW resorts: direct buses.

PARKING

All-day parking at the Magic Kingdom is $5 for day visitors (free to WDW resort guests with presentation of resort ID). Simply bear left shortly after passing through the Auto Plaza; attendants will direct you into one of a dozen lots, all named after Disney characters. Minnie, Sleepy, and Dopey are within walking distance of the TTC; other lots are served by trams. Be sure to note the section and aisle in which you park. Also, know that the parking ticket allows for reentry to the parking area throughout the day.

HOURS

The Magic Kingdom is generally open from 9 A.M. to 7 P.M. However, for the duration of the 25th anniversary celebration (through December 31, 1997), the park is open later than usual. It's best to plan on reaching the park entrance at least half an hour before the posted opening time, particularly during busy seasons. Another way to avoid the morning crush is to put off your visit until 1 P.M. or later. Call 824-4321 for up-to-the-minute schedules.

GETTING AROUND

Walt Disney World Railroad steam trains make a 21-minute loop of the park, stopping to pick up and discharge passengers at stations on the edge of Main Street, Frontierland, and Mickey's Toontown Fair. Horseless carriages, a fire engine, and horse-drawn trolleys take turns offering one-way trips down Main Street. And while the Skyway aerial tram is not necessarily the quickest commute between Tomorrowland and Fantasyland, the ten-minute ride nets a fine bird's-eye view of the park.

93

PARK PRIMER

BABY FACILITIES

The best place in the Magic Kingdom to take care of little ones' needs is Baby Services. This center, equipped with changing tables and facilities for nursing mothers, is located at the Hub end of Main Street next to the Crystal Palace restaurant. Disposable diapers are kept behind the counter at many Magic Kingdom shops; just ask.

CAMERA NEEDS

The Kodak Camera Center on Main Street proffers disposable cameras as well as the requisite film and batteries. It also rents camcorders ($25 per day with a $300 refundable deposit). Two-hour film processing is available here and wherever you see a Photo Express sign. Film is also sold in most Magic Kingdom shops.

DISABILITY INFORMATION

Most shops and restaurants, and many attractions, are accessible to guests in wheelchairs. Convenient parking is reserved for guests with disabilities. Special provisions have also been made to enhance sight- and hearing-impaired guests' enjoyment of the park. The *Walt Disney World Guidebook for Guests with Disabilities* is an invaluable resource, and is available at City Hall. For more information, refer to the "Travelers with Disabilities" section of the *Getting Ready to Go* chapter.

EARLY-ENTRY DAYS

On Monday, Thursday, and Saturday, guests staying at WDW resorts may enter the Magic Kingdom 1½ hours before the official opening time to enjoy Space Mountain and Fantasyland attractions. Early-entry days and attractions are subject to change.

Admission Prices

ONE-DAY TICKET

(Restricted to use only in the Magic Kingdom. Prices include sales tax and are subject to change.)

Adult	$40.81
Child*	$32.86

*3 through 9 years of age; children under 3 free

FERRY VS. MONORAIL

For guests arriving by car or tour bus, it's necessary to decide whether to travel to the Magic Kingdom by ferry or monorail. The monorail makes the trip from the Transportation and Ticket Center (TTC) to the Magic Kingdom in a bit less than the five minutes required by the ferries. However, the ferry often will get you there more quickly during the busier seasons, because long lines can form at the monorail; most people simply don't make the short extra walk to the ferry landing. When there's no line for the monorail, it's your best choice. Vacationers who use wheelchairs should note that while the monorail platforms are accessible, the ramp leading to the boarding area is a bit steep.

FIRST AID

A registered nurse tends to minor medical problems at the First Aid Center, located near the Crystal Palace restaurant at the Hub end of Main Street.

GUIDED TOURS

A four-hour walking tour called Keys to the Kingdom is available during off-peak seasons. The tour offers guests ten and over an on-site orientation to the history and workings of the Magic Kingdom. Guests visit five attractions (waiting in regular attraction lines) and take a peek at the Production Center and the system of tunnels known as Utilidors. Cost is $45, not including park admission. The Keys to the Kingdom tour can accommodate a maximum of 15 guests. When offered, the tour departs daily at 10 A.M. from City Hall, located in Town Square at the start of Main Street. For further details and advance reservations, call WDW-TOUR (939-8687). For same-day reservations stop by City Hall or call 824-4521.

INFORMATION

City Hall, located just inside the park entrance in the cul-de-sac known as Town Square, serves as the park's informal information headquarters. Guest Relations representatives here can answer any questions about the Magic Kingdom. Park guidemaps (including details on the day's entertainment) are available here, and all kinds of arrangements can be made, including priority seating for full-service restaurants.

LOCKERS

Attended lockers are conveniently located underneath the Main Street Railroad Station just inside the park entrance. At the TTC, lockers are available next to the Lost & Found on the west side and beside the bus parking lot on the east side. Cost is $3 per day (plus a $2 refundable deposit) for unlimited use. Items too big to fit into the larger units can be checked at the Guest Relations at the TTC or City Hall.

LOST & FOUND

On the day of your visit, report lost articles at City Hall or at the Guest Relations windows at the TTC. Recovered items can also be claimed at these locations. After your visit, call 824-4245.

LOST CHILDREN

Report lost children at City Hall or alert a Disney employee to the problem.

MONEY MATTERS

The Magic Kingdom has three ATMs: one at SunTrust bank in Town Square, another near Tropical Serenade in Adventureland, and a third at the Tomorrowland Light & Power Co. (the video arcade at Space Mountain's exit). Full-service banking, including foreign currency exchange, is available from 9 A.M. to 4 P.M. at SunTrust. City Hall is also equipped to exchange foreign currency.

Credit cards (American Express, Visa, MasterCard, and The Disney Credit Card) are accepted as payment for admission, merchandise, and for meals at all full-service restaurants and many fast-food locations. Traveler's checks and WDW resort identification cards are also accepted. Only cash is accepted at food carts.

Commemorative 25th anniversary Disney Dollars, available from City Hall in colorful $1, $5, and $10 denominations, are accepted for dining and merchandise throughout Walt Disney World. They can be exchanged at any time for U.S. currency; however, many visitors opt to keep some as inexpensive souvenirs.

PACKAGE PICKUP

Shops can arrange for large or heavy purchases to be transported to a location near Main Street's Emporium for later pickup. The service is available free of charge.

SAME-DAY REENTRY

Be sure to have your hand stamped and to retain your ticket upon exiting the park if you plan to return later the same day.

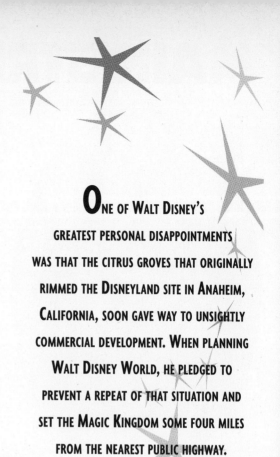

ONE OF WALT DISNEY'S GREATEST PERSONAL DISAPPOINTMENTS WAS THAT THE CITRUS GROVES THAT ORIGINALLY RIMMED THE DISNEYLAND SITE IN ANAHEIM, CALIFORNIA, SOON GAVE WAY TO UNSIGHTLY COMMERCIAL DEVELOPMENT. WHEN PLANNING WALT DISNEY WORLD, HE PLEDGED TO PREVENT A REPEAT OF THAT SITUATION AND SET THE MAGIC KINGDOM SOME FOUR MILES FROM THE NEAREST PUBLIC HIGHWAY.

STROLLERS & WHEELCHAIRS

Wheelchairs–Strollers, located on the right just inside the park entrance, offers one-day rentals of strollers, wheelchairs, and Electronic Convenience Vehicles (ECVs). Cost for strollers and wheelchairs is $5, with a $1 refundable deposit; $30 for ECVs, with a $20 refundable deposit. Quantities are limited. Remember to keep your rental receipt, because it can be used on the same day to obtain a replacement stroller or wheelchair at Epcot, the Disney-MGM Studios, or here at the Magic Kingdom.

TIP BOARD

Located at the end of Main Street closest to Cinderella Castle, the "Main Street Gazette" blackboard is a great source of information on waiting times for the most popular attractions. Check here throughout the day and plan accordingly.

MAIN STREET, U.S.A.

This is the Disney version of turn-of-the-century small-town Main Streets all over the country—freshly painted, full of curlicued gingerbread moldings and pretty details—and, with its baskets of hanging plants and genuine-looking gaslights, a showplace both in the bright light of high noon and after nightfall, when the tiny lights edging all of Main Street's rooflines are flicked on.

What's particularly amazing is that the full variety of furbelows and frills that a real, growing Main Street would have enjoyed has been assimilated into the Disney version. Most of the structures along the thoroughfare are given over to shops, and each one is different, from the wallpaper and layout of displays to the flooring materials, style of chandelier, even lighting level. Some emporiums are big and bustling, others are relatively quiet and orderly; some are spacious and airy, others are cozy and dark. Floors are made of black-and-white tile or of wide oak planks set with wooden pegs; some are covered with Victorian-patterned carpets. Where wallpaper is used, it is striped, or gaudily flowered; in contrast, some walls are paneled in subdued mahogany or oak. The effect is far more sophisticated than first-time visitors might imagine, and it doesn't really matter that some of the "wood" is fiberglass.

Inside and out, maintenance and house-keeping are superb. White-suited sanitation workers patrol the street to pick up litter and quickly shovel up any droppings from the horses that pull the trolley cars from Town Square to the Hub. As in the rest of the Magic Kingdom, the pavement here is washed down every night with fire hoses. There's one crew of maintenance workers whose sole job is to change the little white lights around the roofs; another crew devotes itself to keeping the woodwork painted. As soon as these people have worked their way as far as the Hub, they start all over again at Town Square. The greenish, horse-shaped cast-iron hitching posts are repainted 20 times a year on average—and totally scraped down each time. It's no wonder that professional painters who visit marvel at the quality of work they see.

Some visitors find these details so fascinating it takes them a good deal longer than the 40 minutes spent by the average guest to get from one end of Main Street to the other. There are only three real "attractions" along Main Street, and they are relatively minor compared to the really big deals such as Tomorrowland's Space Mountain and Frontierland's Big Thunder Mountain Railroad and Splash Mountain. But each and every shop has its own quota of merchandise that is meant as much for show as for sale. It's entertaining to watch the cooks stirring up batches of peanut brittle at the Main Street Confectionery. The shop windows, particularly at the Emporium, are also worth a look.

While walking along the street, note the names on the second-story windows. Above Crystal Arts are the names of Roy Disney, Walt's brother, and Patty Disney; above The Shadow Box, that of Dick Nunis, chairman of Walt Disney Attractions. Above the Main Street Athletic Store are the names of Ted Crowell, WDW's former vice president of facilities support, who, among other things, was responsible for supervising maintenance and for the World's own electric generating plants, and of John de Cuir, the Disney artist in charge of production for the paintings filmed for The Hall of Presidents show. Card Walker, the "Practitioner of Psychiatry and Justice of the Peace" mentioned nearby, is the company's former chairman of the executive committee. Other names, as well as those on signs elsewhere in the Magic Kingdom, are also those of real people connected with the company.

Finally, some advice: Before heading toward Cinderella Castle, stop at City Hall to pick up a guidemap with the times and places where live entertainment is scheduled to take place all around the park that day and night. Also, do your shopping in the early afternoon, rather than at day's end when the shops are normally jammed.

Note: Attractions in Main Street, U.S.A., are described in the order that they are encountered upon entering the park.

WALT DISNEY WORLD RAILROAD:

The best introduction to the layout of the Magic Kingdom, the 1½-mile, 21-minute journey on this rail line is as much a must for the first-time visitor as it is for railroad buffs. For the former, it offers an excellent orientation, as it passes through Adventureland and Frontierland and skirts Fantasyland, Mickey's Toontown Fair, and Tomorrowland. The trains make stops here on Main Street and at the Frontierland and Mickey's Toontown Fair stations.

The 1928 steam engine happens to be exactly the same age as Mickey Mouse. Aficionados of railroadiana may remember that Disney himself was among their number—and perhaps, during the early years of television, saw films of him circling his own backyard in a one-eighth-scale train, the *Lilly Belle*, named for his wife. The Walt Disney World Railroad also has a *Lilly Belle* among its quartet of locomotives. The others are named *Roy O. Disney*, *Walter E. Disney*, and *Roger E. Broggie* (a Disney Imagineer who shared Walt Disney's enthusiasm for antique trains). All of them were built in the United States around the turn of the century and later taken to Mexico to haul freight and passengers in the Yucatan, where Disney scouts found them in 1969. The United Railways of Yucatan was using them to carry sugarcane. Brought north once again, they were completely overhauled, and even the smallest parts were reworked or replaced.

MAIN STREET VEHICLES: A number of these can be seen traveling up and down Main Street—horseless carriages and jitneys patterned after turn-of-the-century vehicles (but fitted out with Jeep transmissions and special mufflers that make the putt-putt-putting sound); a spiffy scarlet fire engine, which can be seen in the Firehouse adjoining City Hall when not in operation; and a troop of trolleys drawn by Belgians and Percherons, two strong breeds of horse that once pulled plows in Europe. These animals—between six and ten years old, weighing in at about a ton each, and shod with plastic (easier on their hooves)—pull the trolley the length of Main Street about two dozen times during each of their three to four working days; afterward, they're sent back to their homes at the barn at the Fort Wilderness campground.

MAIN STREET CINEMA: The beauty of this prominent Main Street attraction is that most vacationers bypass it in their rush to get to Space Mountain in Tomorrowland, Pirates of the Caribbean in Adventureland, or other thrill-a-minute attractions. Yet on a steamy summer afternoon—when everyone else is standing in line for these blockbusters—this air-conditioned theater is a fine place to relax. The feature attraction is *Mickey's Big Break*, a ten-minute film that shows how Mickey is chosen for his first starring role. As the story goes, Mickey is one of many actors auditioning for a part in *Steamboat Willie*, the first sound cartoon. Talent agents make their choice—and the rest is history. A vintage Disney cartoon follows the film. There are so many Mickey classics that it's impossible to predict what will be airing and when. But rest assured, *Steamboat Willie* is on the list of those shown. (By the way, Mickey was originally scheduled to be named Mortimer, but Mrs. Disney convinced Walt to make the change.)

Cinderella Castle, Transformed

To celebrate the Magic Kingdom's silver anniversary, Cinderella Castle has become a giant candy-decorated birthday cake, complete with "icing." Lighted nightly, the 25 candles amid pink spires make this quite a sight. For more details, see our special 25th anniversary section, starting on page 15.

Just as the courtly little mouse named Mickey stands for all the merriment in Walt Disney World, this childhood's storybook castle made real represents the hopes and dreams of those youthful years when anything seems possible. That's especially true, given its incredible transformation this year.

At about 180 feet, Cinderella Castle is nearly twice the height of Disneyland's Sleeping Beauty Castle. The castle beneath the icing takes its inspiration not only from the architecture of 12th- and 13th-century France, the country where Charles Perrault's classic fairy tale originated, but also from the mad Bavarian King Ludwig's fortress at Neuschwanstein and designs prepared for Disney's 1950 animated feature *Cinderella*.

Unlike real European castles, this one is made of steel and fiberglass; in lieu of dungeons, it has service tunnels. Its upper reaches contain security rooms; there's even an apartment originally meant for members of the Disney family (but never occupied).

When mounting the curving staircase to King Stefan's Banquet Hall, the parapet-level restaurant; passing underneath its central arches; or viewing it amid fireworks from the Contemporary resort's observation deck, the Castle looks as if it had come straight out of some never-never land of make-believe.

Mosaic murals: The elaborate murals beneath the Castle's archway rank among the true wonders of the World. Designed by Dorothea Redmond and crafted by the mosaicist Hanns-Joachim Scharff, they tell the familiar story of a little cinder girl and one of childhood's happiest happily-ever-afters, using a million bits of Italian glass in some 500 different colors, plus real silver and 14-karat gold. Don't fail to stop and look.

Coats of arms: The one above the Castle on the north wall belongs to the Disneys. Others belonging to Disney executives hang in the foyer of King Stefan's Banquet Hall; curious observers can consult the hostess to learn the heritage of each coat of arms.

Cinderella's Wishing Well: This pleasant alcove nestled along the pathway that leads to Tomorrowland is the perfect spot to gaze at the Castle. Any coins tossed into the water (creating a surprise special effect, of course) are donated to children's charities.

ADVENTURELAND

Adventureland seems to have even more atmosphere than the other lands. That may be a result of its neat separation from the rest of the Magic Kingdom by the bridge over Main Street on one end and by a gallerylike structure (where it merges with Frontierland) on the other; or possibly it's because of the abundance of landscaping. There are Canary Island date palms, small Cape Sable palms, as well as pygmy date tree species, and more. On the Adventureland bridge alone, visitors will see Cape honeysuckle from South Africa, flame vines from Mexico, bougainvillea from Brazil, hibiscus from China, hanging sword ferns, spider plants, and Australian tree ferns, to name just a few flora.

As for the architecture, although it derives from areas as diverse as the Caribbean, Polynesia, and Southeast Asia, there's a strong sense of being in a single place, a nowhere-in-particular that is both familiar and distinctly foreign, smacking of island idylls and tropical splendor. Shops offer imports from India, Thailand, Hong Kong, Africa, and the Caribbean islands.

Strolling away from Main Street, there is the sound of beating drums, the squawks of a pair of parrots, the regular boom of a cannon. Paces quicken. And the wonders soon to be encountered do not disappoint.

Note: Adventureland attractions are described in the order that they are encountered upon entering the land from the Hub and heading away from the Castle.

SWISS FAMILY TREEHOUSE: "Everything we need right at our fingertips," said the father in Disney's 1960 rendition of the classic novel *Swiss Family Robinson*. He was describing the treehouse that he and two of his three sons constructed to house the family after the ship transporting them to New Guinea was wrecked in a storm. When given a chance—several adventures later—to leave the island, all but one son decided to stay on. That decision is not hard to understand after a tour of the Magic Kingdom's version of the Robinsons' banyan-tree home. This is everybody's idea of the perfect treehouse, with its many levels and many comforts—patchwork quilts, lovely mahogany furniture, candles stuck in abalone shells, even running water in every room. (The system is ingenious.)

The Spanish moss draping the branches is real; the tree itself—unofficially christened *Disneyodendron eximus*, a genus that is translated roughly as "out-of-the-ordinary Disney tree"—was constructed entirely by the props department. Some statistics: The

roots, which are of concrete, poke 42 feet into the ground; and some 300,000 lifelike polyethylene leaves "grow" on 1,400 branches, which stretch some 90 feet in diameter. "Boy, Dad sure went out on a limb for that one," quipped a Disney prop worker's son on hearing of his father's task.

JUNGLE CRUISE: Inspired in part by the 1955 documentary *The African Lion*, this ten-minute cruise adventure is one of the crowning achievements of Magic Kingdom landscape artists for the way it takes guests through surroundings as diverse as a Southeast Asian jungle, the Nile valley, the

African veldt, and an Amazon rain forest. Along the way, passengers encounter zebras, giraffes, impalas, lions, vultures, and headhunters; they see elephants bathing, tour a Cambodian temple—and listen to the amusing spiel delivered by the skipper.

For most passengers, this is all just in fun. Gardeners, however, are always especially impressed by the variety of species coexisting in such a small area. To keep some of the more sensitive of subtropical specimens alive, gas-fired heaters and electric fans concealed in the rocks pump hot air into the jungle when temperatures fall to 36 degrees. This adventure, which is best enjoyed by daylight, is one of the Magic Kingdom's more popular attractions, and it does tend to be crowded from late morning until late afternoon, so plan accordingly.

TROPICAL SERENADE: The first of the Audio-Animatronics attractions, this one laid the foundation for attractions such as Great Moments with Mr. Lincoln at the 1964–1965 New York World's Fair. Introduced at Disneyland in 1963, this 17-minute show features four emcees—José, Michael, Pierre, and Fritz—plus some 225 birds, flowers, and tiki god statues singing and whistling up a tropical storm with such animation that even the most blasé folks can't help but smile.

PIRATES OF THE CARIBBEAN: One of the very best of the Magic Kingdom's adventures, this ten-minute cruise through a series of sets depicting a pirate raid on a Caribbean island town is a Disneyland original, added to WDW's Magic Kingdom (in revised form) due to popular demand. Here there are flowerpots that explode and mend themselves, drunken pigs whose legs actually twitch in the porkers' soporific contentment, chickens that look for all the world like the real thing (even when seen at close range); the observant will note that the leg of one resident swashbuckler, dangled over the edge of a bridge, is hairy. Each pirate's face has remarkable personality, and the rendition of "Yo Ho, Yo Ho; a Pirate's Life for Me"—the attraction's theme song— makes what is actually a rather brutal scenario into something that comes across as good fun. Before entering the queue area, be sure to stop and give a nod to the parrot dressed in the pirate costume, near the Pirates of the Caribbean sign.

FRONTIERLAND

With the Rivers of America lapping at its borders and Big Thunder Mountain rising up in the rear, this re-creation of the American frontier encompasses the area from New England to the Southwest, from the 1770s to the 1880s. Hosts and hostesses wear denim, calf-length cutoffs, long skirts, or similar garb. Additionally, the shops, restaurants, and attractions have unpainted barn siding or stone or clapboard walls, and outside there are several wooden sidewalks of the sort Marshal Matt Dillon used to stride along.

Near Pecos Bill Café, the landscape seems desertlike (even on humid summer days), with mesquite providing shade and Peruvian pepper trees nearby; the latter's twisted branches boast clusters of bright-red berries in fall and winter. Jerusalem thorns blossom with sweet-smelling yellow flowers in the spring. Century plants and Spanish bayonets can also be seen. Farther down the Frontierland avenue, slash pines provide some shade, along with other evergreens of a variety known as cajeput, which can be recognized by its spongy, light-colored bark and white flowers.

Note: Attractions are described as they are encountered upon entering the land from the Hub and heading away from the Castle.

DIAMOND HORSESHOE SALOON REVUE: This hour-long show, presented in a re-creation of a western dance hall saloon, is the kind of gig that makes sophisticated folk laugh in spite of themselves. The jokes range from corny to absolutely preposterous, yet seldom fall flat, thanks to the enthusiastic, energetic efforts of the talented crew of singers and dancers who perform here several times each day. Guests may drop in at any point during the performance. For those who want to snack between laughs, there is also a fast-food counter here. See *Good Meals, Great Times* for more details.

FRONTIERLAND SHOOTIN' ARCADE: This arcade is set in an 1850s town in the Southwest Territory. Gun positions overlook Boothill, a town complete with bank, jail, hotel, and cemetery. But silver bullets have given way to infrared beams at the completely electronic shooting arcade. Genuine Hawkins 54-caliber buffalo rifles have been refitted, and when an infrared beam strikes any of the 97 reactive targets, a humorous result is triggered. Struck tombstones rise, sink, spin, or change their epitaphs; hit the cloud and a ghost rider gallops across the sky; a bull's-eye on a gravedigger's shovel causes a skull to pop out of the grave. Sound effects—howling coyotes, creaking bridges, and shooting guns—are created by a digital audio system. Note that admission passes do not include use of the arcade; there is an additional charge here.

COUNTRY BEAR JAMBOREE: An occasional determined sophisticate will remain impervious to the charms of this country-and-western hoedown in Frontierland's big stone-walled Grizzly Hall. But for many guests, with the exception of the 10-to-18 crowd, it's an old favorite. Ostensibly concocted by one Ursus H. Bear after an especially inspiring hibernation season, it is performed by a cast of close to 20 life-size Audio-Animatronics bruins, with results more believable than almost anywhere else in the park, aside from The Hall of Presidents.

Here, Henry, the debonair, seven-foot-tall master of ceremonies, introduces the Five Bear Rugs (a C&W plinking group made up of Zeke, Zeb, Ted, Fred, and Tennessee). A big-bodied, tiny-headed pianist named Gomer plays while the girthy Trixie, the Tampa Temptation, sings "Tears Will Be the Chaser for Your Wine." Teddi Barra floats down from the ceiling crooning "He Doesn't Know the Heart He's Breakin.'" Bubbles, Bunny, and Beulah, in sweet harmony, sing "All the Guys That Turn Me On Turn Me Down." Assorted other bruins entertain, including Terrence, the shank shaker; Wendell, the overbearing baritone; Liver Lips McGrowl; and Big Al, one of the few Audio-Animatronics figures with a following great enough to create a demand for his image on postcards and stuffed animals.

Because the 17-minute Country Bear Jamboree is a popular attraction, lines can get quite long during busy periods. They usually seem longer than they are, however,

101

and it's worth noting that huge groups of people are admitted together so that once a line starts moving, it dwindles fast. Seats in the rear of the house are just as good as seats toward the front, if not a little better.

TOM SAWYER ISLAND: This small landfall in the middle of the Rivers of America has hills to scramble up, a working windmill, Harper's Mill, with an owl in the rafters and a perpetually creaky waterwheel, and a pitch-black (and scary) cave. To get to the island, guests take a raft across the river.

There are oaks, pines, and sycamores here, red maples and elms, and a number of small plants—dwarf azaleas; firethorn, an evergreen shrub that sprouts bright-red berries in December; Brazilian pepper trees, which also grow berries at the end of the year; and American holly plants, which acquire their masses of berries in fall. Dirt paths wind this way and that, and it's easy to get disoriented, especially the first time around. There are also two bridges—an old-fashioned swing bridge and a so-called barrel bridge, which floats atop some lashed-together steel drums. When one person bounces, everybody lurches—and all but the most chicken-hearted laugh. Both bridges are easy to miss, so keep your eyes peeled and ask for directions if the path eludes you.

Across the bridge is Fort Sam Clemens, where there is a guardhouse in which the figure of a ratty-looking drunk is Audio-Animatronically snoring off his last bender, accompanied by a mangy dog, chickens, and a pair of horses. On the second floor of the fort, there are close to a dozen air guns for youngsters to trigger into ceaseless cacophony. This area offers a fine view across the Rivers of America to Big Thunder Mountain Railroad. Keep poking around and you'll find the twisting, dark, and occasionally scary escape tunnel out of the fort. Walk along the pathway on the banks of the Rivers of America, and you're back at the bridges.

The whole island seems as rugged as backwoods Missouri, and, probably as a result, it actually feels a lot more remote than it is—enough to be able to provide some welcome respite from the bustle. One particularly pleasant way to pass an hour here is over lemonade and a snack on the porch at Aunt Polly's Landing. While adults in the party are giving their feet some rest, watching the sternwheelers plying the Rivers of America, kids can go out and burn up some more energy. Restrooms are located at the main raft landing. Note that this attraction closes at dusk.

SPLASH MOUNTAIN: As its name implies, guests are escorted on a waterborne journey through brightly painted backwoods swamps and bayous, down waterfalls, and, finally, over the top of a steep spillway, hurtling

them from the peak of the mountain to a briar-laced pond five stories below. Splash Mountain is based on the animated sequences in Walt Disney's 1946 film, *Song of the South*. The scenery entertains as the story line follows Brer Rabbit through a variety of exploits as he tries to reach his "laughing place." It's tough for a first-timer to take in all the details, since the tension of waiting for the big drop is all-consuming.

There are three tame watery drops during the 11-minute trip, all leading up to the big fall—a 52-foot drop at a 45-degree angle at a top speed of 40 miles per hour—the steepest flume in the world. It is a bit terrifying at the top but once back on the ground it seems most riders can't wait for another trip. (Even though you may get drenched!) By the second or third time around, it's possible to relax and enjoy the interior design and also to take in the spectacular views of the Magic Kingdom from the top of the mountain.

Splash Mountain's designers not only borrowed characters and color-saturated settings from *Song of the South*, but also used quite a bit of the film's Academy Award–winning music in this attraction. As a matter of fact, the song in Splash Mountain's final scene, "Zip-A-Dee-Doo-Dah," has become something of a Disney anthem over the years.

Note: You must be at least 44 inches tall to ride Splash Mountain.

BIG THUNDER MOUNTAIN RAILROAD: This attraction, located partly inside the redstone mountain that pokes into the sky behind the Tom Sawyer Island rafts landing, is something of a cross between Adventureland's Pirates of the Caribbean (a tame but very exciting and scenic boat tour) and Tomorrowland's Space Mountain (an honest-to-goodness roller coaster). As any true coaster buff could tell you, this four-minute ride is a relatively mild one, despite the posted warnings; the thrills are there, but the experience is not so extreme that you'll be left with a determination never to subject yourself to it again. The pleasant rush of adrenaline that comes with some of the swoops and curves, as well as the attractive scenery along the 2,780 feet of track, gives most visitors the opposite reaction.

As with Pirates of the Caribbean, every trip yields new sights, and even another trip in a matter of days is as amusing as the first time. Don't miss the bats, phosphorescent pools and waterfalls, and best of all, Tumbleweed, the flooded mining town (best seen to your left during one of the uphill climbs). Look for about 20 Audio-Animatronics figures here—including realistic chickens, donkeys, possums, a goat, a long john–clad resident spinning through the flood in a bathtub, and a rainmaker whose name is Professor Cumulus Isobar. Careful observers will note a party still going on in a not-yet-sunken second-story room of a saloon, whose weathered look (like that of some other sections of the Magic Kingdom) derives from a judicious mixture of plant food and paint.

The $300,000 worth of real antique mining equipment sprinkled around the attraction's 2½ acres—an ore-hauling wagon, a double-stamp ore crusher, a wooden mining flume, and an old ball mill used to extract gold from ore—were picked up at auctions all over the Southwest, at less than bargain prices, since the high price of gold and the resulting profitability of small-scale mining operations had boosted demand by miners themselves.

The summit of the mountain, whose name refers to an old Indian legend about a certain sacred mountain in Wyoming that would thunder whenever white men took out its gold, is entirely Disney-made. It was in the planning for some 15 years and under construction for 2 years. Hundreds of rock makers contributed, applying multiple coats of cement and paint, throwing stones at the mountain, kicking dirt on it, and banging on it with sticks and picks to make the whole thing resemble the rocks of Monument Valley, Utah—that is, as if Mother Nature herself had created it. Design was largely by Tony Baxter, whose name can be seen on one of the doors in the unloading and boarding area. The area inside the mountain that does not house the tunnels of the ride itself is occupied by the machinery that makes the ride go—pumps, electronic equipment, and part of the computer that runs the show. The total cost was about $17 million, which, give or take a few million, was as much as it cost to build all of California's Disneyland in 1955. Incidentally, that park's version of the attraction, which opened in 1979, is similar, but lacks the flash-flood scene and a few other details. You must be at least 40 inches tall to ride.

Note on timing: Certain aspects of the ride are more convincing after dark. Optimally, you should experience it first at night, then have a second go-round by the light of day. Since the trip is extremely popular, plan to take it in during the 9 P.M. running of SpectroMagic (in season), or just before park closing, when the lines are generally shorter. By day, go during the early morning hours.

LIBERTY SQUARE

The transition between Frontierland on one side and Fantasyland on the other is so smooth that it's hard to say just when you arrive at Liberty Square, yet ultimately there's no mistaking the location. The small buildings are clapboard or brick and topped with weather vanes; the decorative moldings are Federal or Georgian in style; the glass is sometimes wavy, and there are flower boxes in shop windows, brightly colored gardens, neatly trimmed borders of Japanese yew, and masses of azaleas in a number of varieties and shades of white, pink, and red. There are a number of good shops, most notably the Yankee Trader and a new one called Ye Olde Christmas Shop; plus two of the park's most popular attractions, The Haunted Mansion and The Hall of Presidents; and the Liberty Tree Tavern, one of the most charming full-service restaurants in the Magic Kingdom.

Liberty Square is also home to one of the most delightful nooks in all the Magic Kingdom—the small, secluded area just behind Ye Olde Christmas Shop. There are tables with umbrellas, plenty of benches, and big trees to provide shade—and the sound of the crowds seems a million miles away.

Note: Liberty Square attractions are described in the order they are encountered upon entering the land from the Hub and heading away from the Castle.

THE LIBERTY TREE: This live oak (*Quercus virginiana*), not an attraction per se, recalls the trees on which the Sons of Liberty hung lanterns after the Boston Tea Party of 1773. It was found on the southern edge of the Walt Disney World property, and then moved to its present site in one of the more complex of the Magic Kingdom's landscaping operations

Since the tree was so large, lifting it by cable was out of the question—the cable would have sliced through the bark and injured the tree. Instead, two holes were drilled through the sturdiest section of the trunk; the holes were fitted with dowels, and a 100-ton crane lifted the tree by these rods, which were then replaced with the original wood plugs. Unfortunately, the wood plugs had become contaminated. To save the tree, the plugs again were removed, the diseased areas were cleaned out, the holes were filled with cement, and a young oak was grafted onto the tree at its base, where it grows even today. Careful observers will be able to spot the plugs and the portions of the trunk that were damaged. The 13 lanterns hanging on the branches represent the 13 original states.

THE HALL OF PRESIDENTS: This is not one of those laugh-a-minute attractions, like Pirates of the Caribbean or the Country Bear Jamboree; it's long on patriotism and short on humor. But the detail of this 20-minute show certainly is fascinating. After a film (presented on a sweeping 70mm screen) discusses the importance of the Constitution from the time of its framing through the dawn of the Space Age, the curtain goes up on what some guests have mistakenly called the "Hall of Haunted Presidents." A portion of today's Hall of Presidents presentation derives from the Disney-designed Illinois Pavilion's exhibition Great Moments with Mr. Lincoln, from New York's 1964–65 World's Fair.

At the Magic Kingdom show, Bill Clinton and Abraham Lincoln have speaking roles. All 42 chief executives are announced in a roll call and each responds with a nod; careful observers will note the others swaying and nodding, fidgeting, and even whispering to each other during the proceedings.

Costumes were created by two famous film tailors coaxed out of retirement. Not only are the styles those of the period in which each president lived, but so are the tailoring techniques and the fabrics. Some had to be specially woven for the purpose. Each of the Audio-Animatronics figures has at least one change of clothes, and jewelry, shoes, hair texture, and even George Washington's chair are all re-created exactly as indicated by careful research of paintings, diaries, newspapers, and government archives. Perceptive viewers should be able to see the braces on Franklin Delano Roosevelt's legs. The effect is so lifelike that the figures look almost real, even at very close range.

The paintings in the waiting area outside the hall are just a few of the 85 created for the pre–roll call film—in the style of the period during which the event depicted took place. Other paintings can be seen in Main Street's City Hall and in Liberty Square's Liberty Tree Tavern and Columbia Harbour House.

LIBERTY SQUARE RIVERBOAT: The *Richard F. Irvine*, built in dry dock at Walt Disney World and named for a key Disney designer, is a real steamboat. Its boiler turns water into steam, which is then piped to the engine, which drives the paddle wheel that propels the boat. It is not the real article in one respect, however: It moves through the half-mile-long, nine-foot-deep Rivers of America on an underwater rail. The 15-minute ride is more pleasant than thrilling, but it's good for beating the heat on steamy afternoons. En route, a variety of props create a sort of Wild West effect: moose, deer, cabins on fire, and the like. (Best seats are in front or rear and center, so that you can see both riverbanks equally well.)

The trees framing the entrance to Riverboat Landing, which bear crinkly blossoms of bright red most of the year, are crepe myrtles.

THE HAUNTED MANSION: Visitors who expect to get the daylights scared out of them inside this big old house, modeled on those built by the Dutch in the Hudson River Valley in the 18th century, will be a tad disappointed. In deference to the number of small children and other easily frightened souls who tour the Magic Kingdom every day, The Haunted Mansion steers clear of anything too terrifying and a pleasant voiceover keeps the mood light. Even so, the eight-minute experience is among the Magic Kingdom's best. Special effect is

piled upon special effect, and just when you think you've seen it all, there's something new: the raven who appears over and over again; bats' eyes on the wallpaper; the plaque that reads "Tomb, Sweet Tomb"; the suit of armor that comes alive; the horrible transparent specter in the attic; the terrified cemetery watchman and his mangy mutt; the ghostly teapot pouring ghostly tea; the difficult-to-identify flying objects above an image in the crystal ball.

In the portrait hall (which you enter after passing through the mansion's front doors), it's amusing to speculate: Is the ceiling moving up—or is the floor descending? It's one way here, and the other way at The Haunted Mansion in California's Disneyland.

At both places, one of the biggest jobs of the maintenance crews is not cleaning up, but keeping things nice and dirty. Since each mansion's attic is littered with some 200 trunks, chairs, dress forms, shovels, harps, rugs, and assorted other knickknacks, it requires a good deal of dust. This is purchased from a West Coast firm by the five-pound bagful and distributed by a device that looks as if it were meant to spread grass seed. Local legend has it that enough has been used since the park's 1971 opening to bury the mansion. Cobwebs are bought in liquid form and strung up by a secret process.

When waiting to enter, note the amusing inscriptions on the tombstones in the overgrown cemetery.

FANTASYLAND

Walt Disney called this a "timeless land of enchantment," and his successors term it "the happiest land of all"—and it is, for some. Although it's not precisely a kiddieland, it is the home of a number of rides that are particularly well liked by children. The nursery-song cadences of "It's A Small World" appeal to them, as do the bright colors of the trash baskets, the flowers, and the tentlike rooftops; and they delight in the fairy-tale architecture and ambience, reminiscent of a king's castle courtyard during a particularly lively fair. Fantasyland is also one of the most heavily trafficked areas of the park. Parents of younger children should note that many of the attractions are dark and in some cases the special effects may be too intense.

Note: Fantasyland attractions are described in the order that they are encountered upon entering the land via the Castle and proceeding roughly clockwise through the land.

CINDERELLA'S GOLDEN CARROUSEL: Not everything in the Magic Kingdom is a Disney version of the real article. This carousel, discovered at the now-defunct Olympic Park in Maplewood, New Jersey, was built back in 1917. That was the end of the golden century of carousel building that began around 1825 (when the Common Council of Manhattan Island, New York, granted one John Sears a permit to "establish a covered circus for a Flying Horse Establishment"). During the Disney refurbishing, many of the original horses were replaced with horses made of fiberglass. Also, the original horses' legs, which were arranged in a rather decorous pose, were ingeniously rearranged to make the steeds look like real chargers. (Careful examination might reveal some of the cracks by which this change was effected.) For the wooden canopy above the horses, Disney artists hand-painted 18 separate scenes with images of the little cinder girl from Charles Perrault's fairy tale and Disney's 1950 film. Additionally, the original mechanical wooden parts were replaced by metal ones; the thick layer of paint that had obscured some of the finer points of the original carving was stripped away, and the horses were repainted white. The painting alone required about 48 hours per horse.

While waiting for the two-minute ride, it's worthwhile to take the time to study the animals carefully. No two are exactly alike. The band organ, which plays favorite music from Disney Studios (such as the Oscar-winners "When You Wish Upon a Star," "Zip-A-Dee-Doo-Dah," and "Chim-Chim-Cheree"), was made in one of Italy's most famous factories.

LEGEND OF THE LION KING: Based on the animated film, *The Lion King*, this Fantasyland show combines 25 minutes of animation, puppetry, special effects, and music to make guests feel as if they have walked into a cel from the film. In the pre-show area guests meet Rafiki, the wise baboon who serves as the narrator. His voice is provided by stage and television actor Robert Guillaume. A clip from the film is shown and Rafiki recounts the legend that is about to unfold.

Once inside the 500-seat theater, visitors see the movie's Circle of Life scene presented on stage. As the sun rises over Pride Rock, Mufasa assures his son, Simba, that he will always be with him. The characters are depicted by fully articulated puppets—when they speak their mouths move accordingly. Some of the puppets require up to four people to coordinate their head, feet, ear, and mouth movements. The story advances to other scenes, introducing the assorted characters. Some of the more familiar voices you

hear are those of Jeremy Irons as the evil Scar, James Earl Jones as Mufasa, Cheech Marin as Banzai, and Whoopi Goldberg as Shenzi. From the jungle to the plains, guests see Mufasa being trampled by the stampeding wildebeests and pushed to his death by Scar; Scar convincing Simba that he is responsible for his father's demise and must go away; Scar declaring his power over the kingdom; Simba enjoying his freedom with Pumbaa and Timon; and the touching love scene in the jungle with Nala as she tries to convince Simba he must return to take his rightful place as the Lion King.

Guests experience environmental effects, including warm winds during scenes in the Serengeti Plain and mists of rain and cold winds during the jungle nights. The climactic stampede scene begins on the screen; the noise builds and the theater shakes as smoke gives way to darkness. Later, special lighting helps create the image of Mufasa in the sky.

Songs in the show include "Circle of Life," "Hakuna Matata," "Can You Feel the Love Tonight?" and "I Can't Wait to Be King." The music was composed by Elton John with the lyrics written by Tim Rice. Presented by Kodak.

PETER PAN'S FLIGHT: The inspiration for this three-minute attraction was the Scottish writer Sir James M. Barrie's play about the boy who wouldn't grow up, which appeared as a Disney movie in 1953. Riding in flying versions of Captain Hook's ornate ship—which are suspended from an overhead rail once they leave the boarding area—visitors swoop and soar through a short-but-sweet reprisal of the tale. A series of scenes tells the story of how Wendy, Michael, and John get sprinkled with pixie dust and, heading for "the second star to the right and straight on till morning," fly off to Never Land with Tinker Bell. There, they meet Princess Tiger Lily, the evil Captain Hook, his jolly-looking sidekick Mr. Smee, and the crocodile—who has already made off with one of Hook's hands and is on the verge of getting the rest of him as you sail out into daylight.

As in the movie, one of the most beautiful scenes—one that makes this attraction a treat for adults as well as smaller folk—is the sight of nighttime London, dark blue and speckled with twinkling yellow lights, complete with the Thames, Big Ben, London Bridge, and vehicles that really move on the streets. The song that accompanies the trip is "You Can Fly, You Can Fly, You Can Fly," by Sammy Cahn and Sammy Fain.

SKYWAY TO TOMORROWLAND: Entered from near Peter Pan's Flight, this aerial tram transports guests one-way to Tomorrowland in ten minutes. En route it's possible to see the striped tent tops of Cinderella's Golden

Carrousel, Tomorrowland Speedway, and the not-so-wonderful rooftops of the buildings where many Magic Kingdom adventures take place. This attraction is best boarded at its Tomorrowland terminus, where the lines are usually slightly shorter. Guests with disabilities who are able to leave their wheelchairs can take a round-trip ride from Fantasyland.

IT'S A SMALL WORLD: Originally created for New York's 1964–65 World's Fair, with a tunefully singsong melody (written by the Academy Award-winning composers of the music for *Mary Poppins*, among other Disney films), this favorite of young children and seniors alike involves an 11-minute boat trip through several large rooms where stylized Audio-Animatronics dolls—wooden soldiers, cancan dancers, balloonists, chess pieces, Tower of London guards in scarlet beefeater uniforms, bagpipers and leprechauns, gooseherds, little Dutch kids in wooden shoes, Don Quixote and a goatherd, yodelers and gondoliers, houri dancers, dancers from Greece and Thailand, snake charmers, Japanese kite flyers, hippos, giraffes, frogs, hyenas, monkeys, elephants, hip-twitching Polynesians, surfers, and even dolphins—sing and dance to a melody that will run through your head for hours after you float out of their wonderland. Of the two queues that are usually found here, the one to the left is almost always shorter.

SOME WIVES COMPLAIN THAT THEY LOSE THEIR HUSBANDS TO FOOTBALL GAMES EVERY SUNDAY. NOT IRENE KIRKEGARD, FROM MARGATE, FLORIDA. "MY HUSBAND, LARS, GOES TO WALT DISNEY WORLD EVERY OTHER WEEKEND WITH NO EXCEPTION," SHE SAYS.

DUMBO, THE FLYING ELEPHANT: This is purely and simply a kiddie ride—though personages as varied as Romanian gymnast Nadia Comaneci and Muhammad Ali have loved it. The character of the flying elephant was developed for the 1941 film release of *Dumbo*, one oxf the shortest of Disney's animated features and one of the best. It stars a baby elephant born with inordinately large ears and an ability to fly that is discovered after he accidentally drinks from a bucket of champagne. The mouse that sits atop the mirrored ball at the center of the ride's circle of flying elephants is the faithful Timothy Mouse. Inn the film, Timothy becomes Dumbo's manager after the circus folk who had once laughed at the flying elephant hire him to be a big star. The ride lasts two memorable minutes.

MAD TEA PARTY: The theme of this two-minute ride—in a group of oversize pastel-colored teacups that whirl and spin wildly—derives from a scene in the Disney Studio's 1951 movie production of Lewis Carroll's novel *Alice in Wonderland*. During the sequence in question, the Mad Hatter hosts a tea party for his un-birthday. Unlike many other rides in Fantasyland, this is not strictly for younger kids; the 9-to-20 crowd seems to like it best. Be sure to note the soused mouse that pops out of the teapot at the center of the platform full of teacups.

MR. TOAD'S WILD RIDE: Wild in name only, this three-minute attraction is based on the 1949 Disney release *The Adventures of Ichabod and Mr. Toad*, which itself derives from Kenneth Grahame's classic novel *The Wind in the Willows*. It seems that a gang of weasels has tricked that memorable (but gullible) man-about-town Mr. J. Thaddeus Toad into trading the deed to his ancestral mansion for a motorcar that turns out to have been stolen.

In the attraction, flivvers modeled on this very car take guests zigging and zagging along the road to Nowhere in Particular, through dark rooms painted in neon colors and illuminated by black lights, where you witness the redoubtable Mr. Toad trying to get out of the scrape. In the process, you crash through a fireplace, narrowly miss being struck by a falling suit of armor, hurtle through haystacks and barn doors and into a coop full of squawking chickens, then ride down a railroad track on a collision course with a huge locomotive. Some of this is scary enough that some children end up momentarily frightened. By and large, though, this is for kids.

SNOW WHITE'S ADVENTURES: This three-minute attraction near the carousel takes guests on a twisting, turning journey through a few happy moments and a bunch of scary scenes from the Grimm Brothers' fairy tale, which Walt Disney made into the world's first full-length animated feature in 1937. Snow White makes several appearances, as do cheery Audio-Animatronics dwarfs. But the wicked witch—evil, long-nosed, and practically toothless—appears more than once with such suddenness that some youngsters can become really frightened. The adventure concludes on a happy note, as the dwarfs wave goodbye to Snow White and her prince.

MICKEY'S TOONTOWN FAIR

The Magic Kingdom's latest land invites guests to wander through Mickey and friends' new neighborhood—a totally interactive setting that's akin to Disneyland's Toontown. Unlike the characters' old stomping ground here at Walt Disney World, Mickey's Toontown Fair is out in the countryside, far removed from all the pressures of toon stardom. The area, completed in fall 1996, is as imaginative and adorable as its predecessor, Mickey's Starland, and even more fun. The best way to get here is aboard the Walt Disney World Railroad.

Upon entering Mickey's Toontown Fair, it's immediately apparent why Mickey and the gang chose to build their country houses here: because their favorite thing, the county fair, is always in town.

Mickey's Country House has a porch swing that visitors are welcome to sit on. Once inside, guests discover that Mickey, whose sash and coat are neatly pressed and hung on the coatrack, is head judge for the fair. As visitors peer into the kitchen, living room, and gameroom, they see that Donald and Goofy have left their mark throughout the house, most obviously with their botched attempts to help remodel Mickey's kitchen.

To meet Mickey in the **Judge's Tent**, guests go out the back door (others should exit through the garage, which packs some surprises of its own). It's fun to check out the backyard, where Mickey's award-winning garden is bursting with giant vegetables, all of which have Mickey ears (just like the pictures on the seed packs). Before meeting Mickey in the tent, guests see a pre-show video that highlights all of his county fair successes.

Since Minnie and Mickey are next-door neighbors here in the country, **Minnie's Country House** is the next stop. Young kids will love visiting Minnie because her special toon furniture is made of foam, and meant for climbing. As they explore, guests can push a button to listen to her answering-machine messages; open the refrigerator to see many kinds of cheese and feel a blast of cold air; and try in vain to snatch some fresh-baked cookies (it's not a gag, but a clever mirror effect). Guests will discover that Mickey's girlfriend is an avid cook, quilter, painter, and gardener in addition to being the founding editor of *Minnie's Cartoon Living Magazine*. In the garden gazebo behind Minnie's house, visitors can meet the "Martha Stewart of Toontown" in person.

Across the way is **Donald's Boat**, the *Miss Daisy*, which has sprung so many leaks it looks more like a fountain. Anchored in a "duck pond" that's easy to walk across, it's filled with wet surprises; pull the whistle, and water shoots out the top.

At **The Barnstormer at Goofy's Wiseacres Farm**, nearby, a kiddie roller coaster lets little pilots "fly" crop-duster planes on a track that goes around the farm and then, causing quite a ruckus among the hens, *crashes right through his barn*! Guests can see by the shape of the holes through which the coaster enters (and departs) the barn that Goofy himself was the first one to try it. The queue for the ride winds through an adjacent section of the barn that's filled with strange gizmos and whirligigs.

To reach the best character scene yet, head for **Mickey's Toontown Fair Hall of Fame**, a tent filled with champion pumpkins, lima beans, and more—all winning entries from the fair. Beyond this area, three different rooms offer guests a chance to meet any number of Disney characters. Stop in one of the rooms to meet the classic characters, including Goofy, Chip 'n' Dale, and Pluto. Other rooms provide the opportunity to meet either princesses or villains (not in the same room, of course). It's virtually impossible to walk through without meeting the characters, so kids will definitely want to spend time here.

Other areas across the land include **Toon Park**, a playground of foam animal sculptures for young kids to climb; **Pete's Garage**, housing the restrooms; and **Mickey's Toontown Fair Station**, where the Walt Disney World Railroad makes regular stops.

TOMORROWLAND

The original Tomorrowland attempted a serious look at the future. But as Disney planners discovered, it isn't easy to portray a future that persists in becoming the present. So the old Tomorrowland has given way to a friendlier, space-age town whose neighborhood atmosphere is more in keeping with the other lands in the Magic Kingdom. This is the future that never was, the fantasy world imagined by the science fiction writers and moviemakers of the 1920s and '30s. It's a land of sky-piercing beacons and glistening metal, where shiny robots do the work, whisper-quiet conveyances glide along an elevated highway, and even time travel is possible.

Note: All Tomorrowland attractions are described in the order that they are encountered upon entering the land from the Hub and heading (roughly counterclockwise) away from Cinderella Castle.

THE TIMEKEEPER: A fantastic 20-minute multimedia presentation combining a Circle-Vision 360 film with Audio-Animatronics characters and special in-theater effects is hosted by Timekeeper, a wacky, mad scientist robot. Inspired by the likes of Jules Verne and H. G. Wells, who wrote about fantastic visions of the future, Timekeeper has created the world's first and only working time machine (at least as far as we know). Assisting Timekeeper in his time voyage demonstration is 9-Eye, a flying robot camera who is the test pilot for Timekeeper's invention. She has bravely volunteered to fly through history and transmit pictures of what she sees back to guests in the 360-degree time chamber. Guests are able to experience what it was like to hear the young Mozart play his first composition; to fly down a mountain on a speeding bobsled; to see Leonardo da Vinci working on a masterpiece; and to float in a hot-air balloon above Moscow's Red Square, among many other exciting stops on this whirlwind trip through time and space. In a sweep of the 1900 Paris Exposition, guests even meet Jules Verne and H. G. Wells themselves. When Verne hitches a ride with 9-Eye to the present and beyond, he gets to see some of his visions realized. Guests will recognize the voice and zany antics of Timekeeper as those of Robin Williams. Other stars featured are Rhea Perlman as 9-Eye, Jeremy Irons as H. G. Wells, and Michel Piccoli as Jules Verne.

To create this blast through time, filmmakers took the 400-pound Circle-Vision nine-lens camera rig to a number of interesting locations: Innsbruck, Austria, where the rig was mounted on a bobsled and hurled down a 1,200-meter run at 60 miles per hour; Moscow's Red Square for the hot-air balloon scene; the underwater world of the Bahamas; and Vienna, Austria, where the 1900 Paris Exposition was re-created for the historic, albeit fictional, encounter between Jules Verne and H. G. Wells.

ALIEN ENCOUNTER: The centerpiece of Tomorrowland is the Tomorrowland Interplanetary Convention Center, home of the Magic Kingdom's scariest attraction. Created

transported in their midst as the theater goes black. Horrified, the technicians blow up the machine in hopes of destroying the hideous creature. Flickers of light reveal the fearsome alien in the teleporter. But the strain on the equipment has been too great, and guests are plunged into darkness. There is a sound of breaking glass, and the audience realizes that the unthinkable has happened. Next comes a series of creepy sensations designed to convince members of the audience that the monster has found its way to their side. Ultimately, the X-S technicians regain control, but not before guests have been startled enough to jump in their seats.

Note: This 20-minute attraction may be too intense for young children. You must be at least 7 years old and 48 inches tall to enter the attraction.

by Disney Imagineers and director George Lucas, Alien Encounter features some of the most elaborate special effects and show systems ever employed by a theme park.

The premise behind the attraction is a sophisticated one. The Convention Center is hosting X-S Tech, a mysterious corporation from a distant planet. X-S Tech's objective is to impress earthlings, particularly Magic Kingdom guests, with its high-tech products. Visitors learn more about the company in a glitzy corporate video presentation. They also meet Chairman Clench, X-S Tech's CEO. Then they are led into another room for a demonstration of the company's premier product: a teleporter capable of "beaming" people or objects from place to place—even from one planet to another.

At the podium is a robot named S.I.R. To his left and right are bell jars, one of which holds Skippy, a fuzzy, three-foot-tall character. S.I.R. tries to teleport Skippy from one jar to the next, but the demonstration doesn't go very well. He uses too much power, and Skippy's fur is singed and his eyes are rolling.

Despite the minor setback, the folks from X-S Tech continue with their presentation. Guests are shown to a circular auditorium with a large teleporter in the center. Screens around the theater display a live transmission from Planet X, asking visitors to take their seats. Restraints are suddenly lowered onto guests' shoulders. (Don't panic—this is not rough, just scary.) The Planet X broadcast informs guests that X-S Tech intends to demonstrate its invention by teleporting someone from the audience to Planet X. A scanner lights up each seat and lasers sweep the crowd in search of a specimen. Just then, Chairman Clench comes on screen and volunteers. He will have himself teleported to Earth, to meet this Magic Kingdom audience.

Special effects abound as the teleporter is fired up and guests await the arrival of Chairman Clench. But something goes terribly wrong and, instead of Clench, an alien is

TAKE FLIGHT: A whimsical look at the adventure and romance of flight—as seen through the eyes of a child—awaits guests at this 4½-minute attraction (formerly known as Dreamflight). A mixture of two- and three-dimensional media combine with special effects and digitally produced stereo music to take visitors on an entirely delightful journey. The attraction opens with a scene from a giant pop-up book, in which mankind's first attempts at flight are humorously depicted. Three-dimensional aircraft are used in a variety of scenes from the early days of flight. A barnstorming flying circus segment features a man and woman, each standing on a wing and keeping up a tennis match. The next segment highlights a 70mm live-action film, produced in the Northwest exclusively for this attraction.

In the next scene, a section of an M-130 Flying Boat, a plane popular during the late 1930s, is on view. An elegant dining room (particularly by today's standards) is displayed as monitors allow glimpses of the faraway places the M-130 made accessible. In one scene, two dancers perform outside a Japanese temple garden; in another, the sun sets over Paris as a flower merchant packs up his blossoms on the steps of Montmartre. Next stop on the journey is the jet age, in its most pure form. Guests actually ride through a real engine. Digitally prepared graphics and special effects re-create the rotation of the turbine in a realistic fashion.

In another 70mm film segment, visitors get that "you are there" feeling as they seemingly speed down a runway and fly off toward space. The moon, backlit by the sun, provides the lighting for some spectacular views over canyons, valleys, and flat terrain, where the suggestion of cities of the future are depicted. The finale features another pop-up book, measuring 16 by 11 feet, that shows contemporary London and New York. Presented by Delta Air Lines.

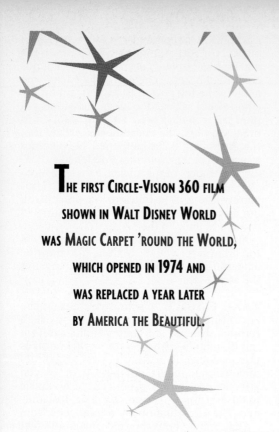

THE FIRST CIRCLE-VISION 360 FILM SHOWN IN WALT DISNEY WORLD WAS MAGIC CARPET 'ROUND THE WORLD, WHICH OPENED IN 1974 AND WAS REPLACED A YEAR LATER BY AMERICA THE BEAUTIFUL.

TOMORROWLAND TRANSIT AUTHORITY: Boarded near Astro Orbiter, these small, five-car trains move at a speed of about ten miles per hour along almost a mile of track, alongside or through most of the attractions in Tomorrowland. If you have any doubts about riding Space Mountain, a ten-minute trip on the Tomorrowland Transit Authority—which travels through the queue area inside and offers a view of the rockets as they hurtle through the darkness—will probably help you decide. Just as important, from a technological and environmental standpoint, is the fact that this train shows off an innovative means of transportation. It is operated by a linear induction motor that has no moving parts, uses little power, and emits no pollution.

ASTRO ORBITER: Here, passengers spin around for two minutes in machine-age rockets, designed to look more like oversize

Buck Rogers toys than 1990s space shuttles. Riders are surrounded by whirling planets as they swing around on high, getting a good view of Tomorrowland.

WALT DISNEY'S CAROUSEL OF PROGRESS: First seen at New York's 1964–65 World's Fair and moved here in 1975, this 20-minute show features a number of tableaux starring an Audio-Animatronics family, and demonstrates the improvements in American life that have resulted from the use of electricity. The audience moves around the scenes as on a carousel, and kids enjoy this effect. An updated final scene has been added, in which guests see what life might be like about five or six years from now: A grandmother plays a virtual-reality game and the oven talks. (These technologically advanced products to be used in homes in the near future are now on display for hands-on inspection at Epcot's Innoventions.)

SKYWAY TO FANTASYLAND: This aerial cable car takes guests from Tomorrowland to a point near Peter Pan's Flight in Fantasyland in ten minutes. The cable car, built by Von Roll Ltd., in Bern, Switzerland, is notable for being the nation's first conveyance of its type able to make a 90-degree turn. If you're going to ride the Skyway, this is the place to get on: The lines at the Fantasyland end are usually slightly longer.

SPACE MOUNTAIN: Rising to a height of over 180 feet and extending some 300 feet in diameter, this gleaming white steel and concrete cone (shaped vaguely like Japan's Mount Fuji) houses an attraction that most people call a roller coaster. Actually, it bears the same sort of resemblance to the traditional thrill ride as the Magic Kingdom does to the garden-variety theme park. It's the Disney version—a roller coaster and then some. While the 2-minute, 38-second ride does not exactly duplicate a trip into outer space, there are some truly phenomenal and quite lovely special effects—shooting stars and strobelike flashing lights among them; and the whole ride takes place in an outer spacelike darkness that gets progressively inkier—and scarier—as the journey progresses.

The six-passenger rockets that roar through this blackness attain a maximum speed of just over 28 miles per hour. Just how terrifying this actually is to any given passenger depends on his or her level of tolerance. In general, the Space Mountain trip seems to inspire in lovers of thrill rides an immediate desire to go again; it's just wild enough to send eyeglasses, purses, wallets, and even an occasional set of false teeth plummeting to the bottom of the track, so be sure to find a safe place for your possessions before the ride starts. It's also turbulent enough to upset the stomachs of those so unwise as to ride it immediately after eating—but not so harrowing that passengers' shaking and weakened knees persist for more than a minute or two after "touchdown." Those in a quandary about whether or not to line up can get a preview from the Tomorrowland Transit Authority; and those who decide to pass after hearing the shrieks and the clatter of the cars from the queue area have their own exit.

After experiencing the space journey, it's interesting to note that the mountain itself occupies a ten-acre site. With the work lights on, the interior of Space Mountain looks humdrum and almost commercially common, with its tangled array of track and supporting scaffolding. Some of the shooting stars are produced quite simply, by aiming a beam of light at a mirrored globe; and legend has it that the meteors visible to guests in the queue area are actually projections of chocolate chip cookies! The whole ride is controlled by a computer, monitored on a board full of dials and a battery of closed-circuit television screens by Disney hosts and hostesses sitting in a control room (whose eerie blue glow is another striking feature of the queue area). As a result, any guest acting in an unsafe manner can be warned, and the ride stopped, if necessary.

Note: Children under seven years old must be accompanied by an adult; guests under 44 inches tall are not permitted to ride; and as the many signs at the attraction warn, you must be in good health, and free from heart conditions, motion sickness, back or neck problems, or other physical limitations to ride. It also is suggested that expectant mothers pass up the trip. Presented by Federal Express.

The Tomorrowland Light & Power Co., a video arcade located at Space Mountain's exit, is a great place to wait for your party if you choose not to ride. A cart here sells video games and toys. An ATM is also available.

TOMORROWLAND SPEEDWAY: Little cars that *vroom* down the tracks at this attraction opposite Cosmic Ray's Starlight Café provide most of the background noise in Tomorrowland. Kids love the ride and will spend as many hours driving the Mark VII-model gasoline-powered cars as they can. Like true sports cars, the vehicles—which cost about $6,000 each—have rack-and-pinion steering and disc brakes; unlike most sports cars, these run on a track. Nonetheless, even expert drivers have a hard time keeping them going in a straight line until the technique is mastered: Just steer all the way to the right, or all the way to the left, and you've got it made. One lap around the track takes about five minutes, and the cars (which are manufactured by a

Disney company called MAPO, short for Mary Poppins) can travel at a maximum speed of about seven miles per hour. Presented by Goodyear.

Note: You must be at least 52 inches tall to drive the cars by yourself.

DID YOU KNOW THAT A YEAR BEFORE WALT DISNEY WORLD OPENED, A PREVIEW CENTER INTRODUCING DISNEY'S FORTHCOMING PARK DREW LARGER CROWDS THAN MANY FLORIDA ATTRACTIONS? THE PREVIEW CONSISTED OF A FILM, SCALE MODELS, AND A SNACK BAR.

SHOPPING

No one travels all the way to the Magic Kingdom just to go shopping. But as many a first-time visitor has learned with some surprise, shopping is one of the most enjoyable pastimes here. Donald Duck key chains and Mickey Mouse lapel pins, Alice in Wonderland dresses for little girls, Walt Disney World sweatshirts, and other Disney souvenir items make up a large portion of the merchandise on display.

But the Magic Kingdom's boutiques and stores stock much more than just Disneyana. Along with the more predictable items in Main Street shops, like film and peanut brittle, it's possible to find cookbooks and stoneware dishes, mock pirate hats and toy frontier rifles, 14-karat gold charms and filigreed costume jewelry. In Adventureland, you can buy imported items from around the world—hand-carved elephant statues from Africa, inlaid marble boxes from India, batik dresses from Indonesia, and more. Shops generally stock items that complement the themes of the various lands.

In many shops, you can watch people at work—a candy maker pouring peanut brittle in the Main Street Confectionery, a glassblower crafting wares in Main Street's Crystal Arts, and the like. And every store offers a selection of items from the inexpensive to the costly: In Tinker Bell's Treasures in Fantasyland, for instance, kids can beg for a $5 windup toy after requests for the larger-than-life-size $250 stuffed animals are denied. Consequently, there's no need to spend a fortune to have a good time. Budget-watchers should note, though, that the temptation to spend yourself into penury is strong, and you need to be careful. It's a good idea to set a limit for each member of your party in advance—and try to stick to it.

Finally, some advice. We recommend shopping in the early afternoon, rather than at day's end when the shops are normally jammed. However, keep in mind that Main Street shops do stay open a half hour after park closing, in case you need any last-minute gifts on the way out of the park. Also note that purchases can be stored for the day in lockers under the Walt Disney World Railroad's depot or, in the case of very large items, behind the desk at City Hall. WDW resort guests may arrange for purchases to be delivered to their hotel rooms free of charge.

Main Street

THE CHAPEAU: This Town Square shop is the place to buy Mouseketeer ears and have them monogrammed, and to shop for visors, straw hats, and assorted other headgear. The hats are fun to try on, even if you don't plan on buying.

CRYSTAL ARTS: Pretty cut-glass bowls, vases, urns, glasses, and plates glitter in the mirror-backed glass cases of this high-ceilinged, brass-chandeliered emporium. An engraver or a glassblower is always at work by the bright light that floods through the big windows. Presented by the Arribas Brothers.

DISNEYANA COLLECTIBLES: Located next to Tony's Town Square restaurant. Limited-edition Disney plates, cels from Disney movies, and other collectibles are sold here.

Where to Eat in the Magic Kingdom

A complete listing of all eateries—full-service restaurants, fast-food emporiums, and snack shops—can be found in the *Good Meals, Great Times* chapter. See the Magic Kingdom section beginning on page 214.

DISNEY & COMPANY: The wallpaper at this shop on Center Street (the cul-de-sac just off Main) is Victorian and the wood-work elaborate; old-fashioned ceiling fans twirl slowly overhead. This shop specializes in children's clothing, but also stocks clocks, watches, and an assortment of dolls and stuffed toys. The selection is not as vast as that at the Emporium, but Disney & Company isn't quite so overwhelming.

DISNEY CLOTHIERS: Disney character merchandise has always been popular, as evidenced by the number of T-shirts, Mouseketeer ears, watches, and sweatshirts sold each year. This shop caters to fashion-conscious shoppers with a love for Disney gear. There is a vast array of men's, women's, and children's clothing and accessories, all of which incorporate Disney characters in some way. There are men's golf shirts with a small Mickey Mouse embroidered on the pocket, and jackets with Mickey embossed on the back. Hats, ties, and dress shirts round out the adult selections. Children's items include socks, suspenders, tops, pants, and bathing suits.

EMPORIUM: Framed by a two-story-high portico, this Town Square landmark, the Magic Kingdom's largest gift shop, stocks a little bit of everything—stuffed animals and toys, an array of dolls, sundries, film, and more. Every customer seems to have an armload of Walt Disney World T-shirts and sweatshirts, towels and handbags, Mouseketeer ears and other hats, and various items emblazoned with Mickey, Minnie, or Walt Disney World logos. The cash registers almost always seem to be busy,

especially toward the end of the afternoon and before park closing. It's a good place to souvenir shop, though, since it's only a few steps from lockers (under the train station) where purchases can be stowed. Don't forget to peer into the windows, which usually feature Audio-Animatronics displays ranging from spirited seasonal themes to character tableaux from the latest Disney movie.

HARMONY BARBER SHOP: The quaint, old-fashioned setting for this working shop (complete with harmonizing quartet) merits a peek even if you have no need for a trim. Nostalgic shaving items are also for sale.

KODAK CAMERA CENTER: This high-ceilinged shop near Town Square is the spot for film, disposable cameras, two-hour film processing, and very minor camera repairs. Gleaming glass-fronted mahogany cases show off the Canon, Minolta, Pentax, Nikon, and other 35mm cameras for sale. Video cameras are available for rent (a deposit is required).

MAIN STREET ATHLETIC STORE: Sports-related gifts and apparel sure to be a hit with the active set are the hallmarks of this shop. Merchandise features logos of popular collegiate and professional teams, along with images of Disney characters gamely pursuing their favorite sports. Guests can also pose behind a variety of backgrounds (ever seen yourself as a boxing champ?) for a unique photo self-portrait.

MAIN STREET CONFECTIONERY: Delicious chocolates are available in this old-fashioned pink-and-white paradise. A delight

A Few Good Silver Souvenirs

- Commemorative park tickets
- 25th anniversary album featuring classic songs from WDW attractions as performed by current artists
- A copy of *Since the World Began*, published by Hyperion
- 25th anniversary CD-ROM, titled *Walt Disney World Explorer*
- Specially commissioned art
- Commemorative edition of The Disney Credit Card, complete with "Remember the Magic" hologram
- 25th anniversary watches, Mouseketeer hats, T-shirts, you name it

Merchandise Hotline

Can't find what you're looking for in the Magic Kingdom? Call the merchandise hotline at 824-5566. Representatives can help locate and direct you to almost any item on the Walt Disney World property, be it Mickey Mouse ears or a Cinderella costume.

at any time of day, but especially when the cooks in the shop's glass-walled kitchen are pouring peanut brittle onto a huge tabletop to cool. Then, the candy sends up clouds of scent you could swear were being fanned right out into the street. Several batches are made each day; the sweet product is for sale in small bags, along with pastilles, jelly beans, marshmallow crispies, nougats, mints, and dozens of other nemeses for a sweet tooth. When your stomach is growling, this is a good place to grab a snack.

MARKET HOUSE: An old-fashioned spot, with pretzels, pickles, honey, and all kinds of tea and snack items arranged in oak cases. The floors are pegged oak, the lighting emanates in part from brass lanterns, and in one corner there's a real old-fashioned hand-crank telephone. Tobacco products are also available.

NEWSSTAND: No newspapers are sold in the Magic Kingdom—even at its newsstand, which is opposite Wheelchairs–Strollers near the park entrance. It's off to your left just inside the turnstiles. What the stand does sell is character merchandise and souvenirs. The selection is fairly limited, but you can usually pick up items you've forgotten during your travels through the rest of the park.

THE SHADOW BOX: Watching silhouette cutters from Rubio Artist Co. snip black paper into the likenesses of children is one of Main Street's more fascinating diversions. There's always a crowd on hand—some folks waiting their turn, some just inspecting the progress and results. Silhouettes cost $5.

UPTOWN JEWELERS: Fine china and other gift items—china figurines, swans, and flowers, all manner of pretty teacups, and Disney character figurines priced from $3.50 to $3,500—are the stock-in-trade of this airy establishment. There's also a selection of good-quality and costume jewelry. One counter stocks wonderful souvenir charms in 14-karat gold and sterling silver:

among them Tinker Bell, Cinderella Castle, and the Walt Disney World logo (a globe with mouse ears). Clocks and watches in all shapes and sizes are available here, including Mickey Mouse watches in a variety of configurations. There are even some pocket watches and a Mickey Mouse telephone. Purchases can be shipped on request.

WHEELCHAIRS–STROLLERS: Immediately inside the turnstiles on the right as you enter the park, this rental concession offers a limited number of strollers and wheelchairs (available on a first-come, first-served basis). Assorted souvenirs may also be purchased.

Adventureland

BWANA BOB'S: A whimsical and colorful hut full of the critters you may have just observed on the Jungle Cruise or at Tropical Serenade.

ELEPHANT TALES: A variety of women's and men's clothing with a safari theme are featured at this shop. Women's accessories and safari plush toys are also available.

ISLAND SUPPLY: Discover nature at its finest through apparel and gifts representing gardening and the great outdoors. The merchandise here has an environmental theme: You'll find wind chimes, herb-garden kits, natural lotions, and a selection of T-shirts made of unbleached cotton.

TIKI TROPICS: This tropical surf shop features a vast assortment of surfing clothing and accessories. Colorful T-shirts, baggies, sharks' teeth jewelry, and even surfboard wax can be found here.

TRADERS OF TIMBUKTU: Located in a marketlike complex in the plaza opposite the Tropical Serenade, this shop displays a selection of the sort of handsome (but inexpensive) trinkets that travelers find while visiting

parts of Africa—carved wooden giraffes and antelope, ethnic jewelry (including carved bangles and malachite-and-elephant-hair baubles), dashikis, and khaki shirts.

Caribbean Plaza

HOUSE OF TREASURE: A good spot to pick up pirates' hats, this swashbuckler's delight adjoins Pirates of the Caribbean on the west and stocks piratical merchandise—toy rifles and brass dolphins, a Pirate's Creed of Ethics printed on parchment, Jolly Roger flags, rings, old-looking maps, pirate dolls, sailing-ship models, ships in a bottle, and eye patches. There's as much here for adults as for youngsters: Women's nautical apparel is available, as are fine nautical gifts such as lamps and brass items.

PLAZA DEL SOL CARIBE BAZAAR: Located next to the Pirates of the Caribbean, this market sells candy and snacks, a variety of straw hats (including colorful oversize sombreros), piñatas, pottery, straw bags, clothing, and artificial flowers.

Frontierland

BIG AL'S: Located along the river, this shop is the place to acquire a variety of leather goods, harmonicas, rock candy, and assorted six-shooters.

BRIAR PATCH: Cuddly creatures from the movie *Song of the South* are featured at this shop, located near the exit to Splash Mountain. Country crafts and a good selection of

Disney character merchandise—including lots of items spotlighting Winnie the Pooh and friends—round out the offerings.

FRONTIER TRADING POST: Outfit a youngster like a true child of the Great Frontier. Cowboy hats or feathered headdresses and moccasins, hefty brass belt buckles, sleeve garters, sheriff's badges, gold nugget and turquoise jewelry, and reproduction pistols and rifles should do the trick. Other western items such as tomtoms, peace pipes, plastic toy horses, and forts are also available. Film and sundries are in stock, too.

FRONTIER WOOD CARVING: The spot for wooden gifts with personalized carvings. Presented by Rubio Artist Co.

PRAIRIE OUTPOST & SUPPLY: Stop by this turn-of-the-century general store for candy and some unusual food, including elk jerky and alligator meat. Decorative items such as candles are also for sale.

TRAIL CREEK HAT SHOP: Hats of all descriptions, plus feathered hatbands and leather goods are on sale at this small emporium tucked away near the Frontierland Shootin' Arcade and the Diamond Horseshoe Saloon Revue. The specialties of the house are western-style hats.

Liberty Square

HERITAGE HOUSE: Early American reproductions predominate in the stock of this store next to The Hall of Presidents. Parchment copies of famous American documents are popular with youngsters. Homeowners might snap up pewter plates and

THE YANKEE TRADER: No first-time Magic Kingdom visitor would expect to buy cast-iron muffin tins and stoneware soufflé dishes here. But this shop, immediately to the right after you turn into the lane leading to The Haunted Mansion, is crammed like a too-small kitchen cabinet with just these kitchen items, and more. There's a great Mickey Mouse waffle iron, among other Disney-themed goods. The shop also has a wealth of countrified cookware and more varieties of jams and jellies than any supermarket shopper would have imagined existed. Gourmands will be pleased to find a cookbook selection that includes not only old favorites, but also unusual volumes of historic recipes. The store is located near the archway entrance to Fantasyland.

YE OLDE CHRISTMAS SHOPPE: A wide selection of Christmas items, including tree-top dolls and souvenir ornaments—both Disney-themed and traditional—is available at this new location year-round.

Fantasyland

FANTASY FAIRE: It's difficult to miss this shop upon leaving the Legend of The Lion King show. It has every item imaginable featuring the characters from *The Lion King*, from plush Simba toys to Timon and Pumbaa T-shirts and souvenirs.

THE KING'S GALLERY: This shop, situated inside Cinderella Castle, is one of the Magic Kingdom's best. The stock includes large tapestries, suits of armor, unicorns of all sizes, cuckoo clocks, Spanish-made swords, German beer mugs with lids, chess sets, and more—very little of it selling at rock-bottom prices. Adding to the intrigue is the presence of practiced artisans demonstrating the technique of Damascening, a form of metalworking originated in Damascus in the sixth century A.D. Painstakingly, these skilled workers dip steel pendants into acid to create tiny pores, then use a combination of sterling silver and 24-karat gold wire to outline designs on the acid-blackened steel.

KODAK KIOSK: A convenient location to buy film and other photo supplies.

SEVEN DWARFS MINING CO.: This souvenir stand next to Snow White's Adventures sells assorted Disney-motif key chains and stuffed animals, plus a colorful collection of Snow White merchandise.

SIR MICKEY'S: Expect to find all sorts of adult-focused character clothing, from T-shirts and sweatshirts to more sophisticated fashions, hats, and accessories in this new shop near the Castle.

candlesticks, creweled items, wooden candlesticks and pepper mills, busts of the early presidents, souvenir spoons, mugs in early-American motifs, wrought-iron knick-knacks, or lovely enameled paintings of clipper ships.

ICHABOD'S LANDING: This small Liberty Square shop gives guests on their way to The Haunted Mansion a taste of things to come, with a stock of horrific monster masks and assorted ghoulish goodies.

LIBERTY SQUARE PORTRAIT GALLERY: In the midst of Liberty Square next to The Hall of Presidents, guests can sit to have their portraits drawn.

Shopping Away from the Parks

THE DISNEY CATALOG: T-shirts, stuffed animals, and other souvenir items can be ordered through The Disney Catalog. Phone 800-237-5751 to receive one.

THE DISNEY STORES: Located in malls all around the country, these shops offer a wide selection of merchandise.

WDW MAIL ORDER: Merchandise found in shops at Walt Disney World is also available by calling 800-272-6201.

TINKER BELL'S TREASURES: One of the more wonderful boutiques in the Magic Kingdom, and a fine toy store by any standard. For sale are stuffed animals, miniature model cars and trucks, character clothing patches, windup and wooden toys, bars of soap emblazoned with Disney scenes, Mickey and Minnie toys and clothing, Alice in Wonderland dresses, Snow White dresses (with Dopey on the skirt), and a positively marvelous array of Madame Alexander dolls. A must.

Mickey's Toontown Fair

COUNTY BOUNTY: A variety of character memorabilia, featuring all the favorites, can be found in this new merchandise location under the big tent. It's also fun to see all the winning entries from previous fairs, such as the largest pumpkin.

Tomorrowland

MICKEY'S STAR TRADERS: One of the best places to go in the Magic Kingdom for Disney-themed items.

MERCHANT OF VENUS: This shop sells the kinds of contemporary decorative gifts that teens and preteens seem to love: futuristic toys, games, jewelry, watches, clothing, and other such items. This is the only shop that carries Alien Encounter merchandise.

GEIGER'S COUNTER: This small shop features a variety of souvenir hats.

URSA'S MAJOR MINOR MART: A small spot tucked away near the Tomorrowland terminus of the Skyway to Fantasyland; great for Disney souvenirs.

JOLIAN PHELAN OF PEMBROKE PINES, FLORIDA, IS A MEMBER OF THE WALT DISNEY COLLECTORS CLUB. AMONG HER DISNEY-THEMED TREASURES, SHE OWNS 100 WATCHES, 20 STATUES, 50 PAIRS OF EARRINGS, AND 100 DOLLS. HER MOST PRIZED POSSESSION? AN AUTOGRAPHED PICTURE OF WALT DISNEY.

ENTERTAINMENT

In this most magical corner of the World, a tempting slate of live performances ranks among the more serendipitous discoveries. The Magic Kingdom's entertainment mix includes dazzling high-tech shows and old-fashioned numbers alike. To keep apprised of the offerings on any given day, it's important for guests to stop at City Hall upon arrival to the park to pick up a current entertainment schedule.

While specifics are subject to change, the following listing is a good indication of the Magic Kingdom's extensive repertoire. As always, we advise calling 824-4321 to confirm entertainment schedules. For information on special events at the Magic Kingdom, see the "Holidays & Special Events" section of Getting Ready to Go. Also, note that from now through the end of 1997, the Magic Kingdom is the focal point for celebrations trumpeting Walt Disney World's 25th anniversary (for all the details, turn to our special section beginning on page 15).

ALL-AMERICAN COLLEGE MARCHING BAND: During weekdays in summer, this band featuring college students from around the country performs throughout the Magic Kingdom in the afternoon and early evening.

CASEY'S CORNER PIANO: A pianist tickles the ivories of a snow-white upright daily at the centrally located Casey's Corner restaurant on Main Street.

DAPPER DANS: A barbershop quartet likely to be encountered while strolling down Main Street. Conspicuously clad in straw hats and striped vests, the Dapper Dans tap dance and let one-liners fly during their short four-part harmonic performances.

DIAMOND HORSESHOE SALOON REVUE: A dance hall such as might have been found in 19th-century Missouri hosts this lively old-time show with cancan dancers several times daily. Guests may drop in at any time during the hour-long performances.

FANTASY IN THE SKY: Even those rare recalcitrant souls who resist fireworks displays as though they were other people's home movies have little quarrel with this spectacular show, which is being presented nightly this year (usually at 10 P.M.) to honor Walt Disney World's 25th anniversary. The program begins with Tinker Bell's Flight, a dramatic sprinkling of pyrotechnic pixie dust over Cinderella Castle that's ideally viewed

Celebratory Parade

The special 25th Anniversary Parade makes its musical procession down Main Street each day at 3 P.M. Every character imaginable is there to celebrate, on floats themed to *Cinderella*, *Beauty and the Beast*, *The Little Mermaid*, *Aladdin*, *The Lion King*, and a finale float with all the rest of the characters and a blast of fireworks. What makes this 25-minute parade unique is that it stops eight times along the route for a "magical moment," in which characters from the floats interact with guests.

from Main Street. The single best vantage point: front and center on the platform of the Walt Disney World Railroad depot.

Fireworks buffs may be interested to know that the 200-odd shells—originally set off over a 15-minute period—are ignited over just 5 minutes in today's productions; with fireworks now bursting at a rate of about one shell every 2 seconds, the experience is all the more exciting. Also, the big symmetrical starburst shells are generally Japanese-made, while the ones whose explosions look as if they had been poured from a pitcher (with a concentrated area of particularly vivid color at the center) are manufactured in England.

FLAG RETREAT: At about 5:10 P.M., a small band and color guard march into Town Square, take down the American flag that flies from the flagpole there, then release a flock of snow-white homing pigeons symbolic of the dove of peace. Watch carefully lest you miss them: As one wag quipped, these are union pigeons; they flap away toward their loft home (behind the Castle) practically before you can say "Cinderella." The entire flight takes just 20 seconds. Some trivia: The carts in which the birds are transported are fashioned from authentic peddlers' carts bought in England for the 1971 Disney film *Bed-knobs and Broomsticks*.

GALAXY SEARCH: The outdoor Galaxy Palace Theater in Tomorrowland hosts this talent show in search of unique entertainment, starring Mickey and his pals.

J. P. AND THE SILVER STARS: This group surfaces from time to time to play familiar tunes on steel drums, bringing a bit of the Caribbean islands to the area near Adventureland's Pirates of the Caribbean. Steel drums, instruments unique to Caribbean music, are essentially barrels.

KIDS OF THE KINGDOM: Performing often in front of the Castle, this group puts on a show featuring lively singing and dancing to classic Disney tunes—plus appearances by such characters as the portly Winnie the Pooh and Mickey Mouse himself. After the show, returning Walt Disney World visitors assemble for a 25th anniversary salute.

RETURNING GUEST TRIBUTE: Held daily in front of Cinderella Castle, this rousing event invites returning guests to cheer the World's 25th birthday.

RHYTHM RASCALS: Specialty songs and comic ditties from the Roaring Twenties on washboards and banjos are their trademark; they usually perform on Main Street.

SWORD IN THE STONE CEREMONY: Several times each day, a child is appointed king or queen of the realm by pulling the magical sword, Excalibur, from the stone in front of Cinderella's Golden Carrousel. Merlin the Magician presides over the ceremony.

WALT DISNEY WORLD BAND: This traditional concert band performs in Town Square every morning and every afternoon just prior to the parade.

Where to Find *the Characters*

Mickey and friends appear next to City Hall on Main Street throughout the day. A queue allows each guest a chance to meet the characters and perhaps have a photo taken. Adventureland is a good spot to find Rafiki and Timon from *The Lion King*. Alice and her friends from Wonderland often show up in Fantasyland. The character meals at Crystal Palace, King Stefan's, and Liberty Tree Tavern offer guests another way to meet their favorites. But the best place to see the characters is at Mickey's Toontown Fair, where guests can meet Mickey, Minnie, and a host of other characters. Be sure to check the park guidemap for updated information.

SpectroMagic

Since its premier during Walt Disney World's 20th anniversary celebration five years ago, this parade has gotten rave reviews and taken its place among WDW's must-sees. Even avid fans of the Main Street Electrical Parade (which, by the way, was shipped to Disneyland Paris) won't be disappointed with this display.

Fiber-optic cable and threads are conduits for shimmering lights that create everything from the strands of "hair" on King Triton's beard on one float to the giant hibiscus blooms and daisy petals on another. Some 600,000 miniature bulbs light in wild, changing patterns, moving in perfect concert with sound effects. Goofy's xylophone keys dance with light at his touch. Mickey's cape becomes a cascade of color sweeping from his shoulders to the base of the float and upward 17 feet above his head. The wonderful spectacle is choreographed to music composed just for the parade.

SpectroMagic borrows its dazzling illusions from the prismatic holographic industry, military lighting developments, electroluminescent and fiber-optic technologies, plus light-spreading thermoplastics, clouds of underlit liquid nitrogen, smoke, and some old-fashioned twinkling lights.

A marvel of the computer age, SpectroMagic is controlled by compact computers, with the audio stored digitally on state-of-the-art microchips. A sequence of electronic triggers activates and coordinates all of the visual and audio effects.

SpectroMagic follows the traditional WDW parade route; of all the spots along the way, the single best vantage point is the very center of the platform of the Walt Disney World Railroad depot. From there, it's possible to see the parade circling Town Square, and then follow it as it makes its way down Main Street. Unfortunately, only a couple of seats here have views that are not obstructed by trees.

The next-best viewing points are the curbs on either side along Main Street. It's very crowded here, and you must claim your foot of curb as much as an hour before the parade (particularly for the busier 9 P.M. running). If you hate crowds, head for Pecos Bill Café; park yourself on one of the restaurant's stools right next to the parade route.

For the 25th anniversary, the parade lights up Main Street nightly. If there are two shows, the 9 P.M. parade is always more crowded than the one at 11 P.M.

Holiday Happenings

It's a rare holiday that passes quietly in the Magic Kingdom. During certain holidays such as Christmas, New Year's Eve, and the Fourth of July, the Magic Kingdom usually breaks curfew, staying open extra-late and stepping up its nighttime entertainment. On these occasions, special performances of SpectroMagic and the Fantasy in the Sky fireworks are often in store. Of course, entertainment plans are subject to change, so it's important to call 824-4321 for up-to-the-minute schedules.

EASTER: A nationally televised holiday promenade on Main Street makes Easter an especially delightful, if a bit crowded, time to visit the Magic Kingdom.

FOURTH OF JULY: The busiest day of the summer—and with reason: There's a double-size fireworks display, whose explosions light up the skies not only above Cinderella Castle, but also over Seven Seas Lagoon.

CHRISTMAS: A towering Christmas tree—a real Douglas fir that is as perfect among trees as Main Street is among small-town thoroughfares—goes up in Town Square, and the entire Magic Kingdom is decked out as only Disney can do it. Throughout the season, the Magic Kingdom hosts a special-admission nighttime celebration called Mickey's Very

Merry Christmas Party. The festivities, complete with hot chocolate and snow, include Mickey's Very Merry Christmas Parade and other holiday shows. There are also special holiday performances during the day. The crowds, of course, are thick. But the decor is beautiful, and the weather is fine (if chilly)—so it's no wonder that some veteran Magic Kingdom fans call this the best time of year.

NEW YEAR'S EVE: It has always been true that on December 31, the throngs are practically body to body. For a celebration of this nature, that's fun. (On an introductory visit, it could be less delightful; first-timers take note.) There is a double-size fireworks display, and the Main Street holiday decorations (including that almost surrealistically perfect Christmas tree presiding over Town Square) are still up. There's plenty of nip in the air as the evening wears on, so dress accordingly.

HOT TIPS

"**T**HERE'S ENOUGH LAND HERE TO HOLD ALL THE IDEAS AND PLANS WE CAN POSSIBLY IMAGINE... BELIEVE ME, IT'S THE MOST EXCITING AND CHALLENGING ASSIGNMENT WE HAVE EVER TACKLED AT WALT DISNEY PRODUCTIONS."

WALT DISNEY (1965)

- Study this chapter before you arrive in the Magic Kingdom so that you're familiar with the park's layout and attractions. Special services are occasionally available to guests during slack seasons, so be sure to peruse any printed information you find in your room.
- Allow plenty of time to sample the Magic Kingdom in small bites. Trying to see it all in a day (or even two) is like eating a rich ice cream sundae too quickly.
- Sunday morning ranks as the most peaceful time to visit the park.
- Consider taking advantage of early-bird admissions to the parks. Each day, sections of one park are open 1½ hours early for WDW resort guests only. But keep in mind that the parks can get crowded on the designated days.
- If you are not staying at a WDW resort, still plan to start out early. Most people arrive between 9:30 A.M. and 11:30 A.M., and the roads and parking lots are jammed. If you're coming at Easter, Christmas, or in summer, plan to arrive before 8:30 A.M., or wait until late afternoon, when things are less hectic. Be at the gates to the Magic Kingdom when they open, and then be at the end of Main Street when the rest of the park opens.
- Wear very comfortable shoes: You'll be spending a lot of time on your feet. (Note that no bare feet are permitted in the park.)
- Shop on Main Street in the early afternoon, not at day's end, when everybody else goes (since shops here are open a half hour after park closing). Besides, the stores are good places to escape the afternoon heat.
- WDW resort guests can have packages delivered to their hotels free of charge.
- Check out the Tip Board at the end of Main Street for information on the waiting times for the most popular attractions.

- Organize your visit so that you don't hop around from area to area, for that wastes time. Plan to eat early or late: before 11 A.M. or after 2 P.M., and before 5 P.M. or after 8 P.M.
- At busy times, take in these not-so-packed attractions: Walt Disney World Railroad, Main Street Cinema, Liberty Square Riverboat, Carousel of Progress, Take Flight, and Tomorrowland Transit Authority.
- Break up your day. Go to one of the water parks, or head back to your hotel (if it's not too far) for some swimming. Be sure to have your hand stamped and hold on to your admission pass and your parking stub.
- If your party decides to split up, set a fixed meeting place and time that can't be confused. Avoid meeting in front of Cinderella Castle, since this area is often congested.
- Many Magic Kingdom attractions have two lines. The one on the left usually will be shorter, since most visitors automatically head for the one on the right.
- For a full-service meal in the Magic Kingdom, make advance priority seating arrangements by calling WDW-DINE (939-3463).
- Don't take food into the park. (There are picnic facilities and lockers at the TTC.)

SPECIAL 25TH ANNIVERSARY TIPS
- Be sure to stop in at the Welcome Center to register and see the exhibit chronicling Walt Disney World's evolution. You will receive a commemorative lithograph.
- If you want to be a part of the 25th Anniversary Parade, choose your spot on the curb at least 45 minutes prior. Guests are randomly picked to participate from along the parade route.
- The Magic Kingdom might be a lot busier than other parts of the World due to all the festivities here. Perhaps purchase a pass that will allow you to "hop" to other parks, so you can break up your time here with other activities, then return to enjoy the Magic Kingdom's extended hours and evening entertainment.

Epcot

magine a place whose entertainment inventory includes both a rich sampling of world cultures and a fun, enlightening journey to the technological frontier. You now have an inkling of the eye-opening and mind-broadening potential of Epcot.

Walt Disney suggested the idea back in October 1966: "Epcot will be an experimental prototype community of tomorrow that will take its cue from the new ideas and new technologies that are now emerging from the creative center of American industry." It would never be completed, he said, but would "always be introducing and testing and demonstrating new materials and systems." Now, more than ever, Walt Disney's dream is a reality. Innoventions, an ever-evolving showplace of the near future, is continually bounding into new territory in its mission to close gaps with technological destiny. A transformed Universe of Energy has emerged. And when Test Track opens this summer, Epcot guests will have a (thrilling) inside track on the fast and perilous world of automobile testing.

The theme park, which opened in 1982, consists of two distinct areas of exploration: Future World and World Showcase. The former examines the newest and most intriguing ideas in science and technology in ways that make them seem not only comprehensible but downright irresistible. The latter celebrates the diversity of the world's peoples, portraying a stunning array of nations with extraordinary devotion to detail.

Think of Epcot as Disney's playground for the curious and the thoughtful. The experiences it delivers—all of them wonders of the real world—never fail to amaze, delight, inspire, and (rest assured) entertain.

 Unless otherwise noted, all phone numbers are in area code 407.

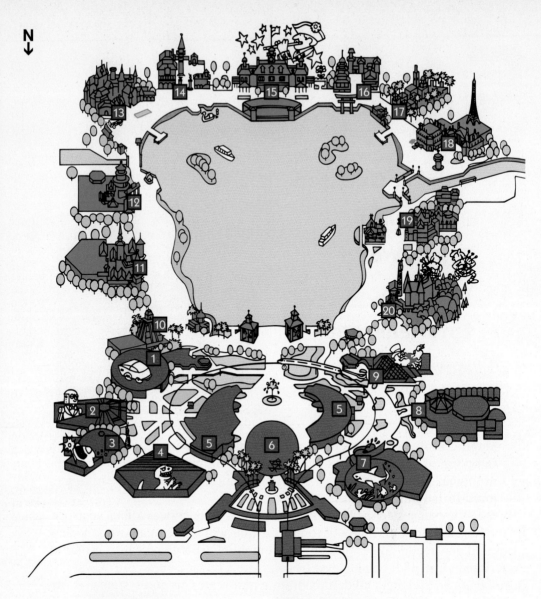

FUTURE WORLD

1 **Test Track**
(opens May 1997)

2 **Horizons**

3 **Wonders of Life**

4 **Universe of Energy**

5 **Innoventions**

6 **Spaceship Earth**

7 **The Living Seas**

8 **The Land**

9 **Journey Into Imagination**

WORLD SHOWCASE

10 **Mexico**

11 **Norway**

12 **China**

13 **Germany**

14 **Italy**

15 **The American Adventure**

16 **Japan**

17 **Morocco**

18 **France**

19 **United Kingdom**

20 **Canada**

GETTING ORIENTED

Double the Magic Kingdom, and you have an idea of the size of Epcot. As for layout, the park is shaped something like a giant hourglass. The nine pavilions of Future World fill the northern bulb, while the international potpourri known as World Showcase occupies the southern bulb. Future World is anchored on the north by the imposing "geosphere" known as Spaceship Earth.

As you pass through Epcot's main entrance plaza, Spaceship Earth looms straight ahead. Pathways curve around either side of the 180-foot-tall geosphere, winding up at Future World's Innoventions Plaza. Here, in addition to a huge show fountain, you see signposts for Innoventions, whose two buildings cradle the east and west sides of the plaza. Beyond this central area, there are two roughly symmetrical north-south avenues; these are dotted with the seven pavilions that form Future World's outer perimeter. Test Track (opens in summer 1997; formerly World of Motion), Horizons, Wonders of Life, and Universe of Energy flank Spaceship Earth on the east, while Journey Into Imagination, The Land, and The Living Seas lie to the west.

In World Showcase, the 11 international pavilions are arranged around the edge of sparkling World Showcase Lagoon, with The American Adventure directly south of Spaceship Earth on the lake's southernmost shore. A walkway from Future World leads to the World Showcase Plaza and the World Showcase Promenade, a 1.3-mile thoroughfare that wraps all the way around the lagoon, winding past each World Showcase pavilion in the process. Proceeding counterclockwise around World Showcase, countries are encountered in the following order: Canada, United Kingdom, France, Morocco, Japan, The American Adventure, Italy, Germany, China, Norway, and Mexico.

HOW TO GET THERE

Take Exit 26B off I-4. Continue on to the Epcot Auto Plaza; take a tram from the parking lot to the park's main entrance.

By WDW Transportation: From the Grand Floridian, Contemporary, and Polynesian: local hotel monorail to the Transportation and Ticket Center (TTC), then switch for the TTC-Epcot monorail. From the Magic Kingdom: express monorail to the TTC, then switch for the TTC-Epcot monorail. From Fort Wilderness and the Disney Village Marketplace: buses to the TTC, then change for the TTC-Epcot monorail. From the Disney-MGM Studios, all other WDW resorts, and the Disney Village Hotel Plaza: buses.

Note that a second Epcot entrance, called the International Gateway, provides entry directly to World Showcase. This gateway, which may be reached via walkways and water launches from the Dolphin, Swan, Yacht Club, Beach Club, and BoardWalk resorts, deposits guests between the France and United Kingdom pavilions.

PARKING

All-day parking at Epcot is $5 for day visitors (free to WDW resort guests with presentation of resort ID). Attendants will direct you to park in one of several lots named in honor of Future World pavilions. Trams circulate regularly, providing transportation from the lots to the main entrance. Be sure to note the section and aisle in which you park. Also, know that the parking ticket allows for re-entry to the parking area throughout the day.

HOURS

Epcot is usually open from 9 A.M. to 9 P.M. However, the two worlds that comprise the park keep different hours: Future World hours are 9 A.M. to 7 P.M. (with the exception of Spaceship Earth and Innoventions, which stay open until 9 P.M.); World Showcase hours are 11 A.M. to 9 P.M. During certain holiday periods and the summer months, hours are extended. It's best to arrive at the park at least a half hour before the posted opening time, particularly during these busy seasons. Call 824-4321 for up-to-the-minute schedules.

GETTING AROUND

Five 66-foot water taxis called the *FriendShip* launches ferry guests across the lagoon. Docks are located at World Showcase Plaza, in front of Germany, and near Morocco. Double-decker buses make frequent stops all along the World Showcase Promenade.

Admission Prices

ONE-DAY TICKET

(Restricted to use only in Epcot. Prices include sales tax and are subject to change.)

Adult..$40.81
Child*...$32.86

*3 through 9 years of age; children under 3 free

BABY FACILITIES

Changing tables and facilities for nursing mothers can be found at Baby Services in the Odyssey Center, between Test Track and Mexico. Also, disposable diapers are kept behind the counter at many Epcot shops; just ask.

CAMERA NEEDS

The Camera Center on the west side of the Entrance Plaza stocks film, batteries, and disposable cameras; it also rents camcorders ($25 per day with a $300 refundable deposit). Two-hour film processing is available here and wherever you see a Photo Express sign. A second camera shop is found in Journey Into Imagination. Film is sold in most Epcot shops.

DISABILITY INFORMATION

Nearly all Epcot attractions, shops, and restaurants are barrier-free. Parking for guests with disabilities is available. Special provisions have also been made to enhance sight- and hearing-impaired guests' enjoyment of the park. The *Walt Disney World Guide for Guests with Disabilities* is available at Guest Relations. For more information, refer to the "Travelers with Disabilities" section of *Getting Ready to Go*.

EARLY-ENTRY DAYS

On Tuesday and Friday, guests staying at a WDW resort may enter Epcot 1½ hours prior to the posted opening time and enjoy selected Future World pavilions—usually Journey Into Imagination, The Living Seas, The Land, and Spaceship Earth. Exact days and attractions are subject to change.

FIRST AID

Minor medical problems can be handled at the First Aid Center, located in the Odyssey Center, between Test Track and Mexico.

INFORMATION

Guest Relations, next to Spaceship Earth, is equipped with guidemaps, a helpful staff, and WorldKey Information Service terminals. Other terminals are near Germany and on the pathway between Epcot's two worlds.

LOCKERS

Attended lockers are found immediately west of Spaceship Earth. Cost is $3 plus a $2 refundable deposit for unlimited use all day.

LOST & FOUND

The department is tucked on the west side of the Entrance Plaza at the Gift Stop. To report lost items after your visit call 824-4245.

LOST CHILDREN

Report lost children at Guest Relations or alert a Disney employee to the problem.

MONEY MATTERS

ATMs are located on the east side of the Entrance Plaza and on the pathway between Future World and World Showcase. Currency exchange can be handled at Guest Relations or at the American Express Travel Office on the west side of the Entrance Plaza. Credit cards (American Express, Visa, MasterCard, and The Disney Credit Card), traveler's checks, and WDW resort IDs are accepted for admission, merchandise, and also for meals at full-service restaurants and many fast-food spots.

PACKAGE PICKUP

Epcot shops can arrange for bulky purchases to be transported to the Gift Stop on the west side of the Entrance Plaza for later pickup. There is no charge for this service.

SAME-DAY REENTRY

Be sure to have your hand stamped upon exiting the park and to retain your ticket if you plan to return later in the same day.

STROLLERS & WHEELCHAIRS

Strollers, wheelchairs, and Electronic Convenience Vehicles (ECVs) may be rented from venues on the east side of the Entrance Plaza and at the International Gateway. Wheelchairs are also available at the Gift Stop. Cost is $5 for strollers, with a $1 refundable deposit; $5 for wheelchairs, with a $1 refundable deposit; and $30 for ECVs, with a $20 refundable deposit. Quantities are limited. Keep your rental receipt; it can be used that same day to obtain a replacement at the Magic Kingdom, the Disney-MGM Studios, or here at Epcot.

TIP BOARD

Check this digital board in Innoventions Plaza throughout the day to learn current waiting times for the most popular attractions.

FUTURE WORLD

A mere listing of the basic themes covered by the Future World pavilions—agriculture, communications, the ocean, energy, health, and imagination—tends to sound a tad academic, and perhaps even a little forbidding. But when these serious topics are presented with that special Disney flair, they become part of an experience that ranks among Walt Disney World's most exciting.

Some of these subjects are explored in the course of lively and unusual Disney "adventures," involving a whole arsenal of remarkable motion pictures, special effects, and Audio-Animatronics figures so lifelike that it is hard to remain unmoved. And Innoventions offers an invitation to sample the near future of technology. The basic elements of Future World are also appealing in their own right, from the palm-dotted Entrance Plaza and the massive buildings of Innoventions to the stupendous fountain just past Spaceship Earth and the many-faceted "geosphere" that has become the universal symbol of Epcot.

There is so much to see and enjoy that it's hard to know just what to do first. Many guests simply stop at Spaceship Earth on their way into Epcot and proceed to wander at random from one pavilion to the next through the morning. As a result, many of the pavilions are frustratingly crowded early in the day—especially Spaceship Earth.

A wise alternative is to choose two or three pavilions from those described in this section, and then to head for World Showcase as soon as it opens at 11 A.M., moving clockwise around the lagoon on one day of your visit and counterclockwise on the next. Then, in the afternoon, when many guests have shifted over to World Showcase, return to Future World. Innoventions is not only a fascinating spot to pass the exceptionally busy hours after lunch, but also a cool refuge when high temperatures prevail outdoors. And although queues can be found during peak seasons at Journey Into Imagination, The Land, Wonders of Life, and Test Track (opening May 1997) throughout most of the late morning and afternoon, the period from late afternoon until Future World closes at 7 P.M is usually less hectic. Keep in mind that certain Future World pavilions—Innoventions and Spaceship Earth—stay open until World Showcase closes, usually 9 P.M.

Future World pavilions are described here as a visitor encounters them while moving counterclockwise (from right to left, which is west to east around the area).

Guest Relations

Located adjacent to Spaceship Earth, this is not only the principal source of Epcot information, but the spot to make meal priority seating arrangements via the easy-to-use touch-sensitive screens. (For specific details, see page 226 of *Good Meals, Great Times*.)

When the terminals are not being used to arrange tables, they can be used to get an overall picture of Epcot, to learn about each pavilion in considerable detail, and to discover nearly everything else that a guest could conceivably want to know about Epcot. If the system's electronic A-to-Z index to shops, restaurants, attractions, and services does not answer a question, it's possible to communicate with a specially trained host or hostess (who is able to hear and see the querying guest with the aid of a microphone and video camera adjacent to the screen). Hosts and hostesses also manage the message service for Epcot guests and keep records of any lost children who may be at Baby Services.

Spaceship Earth

As it looms impressively just above the earth, this great faceted silver geosphere—visible on a clear day from an airplane flying along either Florida coast—looks a little bit like the gigantic spaceship in *Close Encounters of the Third Kind* ready to blast off. It appears large from a distance, and seems even more immense when viewed from directly underneath. It's no surprise that some visitors simply stop beneath it and gawk. The show inside, which explores the continuing search by human beings for ever more efficient means of communication, remains one of Epcot's most visually compelling.

Weighing 16 million pounds, measuring 165 feet in diameter and 180 feet in height, and encompassing 2.2 million cubic feet of space, this geosphere is held aloft by six legs supported by pylons sunk 100 feet into the ground. The distinctive sheen of its covering derives from a quarter-inch-thick sandwich of two anodized aluminum faces and a polyethylene core. This sheath is made up of 954 triangular panels, not all of equal size or shape.

A common misconception about Spaceship Earth is that it is a geodesic dome. Not so. The designers had to make up the word *geosphere* because the structure is unlike any other preexisting building. A geodesic dome is composed of only half a sphere, while Spaceship Earth is almost completely round. In fact, even the word geosphere is something of a misnomer. This extraordinarily large Disney creation is not a perfect sphere; the steelworkers' requirements dictated its slightly uneven dimensions. Presented by AT&T.

SPACESHIP EARTH RIDE: The noted science fiction writer Ray Bradbury, together with a number of consultants and advisers from the Smithsonian Institution, the Los Angeles area's prestigious Huntington Library, the University of Southern California, and the University of Chicago (among others), collaborated with Disney designers in developing this memorable 15-minute journey. It begins in an inky black time tunnel complete with a musty smell that suggests the dust of ages, and continues through history from the days of Cro-Magnon man (30,000 or 40,000 years ago) to the future.

En route, an Egyptian temple shows off the pictorial representations of words and sounds known as hieroglyphics, which were first used around 3,000 B.C., and hieratic writing, a form of script used to write on papyrus. A Phoenician scene set in the ninth century B.C. acknowledges civilization's debt to those tireless traders who introduced a 22-character alphabet (based on sounds) that put written communication, once the province of the intelligentsia alone, within the grasp of the masses. The Romans' pioneering system of roads, the Islamic empire, the efforts of 11th- and 12th-century Benedictine monks to hand-copy religious and classical manuscripts, the Gutenberg press, the Renaissance in Italy, and a number of the 20th century's inventions are represented, and in most cases it's not necessary to be a history scholar to understand why. The Greek theater scene, whose meaning here may not be as widely understood as it should be, reminds viewers that it was the Greeks who refined the alphabet (by the

addition of vowels) and then went on to use the language so expressively. Then, as now, theater was recognized as an important means of examining and transmitting the moral and social questions of the time.

The attraction features some remarkable special effects, such as the flickering candles in the scene where a monk (himself crafted with such precision and authenticity as to appear to be breathing) has nodded off, and the smell of smoke coming from the fall of Rome.

Every scene is executed in exquisite detail. The symbols on the wall of that Egyptian temple really are hieroglyphics, and the content of the letter being dictated by the pharaoh was excerpted from a missive actually received by an agent of a ruler of the period. The actor in the Greek theater scene is delivering lines from Sophocles' *Oedipus Rex*. In the scene depicting the fall of Rome, the graffiti reproduces markings from the walls of Pompeii. In the Islamic scene, the quadrant—an instrument used in astronomy and navigation—is a copy of one from the tenth century. The type on Johannes Gutenberg's press actually moves, and the page that the celebrated 15th-century printer is examining is a replica of one from a Bible in the collection of the above-mentioned Huntington Library. In the Renaissance scene, the book being read is Virgil's *Aeneid*; the musical instruments in that scene are a lute and a *lyra da braccio*, both replicas of period instruments. The steam-powered press in the 20th-century scenes is a reproduction of one that had been developed by William Bullock around 1863, notable because it used paper in continuous rolls rather than individual sheets.

Some visitors wonder as to the identity of the excerpts from the radio and television shows broadcast in this area. Take note: The former include "The Lone Ranger," "The Shadow," a commentary by Walter Winchell, and the Joe Louis–Max Schmeling 1938 boxing rematch. In the fight, it's the first round, and Schmeling, who had inflicted Joe Louis' first loss in a 1936 12th-round K.O., is

on the mat. The referee is counting—and the crowd is going wild. Among the television segments featured are Walter Cronkite's reports from the March 10, 1964, New Hampshire Republican primary; Walt Disney introducing "The Wonderful World of Color"; Ed Sullivan and the Harlem Globetrotters; the Colts versus Browns NFL championship game (1964); and "Ozzie and Harriet," featuring David and Ricky Nelson. Film buffs may recognize clips from the movies *Girl Shy* with Harold Lloyd (1924), *Top Hat* with Fred Astaire and Ginger Rogers (1935), and *20,000 Leagues Under the Sea* (1954).

All these sights are enough to keep necks craning and heads turning as the "time machines" wend their way upward. The most dazzling scene is the ride's finale, when the audience is placed in the heart of a communications revolution amid interactive global networks that tie all the peoples of the world together. Magical special effects, animated sets, and audience-enclosing laser beams are used to create exciting visual sensations. Highlights include glimpses of high-definition TV and virtual-reality classrooms of the future. In one scene, an American boy and a Japanese girl exchange experiences via video telephone.

In the Global Neighborhood exhibit at the end of the journey, guests can interact directly with emerging technologies such as voice recognition, video telephones, and the information superhighway.

Note: The lines for this attraction are usually longest during the morning hours, and at their shortest just before park closing time.

GATEWAY GIFTS AND CAMERA CENTER: These two shops are located near the entrance to Spaceship Earth. The former sells Epcot souvenirs—T-shirts, mugs, toys, etc.—as well as sunscreen, tissues, and the like. Film and various other Kodak products, including disposable cameras, are sold at the Camera Center. Video cameras may be rented here, and same-day film processing is available.

Innoventions

Imagine being able to get your hands on technological goodies fresh off the drawing board—gadgets that will one day change the way you live and work. At Innoventions, you can see, touch, and test products so new they won't be on the market for several months or years. The pavilion is one of Future World's most experiential areas. Equally important, it offers a fun, unintimidating environment where you needn't know how to program a VCR to be able to try out supercomputers, experiment with virtual reality, see a fully automated home in action, or take a shopping spree on the information superhighway.

Within the 100,000-square-foot area, diverse exhibits are presented by major manufacturers. Computers, games, phones, and appliances are among the wide variety of products on display. Exhibits change constantly, making Walt Disney's original dream for Epcot a reality. Representatives from each manufacturer are on hand to answer questions from curious—or even skeptical—visitors. It's also possible to register via computer terminals around the area to receive new product information at home.

Innoventions is separated into two buildings, often referred to as Innoventions East and West. The entire area between the pavilions is filled with color, light, an assortment of spinning mobiles, and sidewalks glistening with fiber-optic lighting effects. Inside, areas are divided by company (a sampling is described below). Since exhibits change often, there may be many different technologies available when you visit. Above all, count on spending quite a while exploring the exhibit areas here (at least a couple of hours). There's so much to see and do that curiosity will often get the better of any schedule here.

Although the exhibits are all very different, two common themes emerge, no matter where guests spend their time. Innoventions offers many opportunities to experience virtual reality in its various applications, from education to games. Another focus throughout, the Internet, ensures that everyone leaving Innoventions understands the technology and how to use it.

A good place to start an exploration is on the west side of Innoventions at a show starring **Bill Nye, the Science Guy**, the host of the popular television show. Seen on screens, he offers an entertaining explanation and overview of the concept and purpose behind Innoventions.

Sega occupies a large space, where kids love to try out the numerous new and proposed video games. Also included is an area just for younger kids, with pint-size games and educational computer programs.

At the **AT&T** area, interactive exhibits deliver a straightforward introduction to the Internet as well as direct TV, a wireless satellite system now accessible through AT&T.

IBM features new ways to think, work, and play with your computer. Try out some of IBM's newest technologies, such as speech recognition and face morphing, plus ThinkPad and Aptiva computers loaded with a host of multimedia software.

Discover magazine holds an annual awards program at Epcot to honor the most innovative minds in science. Guests can learn about the technologies developed by finalists and winners in a permanent display area.

Silicon Graphics has several computers on which guests can try out simulation software, redecorate a room instantly with the click of a mouse via design software, and explore the World Wide Web. This space also presents three virtual-reality experiences, including an Aladdin-themed magic carpet ride demonstration, a virtual tour of an Egyptian tomb, and hands-on virtual skiing.

A see-through Audio-Animatronics figure named Alec Tronic hosts an amusing show in the **Live Wire Theater**, providing an opportunity to observe how the technology works.

The popular **Enel** exhibit takes guests through a computer-based version of St. Peter's Basilica in Rome, to demonstrate how we can "travel" without leaving home.

For an introduction to movies on demand and interactive shopping and games, check out the **Time Warner Full Service Network**. This is the only public forum in the world where guests can freely explore television on demand (in which viewers download desired programs via remote control) until the technology's national rollout in 1998.

Some of the exhibits shown on the west side of Innoventions include the entertaining **House of Innoventions**, presented by Honeywell. In a sample kitchen, living room, bathroom, and bedroom, representatives demonstrate (to no more than 25 guests at a time) the latest ideas to help make home life a little easier and more relaxing by fully automating some of our daily tasks. Some of the products highlighted include home security systems,

Robochef, breakfast express, flash-bake ovens, remote-control toilets (with heated seats), a combination automatic washer-dryer, and an automatic root system irrigation (for plants). But our favorite is Honeywell's Total Home—a computer that fully automates all of the above, plus the lighting, heating, and cooling systems, most appliances, and more.

At **Motorola**, an Audio-Animatronics figure named Sky Cyberguy hosts a funny show, inviting guests to choose one of three paths for a trip on Motorola's Information Skyway. It's also possible to try out wireless two-way radios that allow you to talk to your family at the other end of the exhibit, personal digital assistants, handwriting recognition software, and pagers. But the big attraction here is the popular virtual-reality exhibit, where guests line up to be immersed in a virtual game world while others watch on monitors.

General Electric displays its newest products, from home appliances to jet engines, and offers the opportunity to be "interviewed" by Jay Leno (this one draws a crowd).

Family PC sponsors an exhibit showcasing multimedia technologies. Here, families get a chance to try the latest computer hardware and software. Among the highlights for kids are interactive animated storybooks, including CD-ROMs reprising the latest Disney animated features. **Apple** also has plenty of its latest computers and software on hand for the curious to try.

The **General Motors** display, developed in part by Walt Disney Imagineering, allows guests to "test drive" a new electric vehicle called EV1, enhanced by surround-sound and scenery, and see the inner workings of the technology in a cutaway model.

Another interesting stop is the **Hammacher Schlemmer** display, where guests see how the company tests new products for utility, wearability, and uniqueness. Guests can experience the most sophisticated application of interactive shopping under development. It is so advanced that it will not be on the market for several years.

There are also several restaurants and an espresso bar and bakery in the Innoventions complex. See the *Good Meals, Great Times* chapter for details.

CENTORIUM: This large, sleek shop stocks a vast selection of Epcot and Disney character memorabilia and souvenirs—watches, books, key chains, T-shirts, pencils, hats, and much more—making this the number one source for character merchandise in Epcot. In addition, there are all kinds of items related to other areas of Future World, such as Figment dolls, along with a large selection of Disney-themed sports apparel and children's clothing.

ART OF DISNEY EPCOT GALLERY: Upstairs from Centorium is Epcot's new spot for a unique assortment of Disney collectibles. The shop showcases a wide variety of Disney animation art, including production cels, hand-painted limited-edition cels, sericels, maquettes (character models), fine art serigraphs, and lithographs. In addition, a large selection of decorative items includes renditions of Disney characters by such well-known companies as Lladró.

The Living Seas

A trip four fathoms deep into the Caribbean Sea awaits. The Living Seas is the largest facility ever dedicated to humanity's relationship with the ocean, and was designed by the Disney Imagineers, in cooperation with a board of some of the world's most distinguished oceanographic experts and scientists.

At the entrance is a stylized rockwork marquee that suggests a natural coastline, with waves cascading into tidal pools. Inside, a 125-foot-long sea mural leads to a display depicting advances in undersea exploration,

from Leonardo da Vinci's sketches of underwater breathing devices and submersibles to photos of John Lethbridge's diving barrel and Frederic de Drieberg's 1809 breathing device. Also featured is the diving suit from Walt Disney's classic film *20,000 Leagues Under the Sea*, and the actual 11-foot-long model *Nautilus* used in the movie. Next, a 2½-minute multimedia presentation provides an introduction, saluting the pioneers of ocean research, beginning with early ships, diving bells, submarines, and aqualungs. The show also features a seven-minute film that attempts to demonstrate the critical role of the ocean as a source of energy, minerals, and protein. Some scenes were filmed in very remote parts of the world.

From there, a ride through a simulated Caribbean coral reef environment and the hands-on activities of Sea Base Alpha combine to prolong visitors' stay. The Coral

Reef restaurant offers fresh seafood in a setting where diners look out at the coral reef through acrylic windows 18 feet high and 8 inches thick. Tables are arranged on tiers so that all patrons have an unobstructed view. Presented by United Technologies.

CARIBBEAN CORAL REEF RIDE: To reach the two-passenger sea cabs that make the trip to the coral reef, visitors enter "hydrolators," elevatorlike capsules that actually descend about an inch while creating the illusion of diving deep under the sea. The man-made reef exists in an enormous 6-million-gallon tank (203 feet in diameter and 27 feet deep), where more than 65 species of sea life coexist in a simulated environment that accurately re-creates the chemistry and life-support ecosystems of the Caribbean Sea. Among the 5,000 inhabitants are sea turtles, parrot fish, puffers, barracuda, butterfly fish, angelfish, sharks, croakers, dolphins, and diamond rays.

In addition to the vast array of sea life and vegetation, guests also get to see scuba divers testing and demonstrating the newest diving gear and underwater monitoring equipment as they carry on training experiments with dolphins. Wireless radios allow the divers to talk to onlookers and explain their work. Other undersea attractions include a diver in a JIM suit, the latest in atmospheric diving-wear technology (at Sea Base Alpha, guests have the chance to try one on personally), two one-person submarines, and two mini-robotic submersibles.

Here, scientists had to develop foods to simulate the taste, chemistry, and nutritional value of natural coral. The resulting meal for parrot fish, for example, consists of dry dog food, chickens' laying pellets, a complete amino-acid solution, and a vitamin B-complex solution, all held together by dental plaster. Following the three-minute ride, guests are conveniently deposited at Sea Base Alpha.

SEA BASE ALPHA: This prototype undersea research facility, spread over two levels, includes a visitors center and six modules, each dedicated to a specific subject. One module focuses on ocean ecosystems and shows various forms of adaptation, including camouflage, symbiosis, and bioluminescence. A 6,000-gallon tank displays another coral reef where Bermuda morays, barracuda, and bonnethead sharks swim about. Another module is dedicated to the study of porpoises and manatees. A large holding tank features a step-in port, where guests can see the mammals up close. At another station, a show stars an Audio-Animatronics submersible named Jason who describes for visitors the history of robotics and their use in underwater exploration. In the same area, guests can try on a cutaway JIM suit, and test its maneuverability by doing a series of tasks as part of a game. There are also video screens where visitors can test and expand their knowledge of oceanography.

SEA BASE CONCOURSE: Adjacent to the six modules, the concourse features three displays. The floor-to-ceiling diver lockout chamber is where the crew enters and exits the ocean environment. Visitors can see divers enter the chamber, ascend, and disappear through the ceiling. A full-size mock-up of the latest one-person submersible vehicle, the Deep Rover, is suspended from the mezzanine of the concourse. The Deep Rover is capable of descending more than 3,000 feet below the ocean's surface.

The Land

Occupying six acres, this enormous sky-lighted pavilion examines the nature of one of everybody's favorite topics—food. A film, *Circle of Life,* uses characters from *The Lion King* to deliver an entertaining yet inspirational message about humanity and the environment. A boat ride explores farming in the past and future, including a look at ongoing experiments in raising fish. Guided tours give visitors the chance to learn more about the experimental agricultural techniques actually being practiced in the pavilion and nearby greenhouses, and to get ideas about applications in their own garden. In addition, the subject of nutrition is touched upon in one of Future World's wackiest attractions, a musical show called Food Rocks.

Since this is also the home of two of Epcot's most interesting eating spots—the Garden Grill and the Sunshine Season Food Fair—The Land is understandably popular. During peak seasons, lengthy queues build up for both the boat ride and *Circle of Life.* The best plan is to visit early in the morning, have a quick breakfast at the food court, and perhaps make priority seating arrangements for the character lunch in Garden Grill. Or wait until later in the afternoon, when many people have left Future World for World Showcase. Count on spending about an hour at The Land, or longer if plans include eating here. Presented by Nestlé USA.

LIVING WITH THE LAND: This 13½-minute boat ride through the rain forest and greenhouses in this pavilion opens with a dramatic storm scene. Guests sail through tropical swamps, prairie grain fields, and a family farm. As the boat passes through each amazingly realistic setting, the guide offers commentary on mankind's ongoing struggle to cultivate and live in harmony with the land. Note some of the details that make each setting so convincing, such as water dripping from leaves in the rain forest, sand blowing over the desert, and light flickering from the television set in the farmhouse window.

In the next segment, guests enter a fantastic living-plant research laboratory-solarium. Here, the earth's major food crops, fruits, and vegetables are being grown in high-tech research projects along with rare new crops that may someday help meet the earth's ever-growing dietary needs. The guide on each boat gives an interesting and educational talk on the crops being grown. Also of interest are the experiments being conducted to explore the possibilities of raising fish like other farm products, and the Desert Farm area, where plants receive nutrients through a drip irrigation system that delivers just the right amount of water, and no more—important in an arid climate.

As fantastic and unreal as they appear, all the plants on view in the experimental greenhouses are living. In contrast, those in the biomes (ecological communities) were manufactured in Disney studios out of flexible, lightweight plastic that simulates the cellulose found in real trees. The trunks and branches were molded from live specimens; the majestic sycamore in the farmhouse's front yard, for example, duplicates one that stands outside a Burbank, California, car wash. Hundreds of thousands of polyethylene leaves, made in Hong Kong, were then snapped on. These are fire retardant, as are the blades of grass, which are made of glass fibers implanted into rubber mats. In the South American rain forest scene, the water on the leaves and trunks is supplied by a special drip system that provides a constant flow of moisture.

CIRCLE OF LIFE: This 20-minute film uses animation and live footage to illustrate some of the dangers to our environment, as well as potential solutions. Presented as a fable featuring *The Lion King* favorites Simba, Timon, and Pumbaa, the film takes an optimistic approach to a serious subject. *Circle of Life* is shown in the 428-seat Harvest Theater (near The Land's entrance) on a 23- by 60-foot screen. To set the mood, the movie opens with a stunning live-action animal sequence that recalls the animated "Circle of Life" scene from *The Lion King.*

As the animated part of the film begins, Simba is startled by the shout of "Timber!" and is drenched by the splash of a fallen tree in the water. The culprits are none other than his friends, Timon and Pumbaa, who are clearing the savanna for the development of the Hakuna Matata Lakeside Village. Simba seizes the opportunity to tell the tale, passed on to him by his father, of creatures who sometimes forget that everything is connected in the great Circle of Life: humans. Simba demonstrates to Timon and Pumbaa the consequences of progress, as his lessons are driven home by motion-picture views of humans' mistreatment of the air, water, and land. (Timon: And everybody was *okay* with this?) Simba continues to explain what humans are doing to fix the mistakes of the past and improve the environment, and in the process, convinces Timon and Pumbaa to abandon their development plans. The overall effect is a compelling mix of entertainment and a valuable message about environmental responsibility.

FOOD ROCKS: Classic rock 'n' roll songs have been humorously altered to deliver a nutritional message at this 15-minute mock rock concert. The introduction, presented by

a "heavy metal" group—three four-foot kitchen utensils atop a cartoon stove—perform Queen's "Bohemian Rhapsody" with new lyrics. The show is set in a kitchen of cartoonish proportion, and life-size characters make this an entertaining show. The show is hosted by Füd Wrapper, inspired by rapper Tone Loc. He steers the audience through the kitchen, performing and introducing the guests.

Next, the refrigerator door opens and the whole stage is filled with eerie blue light and fog. A group emerges led by a milk carton wearing dark glasses. They are identified as The Refrigerator Police, and they perform a parody of The Police's hit "Every Breath You Take." The new words come with a message: "Every bite you take, every cake you bake, every milk you shake, every egg you break, will be part of you."

Other musical guests include the Peach Boys, an apple, pear, orange, and peach who harmonize a rendition of "Good Vibrations" called "Good Nutrition;" Pita Gabriel sings to the tune of "Sledgehammer;" and The Sole of Rock 'n' Roll, a fish inspired by Cher, sings a new version of the "Shoop Shoop Song." Neil Moussaka, Chubby Cheddar, the Get-the-Point-Sisters, and (Little) Richard also make humorous appearances.

It's interesting to note that Tone Loc, Chubby Checker, Neil Sedaka, Little Richard, and The Pointer Sisters actually recorded the parodies of their music. In the pre-show area, there are murals featuring fun food facts, three-dimensional food pyramids, and interactive "meal kabobs" where guests can create their own nutritional menus. Six giant "smell boxes" open to reveal the aromas garlic, chocolate, coffee, bacon, orange, and seafood. Don't miss the colorful carpeting with its pattern of forks, knives, and spoons.

GREENHOUSE TOUR: For guests who are interested in a more detailed look at the growing areas at The Land, one-hour guided tours take place throughout the day. The tour travels through four themed greenhouses where plants are grown hydroponically (without soil). Different areas of the greenhouses showcase pioneering research projects undertaken in cooperation with NASA and the U.S. Department of Agriculture. Highlights include two laboratories added in 1994 as part of the tenth-anniversary renovation of The Land. In the biotechnology lab, researchers use tissue culture and genetic engineering to enhance plant life. The integrated pest-management lab offers a look at the science of controlling insect and disease pests in plants. Because this walking tour is an expanded version of The Living with the Land boat ride, the ride is a suggested prerequisite. Reservations, which are required, must be made in person early on the day of the tour, at the podium at the Green Thumb Emporium. Cost is $6 for adults and $4 for children three to nine.

GREEN THUMB EMPORIUM: This little shop between the Sunshine Season Food Fair and Food Rocks stocks merchandise such as hydroponic plants, seeds, books, topiaries, and kitchen accessories, including magnets, place mats, and more.

Journey Into Imagination

The oddly shaped glass pyramids that house Journey Into Imagination (immediately to your right as you face World Showcase Lagoon) are striking. But they pale in comparison with the experiences inside, which are easily among the most whimsical at Epcot. Dreamfinder, a jolly, red-headed, professorial figure—sporting a carrot-colored beard and accompanied by a purple baby dragon called Figment—is only one of the pavilion's delights. He appears in person outside and again inside when he escorts guests through the world of imagination during a 14-minute ride.

There's also a dazzling 3-D movie, called Honey, I Shrunk the Audience. Not to mention the electronic fun house known as Image Works. Or the quirky fountains outside—the Jellyfish Fountains, which spurt streams of water that spread out at the top, looking for an instant like their namesake sea creature; or the Leap Frog Fountains, which send out smooth streams of water that arc from one garden plot to another in the most astonishing fashion. Kids particularly love these.

Plant lovers will recognize the sculpted trees in this garden as *podocarpus*—the same type that is planted in many other locations (but pruned to many different shapes) throughout Epcot.

Count on spending an hour and 15 minutes at the very least at this pavilion—two hours wouldn't be too long at all. During peak seasons, the queue outside seems to be longest from about 10 A.M. to noon and remains fairly lengthy throughout most of the day. Early mornings and late evenings are the least congested times to visit. Presented by Kodak.

JOURNEY INTO IMAGINATION RIDE: It is here that Dreamfinder creates Figment out of a lizard's body, a crocodile's nose, a steer's horns, two big yellow eyes, two small wings, and a pinch of childish delight—and commences the visitor's journey into the world of imagination.

First-timers may perceive the 14-minute ride as a random assortment of scenes that are handsome and scary by turns; but it is actually an organized exploration of how the imagination works and the areas of life in which it functions.

First there is a visit to the Dreamport, the area of the mind to which the senses are constantly sending data to be stored for later use by the imagination. Subsequent scenes depict the way imagination suffuses the worlds of the visual and performing arts, literature, and science and technology. In the course of all this, laser beams dance, lightning crackles, and letters pour out of a giant typewriter like notes from an organ. The images are as fanciful as the imagination itself.

It's interesting to note that the iridescent painting-in-progress on the wall in the visual arts scene—a so-called "polage" produced by refracting light through polarized filters—is the largest of its kind anywhere. When you see flashing lights (about three-quarters of the way through the ride), be sure to sit up straight and smile—your picture is being taken. You'll see your photo at the end of the ride.

IMAGE WORKS: It's a rare Image Works visitor who doesn't experience at least some of the emotion felt by one four-year-old girl who cried every time her parents tried to take her home. That's not surprising, because Image Works is literally crammed with activities that give every visitor the chance to use his or her imagination.

For instance, at Dreamfinder's School of Drama, near the entrance to the Image Works, visitors have the opportunity to be in a TV show. Guests step onto a small stage and, thanks to a Chroma-Key video-effects technique involving foreground and

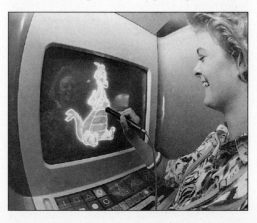

background matting, perform in short video stories. Spectators and performers alike see the results as they happen via video screens. It's always fun to watch the groups of senior citizens, teenagers, or families jumping crazily around on stage following on-screen instructions from Dreamfinder. (And, in fact, having the leisure to spend more than just a few seconds watching these goings-on is sufficient reason to allot more time to your overall Epcot visit.)

Another exhibit at Image Works is Figment's Coloring Book, where guests use computer technology to paint giant coloring-book images of Figment and Dreamfinder. The Sensor is a sort of electronic maze whose various elements react to a visitor's presence by producing lights and sounds. Upon entering the Rainbow Corridor, you'll find a tunnel of neon tubes in all the hues of the rainbow. Image Warp's pneumatically powered Mylar mirrors produce moving versions of old-style fun house reflections in a room wackily illuminated by strobe lights. Then there's the Lumia—a plastic ball seven feet in diameter inside which swirling patterns of light and color appear in response to sounds of different frequencies and intensities. Another feature is Making Faces, a set of screens that allow you to electronically capture your own image and then apply different noses, hairstyles, ears, eyes, even accessories.

At Stepping Tones, hexagonal splotches of colored light on the floor correspond to sounds—a drumroll, a flourish on the harp, a couple of chords sung by a men's chorus, a snippet of hoedown fiddling, and such—emitted when the area is trod upon; the last red hexagon in the room, located in the corner farthest from the entrance, sends out the sound of a beautiful chord played on a harp. In fact, the first tones re-create the music heard in *Close Encounters of the Third Kind*. The floor was "orchestrated" by an avant-garde San Francisco Bay Area composer so that all possible combinations sound interesting at the very least—and the more the merrier. In the Mirage Room, Figment stars in a series of animated sequences using a unique holographic process. At Optical Illusion, you'll see an animated hot-air balloon race between Figment and Dreamfinder.

Other activities include Light Writer, which involves drawing geometric patterns with laser beams, and the Magic Palette, where a special stylus and a touch-sensitive control surface can be used to create all kinds of images, mostly in Day-Glo colors. People often queue up to try these, while the huge kaleidoscopes and the unusual pin screens nearby are practically overlooked. Manufacturing the latter involved putting thousands of straight pins through a screen illuminated with colored lights from below (visitors run their hands across the bottom, thereby creating sweeping patterns of color).

The Electronic Philharmonic, one of the most amusing sections of the Image Works, allows guests to take turns conducting an orchestra. Here's how this works: Each patch of light on the console represents a group of instruments (strings, woodwinds, brass, percussion). Raising and lowering one's hand above that patch of light increases and decreases the volume of the sound produced by that section of the "orchestra." The faster the movement, the louder they play.

Just outside Image Works, note the terrific photography display. The images are winners of Kodak's International Newspaper Snapshot Awards, and well worth a look.

HONEY, I SHRUNK THE AUDIENCE: Welcome to the Imagination Institute, workplace of Professor Wayne Szalinski, the featured character in the two hit "Honey" movies, *Honey, I Shrunk the Kids* and *Honey, I Blew Up the Kid*. Rick Moranis, Marcia Strassman, and the kids reprise their film roles at this 30-minute attraction.

In the pre-show area, guests see a movie about the imagination. Then they are welcomed to the Imagination Institute and given an overview of what they will see inside the theater. Szalinski is to be presented with the Inventor of the Year Award, and will demonstrate several of his inventions. On the way into the theater, guests are given "protective goggles" (3-D glasses), to shield their eyes from flying debris that can come loose during new-product demonstrations.

Once the audience is seated, Szalinski is nowhere to be found. Then he zooms off the screen in his new HoverPod, out of control and miniaturized by his shrinking machine. Szalinski's son Nick steps in to demonstrate the "Dimensional Duplicator," a machine that can make exact copies of anything. As Nick switches on the machine, his little brother Adam drops his pet mouse into the duplicating chamber, hits the number 999, and suddenly hundreds of mice pour out of the screen in an almost 4-D effect that leaves guests squirming. It's so realistic, you might be inspired to stand on your chair!

Nick quickly gets rid of the mice with Professor Szalinski's No-Mess Holographic Pet System, which projects a 3-D cat out into the audience to scare away the mice. The cat morphs into a lynx and finally into a ferocious lion before overheating and exploding. Just then, Szalinski returns, blows himself up to normal size, and demonstrates his new, more powerful shrinking machine. The machine spins out of control and accidentally shrinks the audience and Nick. While the audience is miniaturized the theater shakes with every on-screen footstep. When apparent giants crouch down to ogle guests in the theater, it's a rare person who doesn't feel diminished to ant proportions. The effects are very believable, particularly when Adam picks up the theater and shows it to his mom. Motion effects in the theater add to the realism, as does the full-size pet snake that gets loose. The audience is eventually brought back to normal size, of course, although not without incident. The attraction has one last surprise in store that we won't divulge.

CAMERAS AND FILM: A good selection of film is for sale here, along with cameras, filters, and other photographic essentials.

Test Track

This ground-breaking General Motors pavilion, slated to open in May 1997 in the spot formerly occupied by the World of Motion, is among the most keenly anticipated in Epcot history. For while its predecessor did justice to its mission—regaling guests with a trip through the past, present, and future of transportation—Test Track has greater aspirations. The attraction is not just a thrill ride in a theme park where such things are conspicuous. It is a thrill ride of the highest order, a blockbuster that promises to push Epcot to the fore of visitors' attention. Equally important, Test Track honors the park's larger mission to educate as well as entertain.

More precisely, this new industrial-looking pavilion puts guests through the rather frenetic motions of automobile testing. As ride vehicles progress along the nearly mile-long track, they will whiz down straightaways, hug hairpin turns, accelerate up steep inclines, and face near-collisions—and not always on ideal road conditions. En route, riders learn firsthand how tests are performed in real facilities (called proving grounds) and discover why certain procedures are crucial to automotive safety. Ultimately, they walk away with invaluable insight into cars, not to mention new respect for the complex systems therein.

Before developing the attraction, Disney Imagineers toured GM proving grounds around the country. The result: From

the roll-up doors of its steely facade to the rows of authentic testing equipment inside, Test Track bears more than a passing resemblance to the real thing.

The experience begins with a 20-minute pre-show, a walking tour of the plant that reveals the incredible amount of component testing performed before automakers commit to production. Guests witness 21 true-to-life automotive testing vignettes, with everything from human interface (our courageous, crash-prone counterparts) to tires, brakes, air bags, and even seats being put through their paces. Video monitors explain the purposes of many of the tests.

At the end of this winding queue, visitors are invited 48 at a time into a briefing room. Here, they are directed to climb into their test vehicles, fasten their (standard) seat belts, and prepare to embark on Test Track's five-minute ride segment. Each car seats six. The prototype vehicles, computer-designed and controlled, travel completely independent of one another on the automated test track. Equipped with video and audio, but no steering wheels or brake pedals, they are sporty and buggy-like. The roads themselves bear the familiar yellow lines and signage of the real world, adding to the attraction's realism.

The rough-and-tumble ride begins on the the building's lowest level with an uphill acceleration test over a 16% grade. Then the suspension gets a workout, as the vehicles descend over a very bumpy surface that puts the wheels at odds with one another. Back on the lower level, guests learn by experience how antilock braking systems (ABS) work and, in one of the attraction's more tangible lessons—why ABS are extremely handy when you need to stop suddenly. There are actually two brake tests, one with ABS and one with traditional brakes. Vehicles get going up to 25 miles per hour, then brake to make a quick curve. Without ABS, the vehicles can't negotiate the turn. During environmental testing, riders feel the heat and get the shivers as vehicles pass first through a radiant heat chamber, then a cold chamber. Roadside robots pitch in by spraying the fenders and door panels with water to test for corrosion.

During the road-handling segment, the ride takes a dramatic turn. Vehicles course along a winding road, complete with simulated mountain scenery, and into a darkened tunnel. Passengers hear a horn blast, see the blinding high beams of a tractor trailer, and swerve to avoid the truck. As they emerge and the light level picks up, there is a crash, and guests round a corner to witness a barrier crash test. Their own vehicles then accelerate toward the same barrier. Just when a collision seems imminent, doors open up and the vehicles emerge outside on an elevated track. A long straightaway feeds into a series of heavily banked (about 45-degree) turns and another straight shot that sends vehicles rocketing around the front of the pavilion at top speed. Strobe lights add to the effect. (Displays in the vehicles register real-time data so guests know what tests are being conducted at any given time.) Upon reentering the building, there's one final hurrah before guests disembark: thermal imaging screens that illuminate friction points in the vehicle, pointing to areas prone to excessive wear and tear. So ends a wild and wonderful trip that also happens to be the fastest and, at 5,200 feet, longest Disney ride.

In the post-show area, a demo of smart-car technology, a multimedia presentation on auto assembly, and an automotive boutique are among the highlights. General Motors' latest models and concept cars will also be on display here.

Note: Children under seven years old must be accompanied by an adult; guests under 40 inches tall are not permitted to ride; signs note that passengers must be free of back problems, heart conditions, motion sickness, and other physical limitations to ride. On a separate note, guests visiting prior to the ride's mid-1997 debut can stop by the Test Track Preview Center for a sneak peek of the attraction and a close look at GM cars.

Horizons

For generations, visionaries have been making predictions about life in the future. Jules Verne forecast rockets that would fly like bullets. The 19th-century French artist Albert Robida envisioned subways and dirigible taxis and sketched what life in Paris would be like in 1950. And in the 1930s, pulp science-fiction magazines circulated ideas about automatic barber chairs that would give their owners shoeshines and haircuts, air conditioners that would pipe in alpine chills, robots that would do housework, and suntan lamps and televisions.

The three-acre Horizons show, which draws on the wisdom of countless scientists,

adds its own predictions in a pavilion located between Test Track and Wonders of Life, just beyond Innoventions. After a nod to the visions of earlier centuries in a Looking Back at Tomorrow sequence, the pavilion's continuously moving, suspended, four-passenger vehicles convey guests into the OmniSphere Theatre. Here, on a pair of spectacular hemispherical screens (80 feet in diameter), projectors with special lenses show filmed scenes of a Space Shuttle launch and of growing crystals, together with animated sequences of life in a space colony, a DNA chain, computer chips, and more. All this is a prelude to a voyage through a series of sets demonstrating aspects of life in the future.

At the first destination, called Nova Cite, advanced transportation systems (such as trains that work by magnetic levitation) and sophisticated communication devices (including holographic telephones) keep members of far-flung families in touch with one another.

Next, in the Mesa Verde segment, voice-controlled crop-harvesting robots and genetically engineered fruits and vegetables occupy a once-arid desert. Overhead, "hoverlifts" with spinning blades function as automatic shade controls, and "helium lifters" drop hooks down to fields to collect baskets of the harvest from the robots, and fly the produce off to market. In the future farmer's home, shown nearby, there's an electronic pantry that delivers food to the inhabitants at the push of a button and a home communications center where youngsters can study math (or other subjects) by computer.

In the Sea Castle sequence, depicting a movable—but otherwise islandlike—floating city in the Pacific, schoolchildren take underwater field trips to nearby mining and kelp-farming operations operated by robot devices. And in Omega Centauri, a free-floating colony in space, crystals are grown for use by computers back on Earth and colony inhabitants keep in shape in a health-and-recreation center that features games like zero-gravity basketball (seen in shadow along the rear wall), and rowing and bicycling in simulators that allow space folk the opportunity to pursue their favorite sport in any environment they choose. Boaters, for instance, may shoot the Colorado River's rapids in the Grand Canyon, or paddle a Louisiana bayou, or float through the canals of Venice. Home life is just like that on Earth, but with a couple of twists: When a boy newly arrived at the colony doesn't put on his shoes in the morning, he floats away. (They're magnetic shoes, designed for this zero-gravity environment.) And when the family gets together to celebrate a birthday, those who can't attend in person put in an appearance via a holographic telephone.

There's another fine experience at the ride's conclusion: Visitors pick the journey's ending. Just push a button, and a special audience-polling device inside your vehicle delivers the 30-second experience that the majority of your fellow riders have requested. The car tilts back and vibrates, and the sound effects enhance the sensation of great speed created by fast-moving, close-up filmed visuals of travel on land, by sea, and in space.

Trivia buffs will be curious about the sources of the science-fiction clips presented in the Looking Back at Tomorrow sequence. These include the films *Metropolis* (1926) and *Woman in the Moon* (1928) by the director Fritz Lang; *Mars and Beyond* and *Magic Highways U.S.A.*, shown on the "Disneyland" programs of the 1950s; and Woody Allen's *Sleeper* (1973).

Note: Plans call for significant renovations to Horizons. A completely new attraction is scheduled for this pavilion in the future.

Wonders of Life

The 72-foot-tall steel DNA molecule at the entrance to this popular pavilion beckons guests to humorous and informative experiences related to health. Housed in a 100,000-square-foot geodesic dome and two attached buildings, this attraction allows guests to enjoy both a serious and an amusing look at health, fitness, and modern lifestyles. Wonders also boasts Body Wars, Epcot's first authentic thrill ride—a fast and furious journey through the human body.

From outside the gold-topped dome, the Wonders of Life sign seems to rest on the flumes of water shot up by two fountains. Once inside the building, guests find themselves at the Fitness Fairgrounds. A mobile measuring 50 feet in diameter is suspended from the 65-foot ceiling, where it swings gently in the air currents circulating the building.

At the Fairgrounds, a variety of shows and activities for both children and adults are offered. *Goofy About Health* is an eight-minute multiscreen montage that sees Goofy go from a sloppy-living guy to a health-conscious fellow. Using old Goofy cartoons that haven't been seen for many years, the show traces Goofy's ups and downs, and winds up with new footage of Goofy at his doctor's office. The film is shown in a 100-seat open theater where visitors can come and go as they wish.

At the AnaComical Players Theater, a corny (but nonetheless informative) show is presented by an improvisational theater group. Audience members are asked to participate, and it's all a lot of fun. This theater seats 100 people. The third theater at the Fitness Fairgrounds is enclosed. The 14-minute film shown here, *The Making of Me*, is a story starring Martin Short as a man who wonders how he came into existence. To find out, he travels back in time to the birth of his parents, their first few years together, and their decision to have a child—him. Footage from an actual delivery is part of the film; it is sensitively presented and provides a tangible and touching view of childbirth. It was written and directed by Glenn Gordon Caron, who directed the TV show "Moonlighting" and the film *Clean and Sober*. Parents should be aware, however, that the film is quite graphic and so may not be suitable for some children.

There are plenty of hands-on activities in areas surrounding the theaters. Guests can ride Wonder Cycles, computerized stationary bicycles that enable guests to pedal through a variety of locales including Disneyland and the Rose Parade. At Coach's Corner, golf, tennis, or baseball swings are analyzed, and a professional knowledgeable in each sport offers free, albeit taped, advice to help you on your way. The Sensory Funhouse offers hands-on activities for kids. It's the Disney

version of a children's museum, where education and entertainment go hand in hand.

At the Met Lifestyle Revue, guests punch in such information as age, weight, height, exercise habits, whether they smoke, and perceived stress levels at an interactive computer terminal. The computer then processes the information and offers some advice on how to lead a healthier and less stressful existence.

Frontiers of Medicine, located toward the rear of the Fitness Fairgrounds, features the only completely serious segment of Wonders of Life. Here guests can see some scientific and educational exhibits of leading developments in medicine and health sciences. The exhibits change regularly.

Pure & Simple offers a variety of healthy snacks. Nearby, Well & Goods, Ltd. offers men's, women's, and children's athletic wear, most of which features Disney characters participating in a variety of sports, and some educational materials. Presented by Met Life.

CRANIUM COMMAND: The third major area of Wonders of Life welcomes guests into the mind of a 12-year-old boy in this 17-minute show. The pre-show sets the mood as an animated film explains what you are about to see. General Knowledge is recruiting pilots for an assortment of new brains. There are jokes aplenty, many of which go right over the heads of young kids. Buzzy, our star pilot, fumbles through basic training and gets assigned to the most volatile brain of all, that of an adolescent boy.

Inside a 200-seat theater, the enormously exaggerated head of our 12-year-old subject is piloted by Buzzy, a delightfully corny Audio-Animatronics figure. The two large eyes are actually rear-projection video screens, and it is through them that the audience gets an idea of how a young boy thinks and reacts. The other animated participant, General Knowledge, helps Buzzy learn which portion of the mind is required for a particular situation. The right and left sides for the brain, the stomach, the heart, and the

adrenal gland are all represented by familiar celebrities. Our personal favorite is George Wendt (Norm from "Cheers") operating the stomach. Other characters include Bobcat Goldthwait as the adrenal gland, Dana Carvey and Kevin Nealon (Hans and Franz of "Saturday Night Live" fame) as the heart, Charles Grodin as the left brain, and John Lovitz as the right brain. It's an altogether whimsical and entertaining show—one of the best at Epcot. This is such a fast-paced show with so many details that you'll notice new things even after seeing it many times.

BODY WARS: The same state-of-the-art technology that sends guests on a rollicking five-minute ride through space at the Star Tours attraction at the Disney-MGM Studios also exists at Wonders of Life in the form of this thrill ride. After boarding the vehicles, which are actually the same type of flight simulators employed by military and commercial airlines in pilot training, guests are whisked away on a bumpy, rocky, and exciting ride through the human body. (When instructed to fasten your seatbelt, do so. This is a rough ride.) Movie buffs will think immediately of the film *Fantastic Voyage* and the more recent *Inner Space*. The queue area features exhibits from a fictional company specializing in the latest technology in the miniaturization of people. Guests pass through two special effects portals and are declared ready to do a routine medical probe of the human body—from the inside.

During the course of this bumpy trip, a scientist is dispatched to remove a splinter that has made its way beneath the patient's skin. Guests go along for the ride, but end up on a rescue mission when the scientist is attacked by a white blood cell. Of course, there are some problems along the way, making this trip seem out of control.

Note: This is a rougher ride than Star Tours at the Studios. Signs posted outside Body Wars warn that passengers must be free of back problems, heart conditions, motion sickness, and other such physical limitations. Pregnant women are not permitted to board. There is a minimum height requirement of 40 inches. Children under seven must be accompanied by an adult.

Universe of Energy

Although it's easy to spot this pavilion's mirrored, asymmetrical pyramid, the facade doesn't provide any clue at all to the 36 minutes of surprises in store. One of the most technologically complex experiences at Epcot, the show consists of three motion pictures and a ride-through segment. Not one of these is exactly what guests might expect. This is especially

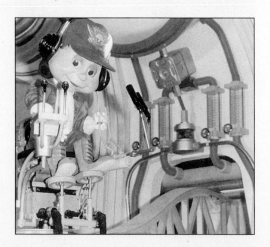

true after the pavilion's 1996 renovation, which repackaged the entire attraction, placing its legendary Audio-Animatronics dinosaurs and lofty environmental message in a decidedly comedic, and much more personal context.

The show begins with a new film, featuring a few folks whom most guests will recognize. A character named Ellen is in her living room watching a game show on which her college roommate Judy is a contestant. Ellen tries to play along at home, but keeps striking out, particularly in the ENERGY category. As she watches, neighbor Bill Nye, the Science Guy, comes over to borrow supplies for an experiment and is aghast at Ellen's ignorance. Bill leaves, and Ellen drifts off to sleep. She dreams she is on the game show competing against her friend Judy and Albert Einstein. The topic is ENERGY, and as Einstein ponders and Ellen fumbles, Judy gives the correct answer and wins. Ellen finishes with a negative score, and wakes up in a sweat.

The second segment, in an adjoining room, introduces two of Disney's most advanced Audio-Animatronics characters to date. Bill Nye is vowing to educate Ellen about the importance of energy. He shows her a brief film about the types of energy used today. Its vivid images of water, fire, burning coal, jet engines, and beautiful yellow flowers are the makings of a fine photo essay—with a twist: The projection surface is made up of 100 solid triangular elements, which rotate in synchronization with the changing images to produce what its creator (Czech filmmaker Emil Radok) described as a "kinetic mosaic."

Ellen is inspired by the film, and decides to go off in search of greater knowledge. Suddenly, the whole seating area rotates, and then breaks up into six smaller sections that move slowly forward—prompting a chorus of oohs and aahs from startled members of the audience. The vehicles embark with Ellen upon an odyssey through the primeval world—an otherworldly region of sulfur-scented air, eerie blue moonlight, unearthly fogs, and lava so ominously authentic that few visitors dare to reach out and touch it.

Huge prehistoric trees crowd the forest. Apatosauruses wallow in the lagoon out front. A lofty allosaurus battles dramatically with an armored stegosaurus a bit farther along, and an elasmosaurus bursts out of a tidal pool with frightening suddenness—all under the vulturelike gaze of winged creatures known as pteranodons. Then Ellen becomes trapped by a dinosaur. She screams for Bill's help, but ultimately manages to free herself, and departs apologizing to the dinosaurs for the intrusion. It's interesting to note that all of the dinosaurs

were created after months of research, including interviews with many well-known paleobotanists and paleontologists. The Audio-Animatronics animals here are the largest of their type ever to be fabricated.

Next, guests move out of the forest and view a fast-paced montage of pictures capturing the history of human civilization, from cave dwellers to the present. The issue of alternative energy sources is raised, and the underlying message communicated is that there is no save-all energy source, but rather many possibilities with promise. The attraction winds up with Ellen returning to the game show of her dreams. This time, she's beating her friend Judy by a long shot. She bets everything in the final round. In order to win, she must name the one energy source that will never be depleted.

Fully as intriguing as the attraction is the advanced technology behind it. The traveling vehicles weigh about 30,000 pounds when fully loaded with passengers. Yet they are guided along the floor by a wire only *one-eighth-inch thick*. Some of the pavilion's energy is generated by two acres of photovoltaic cells mounted on the roof. These cells generate enough energy to run six average homes. Presented by Exxon.

HOME GARDENERS SHOULD NOTE THAT THE SOUTHERN LIVE OAKS IMMEDIATELY TO THE EAST OF THE UNIVERSE OF ENERGY PAVILION WERE AMONG A HANDFUL STARTED FROM ACORNS FOR WALT DISNEY WORLD'S OPENING 25 YEARS AGO. SOME OF THEIR SIBLINGS ARE IN FRONT OF THE AMERICAN ADVENTURE IN WORLD SHOWCASE.

WORLD SHOWCASE

Noble sentiments about humanity and the fellowship of nations, which have motivated so many world's fairs in the past, also inhabit World Showcase. But make no mistake about it: This half of Epcot, located to the south of Future World, is unlike any previous international exposition.

It is instead a group of pavilions that encircle World Showcase Lagoon (a body of water that, incidentally, is the size of 85 football fields) to demonstrate Disney conceptions about participating countries in remarkably realistic, consistently entertaining styles. You won't find the real Germany here; rather, the country's essence, much as a traveler returning from a visit might remember what he or she saw. Shops, restaurants, and attractions are housed in a group of structures that is an artful pastiche of all the elements that give that nation's countryside and towns their distinctive flavor. Although occasional liberties have been taken when scale and proportion required, careful research governed the design of every nook and cranny.

In the shops, many of the wares on display represent the country in whose pavilion they are offered for sale. The food focuses on native cuisine, and the entertainment is as authentic as the Disney casting directors can make it, with native performers commonly featured and new festivities always in the works. Craftspeople are occasionally on hand to demonstrate their art in the appropriate shops. Thanks to special Epcot cultural exchange programs and the personnel

department's efforts to recruit nationals, nearly all the World Showcase staff members in restaurants, shops, and attractions were born in the countries the pavilions represent (or at least spent many years living there) to contribute still more atmosphere.

Home gardeners should be sure to note the World Showcase landscaping: Each pavilion's plantings closely approximate what would be found in the featured nation. The 1.3-mile World Showcase Promenade, which links pavilions on the shores of the World Showcase Lagoon, has its own interesting vegetation, beginning in World Showcase Plaza with 75-foot Washingtonia fan palms, Arizona-California natives that were imported to Central Florida. Underneath them is a garden full of rosebushes. All told, there are more than 10,000 tree roses, teas, grandifloras, and miniatures planted throughout World Showcase. The Y-shaped trees nearby are callery pears. The camphor trees encircling the lagoon on the promenade were planted to provide the walkway with welcome shade.

Keep in mind that since most of Future World closes at 7 P.M., World Showcase may become more congested at this time. We recommend taking in as many shows, rides, and films as possible in the afternoon, and saving the shops for the pleasant evening hours.

Pavilions are described here in the order that they would be encountered while moving counterclockwise (west to east) around the World Showcase Lagoon after crossing the bridge from Future World.

Canada

Celebrating the beauties of America's neighbor to the north, the area devoted to the western hemisphere's largest nation is complete with its own mountain, waterfall, rushing stream, rocky canyon, mine, and splendid garden massed with colorful flowers. There's even a totem pole, a trading post, and an elaborate, mansard-roofed hotel similar to ones built by the Canadian railroads as they pushed west around the turn of the century. All this is imaginatively arranged somewhat like a split-level house, with the section representing French Canada on top, and another devoted to the mountains alongside it and below. From a distance, the Hôtel du Canada, the main building here, looks like little more than a bump on the landscape—as does Epcot's single Canadian Rocky Mountain. But up close they both seem to tower as high as the real thing, thanks to the motion picture designers' technique known as forced perspective, which exaggerates the relative smallness of distant parts of a structure to make the totality appear taller than it really is.

The gardens were inspired by the Butchart Gardens in Victoria, British Columbia, a famous park created on the site of a limestone quarry. The hotel is modeled after Ottawa's Victorian-style Château Laurier.

Willow, birch, sweet gum, plum, and maple trees can all be found in the Victoria Gardens; Canada's hemlocks are represented here by deodar cedars, a Himalaya native that can withstand torrid Florida summers with aplomb.

Lively, engaging entertainment is provided by Canadian folk dancers and the Caledonia Bagpipe Band.

O CANADA!: This 17-minute motion picture, presented in Circle-Vision 360 inside Canada's mountain, portrays the Canadian confederation in all its coast-to-coast splendor—the prairies and plains, sparkling shorelines and rivers, and untouched snowfields and rocky mountainsides. The Royal Canadian Mounted Police also put in an appearance. All the maritime provinces are pictured, with their covered bridges and sailing ships, as is Montreal, with its Old World cafés and imposing churches; the scene in the Cathédrale de Notre Dame, with its organ booming and choirboys in attendance, is particularly stirring. The great outdoors gets equal play. In one scene, Canada snow geese take off all around the screen, and the beating of their wings is positively thunderous. Eagles, possums, mallards, bobcats, wolves, bears, deer, bison, and herds of reindeer all were filmed. Filmed too were steers being roped at a rodeo and the chuck wagon race that takes place every year at that great provincial fair known as the Calgary Stampede. Skiers in the vast and empty Bugaboos, dogsledders, and ice skaters are featured in the winter scenes; in a hockey game, the sound system almost perfectly conveys the scratch of skates on ice and the sharp whack of sticks against a puck. And throughout, the motion picture conveys a sense of the vast size of Canada, providing a you-are-there feeling that makes all of this spectacular scenery still more memorable.

This is partly due to the filming technique called Circle-Vision 360 (also used to obtain footage for the Magic Kingdom attraction, The Timekeeper). It involves a camera rig composed of nine individual cameras arranged around a tubular shaft containing the motor that drives the mechanisms for all the cameras. In some scenes the rig was suspended from a helicopter; when depicting the precision-flying Canadian Snowbirds, Canada's equivalent to the U.S. Air Force's Thunderbirds, it was mounted on a B-25 bomber; in the Calgary sequence, it was placed in one of the racing buckboards; and in the reindeer roundup scene, which took place on the edge of the Arctic Ocean, it was concealed by burlap. Note that there are no seats in this theater.

NORTHWEST MERCANTILE: The first shop to the left upon entering the pavilion's plaza on the way to the Hôtel du Canada features heavy lumberjack shirts, maple syrup, and other wares that trappers might have purchased back in pioneering days. Skeins of rope, tin scoops, lanterns, and a pair of antique ice skates hanging from the long beams overhead set the mood, together with the structure itself. This shop, like the adjacent Trading Post, is built of adze-hewn logs and ornamented by stone statues, masks, and paintings done in the style of the Ojibwa Indians. Located to the store's rear

are Indian artifacts and assorted souvenirs—items like fur vests and moccasins, and sleek-lined sculptures (some made of imitation marble and some carved in soapstone by the Inuit). Notable are several hand-crafted Canadian items that are seldom seen elsewhere in the American market.

United Kingdom

In the space of only a few hundred feet, visitors to this pavilion stroll from an elegant London square to the edge of a canal in the rural countryside—via a bustling urban English street framed by buildings that constitute a veritable rhapsody of historic architectural styles. But one scene leads to the next so smoothly that nothing ever seems amiss. Here again, note the attention to detail: the half-timbered High Street structure that actually leans a bit, the hand-painted "smoke" stains that make the chimneys look as if they had been there for centuries. When a thatched roof is required, it's right where it should be—though the roof may be made of plastic broom bristles because fire regulations prohibit the real thing. London plane trees, so common in British cities, are represented, and a sundial punctuates the promenade. Off to the side is a pair of scarlet phone booths identical to those that used to be found all around the U.K. And there are eight different architectural styles characteristic of the streetscapes, from English Tudor to Georgian and English Victorian.

There is no major attraction in this pavilion; instead, it features half a dozen fine shops and a pub that serves a selection of British-brewed beers and ales that would be the toast of any first class "local" in London itself. There's also plenty of good entertainment, including a group of comedians called the World Showcase Players, who, when not engaged in general clowning on the World Showcase Promenade, coax audience members into participating in their farcical and altogether amusing (if unsophisticated) playlets. In the pub, an entertaining pianist plays, sings just about any request, and interacts with guests late into the evening.

Sharp-eyed visitors with an interest in horticultural matters will have a field day examining the landscaping here. The geometrically trimmed bush in front of the Pooh Corner shop is not an Irish yew, so common to the British Isles, but instead a *podocarpus*; Irish yews don't grow well in Florida. A *podocarpus*, left in its natural shape, also flanks the shop door just to the rear. A similar substitution had to be made for the London plane tree, also not suited to the Epcot climate; its replacement, crowding the half-timbered walls of The Magic of Wales, is a Western sycamore, which looks nearly identical and belongs to the same

Where to Eat in Epcot

A complete listing of all eateries—full-service restaurants, fast-food emporiums, and snack shops—can be found in the *Good Meals, Great Times* chapter. See the Epcot section beginning on page 219.

genus. Don't miss the perennial and herb gardens next to Anne Hathaway's cottage (to the left of the entrance to The Tea Caddy as you face it), and the small path that leads to the garden courtyard. The characters often appear in the garden courtyard. A traditional English hedge maze is found adjacent to the cottage.

POOH CORNER: This delightfully renovated shop now presents the most extensive selection yet of merchandise starring Winnie the Pooh, Piglet, Eeyore, and Tigger, too. Outside, the shop resembles a stone manor built during the last half of the 16th century; the Scottish-stepped gable parapet and the round turrets are inspired by Scotland's Abbotsford Manor, where the novelist Sir Walter Scott lived for a period, wrote his most famous romances, and died in 1832.

THE CROWN & CREST: This shop looks like a backdrop for a child's fantasy of the days of King Arthur, with its high rafters decked out with bright banners, vast fireplace (and crossed swords above), and immense wrought-iron chandelier. Dart boards, fragrance products, "pub mugs," glasses that serve yards of beer, limited-edition chess sets, and coin and stamp sets are the stock in trade at this emporium adjoining Pooh Corner.

PRINGLE OF SCOTLAND: On a sweltering summer day in Central Florida, trying on lamb's wool and cashmere may not hold terrific appeal. But the huge selection of styles and colors in men's and women's sweaters, knitted by Scotland's most famous maker, may well prove enticing despite the temperature outside. Tam-o'-shanters, socks, hats, ties, scarves, mittens, and kilts are only some of the items offered. Don't fail to look at the fascinating tartan map on the wall across from The Crown & Crest; this identifies plaids from Glen Burn and Gordon to Langtree and St. Lawrence.

LORDS & LADIES: Sponsored by the Royal Doulton, Ltd. china makers, this shop (opposite Pringle of Scotland) may be one of the loveliest in Epcot. This is particularly true of the store's elegant Adams Room, embellished with elaborate moldings, hung with a crystal chandelier, and painted in cream and robin's-egg blue. The setting is a perfect background for the selection of superbly crafted collector's statuettes. The figurines' detail is almost photographically perfect, and the prices range from $5 to $12,500. A selection of attractive Royal Doulton china dinnerware is also available.

Don't forget to inspect small, serene Britannia Square just outside the shop entrance furthest from World Showcase Promenade.

But for its somewhat reduced scale and the distinctively Floridian climate, it feels almost like London itself. The crests on the shop's upstairs windows are those of three major U.K. schools—Oxford, Cambridge, and Eton.

THE MAGIC OF WALES: This small emporium offers pottery, slate, jewelry, souvenirs, and handcrafted gifts from Wales. Despite its modest size, it does the highest volume of business (per square foot of size) among the United Kingdom shops.

THE TEA CADDY: Fitted out with heavy wooden beams and a broad fireplace to resemble the Stratford-upon-Avon cottage of Shakespeare's Anne Hathaway, this shop, presented by R. Twinings & Company, Ltd., stocks English teas, both loose and in bags in a variety of flavors. Other items include teapots, biscuits, and candies.

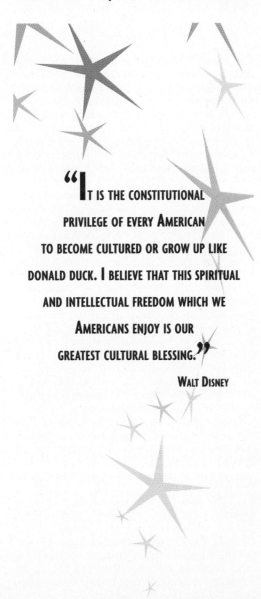

"IT IS THE CONSTITUTIONAL PRIVILEGE OF EVERY AMERICAN TO BECOME CULTURED OR GROW UP LIKE DONALD DUCK. I BELIEVE THAT THIS SPIRITUAL AND INTELLECTUAL FREEDOM WHICH WE AMERICANS ENJOY IS OUR GREATEST CULTURAL BLESSING."

WALT DISNEY

International Gateway

SHOWCASE GIFTS: Disney memorabilia, convenience items, and a package pickup depot are located at this spot near the France entrance.

WORLD TRAVELER: Disney fashions and character merchandise, plus film, 35mm and video camera rentals, and a drop-off for two-hour film processing are conveniently located here.

STROLLER AND WHEELCHAIR RENTAL: Strollers and wheelchairs are available for rent at this location. Remember to keep your rental receipt; it can be used on the same day in the Magic Kingdom, at the Disney-MGM Studios, or again in Epcot should you leave and return at a later hour.

France

The buildings here have mansard roofs and casement windows so Gallic in appearance that you expect to see some sad, bohemian poet looking down from above. A canal-like offshoot of the World Showcase Lagoon seems like the Seine itself; the footbridge that spans it recalls the old Pont des Arts. There's a kiosk nearby like those that punctuate the streets of Paris, a sidewalk café at which to sip a glass of wine and watch the crowds go by, and a bakery whose absolutely heavenly rich aromas announce its presence long before it's visible. Shops sell perfumes, jewelry, crystal, and other luxury items. Their roofs are of real copper or slate, and the cabinetry is crafted finely enough to dazzle even the most skilled woodworker. Galerie des Halles—the iron-and-glass-ceilinged market that Paris once counted as one of its most beloved institutions—lives again (near the Palais du Cinéma exit). But perhaps most special of all are the people. Hosts and hostesses who hail from Paris and the French provinces answer questions in lyrically French-accented English. It's fun to time your visit to take in the shows put on by mimes and clowns (have you ever seen a clown with four legs?).

Some interesting background notes: The dusty rose-colored, lace-trimmed costumes that the hostesses wear were inspired by the dresses in *Le Bar aux Folies-Bergère* by the Impressionist painter Edouard Manet, and the park to the west of the pavilion, with its tall Lombardy poplars, was inspired by neo-Impressionist Georges Seurat's painting *A Sunday Afternoon on the Island of La Grande Jatte*. The main entrance to the pavilion recalls the architecture of Paris, most of which was built during the Belle Epoque ("beautiful age"), the last decades of the 19th century. Then, following the designs of city planner Baron Georges-Eugène Haussmann, thoroughfares were widened and seven stories became the standard height for city buildings. The lane known as La Petite Rue ("the little street") is inspired by small provincial byways. The sinuously curved, Art Nouveau–style facade of the entrance to the arcade between La Signature and Plume et Palette ("pen and palette") recalls the entrances to Paris' great underground transportation system, the Métro. Don't neglect to visit the garden on the opposite side of this arcade—one of the most peaceful spots in World Showcase.

Horticulturally, France offers still other delights, beginning on the World Showcase Promenade. Here a row of Western sycamores that normally grow to 60 or 80 feet—planted in lieu of London plane trees—is being pruned French-style to a height of about 18 feet to develop knots on the end of each branch. These make a distinctive abstract pattern in winter, and in spring send out spiky leaf-bearing shoots that provide bountiful shade in summer. To the west, on the opposite side of the promenade, a small square edged with miniature rose bushes has been planted to outline the shape of a fleur-de-lis.

IMPRESSIONS DE FRANCE: Shown in the Palais du Cinéma, an intimate, elegant little theater that's not unlike the one at Fontainebleau. This enchanting 18-minute travel film takes viewers from one end of France to the other. The film shows off a beautiful tree-dotted estate; fields and vineyards at harvest time; a village flower market and a luscious pastry shop; the ribbed tongue of a glacier and a harbor full of squawking gulls; black-clad Breton women with headdresses made of starched lace shaped into unique styles that reveal the wearer's origin; Paris on Bastille Day—in all some four dozen locations (out of 140 originally shot). Several scenes take place in world-famous landmarks. Viewers visit the Eiffel Tower; Versailles and its gilt Hall of Mirrors (just outside Paris); Mont St. Michel, close to the Brittany-Normandy border in the northwest corner of the country; the French Alps near Mont Blanc, in the southeast; and Cannes, the star-studded resort city on the Mediterranean coast. The automobile competition shown is Cannes' Bugatti Race; the chateau—which Francophiles will immediately recognize as one of those in the Loire River valley—is fabulous Chambord. (This last scene, incidentally, was shot from a helicopter that could fly within three feet of any object being photographed.)

All this is even more appealing thanks to a superbly melodic sound track, consisting almost entirely of the music of French classical composers. These include Jacques Offenbach (1819-1880), known for his operettas; Charles-Camille Saint-Saëns (1835-1921), a conductor, pianist, organist, and composer celebrated for his lush melodies; Claude Debussy (1862-1918), who did with sound what the Impressionist painters did with light; and Erik Satie (1866-1925), known for his piano works. Selections include Debussy's *Syrinx*, the haunting piece for solo flute, and his *Afternoon of a Faun*, which accompany an aerial shot of fertile fields. Listen for Offenbach's *Gaieté Parisienne* in the biking sequence and Satie's *Trois Gymnopédies* in the Alps scene. The Aquarium section from Saint-Saën's *Carnival of the Animals* accompanies the swamp scene, and the same composer's *Organ Symphony* is heard during the Eiffel Tower ascent. The whole is woven together with transitional segments written and arranged by long-time Disney musician Buddy Baker.

The exceptionally wide screen adds yet another dimension. This is not a Circle-Vision 360 film; it was not shot with the nine cameras needed for the motion pictures shown at China and Canada. The France film used only five cameras, and it is shown on a screen made up of five large projection surfaces—200 degrees around. It's one of Epcot's best films.

The wait here is generally not long, except during peak seasons, but it's still best to see the film soon after World Showcase opens or in the early evening.

PLUME ET PALETTE: This spot is one of World Showcase's loveliest shops. The best of the Art Nouveau style is reflected in the curves that embellish the wrought-iron balustrade edging the mezzanine and the moldings that decorate the cherry-wood cabinets and shelves. The woodworking is superb, and each case seems more beautiful than the last. Stained glass in purple, yellow, and lavender ornaments the top of one; stylized tulips painted in delicate antique rose and pale green embellish still others. The curtains are a beautiful dusty pink with white lace.

The decor makes a fine backdrop for an array of merchandise that includes Guerlain cosmetics, fragrances, and bath products. On the mezzanine level, a handful of fine oil paintings (by well-known French landscape artists) are for sale from $300 to $3,000 each, along with attractive prints of French countryside scenes.

LA SIGNATURE: Another beautiful spot, with a chandelier, wallpaper that resembles watered silk, brass-and-crystal sconces, and velvet curtains, this shop stocks a number of collectible miniatures, small china boxes, and intricate tapestries.

GALERIE DES HALLES: Souvenirs—from Eiffel Tower statues to CDs with music by French composers—are the stock in trade at this area located at the exit from the Palais du Cinéma. The area is modeled on Paris's now-demolished Les Halles, originally designed by the architect Victor Baltard (1805–74).

LA CASSEROLE: This shop presents a selection of gifts themed to the artwork of French artists, such as Monet and Renoir. Mugs, tote bags, umbrellas, and picture frames are among the offerings.

LA MAISON DU VIN: Selections in this lovely wine shop range from the inexpensive to the pricey, from *vin ordinaire* going for several dollars to upwards of $290 for a relatively rare vintage. Wine tastings are held here to sample the offerings (a small charge is levied, but you get to keep the glass). Those who don't want to carry their purchases all over World Showcase may have them dispatched to Package Pickup for retrieval at the end of the day.

Morocco

Nine tons of tile were handmade, handcut, and shipped to Epcot to create this World Showcase pavilion. To capture the unique quality of this North African country's architecture, 19 Moroccan artisans were brought to Epcot to practice the mosaic art that has been a part of their homeland for thousands of years. Koutoubia Minaret, a detailed replica of the famous prayer tower in Marrakesh, stands guard at the entrance. A courtyard with a fountain at the center—and flowers everywhere—leads to the Medina (Old City). Between the traditional alleyways and the more modern sections are the pointed arches and swirling blue patterns of the Bab Boujouloud gate, a replica of the one that stands in the city of Fez. An ancient working waterwheel irrigates the gardens of the pavilion and the motifs repeated throughout the buildings include carved plaster and wood, ceramic tile, and brass. Festival Marrakesh takes over the courtyard with belly dancing and Moroccan songs performed by native musicians.

GALLERY OF ARTS AND HISTORY: This museum houses ever-changing exhibits of Moroccan art, artifacts, and costumes.

MOROCCAN NATIONAL TOURIST OFFICE: An information center offers literature useful in planning a visit to Morocco, and the Royal Air Maroc desk makes it easy to book a trip if the mood strikes. There is a three-screen projection area where a continuous slide show depicts the lifestyles and landscapes of the country.

CASABLANCA CARPETS: Hand-knotted Berber carpets, Rabat carpets with brightly colored geometric designs, prayer rugs, wall hangings, and handloomed bedspreads and throw pillows are among the offerings here.

TANGIER TRADERS: Here's the perfect place to buy a fez, plus woven belts, leather sandals, leather purses, and other traditional Moroccan clothing.

MARKETPLACE IN THE MEDINA: Hand-woven baskets, sheepskin wallets and handbags, assorted straw hats, and split bamboo furniture and lampshades are available.

THE BRASS BAZAAR: Brass, brass, and more brass—and it's all shiny. Discover pitchers, planters, pots, and serving sets.

BERBER OASIS: This shop on the promenade spills over with crafted brasswork. Baskets and leather goods abound.

MEDINA ARTS: Stop in this shop for merchandise featuring characters from the animated film *Aladdin*.

Japan

Serenity rules in Japan. Except, of course, when the pavilion resounds with traditional Japanese music performed by a drum-playing duo or group. A small flock of extraordinary stilt-walkers resembling large colorful birds make appearances here as well.

The landscaping, designed in accordance with traditional symbolic and aesthetic values, also contributes to the pavilion's peaceful mood. Rocks, which in Japan represent the enduring nature of the earth, were brought from North Carolina and Georgia (since boulders are scarce in the Sunshine State). Water, symbolizing the sea (which the Japanese consider a life source), is abundant; the Japan pavilion garden has a little stream and a couple of pools inhabited (in good weather) by koi. A small bamboo device at the edge of one of these rivulets regularly fills up with water falling from above, and then, weighted by its contents, empties out and in the process, emanates regular, but somehow soothing, clacking noises. Evergreen trees, which in Japan are symbols of eternal life, are here in force.

Disney horticulturalists created this very Japanese landscape using few plants and trees native to that country because the climate there is so different from that of Florida. The evergreens near the brilliant vermilion *torii* (gate) are native Florida slash pines. The curly-leaved trees by the stream are corkscrew willows. Among the few trees here actually native to Japan are the sago near the courtyard entrance to the Yakitori House; the two Japanese maple trees (identifiable by their small leaves) not far away (near the first stairway from the promenade

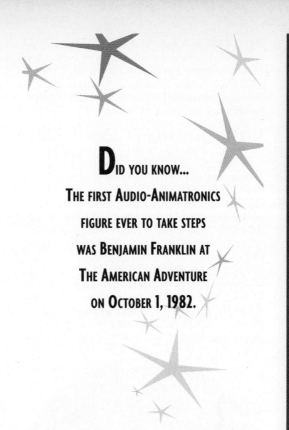

DID YOU KNOW... THE FIRST AUDIO-ANIMATRONICS FIGURE EVER TO TAKE STEPS WAS BENJAMIN FRANKLIN AT THE AMERICAN ADVENTURE ON OCTOBER 1, 1982.

on the left side of the courtyard as you face it); and the prickly monkey-puzzle trees near the walkway to the promenade, on The American Adventure side of the pagoda. Needle-sharp thorns make the latter the only species of tree that monkeys cannot climb.

Visitors who have been to Japan will be interested to observe that most of the structures inside the pavilion have their Japanese antecedents. The pagoda that occupies such a prominent place along World Showcase Promenade was modeled after an eighth-century structure located in the Horyuji Temple in Nara. The striking *torii* on the shore of World Showcase Lagoon derives from the design of the one at the Itsukushima shrine in Hiroshima Bay, one of the most beautiful sites on the inland sea.

BIJUTSU-KAN GALLERY: A changing cultural display, this small art museum has offered, among other exhibitions, "Echos Through Time—Japanese Women and the Arts," a showcase of traditional and contemporary Japanese art forms.

MITSUKOSHI DEPARTMENT STORE: There are kimonos in silk, cotton, and polyester; attractive T-shirts bearing Japanese characters; expensive, almost sculptural traditional headdresses; and an excellent selection of bowls and vases meant for flower arranging. But on the whole, no one would ever apply the term "quaint" to this spacious store set up by Mitsukoshi—an immense, three-century-old retail firm that was once dubbed "Japan's Sears." Some of the china dinnerware is too often seen elsewhere in United States department stores to arouse more than passing interest. It's unfortunate that this familiarity also makes it easy to dismiss some of the other merchandise that has

considerable meaning in Japanese culture. One example is the dolls, of which there are literally rows and rows, priced from $3.50 to $3,000, and clad in elaborate kimonos sashed with wide, stiff obis. These are traditionally given to female children on Girls' Day, a popular Japanese national holiday. The blank-eyed, egg-shaped papier-mâché scarlet masks, which come in a wide range of sizes from small to very large, are part of the traditional New Year celebration. The Japanese color in one eye when making a New Year's resolution, keep the one-eyed "face" in plain view throughout the next 364 days as a reminder of the holiday vow, and celebrate success when the year draws to its close by completing the face.

The structure housing the merchandise was inspired by a section of the Gosho Imperial Palace, which was constructed in Kyoto in the year 794 A.D., and is widely recognized as a fine example of early Japanese architecture.

The American Adventure

When it came to creating The American Adventure, the centerpiece of World Showcase, Disney Imagineers were given a relatively free reign. So the 110,000 bricks of the imposing colonial-style structure that houses the show, a counter-service restaurant, and a shop are of real brick—made *by hand* from soft, pinkish-orange Georgia clay. The show inside stands out because of its wonderfully evocative settings, its innovatively detailed sets, and the 35 superb Audio-Animatronics players, some of the most lifelike ever created by the Disney organization: The American Adventure's Ben Franklin even walks up stairs. The digital sound system is also the most advanced that the Disney organization has ever used, and the show is the most technically complex, involving the world's largest rear-projection screen (72 feet across) and a number of sophisticated sets that rise up from below the stage to the delight and awe of the audience. A superb a cappella vocal group called The Voices of Liberty serenades guests in the building's foyer before each show begins.

Be sure to note the four luxuriant trees out front. They were originally planted in 1969 on Hotel Plaza Boulevard, and have been moved four times in the intervening years. The Disney characters often appear here. Presented by Coca-Cola and American Express.

THE AMERICAN ADVENTURE SHOW: One of the truly outstanding Epcot attractions, this 29-minute presentation celebrates the American spirit from our nation's earliest years right up to the present. The show is kept current. Beginning with the arrival of the Pilgrims at Plymouth Rock and their hard first winter on the western shore of the Atlantic, the Audio-Animatronics narrators—an amazingly lifelike Ben Franklin and a convincing, cigar-puffing Mark Twain—recall certain key people and events in American history—the Boston Tea Party, George Washington and the grueling winter at Valley Forge, the influential black abolitionist Frederick Douglass, the celebrated 19th-century Nez Percé Chief Joseph, and many more. The Philadelphia Centennial Exposition is remembered, along with the contributions of women's rights campaigner Susan B. Anthony, telephone inventor Alexander Graham Bell, and the steel giant and philanthropist Andrew Carnegie. Naturalist John Muir converses on stage with Teddy Roosevelt. Charles Lindbergh, Rosie the Riveter, Jackie Robinson, Marilyn Monroe, and Walt Disney are represented. So are John Wayne, Lucille Ball, Margaret Mead, John F. Kennedy, Martin Luther King Jr.,

Muhammed Ali, and Billie Jean King. The idea is to recall episodes in history, both negative and positive, which most contributed to the growth of the spirit of America, either by engendering "a new burst of creativity" (in the designers' words) "or a better understanding of ourselves as partners in the American experience." The presentation is hardly comprehensive; instead, it's "a hundred-yard dash capturing the spirit of the country at specific moments in time."

Throughout the show, the attention to historical detail is meticulous. Every one of the rear-projected illustrations was executed in the painting style of the era being described. The Chief Joseph and Susan B. Anthony figures are speaking their originals' own words. The precise dimensions of the cannon balls in another scene were carefully investigated—then reproduced. In the Philadelphia Centennial Exposition scene, Pittsburgh's name is spelled without the *h* that subsequent years have added.

For information about how each of the various historical figures actually spoke during his or her lifetime, researchers contacted about half a dozen historians and cultural institutions—the Philadelphia Historical Commission, Harvard's Carpenter Center of Visual Arts, the State Historical Society of Missouri, the Department of the Navy's Ships Historical Branch, and others. When recordings were not available, educated guesses were made: Bell's voice was created on the basis of contemporary comments about his voice's clarity, expressiveness, and crisp articulation, coupled with the fact that his father taught elocution. To select Will Rogers' speeches for the Depression scene, whole

pages of quotes were collected, reviewed, edited, and re-edited; the voice is the humorist's own, from an actual broadcast, as is that of FDR, here heard over the radio in the roadside gasoline-stand scene. That particular scene was suggested by a *Life* magazine photograph; details are accurate down to the price for a gallon of gasoline (18 cents).

One of the most interesting aspects of the show is its inner workings. Underneath the entire theater is a movable carriage device that designers have dubbed "the war wagon." The basement that supports this mechanism is itself supported by pilings driven approximately 300 feet into the ground; it carries ten different sets, and during the presentation

rolls forward or backward to position the appropriate set underneath the stage at the right time. Also, because the height of the space underneath the theater is relatively limited, the sets themselves were specially designed to allow certain sections to contract telescopically as proved necessary. These operations are computer controlled.

The 12 lifesize statues on either side of the stage represent the Spirits of America. These are, on the left, from front to rear, Individualism, Innovation, Tomorrow, Independence, Compassion, and Discovery; and, on the right, from front to back, Freedom, Heritage, Pioneering, Knowledge, Self-Reliance, and Adventure. The 44 flags flanking the Hall of Flags corridor in the escalator area are those that have at some point flown over the United States. Revolutionary War flags, Colonial flags, and even flags representing the countries that had claims to American soil before Independence can be seen. A special highlight of the show is the majestic music played throughout by the Philadelphia Symphony Orchestra. The Golden Dreams sequence includes notable figures such as Muppet creator Jim Henson, Ryan White—the young hemophiliac who succumbed to AIDS after a courageous battle with the disease—and basketball star Earvin "Magic" Johnson.

As one of the most compelling of all the World Showcase attractions, The American Adventure is often quite busy. Seats in the front of the house give the optimal view of the Audio-Animatronics figures (although all seats provide an acceptable view). Perhaps the best time to schedule a visit to the show is soon after World Showcase opens or in the early evening. Be sure to check your guidemap for exact showtimes and arrive early. If you time it right, The Voices of Liberty a cappella group makes for an entertaining wait. Or read the quotes on the walls—Wendell Wilkie, Jane Addams, Charles Lindbergh, Ayn Rand, Archibald MacLeish, Herman Melville, Thomas Wolfe, and Walt Disney all are represented.

ALL-AMERICAN RED, WHITE & BLUE: Visit this shop for nostalgic Americana. Gifts include American flag–colored men's and women's clothing, housewares, baseballs, Coca-Cola products, coins, and books on American history.

AMERICA GARDENS THEATRE: An ever-changing slate of entertainment is presented several times a week in this lakeside amphitheater in front of The American Adventure pavilion. Check your guidemap for details and exact times. Showtimes are also posted on the promenade at the east and west entrances to the amphitheater.

Be sure to note the pruning of the Western sycamores overhead; the old-fashioned pollarding method used, which involves trimming the treetops flat and allowing the lower branches to fill out and interlock, eventually produces a thick canopy. The flower beds outside are planted in appropriately red, white, and blue blossoms.

Italy

The arches and cut-out motifs that adorn the World Showcase reproduction of the Doge's Palace in Venice are just the more obvious examples of the attention to detail lavished on the individual structures in this relatively small pavilion. The angel atop the scaled-down campanile was sculpted on the model of the original right down to the curls on the back of its head—then covered with real gold leaf, despite the fact that it was destined to be set almost 100 feet in the air. The other statues in the complex, including the sea god Neptune presiding over the fountain in the rear of the piazza, are similarly exact. Even the marblelike material used in the facade resembles that used in the real Doge's Palace. And the pavilion even has an island like Venice's own, its seawall appropriately stained with age, plus moorings that look like barber poles, with several distinctively Venetian gondolas tied to them. St. Mark the Evangelist is also remembered, together with the lion that is the saint's companion and Venice's guardian; these can be seen atop the two massive columns flanking the small arched footbridge that connects the landfall to the mainland. The only deviation from Venetian reality is the alteration of the site of the Doge's Palace in reference to the real St. Mark's Square.

The sounds of opera, accompanied by an accordion and guitar, frequently fill the courtyard. But perhaps the most interesting entertainment at this pavilion is The Living Statues, amazing white-robed performers who stand motionless, and then suddenly change poses when you least expect it.

The pavilion is equally interesting from a horticultural point of view. The island boasts a brace of kumquat trees, citrus plants typical of the Mediterranean, and a couple of olive trees that can be seen on both side walls of the Delizie Italiane; originally located in a Sacramento, California grove,

they were moved to Anaheim and then were piled onto a flatbed truck, their branches spreading wide, for the trip to Florida. But they got only as far as the Arizona border. As Disney gardeners tell the story, that state's regulation prohibiting loads beyond a given width is so erratically enforced that no problems had been anticipated. So it came as quite a surprise when the inspector on duty decreed that the trees be trimmed to ten feet. A chain saw soon materialized, and within minutes the ancient olives were shorn. Despite horticulturalists' fears, the trees survived, leaving only their scars to remind visitors of the ordeal; the darker bark is what remains of the original, while the lighter areas are the new growth. The tall, narrow trees that stand like dark columns at various points in the pavilion are Italian cypress, which are extremely common in Italy; Florida slash pines serve as stand-ins for Italian stone pines, which would not grow here.

DELIZIE ITALIANE: This open-air market on the western edge of the piazza is a good spot for a sweet snack of tasty Italian chocolates and other goodies.

IL BEL CRISTALLO: The production of fine glassware has been a tradition in Italy for centuries, so a shop like this one (just off the promenade on the Germany side of the piazza) was a must for the pavilion. On display are typical Venetian glass paperweights and other items, their bright colors trapped in smooth spheres or teardrops of clear or milky glass; small porcelain figurines and flower bouquets so finely crafted that they look almost real; pastel flowers made of beads; and lead crystal bowls and candlesticks. The name of the shop means "the beautiful crystal."

LA CUCINA ITALIANA: This gourmet shop on the west side of the pavilion tempts with an assortment of traditional Italian pastries and desserts. Expect to find red, white, and rosé wines from some of the finest vineyards in Italy. Pasta, olive oils, vinegars, and coffee are just a few of the other provisions available. An eclectic blend of decorative ceramics, cookware, cutlery, and cooking accessories—including items from the "Gourmet Mickey" collection—round out the selection.

LA GEMMA ELEGANTE: Located to the rear of the piazza on its eastern edge, this small shop focuses on jewelry. There are gold and silver chains galore, and some are expensive, but it's also possible to find lovely—and affordable—beads, earrings, and pendants made of Venetian glass; intricate glass-mosaic brooches and pillboxes bearing images of tiny bouquets; cameos; and coral necklaces.

Germany

There are no villages in Germany quite like this one. Inspired variously by towns in the Rhine region, Bavaria, and in the German north, it boasts structures reminiscent of those found in urban enclaves as diverse as Frankfurt, Freiburg, and Rothenburg. There are stair-stepped roof lines and towers, balconies and arcaded walkways, and so much overall charm that the scene seems to come straight out of a fairy tale. The beer hall to the rear is almost as lively as the one at Munich's famed Oktoberfest, especially during the later show. The shops, which offer a range of merchandise from wine and sweets to ceramics and cuckoo clocks, toys, and books—and even art—are so tempting that it's hard to leave the area empty-handed. The various elements that constitute the Germany pavilion are

described here as they would be encountered walking from west to east (counterclockwise) around the cobblestone-paved central plaza, which is formally known as the St. Georgsplatz, after the statue found at its center. St. George, the patron saint of soldiers, is depicted with the dragon that legend says he slew during a pilgrimage to the Middle East.

Try to time your World Showcase peregrinations to bring you to Germany on the hour, when the handsome, specially designed glockenspiel at the plaza's rear can be heard to chime in a melody composed specifically for the pavilion. Check the guidemap to see if a German trio will be performing outside the Biergarten restaurant.

DER BUCHERWURM: This two-story structure, whose exterior is patterned after a merchants' hall known as the Kaufhaus (located in the southern German town of Freiburg in Breisgau), stocks prints and English books about Germany; handsome prints of German cities full of gabled old houses and gloriously spired cathedrals; and an assortment of souvenir items including ashtrays, vases, and spoons bearing images of German cities. The building itself is worth noting. In order to correctly reproduce the statues of the German emperors on its facade, designers hired a photographer who shot from a cherry picker and submitted closeups from a number of angles. (Film and sundries are also available.)

VOLKSKUNST: Small and exceptionally appealing, this establishment is full of a burgher's bounty of German timekeepers, plus a smattering of other items made by hand in the rural corners of the nation. The latter include beer steins in all sizes, from the petite to the enormous and expensive ($2,800); wood carvings made in the southern German town of Oberammergau; bright, fringed Tyrolean scarves; nutcrackers; and a whole collection of "smokers" (carved wooden dolls with a receptacle for incense and a hollow pipe for the smoke to escape).

As for cuckoo clocks, some are small and unprepossessing, and some are so immense that they'd look appropriate only in some cathedral-ceilinged hunting lodge. A must.

DER TEDDYBAR: Located adjacent to Volkskunst, this toy shop would be a delight if only for the lively mechanized displays high up on either side of the entrance and against the rear wall: Some of the stuffed lambs and the dolls in the full-skirted folk dresses (called dirndls) have been animated so that tails wag and skirts swirl in time to German folk tunes. The shop is also home to one of WDW's best selections of toys, including an assortment of expensive stuffed keepsakes from Steiff. Colorful wooden toys are tempting as well, along with all kinds of building blocks. Last but not least, the dolls are simply wonderful.

WEINKELLER: The Germany pavilion's wine shop, situated between the cookie shop and the Biergarten toward the rear of St. Georgsplatz, offers about 250 varieties of German wines produced and bottled by H. Schmitt Söhne, one of Germany's oldest and largest vintners. Wine tastings are held here daily. The selection includes not only those vintages meant for everyday consumption, but also fine estate wines whose prices run into the hundreds of dollars per bottle. These are white (with a few exceptions), because white wine constitutes the bulk of

Germany's vinicultural output. (Only 20% of all German bottlings are red.) The setting itself is quite attractive—low-ceilinged and cozy and full of fir cabinets embellished with carvings of vines and bunches of grapes.

KUNSTARBEIT IN KRISTAL: This shop to the left of Biergarten features Austrian and crystal jewelry, tall beer mugs, wine glasses in traditional German tints of greens and amber, and crystal decanters. Guests can have glassware etched on the spot.

SUSSIGKEITEN: It's a mistake to visit this tiny, tile-floored confectionery shop on an empty stomach: Chocolate cookies, butter cookies, and almond biscuits mix with caramels, nuts, and pretzels on the crowded shelves; and there are boxes upon boxes of *Lebkuchen*, the spicy crisp cookies traditionally baked in Germany at Christmas, not to mention Gummi Bears (which the packages announce as *Gummibaeren*). Children enjoy the animal crackers, which are different from those made in U.S. bakeries. Be sure to note the attractive display of old Bahlsen cookie tins by the door. Incidentally, Bahlsen, the shop's sponsor, was among the first companies in the world to pack baked goods in airtight wrappers to preserve freshness; the firm's logo is an Egyptian hieroglyph that signifies "long life."

DIE WEIHNACHTS ECKE: This is a shop that can set a visitor's mind to thoughts of Christmas—even in the dog days of summer. Ornaments, decorations, and gifts manufactured by various German companies line the shelves of this store.

GLAS UND PORZELLAN: Featuring glass and porcelain items made by the German firm of Goebel, this is an attractive establishment with rope-turned columns, curved moldings, delicate scrollwork, and tiny carved rosettes. But no matter how attractive the background, the stars of the show are the M. I. Hummel figurines that Goebel manufactures. Cherubic, rosy-cheeked children, shown carrying baskets, trays, umbrellas, and other items—depicted as in the drawings of a young German nun named Berta Hummel—are favorites of collectors around the world. There is always an elaborate showpiece at the center of the shop, and a Goebel artist is here to demonstrate the process by which Hummel creations are painted and finished. An excellent display (which includes figurines in all stages of completeness) tells the story.

China

Dominated by a Disney equivalent of Beijing's Temple of Heaven, and announced by a pair of banners that offer good wishes to passersby (the Chinese characters translate: "May good fortune follow you on your path through life and May virtue be your neighbor"), this pavilion conveys a level of serenity that offers an appealing contrast to the hearty merriment of nearby Germany and the gaiety of Mexico. Part of this quiet environment is the byproduct of the soothing traditional Chinese music that plays over the sound system. Live flute, zither, or dulcimer music is performed inside the Temple of Heaven, while agile acrobats do tricks in the courtyard. The attractive gardens also make a major contribution. They are full of rose-bushes native to China, and there is a century-old mulberry tree (to the left of the main walkway into the pavilion), with a pomegranate tree and a wiggly-looking Florida native known as a water oak nearby. In addition, a spacious emporium is devoted to Chinese wares, and two Chinese restaurants add to the overall atmosphere. However, all this is secondary to the fabulous motion picture shown inside the Temple of Heaven—a Circle-Vision 360 film that is one of the best World Showcase attractions.

WONDERS OF CHINA: LAND OF BEAUTY, LAND OF TIME: This 19-minute presentation shows the beauties of a land that few Epcot visitors will ever see firsthand—and does it so vividly that it's possible to see the film over and over and still not fully absorb all the wonderful sights. The Disney crew was the first Western film group to shoot certain sites, and their remarkable effort includes such marvels as Beijing's Forbidden City; vast, wide-open Inner Mongolia and its stern-faced tribespeople; the 2,400-year-old Great Wall; the Great Buddha of Leshan, eight centuries old and dramatically imposing; the muddy Yangtze River and the 3,000-year-old city of Suzhou, whose location on the Grand Canal, which is generally believed to be the largest man-made waterway in the world, encouraged Marco Polo to call it the Venice

of the East. There are shots of the European-style city of Shanghai, as well as Hangzhou, where a handful of Chinese are shown doing their morning exercises along the river's edge. Also shown are Huangshan Mountain, wreathed in fog; the Shilin Stone Forest of jagged rock outcroppings in Yunnan Province; Urumchi, whose distance from the sea in Xinjiang Province earned it the title of the most inland city on earth; Lahsa, in Tibet, and its Potala Palace, boasting a thousand rooms and ten times that many altars. Just as fantastic are the Reed Flute Cave and the bizarrely shaped hills of Kweilin above. To complete the picture, there are fields of snow and of wheat, high meadows and beaches dotted with tropical palms, harbors and rice terraces, calligraphers, checkers and table tennis players, lightning-fast acrobats, championship horseback riders, camels and a panda bear, glittering ice sculptures, and countless bicycles.

Almost every step of the way, the film crews were besieged by curious Chinese, even in near-empty Inner Mongolia. For the Huangshan Mountain sequence, which lasts only seconds, the crew and about three-dozen hired laborers had to carry the 600-pound camera uphill for nearly a mile. The Chinese government would not permit Disney camera operators to shoot aerial footage in some areas, so Chinese crews were sent aloft to record the required scenes, first on videotape and later—after approval from the Disney director in charge of the project—on film. You can see for yourself just how well this collaboration worked.

Be sure to spend some time before viewing the film examining the details that

Village Traders

Located between Germany and China, this open-air shop, notable for its Lion King merchandise, also offers gifts from Africa, India, and Australia. Browse through such souvenirs as boomerangs, handbags, hats, and T-shirts.

embellish the building that houses the theater. The structure's design is based on that of the Hall of Prayer for Good Harvest, the major section of Beijing's Temple of Heaven complex, which was built in the year 1420 (during the Ming Dynasty) and reconstructed after being damaged by lightning in 1896. The name of the World Showcase structure is represented by the characters above the entrance.

The number of stones in the floor was chosen for auspicious associations; the center stone is surrounded by nine stones because nine is considered a lucky number in China. Around the edge of the anteroom rise 12 columns—because 12 is both the number of months in the year and the number of years in a full cycle of the Chinese calendar. Closer to the room's center, there are four additional columns—one for each of the seasons; the japonicus vines entwining each column symbolize long life, while the square beam that they all support alludes to earth; the round beam above signifies heaven. The dragons on the beams allude to imperial strength, while the phoenixes are reminders of peace and prosperity. The measurements and proportions are similarly symbolic. Be sure to stand on the round stone in the absolute center of the anteroom: Every whisper is amplified.

When exiting, pass by the House of the Whispering Willows, an exhibit of ancient Chinese art and artifacts. Changed about every six months, it invariably includes fine pieces from well-known collections. Note that the best times to see the film are during the first couple of hours that World Showcase is open or just before closing.

YONG FENG SHANGDIAN SHOPPING GALLERY: This vast Chinese emporium, located off the narrow, charming Street of Good Fortune at the exit to the film, offers a huge assortment of Chinese merchandise— silk robes, prints, paper umbrellas and fans, embroidered items, change purses, and more. Trinkets, medium-priced items, and expensive antiques are all available in an array that may be matched in few other places in the United States. The calligraphy on the curtains wishes passersby good fortune, long life, prosperity, health, and happiness.

Norway

Set between the Mexico and China pavilions is Norway, the 11th pavilion added to the mix at World Showcase. Built in conjunction with many Norwegian companies, the pavilion celebrates the history, folklore, and culture of one of the western world's oldest countries.

The cobblestone town square is an architectural showcase of the styles of such Norwegian towns as Bergen, Alesund, Oslo, and Setesdal. There's also a Norwegian castle fashioned after Akershus, a 14th-century fortress still standing in Oslo's harbor; the castle here houses the Akershus restaurant. Most can't resist walking into the bakery for a taste of its treats. In a show of modernity, a statue of Norway's living legend, marathoner Grete Waitz, may be found behind the bakery. Shops stock authentic Norwegian handicrafts and folk items: hand-knit woolens, wood carvings, and glass and metal artwork. The World Class Brass comic musicians put on a show in the courtyard.

MAELSTROM: Appropriately, visitors tour Norway by boat—16-passenger, dragon-headed longboats like those Eric the Red and his fellow Vikings used a thousand years ago. The ten-minute voyage through time begins in a tenth-century Viking village where a ship is being readied to head out to sea. Seafarers then find themselves in a mythical Norwegian forest, populated by trolls who cause the boats to plummet backwards downriver, through a maelstrom to the majestic grandeur of the Geiranger fjord, where the vessel narrowly avoids spilling over a waterfall. Ultimately, after a harrowing plunge through a rocky passage, the boats wind up in the North Sea, caught in the fury of a full-blown storm. Lightning flashes reveal an enormous oil rig; as the boat passes the concrete platform legs, the storm calms and a friendly coastal village appears on the horizon.

Survivors disembark there and enter the village. Moments later, guests are invited into a theater where the journey continues on-screen, giving visitors a tangible sense of the natural scenic spectacles and unique personalities that make up modern Norway.

Maelstrom is an exciting ride that has quickly become one of World Showcase's more popular attractions. Try to visit in the evening, when it is least crowded.

STAVE CHURCH GALLERY: Inside the pavilion's reproduction of a wooden stave church, there is a small exhibit that explores Norwegian culture. It's interesting to note that only 30 stave churches remain in Norway today.

THE PUFFIN'S ROOST: A collection of Norwegian gifts, sweaters, activewear, hand-crafted jewelry, fine leather goods, pewter, candy, toys, and trolls are the wares for sale at this shop.

Mexico

The tangle of tropical vegetation surrounding the great pyramid that encloses this pavilion and the Mexican restaurant at the lagoon's edge on the promenade provide only the barest suggestion of the charming area inside. Dominated by a reconstruction of a quaint plaza at dusk, this area is rimmed by balconied, tile-roofed, colonial-style structures. Crowding a pretty fountain area is a quartet of stands selling Mexican handicrafts, and off to the left is an attractive shop stocked with other handsome wares. The Mariachi Cobre band keeps things lively (both inside and out). To the rear, the San Angel Inn, a corporate cousin of the famous Mexico City restaurant, serves authentic Mexican fare. Behind it, the pavilion's main show chronicles Mexican culture from earliest times right up to the present. Take a look at the cultural exhibit inside the pyramid entrance on the way in. Note that the pyramid itself was inspired by Meso-American structures dating from the third century A.D. The serpent heads on either side of the stairway evoke the Aztec god Quetzalcoatl.

EL RIO DEL TIEMPO: THE RIVER OF TIME: Over the course of this six-minute boat trip, liberally sprinkled with vignettes of pre-Columbian, Spanish Colonial, and modern Mexican life, visitors greet a Mayan high priest, watch stylized dances by performers in vivid costumes, and are assailed by vendors at a lively market. A band costumed to look like skeletons entertains at one juncture (in a reference to the Day of the Dead, a holiday celebrated in Mexico with candies and sweets shaped like skulls or skeletons). In addition, there are a handful of film clips depicting present-day Acapulco (with its cliff divers and flying dancers), Tulum, Manzanillo (and its speedboats), and Isla Mujeres (with its gorgeous sea life). The cheery montage of film, props, and Audio-Animatronics figures is reminiscent of the Magic Kingdom's It's A Small World. During peak seasons, long lines, which prevail from late morning on, usually thin out in the afternoon as the crowds drift into the more distant parts of World Showcase. If you are in the area, skip the boat ride the first time around and return in the evening or late in the afternoon when the crowds are likely to be far smaller.

PLAZA DE LOS AMIGOS: Brightly colored paper flowers, sombreros, wooden trays and bowls, peasant blouses, baskets, and pottery make this *mercado* (shopping area) at the plaza's center as bright and almost as lively as one in Mexico itself. The colorful papier-mâché piñatas that figure so strongly in the scenery here are so popular that Epcot has to buy them from suppliers by the truckload. Irresistible.

ARTESANIAS MEXICANAS: This shop stocks more expensive versions of some of the merchandise sold in the *mercado*—onyx ashtrays, bookends, plaques, and unique Mexican decorative gifts.

EL RANCHITO DEL NORTE: Gifts and souvenirs from northern Mexico are the featured items at this spot.

LA FAMILIA FASHIONS: Mexican fashions and accessories for women and children, malachite, plus silver and turquoise jewelry are available.

World Showcase Plaza

PORT OF ENTRY: Features Olympic-themed and Team Disney casual clothing, plus other sports-related products.

DISNEY TRADERS: Merchandise combining the charms of Disney characters and World Showcase themes are the primary stock-in-trade. Sunglasses, film, cigarettes, and sundries are also available.

ENTERTAINMENT

Epcot presents an intriguing array of live performances each day, making it important for guests to consult an entertainment schedule, which is incorporated in the current park guidemap. While the overall lineup is constantly changing, certain shows—the not-to-be-missed IllumiNations, for one—are fixtures. The following listing offers an indication of Epcot's crowd-pleasing potential. For information about special events at Epcot, see the "Holidays & Special Events" section of *Getting Ready to Go*. Through the end of 1997, special goings-on will be happening propertywide to herald WDW's 25th anniversary (for all the details, turn to our special section beginning on page 15). For up-to-the-minute schedules call 824-4321.

AMERICA GARDENS THEATRE: The lagoonside venue at The American Adventure in World Showcase hosts high school choirs and international dance companies alike. Check a schedule for current offerings.

FOUNTAIN OF NATIONS: This dramatic fountain in Future World's Innoventions Plaza breaks into a computer-choreographed water ballet every 15 minutes.

FUTURE WORLD ENTERTAINMENT: Expect increased visibility for ever-changing performances designed to bring more fun to Future World. Future Corps, an impressive drum and bugle corps, performs nearly every day. Popular additions include the Jammitors, a unique group that uses trash cans as a drum set, and The Innoventors, strangely dressed and wacky street characters.

ILLUMINATIONS 25: A spectacular display of lasers, fireworks, and dancing fountains to the accompaniment of symphonic music, this show is a sure highlight of any Epcot visit. For Walt Disney World's 25th anniversary, extraordinary additions to the beloved show include new celebratory music from around the world, a grand fireworks display that creates the image of a cake over the lagoon, and a special "Circle of Life" finale. The nightly extravaganza, visible from anywhere on the World Showcase Promenade, is scheduled at closing time year-round. To snare a prime viewing spot (we recommend the island between Italy and The American Adventure), claim it about 45 minutes before showtime.

WORLD SHOWCASE PERFORMERS: It's all but impossible to complete a circuit of World Showcase without catching a few performances en route. Keep an eye on the schedule to take in live entertainment at each pavilion, often presented by natives of the country represented. Among the possibilities: worldly comedians, a nomadic troupe of stilt-walking "birds," French mimes, a Mexican mariachi band, Moroccan belly dancers, Chinese acrobats, Canadian bagpipers, and more. A bus full of Caribbean songsters travels the promenade. For details, see descriptions in the "World Showcase" section of this chapter.

Holiday Happenings

During certain holidays such as the Fourth of July, Christmas, and New Year's Eve, Epcot usually stays open extra-late and presents added entertainment for the occasion.

Note, too, that World Showcase keeps an international holiday calendar. January visitors might celebrate Scottish Heritage Day or Chinese New Year. In February there's Carnival du Quebec. May visitors might cheer Cinco de Mayo in Mexico or Independence Day in Norway. July packs France's Bastille Day, Japan's Tanabata Festival, and Canada Dominion Day in addition to the U.S.A.'s Fourth of July. Oktoberfest and Morocco's Independence Day also get their turn.

As always, precise entertainment plans are subject to change, so it's important to call 824-4321 to confirm schedules.

CHRISTMAS: Epcot celebrates big, with a nightly tree-lighting ceremony, a wondrously lighted archway that hugs the pathway to World Showcase Plaza, a candlelight choral processional, and a special edition of IllumiNations among the traditional elements of its Holidays Around the World festivities. The holiday IllumiNations features a special score complete with Tchaikovsky's "Nutcracker Suite," a Chanukah medley, and a dramatic "Let There Be Peace on Earth" finale.

HOT TIPS

• Stop by Guest Relations for a guidemap. Consult the entertainment schedule to be sure you won't miss any of the special shows.

• The best time to visit World Showcase is as soon as it opens (usually at 11 A.M.). See Future World in the late afternoon until it closes (usually at 7 P.M.). Remember that lines throughout Epcot are longest during midday, and shortest during the early evening.

• During peak seasons, preferred priority seating times at Epcot's full-service restaurants book quickly. So be sure to arrive at Epcot early to get a jump on the day and help assure that you get the restaurant and seating time of your choice. Remember, too, that non-prime dining hours are often available to those making late arrangements, so adjusting your eating schedule may well help you to visit the restaurant of your choice. Most World Showcase restaurants seat guests until park closing. Guests can also make advance plans by calling WDW-DINE (939-3463).

• Check the Tip Board in Innoventions Plaza for current waiting times for the most popular attractions, and alter your touring plans accordingly.

• Save the shops in World Showcase for the afternoon when just about everything else is very crowded.

• Guests staying at WDW resorts can have purchases delivered to their hotels at no extra charge.

• Don't queue for the World Showcase Promenade buses. You'll get where you're going faster by walking.

> **"E**PCOT WILL ALWAYS BE A SHOWCASE TO THE WORLD FOR THE INGENUITY AND IMAGINATION OF AMERICAN FREE ENTERPRISE.**"**
>
> WALT DISNEY

• Don't try to see all the World Showcase films in one day, especially if you're traveling with children.

• Be sure to allow extra time for Image Works at Journey Into Imagination, Innoventions, and Sea Base Alpha at The Living Seas.

• The jumping fountains outside the Journey Into Imagination pavilion are a favorite with children of all ages.

• Note that Spaceship Earth and Innoventions stay open after the rest of Future World closes (usually 7 P.M.), making the evening hours a good time to take in these attractions. The Fountain View Espresso & Bakery, Pasta Piazza Ristorante, and the Electric Umbrella restaurants also stay open until 9 P.M.

Where to Find the Characters

In Future World, characters host each meal at The Land's Garden Grill restaurant (see *Good Meals, Great Times* for details). Also, find Goofy at Wonders of Life, Timon and Rafiki at The Land, and Dreamfinder and Figment at Journey Into Imagination. Mickey appears at the Centorium. In World Showcase, characters favor the country of their literary origin. Discover *Snow White* characters in Germany, familiar faces from *Beauty and the Beast* and *The Hunchback of Notre Dame* in France, friends from *Aladdin* in Morocco, and *Pinocchio* stars in Italy. The United Kingdom is home to Winnie the Pooh, Alice in Wonderland, Mary Poppins, and others. Check a guidemap for current places.

Disney-MGM Studios

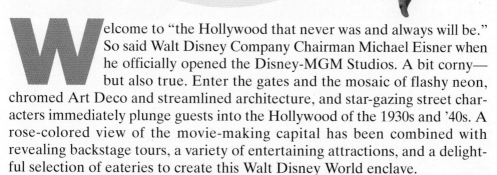

Welcome to "the Hollywood that never was and always will be." So said Walt Disney Company Chairman Michael Eisner when he officially opened the Disney-MGM Studios. A bit corny—but also true. Enter the gates and the mosaic of flashy neon, chromed Art Deco and streamlined architecture, and star-gazing street characters immediately plunge guests into the Hollywood of the 1930s and '40s. A rose-colored view of the movie-making capital has been combined with revealing backstage tours, a variety of entertaining attractions, and a delightful selection of eateries to create this Walt Disney World enclave.

The Disney-MGM Studios is situated on a 110-acre site southwest of Epcot. The water tower, known to punsters (for obvious reasons) as the "Earffel Tower," is reminiscent of the structures looming over most Hollywood studios of the Golden Era. Here, however, it gets that special Disney touch—it's capped by a Mousketeer-style hat.

What makes this area of Walt Disney World different from other Disney theme parks is the extent to which guests can participate in the attractions. Our best advice is to volunteer, wherever and whenever possible. It's fun, and it adds enormously to the experience.

The Studios is still expanding and evolving. If the Magic Kingdom is the home of the classics, this park is the place where Disney's latest animated hits debut as creative shows, parades, and attractions. It's also where the contemporary characters make their first live appearances.

 Unless otherwise noted, all phone numbers are in area code 407.

DISNEY-MGM STUDIOS

163

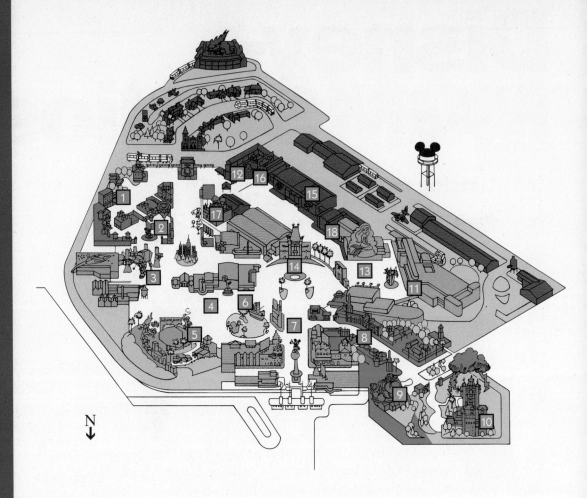

N

1 The Hunchback of Notre Dame—
   A Musical Adventure

2 Jim Henson's Muppet★Vision 3-D

3 Star Tours

4 Monster Sound Show

5 Indiana Jones Epic Stunt Spectacular

6 SuperStar Television

7 Hollywood Boulevard

8 Sunset Boulevard

9 Beauty and the Beast Stage Show

10 The Twilight Zone Tower of Terror

11 The Magic of Disney Animation

12 Studio Backlot Tour

13 Voyage of the Little Mermaid

14 The Great Movie Ride

15 Working Sound Stages

16 Backstage Pass to
    101 Dalmatians

17 Honey, I Shrunk the Kids
    Movie Set Adventure

18 The Making of...

GETTING ORIENTED

While the Disney-MGM Studios is about half the size of Epcot, the park has a sprawling layout with no distinctive shape or main thoroughfare. Even so, the Studios is easily navigated, with just a handful of broad avenues veering off toward different attractions, restaurants, and shops.

The park entrance is at Hollywood Boulevard. This shop-lined avenue leads straight to Hollywood Plaza, address of the Studios' most central landmark, a replica of Mann's Chinese Theatre that doubles as the site of The Great Movie Ride. Walking along Hollywood Boulevard toward the plaza, you'll come to the first major intersection, Hollywood Junction. Here, a wide, palm-fringed thoroughfare known as Sunset Boulevard (the Studios' newest block) branches off to the right. Anchoring Sunset Boulevard's far end is the Hollywood Tower Hotel, home of The Twilight Zone Tower of Terror. The strip is also graced with several shops, the Sunset Ranch Market, and the Theatre of the Stars amphitheater, where the Beauty and the Beast Stage Show is performed.

Stand in Hollywood Plaza facing the Chinese Theatre, and you'll notice an archway off to your right; this leads to Mickey Avenue. A self-contained area with a backstage feel to it, Mickey Avenue entices with tours of working animation and television studios. If you make a left off of Hollywood Boulevard and proceed clockwise past Echo Lake, you are on course for such participatory attractions as SuperStar Television, Monster Sound Show, Indiana Jones Epic Stunt Spectacular, and Star Tours. (The opposite side of the small lake is given mainly to dining spots.) Just beyond Star Tours there is one last entertainment zone. The highest-profile attractions here: Jim Henson's Muppet*Vision 3-D, The

Hunchback of Notre Dame—A Musical Adventure, and a facade of a Manhattan block called New York Street. Walk left past the skyscraper end of New York Street, and you're on a quick track back to Hollywood Plaza and the Chinese Theatre.

HOW TO GET THERE

Take Exit 26B or Exit 25 off I-4. Continue about a half mile to reach the parking area. Take a tram to the park entrance.

By WDW Transportation: From the Dolphin, Swan, Yacht Club, Beach Club, and BoardWalk: water launches. From Fort Wilderness and the Disney Village Marketplace: bus to the Transportation and Ticket Center (TTC), then transfer to the Disney-MGM Studios bus. From the Magic Kingdom, Epcot, all other WDW resorts, and the Disney Village Hotel Plaza: buses.

PARKING

All-day parking at the Studios is $5 for day visitors (free to WDW resort guests with presentation of resort ID). Trams circulate regularly, providing transportation from the parking area to the park entrance. Be sure to note the section and aisle in which you park. Also be aware that the parking ticket received allows for reentry to the parking area throughout the day.

HOURS

The Disney-MGM Studios is usually open from 9 A.M. to 7 P.M. During certain holiday periods and the summer months, hours are extended. It's best to arrive at the park at least a half hour before the posted opening time, particularly during these busy seasons. Depending on the season, some attractions do not open until late in the morning. Call 824-4321 for up-to-the-minute schedules.

Admission Prices

ONE-DAY TICKET

(Restricted to use only in the Disney-MGM Studios. Prices include sales tax and are subject to change.)

Adult	$40.81
Child*	$32.86

*3 through 9 years of age; children under 3 free

DISNEY-MGM STUDIOS

BABY FACILITIES

Changing tables and facilities for nursing mothers can be found at Baby Services, which is tucked inside the Guest Relations building near the park entrance. Disposable diapers are kept behind the counter at many Studios shops; just ask.

CAMERA NEEDS

The Darkroom on Hollywood Boulevard stocks film, batteries, and disposable cameras; it also rents camcorders ($25 per day with a $300 refundable deposit). Two-hour film processing is offered here and wherever you see a Photo Express sign. Film is sold in most Studios shops.

DISABILITY INFORMATION

Nearly all attractions, eateries, and shops are barrier-free. Convenient parking is reserved for guests with disabilities. Provisions have been made to enhance sight- and hearing-impaired guests' enjoyment. The *Walt Disney World Guidebook for Guests with Disabilities* is available at Guest Relations. For more information, see the "Travelers with Disabilities" section of *Getting Ready to Go*.

EARLY-ENTRY DAYS

On Wednesday and Sunday, guests staying at WDW resorts may enter the Disney-MGM Studios 1½ hours prior to the official opening time to enjoy such attractions as Tower of Terror, The Great Movie Ride, and Star Tours. Early-entry days and attractions are subject to change.

FIRST AID

Minor medical problems can be handled at this station, located in the Guest Relations building at the park entrance.

INFORMATION

Guest Relations, located just inside the park entrance, offers the requisite guidemaps and ever-resourceful staff. To make same-day dining arrangements for certain Studios eateries, go to the booth at the junction of Hollywood and Sunset boulevards.

LOCKERS

Attended lockers, found at Oscar's Super Service near the entrance, cost $3 per day (plus a $2 refundable deposit) for unlimited use.

LOST & FOUND

Located in a building near the park entrance, past the turnstiles on the right. To report lost items after your visit, call 824-4245.

LOST CHILDREN

Report lost children at Guest Relations or alert a Disney employee to the problem.

MONEY MATTERS

There is an ATM next to Oscar's Super Service at the park entrance. In addition to cash, credit cards (American Express, Visa, MasterCard, and The Disney Credit Card), traveler's checks, and WDW resort IDs are accepted for admission, merchandise, and also for meals at full-service restaurants and at many fast-food spots.

PACKAGE PICKUP

Shops can arrange for cumbersome purchases to be transported to Oscar's Super Service at the park entrance for later pickup. There is no charge for this service.

SAME-DAY REENTRY

Be sure to have your hand stamped upon exiting the park and to retain your ticket if you plan to return later in the same day.

STROLLERS & WHEELCHAIRS

Strollers, wheelchairs, and Electronic Convenience Vehicles (ECVs) may be rented from Oscar's Super Service, located just inside the park entrance on the right. Cost for strollers and wheelchairs is $5, with a $1 refundable deposit. Remember to keep your receipt, which can be used on the same day for a replacement at the Magic Kingdom, Epcot, or here at the Studios (at The Costume Shop). Cost for ECVs is $30, with a $20 refundable deposit. Note that quantities are limited.

TIP BOARD

Check this board at the junction of Hollywood and Sunset boulevards to learn current waiting times for the most popular attractions. Also look here for showtimes. Hosts and hostesses stand by to provide additional information and to make same-day dining arrangements for some of the Studios' full-service restaurants.

THE MAIN ATTRACTIONS

The Disney-MGM Studios has a brand of attractions altogether unique. Some offer guests behind-the-scenes looks at the creative and technical processes that generate television, movies, and animation. Others go so far as to allow guests to gain a bit of showbiz experience along with the insight. Still others resurrect popular characters and stories in new forms—from stage shows to thrill rides.

Because many of the shows and attractions at the Studios are presented at scheduled times throughout the day, it's especially important to consult a guidemap and the park's Tip Board for starting times. Attractions are described below roughly in the order they might be visited in a sweep of the park's major sections: Sunset Boulevard, Mickey Avenue, the area stretching from Hollywood Boulevard to Star Tours, and the New York Street vicinity.

The Twilight Zone Tower of Terror

The Hollywood Tower Hotel is the decrepit home of the Studios' newest thrill ride. A relic of Hollywood's Golden Age, the hotel clearly has had some problems. On the facade of the 199-foot-tall building (the tallest attraction at any Disney theme park) hangs a sparking electric sign. As the legend goes, lightning struck the building during a violent storm on Halloween night in 1939. An entire guest wing disappeared along with an elevator carrying five people. The disappearances remain a mystery.

The line for the ride winds through the once glorious lobby, where dusty furniture, cobwebs, and newspapers circa 1939 add to the eerie atmosphere. As guests enter the library, they see a television set brought to life by a bolt of lightning. Rod Serling intones a typical monologue, inviting them to enter another part of the building—and The Twilight Zone. He introduces the one-time staff and guests of the hotel (who will reappear later in the trip). During his spiel, Serling informs you that the maintenance elevator is the only working elevator in the hotel.

Visitors are led through an old hallway toward the boiler room to enter the ride elevator. (This is your only chance to change your mind about riding. Guests who decide to forego the trip can take a real elevator to the exit.) Once inside, passengers are seated on benches equipped with safety bars. The doors close and the elevator begins its ascent. At the first stop, the elevator doors open and guests have a view down an endless hotel corridor. Among the many special effects is a ghostly visit by the hotel guests who vanished. Suddenly, the view of the hall disappears and is replaced by a sky full of stars. The doors close again and you continue your trip skyward.

At the next stop, you enter the Fifth Dimension, a combination of eerie sights and sounds reminiscent of "The Twilight Zone" TV series. In fact, Disney Imagineers watched each of the 156 original "Twilight Zone" episodes at least twice (over 174 hours) for inspiration. Notice the clock that ticks incessantly as it hangs in midair, and the giant eyeball (watch it closely and you may see your image floating inside). This part of the ride is a disorienting experience, in part because the elevator is actually moving horizontally.

After this, you near the dreaded drops. What happens next depends upon the whim of Disney Imagineers, who have programmed the ride so that the drop sequence can easily be changed by computer. At press time the

ride was taking an immediate plunge (of about eight stories) before traveling quickly back up to the 13th floor. When the elevator reaches the top (at a height of about 157 feet) passengers can see the Studios below. The flash of light you see is a camera capturing your look of horror, while the noises you hear may have you convinced the elevator cables are breaking. The doors shut again and you plummet 13 stories. The drop is over in about $2^{1}/_{2}$ seconds, but it always seems longer. The elevator shaft is pitch black, and the use of sound, wind, and flashing lights maintains the sense of speed even as you are slowing down.

Just when you think it's over, the vehicle suddenly launches skyward, barely stopping before it plunges 13 stories again (creating a sensation similar to one you'd feel on a roller-coaster). As you prepare to exit the elevator, Rod Serling offers a tip: Next time you enter an old hotel, be sure to use the stairs.

From the time you enter the building, the entire trip takes about 12 minutes. Note that you must be at least 40 inches tall to go on the ride. It is not recommended for pregnant women, those with a heart condition, or people with back and neck problems.

On the way out, you'll pass through Tower Hotel Gifts, where key chains, T-shirts, and other merchandise with the Hollywood Tower Hotel logo are for sale. This is also the place to buy the photo taken at the top of the tower. Two bits of interesting trivia: The motors running the ride vehicles are three times as powerful as those that propel the elevators at New York City's 110-story World Trade Center; the cameras that take the pictures of horrified guests are mounted behind the Hollywood Tower Hotel sign.

Beauty and the Beast Stage Show

Here's the show that gave birth to the hit Broadway musical. Five times each day, Belle, Gaston, Mrs. Potts, Lumière, and the cast of the Disney film *Beauty and the Beast* come to life at the 1,500-seat Theatre of the Stars amphitheater on Sunset Boulevard. The 30-minute show is as entertaining as they come. The staging is just right and the music simply addictive as it traces the classic tale—from Belle's dissatisfaction with her provincial life in a small French town to the climactic battle between the staff of the Beast's castle, and Gaston and the townspeople. Lumière and friends perform the song, "Be Our Guest," with a delightful display of giant dancing spoons and Jell-O molds. The costumes of Lumière, Mrs. Potts, and Cogsworth are exceptional and the special effects that transform the Beast into a dashing prince are quite effective. A happy-ending finale, complete with a send-off of white doves, is a delight.

The Magic of Disney Animation

This is one of the finest, funniest, and most entertaining of all the attractions at the Studios. In a 35-minute tour, guests learn about the animation process and get to see Disney animators at work on a forthcoming film. The animators who work in the building generally work only weekdays, quitting between

5 P.M. and 6 P.M. each night, so you might try to time your visit accordingly.

In the lobby, duplicates of 12 of the many Oscars won by the Disney Animation Team are on display, along with a revolving collection of character drawings and original cels from recent Disney animated features as well as works-in-progress. From the lobby, guests move into the Disney Animation Theater, where an uproariously funny film starring Robin Williams and Walter Cronkite offers a lesson in the basics of animation. Through the eyes of Williams, it even allows guests a look at what it's like to be a cartoon character.

The producers of this film say that each scene was a struggle to complete, because Walter Cronkite had trouble keeping a straight face. Williams is at his best as one of the lost boys from *Peter Pan*. His nonstop banter is so quick and comical that a second trip may be necessary to take it all in. In one segment, he's turned into a variety of recognizable characters, including Mickey Mouse. "I can even be a corporate symbol," he proclaims in his best Mickey Mouse voice. All in all it's great fun, and Cronkite is an absolutely perfect straight man.

The film is followed by a walk through the working animation studios, where Williams and Cronkite continue to narrate on overhead monitors. First stop is the story room, where animators develop story lines. Next, it's on to the drawing boards where Mickey, Minnie, and other characters undergo the metamorphosis from pencil sketch to moving picture. Working at their desks in full view of visitors, animators are seen creating the drawings that will later appear in real films. Guests might see animators at work on *Hercules*, the 1997 summer release, or *The Legend of Mulan*, a future release which is to be the first feature created and produced exclusively here at the Studios.

Visitors also view the cleanup room, the special-effects area, and the special camera that's used to transfer drawings to cels. Then artists can be seen hand-painting up to 25 different colors onto these transparent sheets. To produce one 24-minute film, the animation team must complete 34,650 drawings, and add scenes from at least 300 background paintings before completing the work with musical scores and special effects. Offering still further insight into animators' realm is a new segment in which guests either meet a Disney artist or view an interesting video clip.

Stop in at the Animation Gallery, where original Disney animation cels, exclusive limited-edition reproductions, books, figurines, and other collectibles are for sale. In addition, a Disney artist can be seen painting cels that can be purchased on the spot.

Voyage of the Little Mermaid

One of the Studios' most popular attractions, this 15-minute live musical production adapted from the animated instant classic is presented in a theater with an underwater feel to it. Characters such as Flounder, Sebastian, sea horses, snails, and an octopus are artfully brought to life by puppeteers dressed completely in black so that only the creatures are visible. They open the show with the lively song, "Under the Sea," then clips from the

movie are shown in the background as actors join the puppets on stage to help tell the tale.

Ariel the mermaid is the star of the show and performs songs from the film, including "Part of Your World." Prince Eric also makes an appearance, and an enormous Ursula glides across the stage and steals Ariel's voice. Of course, the happy ending prevails. The story line is a bit disjointed, and hops from scene to scene, but most viewers are sufficiently familiar with the plot, so this doesn't detract from the show.

There are some excellent special effects inside the theater, including cascading water, lasers, and a lightning storm that may be a bit intense for younger children. Some of the effects—particularly those created by lasers that make you feel as though you really are under the sea—are best seen from the rear of the theater. Expect to wait a while for this popular show.

The Making of...

Moviegoers have long been intrigued by the filmmaking process, particularly as it relates to animation. Be it Mickey Mouse or Snow White, Beauty or the Beast, audiences clamor for information on what it takes to bring their favorite characters to life. The answers, at least for Disney's latest hits, are found here.

The Making of... begins on actual sound-stages, but leads to a movie screening that gives guests a fascinating, behind-the-scenes glimpse at the intricacies of filmmaking. While the attraction occasionally explores live-action releases, animated features predominate. Typically, it introduces the actors behind characters' voices; the composers and lyricists responsible for the memorable tunes; and the animators themselves, who go to great lengths to "get into" the characters they draw. For example, one senior animator for *Pocahontas*, charged with creating the mischievous Meeko, immersed himself in the world of raccoons, filling his office with raccoon posters, puppets, and stuffed animals.

The film yields lots of interesting, and perhaps surprising, bits of information. Guests come away with an appreciation for the work involved in producing a Disney film. For example, consider the extensive time computer animators for *Toy Story* spent creating the characters and making them move realistically (Woody has 200 controls for his face alone), and designing the film's scenery (there are 1.2 million computer-generated leaves on the trees in Andy's neighborhood).

This attraction is updated periodically to keep up with the latest Disney releases. Depending on when you visit, you might see *The Making of Hercules* or *The Making of The Legend of Mulan*. The Walt Disney Theater entrance is on Mickey Avenue and the show lasts about 15 minutes.

Studio Backlot Tour

Guests go backstage to see—and experience—some little-known aspects of television and movie production on a tour of real sets and prop stations. Highlights include two special-effects sequences in which guests learn first-hand how show designers create natural disasters and waterborne scenes on a studio set. Crowds seem to thin out during the late afternoon hours, so if the line is long, your time will be better spent at one of the other attractions until then.

First stop is an outdoor special-effects area, where two guests are tapped to hit the high seas. The six-minute show demonstrates the effects required to reproduce battle scenes at sea in a water tank. Pyrotechnics, simulated depth charges, and torpedo blasts combine in an action-packed display.

Guests then wait in a queue area to board the trams that travel to the backlot area. (Note that when boarding the trams, those who sit on the left side will get wet at Catastrophe Canyon, while those on the right will stay dry. Choose accordingly.) This 25-minute tour segment passes by television and movie production departments, where actual work is being done. The tram then winds through a tunnel, where guests can get a good look at the wardrobe department. More than 100 designers produce the costumes for all of Disney's motion picture, television, and entertainment projects—and with 2.25 million garments, Walt Disney World has the world's largest working wardrobe. Several famous costumes are on display, including Kimberly Williams' wedding dress from the movie *Father of the Bride*.

The tram then passes through the camera, props, and lighting departments, where equipment is stored until it is needed either on or off the studio's sets. Disney's camera equipment is so advanced that many visiting network television crews often borrow it when covering Space Shuttle launches at the Kennedy Space Center, about 70 miles to the east. A look into the scene shop reveals carpenters at work on sets that are later finished on the soundstages.

The tram turns into the backlot residential street where empty, hollow facades give the outward appearance of a lovely neighborhood. Used mainly for exterior shots, the houses on this street include Vern's home from *Ernest Saves Christmas*. There's also the facade of "The Golden Girls" home and the house from "Empty Nest."

As trams head for the highlight of the tour, the guide explains how landscapes can be created by set designers to fill a given need. He or she then asks, "Where in Central Florida can you find an active oil field in the middle of a dry, rocky, barren desert canyon prone to flash floods?" The answer is Catastrophe Canyon, which produces some of the best special effects most visitors will ever experience. As the guide will tell you, crews are filming a movie in which a backstage tram gets stuck in the canyon during a flash flood. But supposedly it's safe to go in because they're not filming today. Astute guests will notice that the oil company, Mohave, is the same one represented at Oscar's Super Service on Hollywood Boulevard.

In a spectacular series of special effects, a rain storm begins; then there's an explosion, complete with flames that are so hot even riders on the right side of the tram feel them; followed by a flash flood that is so convincing it forces everyone to lean the other way. The road underneath the tram shifts and dips hydraulically, lending even more reality to the adventure. A later behind-the-scenes look reveals the tanks, capable of releasing enough water to fill ten Olympic-size swimming pools. Some of the water is blown out by air cannons, which can shoot 25,000 gallons of water over 100 feet. To put that in better perspective, if a basketball were stuck into one of the cannons, it could be shot over the top of the Empire State Building.

From Catastrophe Canyon, the tram rides by New York Street, where meticulously reproduced facades line the urban streets. Though the brickwork looks authentic, these backless facades are constructed mostly of fiberglass and styrofoam. The skyscrapers, including the Empire State Building and the Chrysler Building, are actually painted flats. Forced perspective (the same technique that makes Cinderella Castle appear much taller than it is) makes the 4-story Empire State Building appear as if it's the genuine 104-story structure. Though clearly a New York reproduction, the facades can be altered to fit the role for Any City, USA. Tour groups often encounter film crews setting up or taking down equipment from shoots done on the lot. If crews are not filming, guests can explore New York Street on foot.

DID YOU KNOW...
WHEN THE DISNEY-MGM
STUDIOS OPENED IN 1989, IT HAD JUST FIVE
ATTRACTIONS AND ONE EXHIBIT.

Backstage Pass to 101 Dalmatians

This 35-minute behind-the-scenes look at moviemaking is a walking tour that begins with a funny video clip about the process of casting dogs for roles in the featured live-action film. Guests are then led into a room called the Special Effects Creature Shop, where they see all kinds of props that were used to produce Disney's *101 Dalmatians*. The guide explains how certain props, such as Audio-Animatronics puppies, helped film-makers create action scenes that otherwise would have been virtually impossible to shoot. A video reveals how the extremely curious and lively real puppies interacted with the Audio-Animatronics animals on the set.

Before the tour proceeds to the Special Effects Stage for the next segment, two children are chosen from the crowd to participate. Guests learn how film shot against a blue screen can then be superimposed onto any background chosen by the producers. Then the children take their appointed positions and are filmed interacting with *101 Dalmatians* props. This footage is cut in with real scenes from the movie and shown on screen.

Then it's on to the soundstages, where specially designed, soundproof catwalks allow visitors to gawk and talk all they want. The tour takes in three soundstages, where filming may be in progress for movies or television shows. It is also possible, however, that nothing will be happening on the set. In this case, guests will view a short video about the challenges of orchestrating action scenes involving hundreds of puppies (each of which had its own trainer).

From this area, guests are led into a walkway where they see a short film introducing the character Cruella de Vil (played by actress Glenn Close). At the film's conclusion, guests visit a large room overflowing with props and sets used to create Cruella's world, and the guide explains how these elements helped establish her lusciously villainous character. In addition to costumes and part of the set of the de Vil mansion, guests will get a close look at Cruella's fantastic car, built especially for the film.

American Film Institute Showcase

Costumes, props, and set pieces used in recent as well as classic movies and television shows are on display in this ever-changing exhibit. Although showcased items may be different when you visit, displays have included costumes from *Mary Poppins*, the police car from *Dick Tracy*, the caricature mural from *Three Men and a Baby*, concept artwork from *Toy Story*, live-action sets and stop-motion puppets from *James and the Giant Peach*, and a tool belt from the hit television show, "Home Improvement." Other props have come from *Who Framed Roger Rabbit*? and *Crimson Tide*, and a new interactive area demonstrates the five phases of movie making. Souvenirs sold here include items with the "Home Improvement" logo, plus movie memorabilia (such as personalized directors' clapboards and film reel frames).

The Great Movie Ride

Housed in a full-scale reproduction of historic Mann's Chinese Theatre, this 22-minute attraction captivates guests' imagination from the start. The queue area winds through the precisely reproduced lobby and into the heart of filmmaking, where guests will see some famous movie scenes on a large screen. (Note that if the queue extends outside the building, you're in for a long wait. It takes about 25 minutes to reach the ride vehicles once you've entered the theater.)

More than 60 dancing mannequins atop a large-tiered revolving cake greet guests in a replay of the "By a Waterfall" scene from the Busby Berkeley musical *Footlight Parade*.

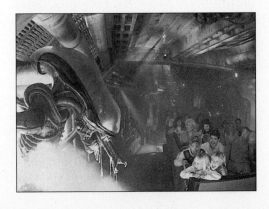

Gene Kelly's most memorable performance from *Singin' in the Rain* is the next scene, in which rain seems to drench the soundstage but doesn't dampen the spirits of the Audio-Animatronics representation of Kelly, who sings his heart out. Then Mary Poppins and Bert the chimney sweep entertain, as Mary floats from above via her magical umbrella and Bert sings the tune "Chim Chim Cher-ee" from a rooftop.

From the world of musical entertainment, guests segue to adventure. James Cagney re-creates his role from *Public Enemy* as the ride proceeds along Gangster Alley. A Prohibition-style mob shootout begins and guests find themselves in the midst of an ambush. An alternate route leads to a western town, where John Wayne can be seen on horseback eyeing some would-be bank robbers. When the thieves blow the safe and flames pour from the building, the heat can be felt even from the trams.

The ride vehicles whisk guests past danger and into the spaceship *Nostromo* from the film *Alien*. Officer Ripley guards the corridor while a convincing monster threatens riders with its slimy body from overhead. (Note that this scene and the gangster and western scenes are presented in a darkened setting and may be upsetting to younger children.) Next stop is the Well of Souls from *Raiders of the Lost Ark*, where Harrison Ford and John Rhys-Davies struggle to remove the ancient ark from its sepulcher. There is also a Tarzan scene in a jungle, and the legendary farewell scene with Rick and Ilsa from *Casablanca* is depicted, complete with a real airplane that looks just like the one used in the movie.

Guests are taken from the airfield to the swirling winds of Munchkinland, where a house has just fallen upon the Wicked Witch of the East. Her sister, as portrayed by Margaret Hamilton, appears in a burst of black smoke. This Audio-Animatronics figure represents the third generation of this technology, and she is impressively lifelike. But happy endings prevail and guests follow Dorothy, the Tin Man, the Cowardly Lion, the Scarecrow, and Toto along the Yellow Brick Road to the Emerald City of Oz. As the ride draws to a close, fans can enjoy a film montage of memorable moments from Academy Award–winning films.

The 50 Audio-Animatronics figures created for this ride were crafted by many of the same artists who created the characters in The Hall of Presidents in the Magic Kingdom. Their attention to detail is amazing. John Wayne's horse and rifle, for example, match those he used in his westerns. The costumes worn by the Julie Andrews and Dick Van Dyke Audio-Animatronics figures are modeled after the originals from *Mary Poppins*. And Gene Kelly personally inspected his likeness before it was shipped to Florida.

SuperStar Television

Roles in famous television shows are up for grabs at this remarkable attraction. In the outdoor pre-show area, a host or hostess chooses members of the audience to star in a variety of famous television scenes. Note: Most would-be stars are picked from nearer the front of the area; a few more roles are filled inside the theater. While just being in the audience will provide a lot of laughs, if there's even a little ham in you, move up front and volunteer loudly.

Audience members are led into a 1,000-seat theater reminiscent of the days of live television broadcasting. At the same time, would-be stars head backstage for costuming, makeup, and meetings with the directors.

The stage has several sets, and as the camera operators film the actors in their various roles, the audience watches on eight six-foot-wide projection screens suspended from the ceiling. The pictures on the screens vary significantly from the live events on stage because the use of "blue-screen" electronic techniques allows backstage editors to merge the live action with historic clips from the classic shows.

The first scene features a gentleman guest in the news reporter's seat on the "Today" show on July 17, 1955, the day Disneyland opened. Applause signs flash when appropriate, and audience members respond enthusiastically for their fellow tourists. Next, a woman guest gets to play the Ethel Mertz part opposite Lucille Ball's Lucy Ricardo in what is perhaps the single most famous scene from "I Love Lucy." Complete with white smock and tall white hat, the guest star tries to wrap chocolates as they quickly come along a conveyor belt, and though seen dozens of times, the scene is still funny, even with an amateur in the role of Lucy's second banana.

Another guest plays the part of Al Borlund opposite Tim "the Tool Man" Taylor in a scene from "Home Improvement." Several youngsters are chosen to star in the opening theme song from "Gilligan's Island." Other scenes include a classic from "Cheers," in which Woody the bartender, Norm, and Cliff star with four guests. One lucky youngster has the opportunity to hit a grand-slam homerun at New York's Shea Stadium and then be interviewed by the late Howard Cosell.

There are no bad seats in the house, as the eight monitors can be seen easily by the entire audience. This attraction tends to be less crowded during the morning hours, so try it then, and if time permits, go again; each new cast brings a fresh flavor to the presentation. The entire attraction takes about 45 minutes, from the choosing of stars till the end. Presented by Sony.

Monster Sound Show

Parents, don't be fooled by the name. There is nothing scary about this attraction, where guests have the opportunity to create the sound effects for a short film, with predictably funny results.

The pre-show begins outside the theater with a short video presentation starring David Letterman in a funny introduction to what's inside. His comments close with an atypical (for a Disney attraction) warning that, "If you break anything, security guards in mouse suits will beat you senseless."

Upon entering the 270-seat theater, the host chooses several "Foley" artists from the audience. (Foley is the Hollywood sound-effects system named for its creator, Jack Foley.) The audience is then treated to a cute comedy-mystery film starring Martin Short and Chevy Chase that includes the sounds of thunder, rain, creaking doors, and falling chandeliers. As the film is shown again, the amateur sound

crew does its best to match the proper sound effects to the action on the screen. The third viewing of the film features the new sound track created by the studio's newest Foley artists. The thunder never seems to match the storm and the crash of the chandelier most often takes place as the creaking door opens, but that's the point and it's all a lot of fun.

The 15-minute show features many original gadgets created by sound master Jimmy Macdonald. He invented more than 20,000 sound gadgets during his 45 years with the Walt Disney Studios in California, and also became the voice of Mickey Mouse during the 1940s. There are some special artifacts on display, including Tinker Bell's chimes, a door used in *Alice in Wonderland*, and the coconut shells used to produce the hoofbeats in the *Legend of Sleepy Hollow*. But most of the sounds guests hear are created by the ingenious use of barrels, nails, sandpaper, and other gadgets that go bonk, buzz, zip, or bump.

The post-show area, SoundWorks, offers some hands-on fun for the rest of the audience. Earie Encounters allows visitors to reproduce the flying-saucer sounds from the 1956 film *Forbidden Planet*. At Movie Mimics, guests can dub their voice over that of Roger Rabbit and other stars; and at Soundsations, our personal favorite, "3-D Audio" puts guests in an enclosed room filled with sound so realistic that the wind from a hair dryer can almost be felt. Presented by Sony.

Indiana Jones Epic Stunt Spectacular

Earthquakes, fiery explosions, and assorted other dramatic events give guests some insight into the science of movie stunts and special effects at this impressive 2,000-seat amphitheater. Stunt men and women re-create scenes from Indiana Jones films to demonstrate the skill required to keep audiences on the edge of their seats. Show director Glenn Randall, who served as stunt coordinator of such well-known adventure films as *Raiders of the Lost Ark*, *Indiana Jones and the Temple of Doom*, *Poltergeist*, *Never Say Never Again*, *E.T.*, *Firestarter*, and *Jewel of the Nile*, calls the show "big, visual excitement."

But the 30-minute show isn't all flying leaps. Guests also see how the elaborate stunts are pulled off—safely—while the crew and an assistant director explain what goes on both in front of and behind the camera.

In one segment, a scene from *Raiders of the Lost Ark* is staged. A 12-foot tall rolling ball chases a Harrison Ford lookalike out of the temple. There is steam and flame so intense that the audience can feel the heat. The crew then dismantles the set, revealing the remarkable lightness of movie props, as two assistants roll the ball uphill for the next show.

In a scene at a busy Cairo street market, "extras" chosen from the audience help to play out the famous scene in which Indiana Jones pulls a gun while others are fighting with swords. The explosive action continues, and leads to a sensational desert finale in which the hero and his sweetheart make a death-defying escape.

There are moments during this presentation when the audience might wonder if, just for a minute, something has gone wrong. But by revealing tricks of the trade, the directors and stars show that what appears to be very dangerous is actually a perfectly safe, controlled bit of movie magic. It's a great show.

Star Tours

Having witnessed the unyielding popularity of this attraction at Disneyland, California, Disney made the decision to open a counterpart here. The attraction, which was inspired by George Lucas' *Star Wars* film trilogy, offers guests the chance to board StarSpeeders that are actually the same type of flight simulator regularly employed by the military and commercial airlines to train pilots. By synchronizing a stunning film with the virtually limitless motion of the simulator, the ride allows guests to truly feel what they see. (Note that when instructed to put on your seat belt, do so. This is a rough ride.)

Visitors enter an area where the famed *Star Wars* characters R2D2 and C-3PO are working for a galactic travel agency. They spend their time in a bustling hangar area servicing the Star Tours fleet of spacecraft. Riders board the 40-passenger craft for what is intended to be a leisurely trip to the Moon of Endor, but the five-minute ride quickly develops into a harrowing flight into deep space, including encounters with giant ice crystals and laser blasting fighters. The flight is out of control from the start, as the rookie pilot comically proves that Murphy's Law applies to the entire universe.

The sensations are extraordinary and the technology quite advanced. (By the way, this same technology is used at Body Wars in the Wonders of Life pavilion in Epcot's Future World. There guests take a rollicking ride through the human body.)

Signs at Star Tours warn that passengers must be free of back problems, heart conditions, motion sickness, and other physical limitations. Pregnant women are not permitted to board. There is a minimum height requirement of 40 inches, and children under seven must be accompanied by an adult; children under 3 are not permitted to ride.

Jim Henson's Muppet✳Vision 3-D

One of the most entertaining attractions at the Disney-MGM Studios, this spectacular 3-D movie is quite remarkable. Like so many Disney attractions, a lot of the appeal is in the details. A very funny 12-minute preshow gives some clues of what's to come. Characters including Scooter, Gonzo, and Sam Eagle entertain on overhead screens.

Inside the theater constructed specifically for this show, many will notice that it looks

Where to Eat at the Studios

A complete listing of eateries at the Studios—full-service restaurants, fast-food emporiums, and snack shops—can be found in the *Good Meals, Great Times* chapter. See the Disney-MGM Studios restaurant section, which begins on page 227.

just like the one from the television series "The Muppet Show." Even the two curmudgeonly old fellows are sitting in a balcony, bantering with each other and offering some negative but humorous commentary on the film. The comedy comes directly from Muppet Labs, presided over by Dr. Bunson Honeydew—and his long-suffering assistant, Beaker—and introduces a new character, Waldo, the "Spirit of 3-D." The 3-D effects are convincing and most viewers can't resist reaching out at least once. Among the highlights are Miss Piggy's hilarious solo, which Bean Bunny turns into quite a fiasco. Sam Eagle's grand finale leads to trouble as a veritable war breaks out, and with an appearance by everyone's favorite Swedish Chef, a cannon blasts the screen from the rear balcony.

But the 3-D effects, spectacular as they are, are only part of the show: There are appearances by live Muppet characters, a clutch of fiber-optic effects, fireworks, and lots of very funny details built into the walls that surround the seating area of the huge theater. There are carryings-on for most of the senses—sight, smell, and touch, among them—and it's hard to know where to look first, making this more like a "4-D" experience. We're glad that they've put the 12-minute show in such a large theater, to allow the crowds to enjoy it without too long a wait.

The Hunchback of Notre Dame— A Musical Adventure

The Studios' newest showpiece, a 30-minute musical based on Disney's animated feature *The Hunchback of Notre Dame*, is performed in the shaded comfort of the Backlot Theater—a newly canopied bleacher-style theater located just beyond New York Street. The show takes guests to the catacombs of 15th-century Paris, where gypsies reprise the age-old tale of the bell ringer Quasimodo and his struggle to find love and happiness.

Clopin, the King of the Gypsies, is the narrator. It is he who parts the curtains for this "play within a play," inviting guests to watch as a troupe of gypsies endearingly reenact the bittersweet love story of Quasimodo and Esmeralda. While gypsy magic plays a part throughout, the show is characterized by an imaginative simplicity akin to street theater. Long runway ramps that bring characters into the audience enhance the feeling of being part of the performance. Those who have seen the movie will recognize the opening notes of "The Bells of Notre Dame," the song that signals the start of the performance.

The curtain opens to a gypsy campsite beneath the city. Here, Clopin and the gypsies create a colorful set filled with such treasures

as Persian rugs and jewels that they've "picked up." The gypsies impart the details of Quasimodo's life in the cathedral's bell tower, telling the story through song, costumes, masks, giant puppets, and dance. As the show evolves, the gypsies' theatrics reveal Quasimodo's oppression at the hands of Judge Claude Frollo, his love for the beautiful Esmeralda, and the kindness of Phoebus, the guard who helps the lonely bell ringer. Along the way, eye-catching effects, such as Esmeralda's disappearing in a puff of smoke and reappearing across the stage, keep guests wondering what will happen next.

Lest there be too much sorrow, the set again transforms and a wonderfully lively scene steals away to the streets of Paris for a thoroughly rambunctious revival of the Festival of Fools. Comic relief is also provided in the form of three gargoyles, Victor, Hugo, and Laverne, who act as Quasimodo's collective conscience. A point of interest: The first two gargoyles' namesake is author Victor Hugo, while Laverne's heritage is the Andrews Sisters. The show includes many of the film's memorable tunes, including "Topsy Turvy," "A Guy Like You," and, of course, "God Help the Outcasts."

Honey, I Shrunk the Kids Movie Set Adventure

The set for the backyard scenes of the popular Disney movie has been re-created as an oversize playground for kids. Stalks of grass soar 30 feet high and enormous tree stumps and LEGO toys provide unusual climbing opportunities. Kids especially love to climb into the discarded film canister and slide back out along an oversize reel of film. A hose with a small leak also provides entertainment as it squirts in a slightly different location each time. It's all great fun, and the props serve to make the kids look and feel very tiny indeed.

SHOPPING

Hollywood Boulevard

CELEBRITY 5 & 10: Modeled after a 1940s Woolworth's, this large shop carries trinkets, costume jewelry, picture frames, shirts, jackets, aprons, teddy bears, magnets, and memorabilia associated with old Hollywood. This is also a good place to pick up a director's clapboard and other non-Disney, film-related merchandise.

COVER STORY: Just through The Darkroom, this is where guests can have their images put on the front cover of a large selection of magazines. Costumes and appropriate accessories are provided by the shop.

CROSSROADS OF THE WORLD: In the middle of the entrance plaza, Mickey Mouse keeps watch from atop this Hollywood Boulevard landmark. The small kiosk deals in souvenirs, sunglasses, film, raingear, sundries, and information.

THE DARKROOM: The Art Deco facade of this shop allows guests to enter through an aperture-like doorway. Here, Kodak VHS video cameras are available for rent at $25 per day, with a refundable deposit of $300. Deposits can be charged on American Express, MasterCard, or Visa. Blank tapes must be purchased separately. Although no 35mm cameras are available for rent, disposable cameras, film, and accessories are sold.

KEYSTONE CLOTHIERS: Ranging from flashy to classy, women's fashions and accessories are the specialties of this shop. A favorite item sold here is a Mickey Mouse umbrella that sprouts two ears when opened.

L.A. CINEMA STORAGE: A great source for kids' stuff, with a wide variety of children's clothing (we love the denim shirts embroidered with characters). Many items feature characters from recent animated films, but classic characters, especially Pooh and friends, have a presence as well.

LAKESIDE NEWSSTAND: One-stop shopping for Disney-MGM Studios logo merchandise and other souvenirs.

MICKEY'S OF HOLLYWOOD: The place to find T-shirts, sweatshirts, hats, plush toys, watches, socks, wallets, tote bags, books, mugs, and sunglasses, plus items emblazoned with the Disney-MGM Studios logo or Walt Disney Studio logo.

MOVIELAND MEMORABILIA: Located just to the left of the main entrance, this kiosk stocks stuffed toys, hats, books, sunglasses, film, key chains, and other souvenirs.

OSCAR'S CLASSIC CAR SOUVENIRS & SUPER SERVICE: The 1949 Chevrolet Tow Truck parked out front gets plenty of attention. Automotive memorabilia, mugs, models, and key chains are for sale. The truck, by the way, is not. Services offered here include stroller and wheelchair rental, lockers, and infant products, plus a stamp machine.

SID CAHUENGA'S ONE-OF-A-KIND: Authentic antiques and curios are the stock-in-trade here. Autographed photos, old movie magazines and posters, and assorted Hollywood memorabilia are among the celebrity-oriented collectibles with which Sid is willing to part—for a price.

SWEET SUCCESS: Specialty candies and more traditional treats are available at this sweet-smelling shop.

Sunset Boulevard

LEGENDS OF HOLLYWOOD: A tribute to legends of film. Celebrity items, photographs, classic film videos, autographed books, and movie paraphernalia are the focus here. Disney stock includes adult and children's books, CDs, videos, and computer games.

MOUSE ABOUT TOWN: The best source for casual men's apparel featuring the famed mouse subtly embroidered onto dark-colored sportswear, button-down shirts, polo shirts, and jackets. We particularly like the Tommy Hilfiger–inspired Mickey logo.

ONCE UPON A TIME: The exterior of this shop replicates the Carthay Circle Theatre in Hollywood, where *Snow White* premiered in 1937. The focus is on the classic Disney characters: Mickey, Minnie, Donald, Goofy, and of course, Snow White and the seven dwarfs. Look for unique collectible items, such as limited-edition porcelain characters.

SUNSET CLUB COUTURE: The largest collection of character jewelry and watches. A sophisticated selection of mostly Mickey watches includes many limited-edition pieces and some great pocket watches. Collectors should note the custom-made character watches, which a Disney artist draws on the spot. Jewelry highlights stylized Mickey designs (cutout gold ears, marcasite ears).

SUNSET RANCH: This open-air shop carries a variety of character hats, totes, and apparel, plus sunscreen, film, and sundries.

Beyond the Boulevards

ANIMATION GALLERY: Don't overlook this shop in the Animation Building, where limited-edition figurines, Disney animation cels, and other collectibles ensure great browsing, even if buying isn't on your mind.

BUY THE BOOK: This cozy newcomer next to Sci-Fi Dine-In is patterned after its namesake bookstore from the TV show "Ellen"; it even has some authentic props. Specialty coffees and all sorts of page-turners are on hand; occasional book signings are held.

ENDOR VENDORS: The shop outside Star Tours offers intergalactic souvenirs tied to the *Star Wars* films and the Star Tours attraction, some of which are hard to find anywhere else.

FOTOTOONS: After the Studio Backlot Tour, visitors can have their photo combined with an image of a cartoon character.

GOLDEN AGE SOUVENIRS: Between Monster Sound Show and SuperStar Television, this small shop stocks Disney character merchandise.

INDIANA JONES ADVENTURE OUTPOST: Right next to the attraction, discover an assortment of adventure clothing and memorabilia with the Indiana Jones insignia.

IT'S A WONDERFUL SHOP: Tucked away in a corner behind Muppet*Vision 3-D, this "snow-covered" shop—with ornaments galore—feels like Christmas year-round.

THE LOONY BIN: A perfect stop after the Studio Backlot Tour. Lots of Roger Rabbit merchandise and some gag gifts are for sale. There's a host of hands-on fun in the form of props from the movie *Who Framed Roger Rabbit?* that kids just love.

STAGE 1 COMPANY STORE: Near the exit of Muppet*Vision 3-D, guests can find merchandise with the likenesses of Muppets (Miss Piggy, Kermit, Fozzie Bear) in addition to a variety of Disney character items.

THE STUDIO STORE: In the Animation Courtyard, expect to find T-shirts, sweatshirts, hats, and accessories inspired by the newest animated film releases—*The Hunchback of Notre Dame* and others.

UNDER THE SEA: In front of Voyage of the Little Mermaid, look for T-shirts, sweatshirts, bathing suits, towels, and more featuring Ariel, Sebastian, Flounder, and friends.

Where to Find *the Characters*

You'll often find Disney characters—such as Quasimodo and Esmeralda, Woody and Buzz, Belle and the Beast, and Aladdin and Jasmine—strolling along Mickey Avenue. And Mickey is almost always standing by for photo opportunities on Sunset Boulevard. Another fun way to meet the characters is at the Soundstage restaurant. As always, check the park guidemap for the most current details.

ENTERTAINMENT

As you might expect from a park fashioned in the image of Hollywood's heyday, the Disney-MGM Studios knows how to put on a show. (The great movie music that's piped into the park when small bands aren't strolling through certainly sets the stage.) Celebrity appearances are a distinct possibility as well. Basically, in these parts, it's showtime all the time. So guests should be sure to pick up a guidemap at Guest Relations first thing, not only to check attraction starting times, but also to find out what other entertainment is on tap.

While specifics are subject to change, the following listing is a good indication of the Studios' stage presence. As always, we advise calling 824-4321 to confirm entertainment schedules. For information on special events at the Studios, see the "Holidays & Special Events" section of *Getting Ready to Go*. Also, note that through the end of 1997, celebratory shows and events will be happening property-wide to mark WDW's 25th anniversary (for details turn to our special section beginning on page 15).

SORCERY IN THE SKY: During seasons when the park is open late, this ten-minute fireworks display lights up the sky over the Chinese Theatre. The show is set to music from *Fantasia* and other classic films, with narration by Vincent Price. Best viewing spots are along Hollywood Boulevard.

STREETMOSPHERE CHARACTERS: This troupe of performers infuses Hollywood Boulevard with old-time Tinseltown ambience. Would-be starlets searching for their big break, starry-eyed fans seeking guests' autographs, and gossip columnists chasing leads entertain daily.

TOY STORY PARADE: A colorful, whimsical 15-minute procession marches down Hollywood Boulevard daily at 1 P.M. to the tune of "Strange Things (Are Happening to Me)" and "You've Got a Friend in Me." Sarge and his troops scope out the parade route. Other favorite characters from the film follow, as Mr. Potato Head and Hamm balance on a stack of games while Slinky the Dog weaves back and forth along the street. Buzz Lightyear stands high atop his spaceship, with awestruck green aliens below. Bringing up the rear is Woody, who speaks to the crowd with the help of Mike (the tape recorder) from a huge wagon of blocks. A jumbo Etch-A-Sketch reads "Goodbye" and "The End" as two green army soldiers carry a jump rope to mark the end of the parade.

Holiday Happenings

Like Epcot and the Magic Kingdom, the Disney-MGM Studios usually stays open extra-late to mark certain holidays such as New Year's Eve, the Fourth of July, and Christmas. During these times, special nighttime entertainment such as Sorcery in the Sky fireworks is often in store. Of course, entertainment plans are subject to change, so it's important to call 824-4321 for up-to-the-minute schedules.

CHRISTMAS: Lights, Camera, Christmas! is the Studios' brilliant, twinkling homage to the season. An extraordinary luminous holiday display featuring more than two million lights (owned by Little Rock businessman Jennings Osborne and his family) sets the backlot area of the Studios aglow. The display is lighted nightly throughout the season. Check a guidemap for exact times.

HOT TIPS

• Arrive at the Disney-MGM Studios before the posted opening time. The gates usually open about 8:30 A.M.

• Check the Studios Tip Board often to get an idea of showtimes and crowds.

• See Muppet*Vision 3-D, Voyage of the Little Mermaid, and Star Tours early in the day before the crowds build up.

• Tower of Terror is a popular attraction with very long lines. Ride it early in the day—and never right after a meal.

• For a full-service meal, make priority seating arrangements when you arrive at the park, at either the Tip Board or the desired eatery: 50's Prime Time Café, Hollywood Brown Derby, Sci-Fi Dine-In Theater, or Mama Melrose's. Or make advance plans by calling WDW-DINE (939-3463) up to 60 days ahead.

• Snag a good spot along Hollywood Boulevard to see the afternoon parade.

• The shops on Hollywood Boulevard are open a half hour past park closing.

Everything Else in the World

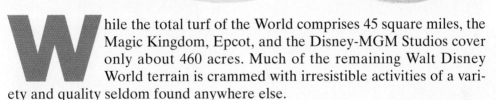

While the total turf of the World comprises 45 square miles, the Magic Kingdom, Epcot, and the Disney-MGM Studios cover only about 460 acres. Much of the remaining Walt Disney World terrain is crammed with irresistible activities of a variety and quality seldom found anywhere else.

There's superb golf and tennis, beaches for sunbathing, lakes for speedboating and sailing, canoes for rent and winding streams to paddle along, bicycles for hire, campfire sites, nature trails, and picnic grounds. The recreation options continue with River Country, Disney's old-fashioned swimming hole; Typhoon Lagoon, a state-of-the-art water park complete with surfing lagoon; and Blizzard Beach, a thrilling watery wonderland that translates the hallmarks of a ski resort to the realm of swimming.

Add to all that Pleasure Island, an after-dark entertainment complex, and the Disney Village Marketplace, a one-stop-suits-all assortment of shops and restaurants, and the list still isn't complete. A host of programs invite youngsters and adults to slip behind the scenes and learn about the workings of the World. Finally, the Disney Institute gives guests an altogether new way to vacation in the World. A resort geared to discovery, it offers the opportunity to dabble in animation, culinary arts, and all manner of other areas. As Michael Eisner said at the 1996 dedication of the Institute, "It's like putting the cherry on top of the cake at Walt Disney World."

 Unless otherwise noted, all phone numbers are in area code 407.

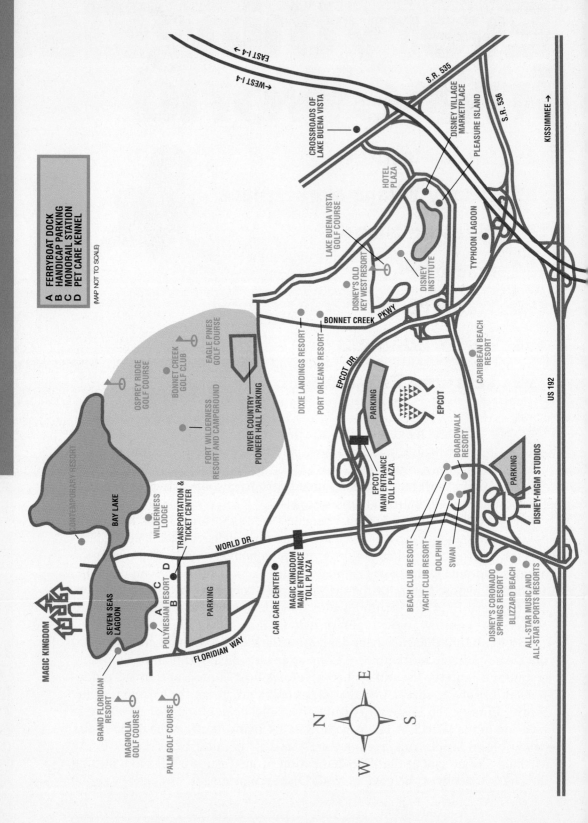

A   FERRYBOAT DOCK
B   HANDICAP PARKING
C   MONORAIL STATION
D   PET CARE KENNEL

(MAP NOT TO SCALE)

MAGIC KINGDOM

SEVEN SEAS LAGOON

GRAND FLORIDIAN RESORT

MAGNOLIA GOLF COURSE

PALM GOLF COURSE

CONTEMPORARY RESORT

BAY LAKE

WILDERNESS LODGE

TRANSPORTATION & TICKET CENTER

POLYNESIAN RESORT

PARKING

WORLD DR.

FLORIDIAN WAY

CAR CARE CENTER

MAGIC KINGDOM MAIN ENTRANCE TOLL PLAZA

OSPREY RIDGE GOLF COURSE

BONNET CREEK GOLF CLUB

EAGLE PINES GOLF COURSE

FORT WILDERNESS RESORT AND CAMPGROUND

RIVER COUNTRY PIONEER HALL PARKING

DIXIE LANDINGS RESORT

PORT ORLEANS RESORT

BONNET CREEK PKWY

EPCOT DR.

PARKING

EPCOT MAIN ENTRANCE TOLL PLAZA

EPCOT

BOARDWALK RESORT

PARKING

DISNEY-MGM STUDIOS

BEACH CLUB RESORT

YACHT CLUB RESORT

DOLPHIN

SWAN

CARIBBEAN BEACH RESORT

US 192

DISNEY'S CORONADO SPRINGS RESORT

BLIZZARD BEACH

ALL-STAR MUSIC AND ALL-STAR SPORTS RESORTS

CROSSROADS OF LAKE BUENA VISTA

EAST I-4 →
← WEST I-4

S.R. 535

DISNEY VILLAGE MARKETPLACE

PLEASURE ISLAND

HOTEL PLAZA

LAKE BUENA VISTA GOLF COURSE

DISNEY'S OLD KEY WEST RESORT

DISNEY INSTITUTE

TYPHOON LAGOON

S.R. 536

KISSIMMEE →

N E
W S

DISNEY INSTITUTE

Tucked away in a tranquil lakeside enclave is the Disney Institute, the place that launched an entirely new type of Walt Disney World vacation. This resort, which opened in February 1996, engages guests in more than 60 innovative programs ranging from animation and wilderness exploration to topiary gardening, rock climbing, and the culinary arts.

Guests choose from nine different program areas, including one designed for youths, to create a customized vacation. The Disney Institute provides a creative environment that inspires guests to try something new. While some are cooking up a healthy feast, others are scrambling up a rock face. As one member of the family is hosting a radio show, another is giving acting a shot. While some guests hone their photography skills, others are learning self-defense, improving their golf game, and taking a stab at computer animation. Contributing to the environment of experimentation are artists-in-residence, who bring their expertise to workshops during the day and then perform at night.

Getting Oriented

Guests participating in programs stay in the surrounding villas as part of an intimate lakeside community. The Institute's own architecture is reminiscent of a quaint American village, with a town green as the center of all activity. Facilities include a state-of-the-art cinema, outdoor amphitheater, performance center, closed-circuit television and radio station, 28 program studios, and a youth center. Note the inscriptions surrounding signs at the Institute, which offer inspirational quotes.

Sports & Fitness Center: This 38,000-square-foot center boasts an indoor exercise pool, a basketball court, two large aerobics rooms, and a wealth of state-of-the-art Cybex weight training equipment and cardiovascular machines. (Use of the center is complimentary to those participating in programs.) The Institute also encompasses four clay tennis courts, six swimming pools, and the Lake Buena Vista golf course. Within the fitness center, a full-service spa invites guests to indulge in an extensive array of facials, massage, aromatherapy, body therapies, and hand and foot treatments (all of which are priced à la carte). Locker rooms include a steam room, sauna, and whirlpool.

The Programs

Here's the fun part. Guests get to design their own vacation by choosing from a menu of fascinating programs. Instructors are experts in their field, and the student-instructor ratio ensures plenty of personal attention. The idea is that participants get to try something different, taking home with them newfound skills, creations, and insights. Our advice: Bring a large suitcase. On a recent trip we came home with a topiary, rosemary-infused oil, a best-seller, a dried floral arrangement, and new perspective.

Culinary Arts: In these popular programs, guests can try preparing regional cuisine, entertaining, pairing food and wine, or executing new techniques, all at individual cooking stations with chefs leading the way. A bonus: At program's end, participants can eat their creations (and take home the recipes).

Design Arts: Workshops explore the principles of design used in interiors, architecture, and landscaping. Guests might try painting a faux finish or embarking on an antiques treasure hunt.

Entertainment Arts: Discover the creative processes behind the scenes of animation, radio and audio, television and video, photography, and show biz. Participants get to draw a Disney character or create its voice; act as a deejay in a production that will air on the Disney Institute radio station; or practice photographing a family member.

Gardening and the Great Outdoors: These programs celebrate nature, with particular focus on gardens. Guests can go bird-watching, take a morning nature walk, or join a "swamp party" in the wilderness. Gardening courses invite visitors to study Disney landscape design techniques and growing methods, and perhaps take home a self-made portable garden or topiary.

Lifestyles: These sessions focus on family life and self-discovery. The range of experiences includes tracing a family tree, creating a computer storybook, ballroom dancing, and meditation. Guest instructors offer their ideas about money management, time and organizational skills, and relationships.

Performing Arts: A changing roster of artists-in-residence offer interactive workshops in music, film, theater arts, dance, and the spoken word. Guests may see an open rehearsal, film screening, or noted speaker.

Sports and Fitness: Extensive programming is available, including sports clinics, aerobics, golf, tennis, outdoor programs, relaxation techniques, rock climbing, self defense, strength training, and water exercise. Many sessions do not require pre-registration, so allow time to take advantage of facilities and join scheduled classes.

Story Arts: Discover the Disney art of telling a great story through a variety of media. Learn journal writing techniques, create a handmade book, or tap your inventive side as an "Imagineer."

Youth Programming: Kids 10 to 17 have special courses geared just for them in many of the different program areas. Examples of the fun experiences offered include a Disney Institute scavenger hunt, cooking for starving students, radio broadcasting, rock climbing, and comic strip illustration. Disney Day Camp provides program options for kids 7 to 9; see page 199 for details.

Entertainment

Through the artist-in-residence program, guests have the opportunity to witness the creative process. Accomplished musicians, dancers, writers, and filmmakers stay at the Institute for a few days, holding workshops (and taking programs themselves) during the day, and entertaining in the evening. Seeing one of their performances is the perfect ending to a Disney Institute day, particularly in the intimate Performance Center, so be sure to check the program and events board (in the town green) to see what's on tap. Whatever is planned, trust us when we say it is not to be missed.

Essentials

Institute guests stay in Bungalows and Town Houses at The Villas at the Disney Institute. For room configurations, see page 69 of *Transportation and Accommodations*.

Where to eat: Seasons Dining Room offers full breakfast, lunch, and dinner menus for the convenience of guests. See *Good Meals, Great Times* for details.

Shopping: Dabblers in the Welcome Center has items related to Institute programs.

Rates: Accommodations are based on double occupancy; rates also include unlimited programs, use of facilities including the Sports & Fitness Center (but excluding spa treatments), taxes, and baggage gratuities, plus a one-day theme park ticket. Single rates are available. An optional meal plan is offered. The Institute is designed for guest arrival on Monday or Friday, but can accommodate those who prefer to arrive on other days.

Bungalows start at $499 for three nights, $652 for four nights, and $1,111 for seven nights. One-bedroom Town Houses start at $573 for three nights, $750 for four nights, and $1,282 for seven nights. Two-bedroom Town Houses start at $678 for three nights, $890 for four nights, and $1,527 for seven nights. Cost per additional person sharing the same accommodation is $275 for three nights, $353 for four nights, and $587 for seven nights. Rates are higher during peak seasons. All prices are subject to change.

Reservations: It's wise to pre-register for programs; however changes can be made upon arrival (based on availability). For information and reservations, call 800-496-6337.

Day Programs at the Institute

If you can't spend a week, then at least come for the day. Programs designed to offer a "day in the life" allow guests to sample programs, use the Sports & Fitness Center, and catch the extraordinary evening performances. The introductory rate, $49, is likely to go up in the coming year. Reservations are necessary; call 827-4800 up to two weeks in advance.

Another package offers a more literal taste of the Institute, with dinner at Seasons Dining Room plus an evening performance. Cost is about $25 per person; call 939-3463 for reservations.

DISNEY VILLAGE MARKETPLACE

Located on the shores of Buena Vista Lagoon, the Disney Village Marketplace is a relaxing setting for one-stop shopping, and much more. The attractive waterside enclave is sprinkled with gardens, including 17 whimsical topiaries (look for the Cheshire Cat and Lumière). Distractions abound. While some guests will want to have lunch in one of the themed restaurants, others may grab a bite from the Gourmet Pantry and lunch at one of many waterfront tables. Between shops, some gravitate toward the marina for boating or fishing. Kids enjoy seeking out the interactive fountains and Hidden Mickeys throughout the area, especially the big one whose jets shoot up in the (drenching) shape of Mickey's head. Younger kids can be let loose at the innovative playground. And adults will want to allow time for a drink in one of the Marketplace's atmospheric lounges. See the *Good Meals, Great Times* chapter for lounge and restaurant information.

Changes within the last year have shuffled and expanded the attractions here. Among the recent additions to the Marketplace's roster of diversions is the Rainforest Café, a themed restaurant complete with waterfalls, thunder and lightning, and tropical birds to simulate a rainforest environment. As for the shops, the most popular ones have new homes with more elbow room; the Christmas Chalet, for example, has nearly doubled in

size. Others have left to make room for new shops such as Summer Sands and Authentic All Star. But the biggest shop development (literally) is Mickey's Character Shop, which has tripled its dimensions to become the World of Disney—the largest character emporium in the world.

All this change is part of the major expansion that will ultimately blur the lines between the Disney Village Marketplace and Pleasure Island next door to create one huge entertainment district. The transformation is expected to be completed by the end of 1997. By then, a Virgin megastore at the Marketplace will have upped the superstore presence. Pleasure Island's movie theater complex will have ballooned to a grand total of 24 screens. And a third area will have been added, including several high-energy venues. The main attractions include House of Blues, partly owned by Dan Aykroyd; Wolfgang Puck's Café, which will mark the L.A. chef's Florida debut; and Lario's, a restaurant-nightclub created by singer Gloria Estefan and her husband, Emilio. The district's three distinct entertainment zones will connect via walkway.

Despite all there is to do here, the pace is far more leisurely than that of the theme parks. The best way to take it all in is simply to wander at will. Note that weekends are fairly busy in these parts.

Essentials

GUEST SERVICES: Located in World of Disney, this information center is also the place for priority seating assistance, lost and found, film and stamp sales, photo processing, an ATM, wheelchair and stroller rental, theme park ticket purchase, and gift wrapping.

HOW TO GET THERE: The Marketplace is easily accessible from Exit 26B off I-4.

By WDW Transportation: From The Villas at the Disney Institute: walkway or bus. From Port Orleans, Dixie Landings, and Old Key West: boats or buses. From the Magic Kingdom, Epcot, the Grand Floridian, Contemporary, and Polynesian: monorail to the TTC, then transfer to Disney Village bus. From the Disney-MGM Studios, the Wilderness Lodge, and Fort Wilderness: bus to the TTC, then switch for Disney Village bus. From all other WDW resorts: buses. For more information about WDW transportation, see *Transportation & Accommodations*.

Shopping

The Disney Village Marketplace boutiques stock everything from toys and books to fashions and accessories for the whole family. Many stores carry the staggering range of Disney character merchandise; others don't even hint at Disneyana. The descriptions below suggest the types of things that each store offers. The shops are open daily from 9:30 A.M. to 11 P.M., and even later during certain seasons. Note that delivery of purchases to a WDW resort is complimentary.

THE ART OF DISNEY: Disney animation cels, porcelain figures, ceramics, and unique collectibles are the goods available at this gallery next to 2R's Reading and Riting.

AUTHENTIC ALL STAR: This shop is a preview of the celebrity athlete–owned Official All Star Café that's opening in May 1997 as part of Disney's Sports Complex. Hats, shorts, sweatshirts, jackets and other sports gear are among the logo merchandise sold.

THE CAPTAIN'S TOWER: At the center of the Disney Village Marketplace, this open-air shop is the focal point for major promotions. The merchandise changes three to four times a year depending on special events and the latest fashion trends.

CHRISTMAS CHALET: If anything can set a mind to dreaming of white Christmases when the mercury is hitting 95 degrees outside (and the humidity is just about the same), this lovely shop is it. Ringing the edges of the rooms are small treasures in traditional reds and greens—ornaments made of wood, metal, glass, and felt, and even some covered with feathers. The selection is one of the best of its type anywhere, considering that the shop doubled in size this past year. In addition, there are character collectibles and other unique Christmas trinkets.

DISCOVER: Concern for Mother Nature is fully demonstrated in the relaxed atmosphere of this environmentally aware emporium. Among the offerings are birdhouses, herb-garden kits, wind chimes, educational toys for children, environmentally oriented music, and other unique gift items.

EUROSPAIN: An array of handcrafted gifts and decorative items from prestigious Spanish artisans and designers. This shop sells roughly the same sort of cut-glass merchandise available at Main Street's Crystal Arts in the Magic Kingdom. Large green, blue, or red cut-glass bowls and vases are available, along with clear-glass mugs, glass sculptures, and other items engraved to customers' specifications with initials, messages, or pictures. If you bring a favorite photograph to this shop, the engraver can have it reproduced on a plate or other item. Presented by Arribas Brothers.

GOURMET PANTRY: Though escargots and smoked oysters can be found here, there are also breads and pastries, meats and cheeses, cereals, yogurt, beer and soft drinks, and many more items—both mundane and exotic. Unusual teas and specially blended, freshly ground coffees are also available, and occasional free tastes are offered to passersby. Assorted chocolates, jelly beans, cookies, and fudge are sold both prepackaged and in an area where shoppers can select their own favorites. The shop stocks a large selection of wines and spirits. Godiva chocolates, specialty sandwiches, and salads are also available. The line of Gourmet Mickey cookware and utensils is fully represented. Also, many varieties of cooking sauce, dressing, and spice, plus jams, honey, and a supply of Mickey-shaped pasta, round out the offerings. Guests at the nearby villas, take note: Purchases can be delivered to your villa; if you aren't going to be there, the delivery person will even stash perishables in your refrigerator. To order by phone, call 828-3886.

GREAT SOUTHERN CRAFT CO.: A small showplace of Americana gift items. There is fine handmade pottery, plus country and folk crafts. Observe as artists create unique hand-carved candles on the spot.

HARRINGTON BAY CLOTHIERS: Designed like a Bermuda plantation home, this shop stocks traditional and casual men's clothing from designers such as Nautica and Tommy Hilfiger. Located near the Captain's Tower, close to the parking lot.

MICKEY'S PHOTO STUDIO: Here guests can dress up in antique-style outfits and pose for old-fashioned portraits.

Shopping at the Crossroads

Constructed by the WDW folks, the Crossroads of Lake Buena Vista shopping center, located adjacent to the Disney Village Hotel Plaza, is a convenient dining and shopping area. The retail center is anchored by a Gooding's supermarket, which is open 24 hours a day and has a full-service pharmacy (open 10 A.M. to 6 P.M. weekdays). Guests at the nearby villas will find this an especially convenient stop.

Shops here stock clothing, swimwear, sunglasses, athletic shoes, and electronics. Character Connection offers the requisite Disney merchandise. There is also a bookstore, a card shop, and an express-photo shop. Eateries include T.G.I. Friday's, McDonald's, Taco Bell, Perkins, Pizzeria Uno, Red Lobster, Pebbles, Johnny Rockets, Chevy's Mexican Restaurant, Pacino's, and Jungle Jim's.

In addition to the shops and services, there's Pirate's Cove Adventure Golf, a miniature golf course.

RESORTWEAR UNLIMITED: This shop features bright and classy fashions. An assortment of sportswear and swimwear is enhanced by bold jewelry, hats, and handbags. Lancôme cosmetics are also available.

SUMMER SANDS: A beach lover's delight, this newcomer stocks swimwear, Florida clothing and souvenirs, jewelry, sun-care products, straw hats, and bags.

TOYS FANTASTIC: This fun spot stocks a wide variety of Mattel toys and games, including the newest playthings featuring Disney characters, a full line of Hot Wheels action toys, and Barbie fashions.

2R'S READING AND RITING: A large selection of hardcover and paperback books on just about any subject can be found here. Located near the WDW bus drop-off, the shop also stocks a great selection of greeting cards and stationery. In keeping with the nationwide bookstore trend, you can order coffee or cappuccino to sip while browsing.

TEAM MICKEY'S ATHLETIC CLUB: The locker-room decor offers the perfect setting for sports clothing, activewear, and sports equipment. This is the place to find T-shirts, sweatshirts, and other items with Disney University logos, as well as Mickey and Goofy in sporting poses (playing golf or tennis, for example) emblazoned on shirts. There is also a large selection of athletic footwear.

WORLD OF DISNEY: More than 38,000 square feet of retail space filled with Disney merchandise provides the widest variety of Disneyana anywhere. The Disney characters are available stuffed, in porcelain, and immortalized on everything from T-shirts and hats to towels, blankets, and carry-all bags. The amount of space not only makes for more comfortable shopping; it also inspired Disney to provide entertainment. Upon entering the superstore, look up at the colorful aircraft 50 feet overhead, each piloted by a different Disney character. Check out the huge video screen for movie showings and the 24-foot wall of stuffed animals. Twelve themed rooms provide the backdrop for the dizzying array of goods. For example, the enchanted dining room from *Beauty and the Beast* is re-created in the culinary section. Villains turn up at the watch and jewelry counter. The murals in the room specializing in kids' clothing and costumes tell the story of *Alice in Wonderland*. And fairies from *Cinderella* and *Sleeping Beauty* float through the intimate-apparel department. Engraving and personalization services are available for many items. A concierge desk can help locate just about any item in the store, then make arrangements for delivery home or to a WDW resort.

Lakeside Activities

Buena Vista Lagoon, the 35-acre expanse that borders this village of cedar-shingled shops, gives the Marketplace much of its atmosphere: When the sidewalks radiate heat, the water looks cool and inviting; in the slanting rays of the late afternoon sun, it glistens like a sheet of silver.

There's always something going on. Little Water Sprites zip to and fro, speeding across the lake, while more laid-back folks float gently along in pontoon or canoe boats, and still others fish off the dock.

It's pleasant to sit and watch all this activity from the waterside benches and tables; over ice cream or frozen yogurt at Donald's Dairy Dip on the lake's west shore; or over Maryland crab cakes and fresh frozen strawberry margaritas at Cap'n Jack's Oyster Bar.

Those who would rather participate need walk only a few steps to the marina, where several types of boats can be rented from morning until dusk. Opening and closing hours change from season to season; call 828-2204 for details. No swimming is permitted. (Prices are subject to state tax.)

CANOPY AND PONTOON BOATS: Providing serenity rather than thrills, the 16-foot canopy boats accommodate up to eight adults, while 20-foot pontoon boats hold up to ten adults. Some people stock up on picnic supplies at the Gourmet Pantry and turn an afternoon sail into a party. Cost ranges from $19 to $22 per half hour.

FISHING EXCURSIONS: A guided two-hour catch-and-release fishing trip aboard a pontoon boat with room for five anglers departs from the Disney Village Marketplace marina several times daily. The fee per boatload—$137 for two hours ($50 for each additional hour)—includes guide, gear, bait, and refreshments. Reservations are required at least 24 hours in advance. Call 828-2204 or 828-2461. Fishing is also permitted off the dock, and cane poles are available for rent ($3.75 per half hour).

WATER SPRITES: These tiny craft are extremely popular. Though they don't really move very fast, they feel as if they do; in any event, they get up enough speed to allow renters to cover quite a lot of territory on Buena Vista Lagoon. Half-hour rentals cost about $16. There are usually lines of people waiting for boats between 11 A.M. and 4 P.M.; plan accordingly. The minimum age to rent or drive one of these boats (even accompanied by an adult) is 14.

Where to Eat at the Marketplace

A complete listing of all restaurants, bars, and snack spots can be found in the *Good Meals, Great Times* chapter. See the Disney Village Marketplace restaurant listing, including the new Rainforest Café, beginning on page 238.

PLEASURE ISLAND

A six-acre island nighttime entertainment complex delivers a wealth of options that nicely top off a day in the parks. In addition to seven nightclubs, there are several restaurants, an unusual variety of shops, and a multiplex cinema.

Pleasure Island is connected to the Disney Village Marketplace by three footbridges. A huge expansion project will blend the two areas into one double-size entertainment district set to debut in late 1997. On the Pleasure Island side of the fence, three venues will combine to create a dynamic new area behind the AMC Theatres. Lario's and House of Blues will be the newest nightclubs to hit the scene, while Wolfgang Puck's Café brings yet another dining option. See the box below for details about the expansion.

The nightclubs open between 7 P.M. and 8 P.M., and don't close until 2 A.M. There is no fee to explore Pleasure Island before the clubs open or to dine at its restaurants. A single admission of $17.97 (including tax) allows access to all clubs and the nightly street party. Length of Stay Passes and Five-Day World Hopper Passes include Pleasure Island admission. An annual pass costs $43.41 ($36.95 for a renewal). Guests under age 18 must be accompanied by a parent.

Specialty drinks, beer, wine, and soft drinks are available at all of the clubs. The drinking age in Florida is 21. Guests who are 18 and over will be admitted to the clubs (except Mannequins), but will not be served alcohol. A valid U.S., foreign, or international driver's license with a photo, an active U.S. military identification card, or a passport must be presented as proof of age.

Clubs

ADVENTURERS CLUB: "Explore the unknown, discover the impossible," states the credo posted at the entrance. The place is modeled on the paneled libraries and elegant salons of similar clubs of the 19th century, and is jam-packed with memorabilia. Just about all the items on display were collected at garage sales, antiques shows, and shops all around the world by Disney Imagineers. The cozy recesses hide rooms where the masks on the walls come to life; current club members, including an inept pilot and a world-renowned bug expert, mingle—with amusing results.

The two-story club is littered with "stuff," so stroll around and snoop all you like. If you have a seat on one of the stools at the bar, ask the bartender to work his or her magic; your stool (or that of an unsuspecting friend) may very slowly sink toward the floor. In the library, a haunted organ sets the scene for outrageous storytellers. The show is a little corny, but entertaining.

COMEDY WAREHOUSE: A comedy troupe performs five times each evening from 7 P.M. to 1 A.M. There are five comedians and one musician. It's a funny, entertaining show that features improvisational comedy based on audience suggestions. Guests perch on stools in a tiered arena, so every seat offers a good view, even if the stools are a little tough on bad backs. Popcorn is the snack of choice.

8TRAX: The seventies are back. Rock 'n' roll music from the early 1970s and sounds from the disco era fill this dance spot. To keep things in the 1970s mode, the staff dresses in polyester.

MANNEQUINS DANCE PALACE: This is the place to head to dance the night away. Guests enter through an elevator that rises to the third floor. Lights, contemporary dance music, and an overall exuberant atmosphere dominate the scene. The name of the club is derived from the many mannequins serving as props. Each of the figures is tied to dance in some way. There are several "cats" from the musical of the same name, and wonderful re-creations of Deborah Kerr and Yul Brynner dressed as Anna and the King of Siam in the "Shall We Dance?" scene from the film *The King and I.*

Nightlife Explosion

By the end of 1997, a bright new nightlife strip will totally energize the area behind the AMC Theatres. The hottest things happening at this end of Disney's entertainment district are the club openings. Lario's, created by Gloria Estefan and her husband Emilio, will emphasize Cuban rhythms (like its popular Miami Beach sister). The more laid-back House of Blues, part-owned by bona fide Blues Brother Dan Aykroyd, will highlight a wide array of live music, including blues and jazz.

The new area will not have a separate admission price, but individual venues may charge a cover. Both spots will double as restaurants; for details, see the *Good Meals, Great Times* chapter.

The main dance floor is actually a turntable, and the music is provided by a deejay whose audio booth is about as high-tech as they come. The lighting is a major attraction, with 60 robotically controlled lighting instruments, and a matrix of lights behind the stage that has been dubbed "the toaster oven" by Disney Imagineers (because it warms the entire room when lit). There are also machines that can create bubbles, hurl confetti, or even make it snow. **Note:** This club is restricted to guests 21 and older.

NEON ARMADILLO MUSIC SALOON: Live country music is performed nightly, and the dance floor is nearly always full. The Southwest decor is highlighted by a wonderful brass chandelier in the shape of a spur and inlaid wood tabletops decorated in Navajo-blanket patterns.

PLEASURE ISLAND JAZZ COMPANY: Reminiscent of jazz clubs from the 1930s, this one is situated in a building that looks like an old warehouse. There is live entertainment nightly featuring jazz tunes from the 1930s to the present. Guests sit at small cocktail tables on comfortable padded chairs. The music is not too loud, so conversation is possible. Tapas-style appetizers are available.

ROCK 'N' ROLL BEACH CLUB: A novel combination of dancing, noshing, and surfer-style decor awaits guests here. The dance floor is located on the lowest level of the building, and there are billiard tables and games on the second and third floors.

Live bands perform hits from the 1960s to the present. The band plays 45 to 50 minutes each hour, and a deejay takes over during the breaks to offer uninterrupted musical entertainment. The atmosphere is a little frenetic but nonetheless exciting.

Entertainment

As if seven nightclubs weren't enough, Pleasure Island is on the verge of providing even more evening diversions. It has made a successful bid to attract nationally known artists, who perform here on the West End Stage. There's at least one name talent each month. Selected summer weekends and various other times bring live reggae music to the island's waterfront. As part of the expansion, a 1,500-seat performing arts theater is expected to open by late 1997, providing yet another entertainment venue.

AMC THEATRES: Current movies are shown at this multiplex cinema. The ten theaters—set to more than double this year to 24 screens—feature an exceptional sound system that was developed by George Lucas.

LATE-NIGHT STREET PARTY: Every night at Pleasure Island is like New Year's Eve. There is a fireworks show with special-effects lighting and confetti, and a talented troupe of dancers entertains on the streets.

WEST END STAGE: Bands, including some top-name groups, perform at this covered stage nightly. The Island Explosion, Pleasure Island's own dance troupe, also entertains at this venue.

Where to Eat at Pleasure Island

A complete listing of restaurants, bars, and snack spots can be found in the *Good Meals, Great Times* chapter. See the Pleasure Island restaurant listing, including the new Fulton's Crab House and a sneak preview of dining options to come, beginning on page 236. Restaurants here are open from about 11:30 A.M. to midnight.

Shopping

The variety of merchandise at Pleasure Island's shops is a little more eclectic than that found at the other WDW emporiums. Shops are open from 11 A.M. to 2 A.M.

AVIGATOR'S SUPPLY: The Adventurers Club logo is emblazoned on a wide variety of merchandise, including T-shirts, sweatshirts, magnets, and tote bags.

CHANGING ATTITUDES: This shop reveals its hip, young style with an assortment of T-shirts, accessories, jewelry, tote bags, and other goods.

DOODLES: Hats, horns, and other party items are available here. Logo merchandise from the various clubs is also for sale.

DTV: A collection of fun and colorful contemporary fashions featuring Mickey Mouse and his friends is available here.

ISLAND DEPOT: The shop features popular surfwear and activewear, including T-shirts, shorts, backpacks, and hats, plus casual watches and jewelry. The No Fear and Mossimo collections are here.

MUSIC LEGENDS: Compact discs, T-shirts, and memorabilia from the early days of rock 'n' roll to heavy metal and hip-hop are available at this spot. There are three sections highlighting different types of music. If a well-known band is featured at the West End Stage, you'll find its latest releases, as well as any T-shirts and souvenir merchandise here.

PROPELLER HEADS: Pleasure Island's arcade, open from 10 A.M. to 2 A.M., features the usual array of blipping and bleeping video games popular with younger guests.

REEL FINDS: Movie- and television-themed memorabilia constitute the stock at this star-studded spot. Items once owned by celebrities of both big- and small-screen fame are on display.

SUPERSTAR STUDIOS: Star in your own music video. Guests lip-sync favorite songs for either audio or video recordings. A particular favorite with teens.

SUSPENDED ANIMATION: Posters, prints, lithographs, cels, and original Disney animation art are sold here. It's a pleasant place to browse.

Getting to Know the BoardWalk

Guests have a second after-dark destination in the new BoardWalk entertainment district, whose innovative clubs are a fine complement to those at Pleasure Island and a real boon to Walt Disney World nightlife. There is no charge to enter the premises, so go for a nostalgic stroll on the boards and check out all the restaurants, shops, and clubs along the lively waterfront strip. For complete details on BoardWalk dining options, see the *Good Meals, Great Times* chapter.

A dance hall heritage is readily apparent from the huge marquee outside **Atlantic Dance**. The ten-piece band highlights music from the 1940s through the '90s. It's a place to dance all night, or sip champagne while sampling hors d'oeuvres on one of two balconies overlooking the water.

Taste hand-crafted specialty ales in **Big River Grille & Brewing Works**, a working brew pub. As the brewmaster creates the three flagship ales and two seasonal brews, guests can observe the entire brewing process through floor-to-ceiling windows. A full menu of pub grub, including shepherd's pie and beer bread, complements the ales.

Sports fans should cheer the arrival of the interactive **ESPN Club**. More than 70 televisions broadcasting live sports events (even in the restrooms) ensure that guests always know the score. A sports commentator hosts trivia contests, interviews celebrity athletes, and entertains during commercial breaks. A limited menu, including ballpark favorites, is served in an arena-style dining area.

Two dueling pianos encourage sing-alongs at **Jellyrolls**. Guests are likely to hear anything from '70s standards to recent hits at this lively bar with nonstop live entertainment. A limited menu is offered.

TYPHOON LAGOON

A furious storm once roared 'cross the sea,
Catching ships in its path, helpless to flee,
Instead of a certain and watery doom,
The winds swept them here to Typhoon Lagoon!

So reads the legend (looking a bit like an old Burma-Shave road sign) that guests see as they drive into Typhoon Lagoon, a 56-acre state-of-the-art aquatic theme park. The watery playground was inspired by an imagined legend: A typhoon hit a small resort village years and years ago, and the storm—plus a resultant earthquake and volcanic eruption—left the village in ruins. The local residents, however, were resourceful and rebuilt their town as best they could.

Whether the typhoon ever actually took place doesn't really matter, because this is a delightful place to spend a day. The surf lagoon is larger than two football fields, speed slides whisk guests through caves, other slides offer twisting journeys, white-water routes invite groups to ride the rapids, and miniature slides entertain kids.

The centerpiece of Typhoon Lagoon is one of the world's largest man-made watershed mountains, Mt. Mayday. Precariously perched atop its peak is the *Miss Tilly*, a marooned shrimp boat originally from Safen Sound, Florida. The smokestack on *Miss Tilly* erupts every half hour, shooting a 50-foot flume of water into the air. Guests who make the 85-foot climb up Mt. Mayday are rewarded with a great view of the action below.

What follows is a description of all the activities at Typhoon Lagoon. What we'll leave to your imagination is the joy of pulling up a lounge chair and people-watching.

TYPHOON LAGOON: The main swimming area spreads out over 2½ acres and contains 2.75 million gallons of water, making this the world's largest wave pool. The Caribbean-blue lagoon is surrounded by a white-sand beach, and its main attraction is the waves that come crashing to the shore. Guests are welcome to bodysurf—just ride the waves with their bodies. Water collects in 12 huge chambers above the lagoon and falls through trap doors, creating the waves. There are also two tidal pools, Whitecap Cove and Blustery Bay, where less adventurous guests can loll about in water made for bobbing, not riding.

CASTAWAY CREEK: This 2,100-foot circular river that winds through the park offers a lazy, relaxing orientation to Typhoon Lagoon. Tubes are free and are the most enjoyable way to make the trip along the three-foot-deep waterway. The ride takes guests through a rain forest where they are cooled by mists and spray; through caves and grottoes that provide welcome shade on hot summer days; and through an area known as Water Works, where "broken" pipes from a water tower unleash showers on passersby. The current is calm, and aside from a few floating props, the journey is unimpeded. There are exits along the way where guests can hop out for a while and do something else, or just dry off a bit and then jump right back in. It takes 25 to 35 minutes to ride around the park without taking a break.

GANGPLANK FALLS, KEELHAUL FALLS, AND MAYDAY FALLS: These three white-water rides offer guests a variety of trips aboard inner tubes. All the slides course through caves and waterfalls, and past intricate rock work, making the scenery an attraction in itself. Gangplank Falls gives families a chance to ride together.

HUMUNGA KOWABUNGA: These two speed slides, reported to have been carved into the landscape by the historic earthquake, will send guests zooming through caves at speeds of 30 miles per hour. The 214-foot slides offer a 51-foot drop, and the view from the top is a little scary. But it's over before you know it, and once-wary guests hurry back for another try. Modest maidens beware! A one-piece suit is far safer than a two-piece suit. Guests are also warned that they should be free of back trouble, heart conditions, and other physical limitations to take the trip. Pregnant women are not permitted to ride.

STORM SLIDES: The Jib Jammer, Rudder Buster, and Stern Burner body slides send guests off at about 20 miles per hour down winding fiberglass slides, in and out of rock formations and caves, and through waterfalls.

It's a somewhat tamer ride than Humunga Kowabunga, but still offers a speedy descent. The slides run about 300 feet, and each offers a different view and experience. Altogether, it's a cooling and enjoyable trip.

SHARK REEF: Guests obtain free snorkel equipment for a swim through an artificial coral reef where they come face to face with sharks and lots of fish. The reef is constructed around a sunken, upside-down tanker (where guests who don't care to swim among the fish can get a close look from the portholes). There are 362,000 gallons of seawater around the reef. The sharks, by the way, are small leopard sharks and bonnethead sharks, both passive members of the species. They don't eat anything bigger than they are. Guests must shower before entering the reef's depths.

KETCHAKIDDEE CREEK: Open only to those four feet tall or under (unless accompanied by a small child), this kiddie area offers comparable rides scaled down for pint-size visitors. Children *must*, however, be accompanied by an adult. There are slides, fountains, waterfalls, squirting whales and seals, a mini rapid ride, and a grotto with a thin veil of water that kids love to run through again and again.

Essentials

WHEN TO GO: Typhoon Lagoon gets very crowded early in the day. Once the park reaches a certain capacity, only guests using WDW transportation will be admitted. When the park reaches peak capacity, no one will be admitted until crowds subside (usually after 3 P.M.). Hours vary seasonally, with extended hours in effect during the summer months. All pools are heated in the winter. Note that Typhoon Lagoon is usually closed for refurbishment during certain winter months, typically November and December.

The park may also close due to inclement weather. Call 824-4321 for schedules.

HOW TO GET THERE: Buses are available from the TTC, and all WDW resorts except the Grand Floridian, Contemporary, Polynesian, Wilderness Lodge, and Fort Wilderness (which require transfers at the TTC).

LOCKER ROOMS: Restrooms with showers and lockers are located near the entrance. Other restrooms are available farther into the park. These are labeled "Buoys" and "Gulls." Small lockers cost $3 plus a $2 deposit to rent for the day, while large lockers cost $5 plus a $2 deposit. Towels rent for $1, and life jackets are available with a $25 refundable deposit.

WHERE TO EAT: There are two restaurants at Typhoon Lagoon, both offering similar fare and outdoor seating at tables with colorful umbrellas. Leaning Palms, which was known as Placid Palms before the typhoon hit, was renamed to fit its somewhat unorthodox architecture. Burgers, hot dogs, salads, ice cream, and assorted snacks are sold here. Typhoon Tilly's Galley & Grog offers a similar menu and has a separate area just for ice cream and frozen yogurt. Let's Go Slurpin offers frozen drink specialties and spirits. Also on hand are picnic areas, where guests can bring their own food or enjoy a sampling from the restaurants. Note that no alcoholic beverages or glass containers can be brought into the park.

FIRST AID: A first-aid station capable of handling minor medical problems is located just to the left of Leaning Palms.

BEACH SHOP: Singapore Sal's, located to the right of the main entrance, is set in a ramshackle building left a bit worn by the typhoon. Bathing suits, sunglasses, hats, towels, sunscreen, souvenirs, thong sandals, and beach chairs are among the wares here.

Admission Prices

ONE-DAY TICKET
(Prices include sales tax and are subject to change.)

Adult	$25.39
Child*	$19.03

ANNUAL PASS

Adult	$90.05
Child*	$72.03

Note: Admission is included with a Length of Stay Pass or a Five-Day World Hopper Pass.

*3 through 9 years of age; children under 3 free

BLIZZARD BEACH

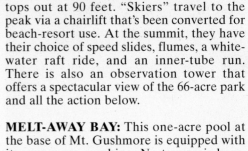

The newest water park at Walt Disney World (it opened in April 1995) is said to be the result of a freak winter storm that dropped a mountain of snow on the western side of the WDW property. As plans were quickly made for Florida's first ski resort, temperatures soared and the ice and snow began to melt. Designers were ready to close the new resort when they spotted an alligator sliding down the slopes and realized that the melting snow created the tallest, fastest, and most exhilarating water adventure park in the world. The slalom and bobsled runs became downhill water slides. The ski jump is now the world's tallest (120 feet), fastest (60 miles per hour), free-fall speed slide. Instead of skiers, the chairlift carries swimmers to the top.

Once again, Disney Imagineers have concocted an interesting tale to explain the existence of their latest creation. And, of course, it doesn't really matter if the legend is true. This is the most action-packed water park yet, with enough cool activities for the entire family to fill at least a day.

The centerpiece of Blizzard Beach is the snow-capped Mt. Gushmore and its Summit Plummet, visible from almost anywhere in the park. Most of the more thrilling runs are found on the slopes of this mountain, which tops out at 90 feet. "Skiers" travel to the peak via a chairlift that's been converted for beach-resort use. At the summit, they have their choice of speed slides, flumes, a white-water raft ride, and an inner-tube run. There is also an observation tower that offers a spectacular view of the 66-acre park and all the action below.

MELT-AWAY BAY: This one-acre pool at the base of Mt. Gushmore is equipped with its own wave machine. No tsunamis here, however, just a pleasant bobbing wave. The pool is constantly fed by "melting snow" waterfalls.

CROSS COUNTRY CREEK: This meandering 3,000-foot waterway circles the entire park. A slow current keeps visitors moving along. Inner tubes, which are free, are the most pleasant way to travel. The ride includes a trip through a bone-chilling ice cave, where guests are splashed with the "melting ice" from overhead.

SUMMIT PLUMMET: The big thrill ride begins 120 feet in the air on a platform built 30 feet above the top of Mt. Gushmore. It looks just like a ski jump. Brave souls travel about 60 miles per hour down the 350-foot slide. Near the top, guests pass through the ski chalet. To those watching from below, riders seem to disappear into an explosion of mist. Female riders would be wise to make the trip in a one-piece suit.

SLUSH GUSHER: A tamer trip down Mt. Gushmore can be undertaken next door to Summit Plummet. Although shorter and less severe than its neighbor, this double-humped slide still offers a brisk journey through a snow-banked mountain gully. Topping out at 90 feet, Slush Gusher is the tallest slide of its kind.

TEAMBOAT SPRINGS: The longest family white-water raft ride in the world takes five-passenger rafts down a twisting, 1,400-foot series of rushing waterfalls.

TOBOGGAN RACERS: An eight-lane water slide sends guests racing over a number of dips. Guests lie on their stomachs on a mat and travel headfirst down the 250-foot route.

SNOW STORMERS: A trio of flumes descends from the top of the mountain. Guests race down on a switchback course that includes ski-type slalom gates.

RUNOFF RAPIDS: On this inner-tube run, guests careen down three different twisting, turning flumes, one completely in the dark.

COOL RUNNINGS: No bunny slopes here. Riders can bank on hurtling and whirling over lots of moguls on these twin inner-tube slides.

DOWNHILL DOUBLE DIPPER: Guests travel down these two parallel 230-foot-long racing slides at speeds of up to 25 miles per hour. The partially enclosed water runs feature ski-racing graphics, flags, and time clocks.

SKI PATROL TRAINING CAMP: An area designed specifically for preteens. Frozen Pipe Springs looks like an old pipe and drops sliders into eight feet of water. The Thin Ice Training Course tests agility skills as kids try to walk along broken "icebergs" without falling into the water. At the Ski Patrol Shelter, guests grab on to a T-bar for an airborne trip. At any point in the ride they can drop into the water below.

TIKE'S PEAK: A kid-size variation of Blizzard Beach, this attraction features miniature versions of Mt. Gushmore's slides and a snow-castle fountain play area.

Essentials

WHEN TO GO: As the World's newest water park, Blizzard Beach becomes very crowded early in the day. Once the park reaches a certain capacity, only guests using WDW transportation will be admitted, so plan accordingly. When the park reaches peak capacity, no one will be admitted until crowds subside (usually after 3 P.M.). Hours vary seasonally, with extended hours in effect during the summer months. All pools are heated in winter. Note that Blizzard Beach is usually closed for refurbishment during certain winter months, typically January and February. The park may also close due to inclement weather. For current schedules, call 824-4321.

HOW TO GET THERE: Direct buses are available from the TTC and all Walt Disney World resorts.

LOCKER ROOMS: Restrooms with showers are located near the main entrance. Other restrooms and dressing rooms are located around the park. Small lockers cost $3 plus a $2 deposit to rent for the day, while large lockers cost $5 plus a $2 deposit. Towels rent for $1, and life jackets are available with a $25 refundable deposit.

WHERE TO EAT: Burgers, hot dogs, fruit salads, and drinks are available at Lottawatta Lodge, a fast-food restaurant located in the main village area. Two other snack stands with limited offerings are located in more remote areas: Avalunch and The Warming Hut offer snacks and soft drinks. There are also picnic areas for those who prefer to pack their own. Note that no alcoholic beverages or glass containers are permitted in the park.

FIRST AID: Minor medical problems are handled at this station near the main entrance.

BEACH SHOP: The Beach Haus, near the main entrance, stocks bathing suits, T-shirts, shorts, sunglasses, hats, suntan lotion, beach towels, and all the other accoutrements needed for a day in the park. Logo merchandise is in large supply.

Admission Prices

ONE-DAY TICKET
(Prices include sales tax and are subject to change.)

Adult	$25.39
Child*	$19.03

ANNUAL PASS

Adult	$90.05
Child*	$72.03

Note: Admission is included with a Length of Stay Pass or a Five-Day World Hopper Pass.

*3 through 9 years of age; children under 3 free

FORT WILDERNESS

In a part of the state where campgrounds tend to look like pastures—barren and very hot—the Fort Wilderness campground, located almost due east of the Contemporary resort, is an anomaly—a forested 700-acre wonder of tall slash pines, white-flowering bay trees, and ancient cypress hung with streamers of Spanish moss. Seminole Indians once hunted and fished here.

In all, there are some 1,192 woodsy campsites arranged in several campground loops; among them, Fleetwood units are available for rent, completely furnished and fitted with all the comforts of home. For information about both lodging options, see *Transportation & Accommodations*.

Scattered throughout the campground loops are a number of sporting facilities, including two tennis courts, and myriad tetherball, basketball, and volleyball courts. Fort Wilderness has riding stables, two swimming pools, a marina full of boats, a canoe livery, a beach, bikes and electric golf carts for rent, and a nature trail. Some of these facilities are available for the use of campground guests only; some are open to guests at WDW-owned resort hotels and villas as well; some can also be enjoyed by guests lodging at the establishments at the Disney Village Hotel Plaza as well as off the property.

There's also a petting farm where goats, ducks, and other farm animals run free inside a white-rail fence, and it's fun to walk through the barn that houses the large, sleek horses that pull the Magic Kingdom's Main Street trolleys.

Two stores—namely, the Settlement Trading Post and the Meadow Trading Post—stock campers' necessities, groceries, and some Disney souvenirs. And then there's Pioneer Hall, widely known as the home of the Hoop-Dee-Doo Musical Revue dinner show (described in *Good Meals, Great Times*). This rustic structure (made of western white pine shipped all the way from Montana) also has a cafeteria and lounge.

Last but not least in the Fort Wilderness catalog is River Country. This eight-acre expanse of water-oriented recreation embodies everyone's idea of the perfect swimming hole. It's a separate attraction, with its own hours and admission fees.

BEACHES AND SWIMMING: The clear waters of Bay Lake, which lap the 315-foot white-sand beach at the north end of the campground, are delightful. Swimming is allowed inside the roped-off areas, and there are also two pools for campers' use. Note that beaches and pools are open to Fort Wilderness guests only.

BIKE RENTALS: Tandems and other bikes can be hired at the Bike Barn for trips along the bike paths and roadways of Fort Wilderness—or just for getting around. Cost is $3 per hour or $10 per day; $15 for overnight.

BLACKSMITH SHOP: The pleasant fellow who shoes the draft horses that pull the trolleys down Main Street in the Magic Kingdom is on hand at some time every day to answer questions and talk about what he does; occasionally guests can watch him at work, fitting the big animals with the special polyurethane-covered, steel-cored horseshoes that are used to protect the horses' hooves.

BOATING: Fort Wilderness is ribboned with tranquil canals, some out in the open and some canopied by trees, which make for delightful canoe trips of one to three hours—or longer if you take fishing gear and elect to wet your line. Canoe rentals are available at the Bike Barn for $4 per hour or $10 per day. Pedal boats ($5 per half hour or $8 per hour) can also be rented here for use in the canals. For a trip around Bay Lake, zippy little Water Sprites, sailboats, and pontoon boats are available for rent at the marina, at the north end of the campground. (See the *Sports* chapter for details and fees.)

CAMPFIRE PROGRAM: Held nightly near the Meadow Trading Post at the center of the campground, this evening entertainment program features Disney movies, a sing-along, and cartoons. It's open to WDW resort guests only (no charge). Also, Chip 'n' Dale always put in an appearance.

ELECTRIC CART RENTALS: Available at the Bike Barn ($35.51 for 24 hours) for sightseeing or transportation. Renters must be 18 years old and have a valid driver's license. Reservations are necessary; call 824-2742.

ELECTRICAL WATER PAGEANT: This twinkling cavalcade of lights (described in more detail in the *Good Meals, Great Times* chapter) can be seen from the beach here nightly at 9:45 P.M.

FISHING EXCURSIONS ON BAY LAKE: Walt Disney World's restrictive fishing policy means plenty of angling action—largemouth bass weighing two to eight pounds, mainly—for those who sign up for the special 8 A.M., 11:30 A.M., and 3 P.M. fishing excursions. The fee is $137 for up to five people for a two-hour excursion (each additional hour is $50) and includes gear, a guide, and refreshments; no license is required. Note that all fishing is strictly catch-and-release. Call 824-2621 for reservations.

FISHING IN THE CANALS: In addition to largemouth bass, catfish and panfish can be caught here as well. Those without their own gear will find cane poles and lures for sale at the trading posts; equipment is also available for rent at the Bike Barn. Cane poles are $2 per hour or $4 for the whole day. Rods and reels are $4 per hour or $8 per day. No license is required. Fort Wilderness resort guests may toss their lines in right from the shore.

HAYRIDES: The hay wagon departs from Pioneer Hall at 7 P.M. and 9:30 P.M. and carries guests on a trip through wooded areas near Bay Lake. Each ride lasts about an hour, and concludes back at Pioneer Hall. Tickets can be purchased from the hayride host. The price is $6 for adults; $4 for children 3 to 9. Children under ten must be accompanied by an adult.

LAWN MOWER TREE: The tree that somehow, mysteriously, grew around a lawn mower is a Fort Wilderness point of interest worth hunting down. It's just off the sidewalk leading to the marina.

PETTING FARM: This fenced-in enclave just behind Pioneer Hall is home to some friendly goats, sheep, rabbits, chickens, and other assorted barnyard critters. (A colony of prairie dogs didn't work out because its members persisted in burrowing out of their compound; no sooner would their Disney caretakers try to thwart them—by digging a bigger hole and installing a below-ground-level wire fence—than the little creatures would gnaw through it.) Pony rides are available between 9 A.M. and 5 P.M. for $2. Though mainly designed for youngsters, the Petting Farm is also fun for adults, and it's a good place to pass the time while waiting for seating at the Hoop-Dee-Doo Musical Revue in nearby Pioneer Hall.

TENNIS: Two tennis courts are available; play is on a first-come, first-served basis.

TRAIL RIDES: Horseback trips depart four times daily from the front of the campground and take riders on a leisurely, meandering ride through the Florida wilderness, where it is not uncommon to see birds, deer, and even an occasional alligator. Galloping is not part

Hoop-Dee-Doo Musical Revue

Sturdy, porch-rimmed Pioneer Hall is best-known Worldwide as the home of the Pioneer Hall Players, an energetic troupe of singing, dancing, wisecracking entertainers who keep audiences chuckling, grinning, and whooping it up for two hours during a procession of barbecued ribs, fried chicken, corn-on-the-cob, strawberry shortcake, and other stomach-stretching vittles. If you have time for only one of the Disney dinner shows, make it this one (for more details see *Good Meals, Great Times*). Reservations are hard to come by. See the reservation chart on pages 22 and 23 for details.

of the game, so you don't need riding know-how to sign up. Cost is $17 per person for both day visitors and for guests at WDW-owned properties. No children under nine are allowed to ride. There is a weight limit of 250 pounds. Reservations are necessary; phone 824-2621 up to two weeks in advance.

TRI-CIRCLE-D RANCH: This corner of Fort Wilderness is the place that the world champion Percherons and all the draft horses that pull trolleys down Main Street in the Magic Kingdom call home. You can watch them chomping placidly on their food, and occasionally see young colts and fillies as well. The Tri-Circle-D insignia above the barn door—two small circles, Mouse-ears style, atop a large one with the letter *D* inside—is also the WDW brand.

VOLLEYBALL, TETHERBALL, AND BASKETBALL COURTS: Open only to guests at WDW-owned properties, these are scattered throughout the camping loops. No charge.

WATERSKI TRIPS: Ski boats with drivers and equipment can be hired (including instruction) for $82 an hour at the marina. There is a minimum of two people and a maximum of five. Reservations are necessary and can be made up to two weeks in advance. Call 824-2621.

WILDERNESS SWAMP TRAIL: A three-quarter mile trail, this smooth footpath into the woods skirts the marshes along the shore of Bay Lake, then plunges into a forest full of tall, straight-standing cypress trees. It is near Marshmallow Marsh, at the northern end of the campground.

Essentials

HOW TO GET THERE: From outside the World, take Magic Kingdom Exit 25 off I-4 onto U.S. 192, go through the Magic Kingdom Auto Plaza, and, bearing to your right, follow the Fort Wilderness or River Country signs. This is the most expeditious way to go, even for WDW resort guests.

By WDW Transportation: There's a direct bus (or bike path) from the Wilderness Lodge to Fort Wilderness. From Epcot, the Contemporary, Polynesian, and Grand Floridian resorts, take the monorail to the Transportation and Ticket Center (TTC), and transfer for the bus to Fort Wilderness. From Disney-MGM Studios, the Disney Village Marketplace, and Disney Village Hotel Plaza establishments, take a bus to the TTC. Change there to the bus to Fort Wilderness. From all other WDW resorts take a bus to the Disney Village Marketplace, switch for the bus to the TTC, then take the Fort Wilderness bus. Allow yourself plenty of time to make transfers.

Boats are also available from Magic Kingdom marinas (about a 30-minute ride) and from the Contemporary resort (about a 25-minute ride). For more details about WDW Transportation, see *Transportation and Accommodations*.

WHERE TO EAT: For a complete list of restaurants found at the Fort Wilderness campground, see page 232 in the *Good Meals, Great Times* chapter. The Settlement Trading Post, located not far from the beach at the north end of the campground, and the Meadow Trading Post, located near the center of Fort Wilderness, also offer food staples.

RIVER COUNTRY

It's next to impossible to go through childhood reading such classic books as *The Adventures of Tom Sawyer* and *The Adventures of Huckleberry Finn* (and other great tales of growing up) without developing a few fantasies about what it would be like to swim in the perfect swimming hole. A group of Disney Imagineers concocted a Disney version on a somewhat larger scale at River Country, a water-oriented playground that occupies a corner of Bay Lake at Fort Wilderness campground.

Fred Joerger—the same Disney rock builder who created Big Thunder Mountain, Schweitzer Falls at the Jungle Cruise, and the caves of Tom Sawyer Island in the Magic Kingdom—also helped design the rocks used to landscape one of the largest swimming pools in the state. The rocks, scattered with real pebbles acquired from stream beds in Georgia and the Carolinas, look so real that it's hard to believe they aren't.

More to the point, the place is great fun. Slipping and sliding down the curvy water chutes at top speed; getting spun around in the whirlpools of White Water Rapids; and slamming into the water from the swimming pool's high slides make even careworn grownups smile, grin, giggle, chortle, and roar with delight. People who climb to the top of the water-slide ridge with trepidation may embark on a lightning-fast ride only because it seems too late to back out, but at the bottom they rush back for more. Line-haters queue up—over and over again. Those who associate lakes with muck and weeds get ecstatic over the way the soft sand on the River Country bottom squishes between their toes.

WHAT TO DO: There are several sections to River Country—the 330,000-gallon swimming pool; Bay Cove (a.k.a. the Ol' Swimmin' Hole), the big walled-off section of Bay Lake that most people consider the main (and best) part of River Country; an adjoining junior version of the above for small children, with its own beach; and the grassy grounds, with picnic tables and a squirting fountain in which to play. On the edge of the lake there's also a boardwalk nature trail through a lovely cypress swamp, and a wide (if not terribly long) white-sand beach.

The large swimming pool that's known as Upstream Plunge is heated in winter. It has a pair of Slippery Slide Falls water slides that begin high enough above the water to make an acrophobe climb right down again. They plunge at such an angle that it's impossible to see the bottom of the slide from the top. Daredevils who don't chicken out are shot into the water from a height of about seven feet—hard enough, as one commentator observed, to "slap your stomach up against the roof of your mouth." Gutsy kids adore the experience; those who like their thrills a bit tamer might prefer to watch.

The heart of River Country, Bay Cove, is actually a part of Bay Lake (and quite chilly during cooler months). It's fitted out with rope swings, a ship's boom for swooping and plunging, and assorted other constructions designed to put hearts into throats as swimmers plunge from air to water. The big deals, however, are the two flume rides—one 260 feet long (accessible by a boardwalk and stairway to the far right of the swimming hole as you face it) and a smaller one, 100 feet shorter (accessible by a stairway to the left)—and the white-water raft ride.

The flumes, which are like overgrown, steep-sided water slides, corkscrew through the greenery at the top of the ridge known as Whoop-'N-Holler Hollow, sending even the most stalwart shooting into the water, usually like greased lightning. White Water Rapids, as the white-water raft ride mentioned above is known, involves a more leisurely trip through a series of chutes and pools in an inner tube from the crest of Raft Rider Ridge (adjoining Whoop-'N-Holler Hollow) into Bay Cove. It's not a high-speed affair like the flumes, but some people like it better. The pools are contoured so that the water swirls through them in whirlpool fashion. You tend to get caught in the slow circling water, and when other tubers come sliding down the chutes at you, arms and legs get all tangled up.

197

Essentials

WHEN TO GO: Daytime temperatures in Orlando are such that it's possible to enjoy River Country almost all year round, though it is perhaps most pleasant in spring when the weather is getting hot but the water is still cool. In summer, the place can be very busy indeed. Ticket windows close as the crowd approaches a certain capacity. During the busiest seasons, that may happen as early as 11 A.M. It's worth noting, however, that those who already have tickets will be admitted anyway, until the park has reached peak capacity. Things usually quiet down after 3 P.M. River Country is usually closed for refurbishment during certain cooler months, typically September and October. Note that the park may also close due to inclement weather. River Country closes at 7 P.M. during the summer. Call 824-4321 for up-to-the-minute schedules.

HOW TO GET THERE: From the Transportation and Ticket Center, buses drop off passengers within walking distance of River Country. It's also possible to go by boat. Launches leave regularly from the dock near the gates of the Magic Kingdom. Guests arriving at River Country by car may take a bus from the Fort Wilderness visitor parking lot to the entrance.

LOCKER ROOMS: Men's and women's dressing rooms with showers and lockers are available. Small lockers cost $3 plus a $2 deposit to rent for the day; large lockers cost $5 plus a $2 deposit. Towels are available for rent at $1 each at the concession window, but they're small, so you'll probably want to bring at least one beach towel.

WHERE TO EAT: Pop's Place has hot dogs, quarter-pound burgers, salads, beer, and soda. The Waterin' Hole offers a limited selection during peak seasons. Picnicking is permitted (but no alcohol or glass containers can be brought into the park). Eat on the beach or seek out one of the tables on the shady lawns.

FIRST AID: A first-aid station capable of handling minor medical problems is located near the locker rooms.

BEACH SHOP: Film, towels, sand pails, sunscreen, and other beach essentials are available at the River Relics stand.

Admission Prices

ONE-DAY TICKET
(Prices include sales tax and are subject to change.)

Adult	$15.64
Child*	$12.19

ANNUAL PASS

Adult	$58.57
Child*	$58.57

Note: Admission is included with a Length of Stay Pass or a Five-Day World Hopper Pass.

*3 through 9 years of age; children under 3 free

LEARNING PROGRAMS

A variety of educational programs offer behind-the-scenes looks at the Walt Disney World Resort. Disney Day Camp provides youthful spins on several Disney Institute programs for kids ages 7 through 9. Wonders of Walt Disney World programs invite young people ages 10 through 15 to step backstage for a look at wildlife, art, entertainment, and international cultures. Still other options give adults a chance to study the culture and landscapes of Epcot's World Showcase, or to participate in a series of multi-day business and education seminars. A brief description of available programs follows.

DISNEY DAY CAMP FOR KIDS 7 TO 9

The Disney Institute offers a number of 3½-hour field trips especially for younger kids; designed to complement the Institute's offerings for older youth, the programs are available both to families staying at the Disney Institute and day visitors. Participation is included in Disney Institute vacation rates (see page 181 for complete details about the Institute); for day visitors, the cost is about $50 per child for one day with either one or two programs ($5 more with boxed lunch). For reservations or additional Disney Day Camp information, call 827-4800.

ArtSurround (Sunday and Thursday) journeys to Epcot's World Showcase, where kids see works of art, and learn about artists' many different inspirations, from nature to music, motion, and emotion.

Broadway Bound (Tuesday and Friday) offers kids a glimpse of show biz and what it takes to hit the big time.

Disney's Orient Express (Tuesday and Saturday) takes kids on a trip to the Orient via Epcot's World Showcase. En route, they discover the music, art, and history of Japan and China.

Face Magic (Wednesday and Friday), which takes place backstage at the Disney-MGM Studios, reveals how makeup artists create illusions and special effects; then kids get to apply their newfound knowledge to their own faces.

Swamp Stomp (Monday and Saturday) escorts kids through a cypress swamp. During this nature safari, they keep watch for native animals, and learn about measures that can be taken to protect the environment.

Stealing the Show (Monday and Thursday) invites kids to take center stage for improvisation games, mime exercises, and rhythm drills much like those professional actors use to hone their skills.

Tiles, Temples, & Treasures (Sunday) brings kids to Epcot's World Showcase, where they explore what life is like in Mexico and Morocco.

WONDERS OF WALT DISNEY WORLD FOR KIDS 10 TO 15

Wonders of Walt Disney World education programs spark the imaginations of students interested in learning about wildlife, art, entertainment, or international cultures. Each six-hour learning program was developed in cooperation with leading educators. In many cases, students can earn school credit or an excused absence for completing the program. The cost is $79 and participants receive a book with follow-up activities, access to the theme parks and backstage areas during the program, lunch, and a personalized certificate of completion. Program content and prices are subject to change without notice. For individual reservations, call 354-1855. For special rates for groups of 11 or more, call 824-4730. Choose from the following four programs.

Wildlife Adventure: Exploring the Environment (Tuesday and Thursday) essentially takes students on a safari through the pristine Walt Disney World conservation area. Environmental issues are discussed while kids observe alligators, birds, and other creatures in their natural habitat.

Art Magic: Bringing Illusion to Life (Monday through Friday) shows how WDW artists create the illusion of reality in movies and theme parks. This program includes a behind-the-scenes look at the animation process. Following a discussion about the steps involved in developing an animated film, kids get to paint a keepsake Mickey Mouse cel. The students then see the use of theme, color, and forced perspective in the parks. The day concludes with tips on drawing Disney characters.

Show Biz Magic: The Walt Disney World of Entertainment (Monday through Thursday) introduces kids to the diversity of WDW entertainment. Discussions on show preparation and auditions are reinforced through talks with performers from a variety of entertainment areas. Highlights include a visit to a costuming department and a trip into the tunnel system beneath the Magic Kingdom.

Passport: A Secret Mission to Other Lands (Wednesday and Friday) brings to life the traditions, art, culture, and history of Epcot's World Showcase. As students travel from country to country, they have the chance to talk with international cast members, study architectural styles, learn how to communicate in other languages, and uncover the secrets behind the re-creations of world-famous landmarks here.

Adult Learning Programs

Adult Learning Programs escort guests 16 and older behind the scenes. Among the program choices is a guided tour that ventures backstage at each of the theme parks, and a hands-on introduction to the art of animation. Still other learning tours focus on Epcot, revealing clever design techniques as well as meticulous gardening strategies that contribute to the cultural authenticity of World Showcase. Programs geared toward business professionals round out the options.

Content and prices of the Adult Learning Programs described below are subject to change without notice. For information and reservations for all but the Disney University Professional Development Programs, call WDW-TOUR (939-8687).

Hidden Treasures of World Showcase (Sunday, Wednesday, and Friday) escorts guests on a richly detailed tour of Epcot's World Showcase. Participants discover the often overlooked art, architecture, costumes, landscape, and entertainment of the meticulously created international pavilions. The tour lasts about 3½ hours, and costs $25 per person in addition to theme park admission.

Gardens of the World (Monday, Tuesday, Thursday) is hosted by a Disney horticulturist. This 3½-hour program, especially popular among gardeners, guides guests through a study of the plants, flowers, and trees of Epcot's World Showcase. Cost is $25 per person in addition to theme park admission.

Backstage Magic (Monday and Wednesday) is a six-hour exploration of the backstage areas of Walt Disney World, including behind-the-scenes views of theme park attractions and an animation studio, plus a tour of the Magic Kingdom's Utilidors (underground tunnels). Cost is $160 per person.

Inside Animation (Tuesday and Thursday) is a 2½-hour program that takes place at the Disney-MGM Studios. Participants learn about the art of animation, discover how the classics are brought to life, and create their own Mickey Mouse cel. Cost is $45 per person in addition to theme park admission.

Disney University Professional Development Programs offer a variety of programs designed specifically for business and education professionals. Programs help participants see how Disney methods can be adapted to their organizations or classrooms. For additional information, contact Disney University Professional Development Programs; Box 10,093; Lake Buena Vista, FL 32830-0093; 363-6000 or fax 824-4866.

World Tours

In addition to the above-mentioned options, a constantly changing lineup of learning programs offers guests a range of behind-the-scenes tours in all three theme parks. They range from two hours to nearly seven, and cost between $25 and $160. For reservations or more information, call WDW-TOUR (939-8687).

Sports

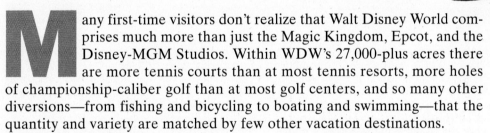

Many first-time visitors don't realize that Walt Disney World comprises much more than just the Magic Kingdom, Epcot, and the Disney-MGM Studios. Within WDW's 27,000-plus acres there are more tennis courts than at most tennis resorts, more holes of championship-caliber golf than at most golf centers, and so many other diversions—from fishing and bicycling to boating and swimming—that the quantity and variety are matched by few other vacation destinations.

So while the golfers in the family are pursuing a perfect swing on one of five first-rate 18-hole courses, tennis buffs can be wearing themselves out on the courts, sailors can be sailing, waterskiers can be skimming back and forth across powerboat wakes, and anglers can be dangling a cane pole in a canal in hopes of bringing in a big bream.

Instruction (formal and impromptu), as well as guides, drivers, and assorted leaders and supervisors, make every sport as much fun for rank beginners as for hard-core aficionados. Moreover, the ready accessibility of WDW sporting activities—via an excellent system of public transportation (see *Transportation & Accommodations*)—means that no visiting family or group member need curtail play time to chauffeur others around.

Note: Prices given in this chapter are subject to change, and do not include applicable state tax.

 Unless otherwise noted, all phone numbers are in area code 407.

A MATTER OF COURSES

Most people don't immediately think of Walt Disney World when they contemplate a golf vacation. Yet there are six superb courses here: The Magnolia, the Palm, and the Oak Trail are situated across from the Polynesian resort and extend nearly to the borders of the Magic Kingdom. Just a short drive away is the Lake Buena Vista course, whose fairways are framed by the Disney Institute and Old Key West resort. Osprey Ridge and Eagle Pines play from the Bonnet Creek Golf Club near Fort Wilderness.

While the original Joe Lee–designed courses (the Palm, Magnolia, and Lake Buena Vista) won't set anyone's knees to knocking in terror from the regular tees, all three are demanding enough to merit the status of an annual stop on the PGA Tour tournament trail. And the annual LPGA HealthSouth Inaugural is contested on the Lake Buena Vista course.

Osprey Ridge was designed by Tom Fazio to offer a reasonable challenge for beginners as well as more advanced players. Eagle Pines, designed by Pete Dye, is a "low profile" layout built level with, or lower than, the surrounding land.

Depending on the tee from which a golfer opts to play, the Disney courses will prove challenging and/or fun, and all are constructed to be especially forgiving for the mid-handicap player. What's more, they're remarkably interesting topographically, considering that the land from which they were carved was about as hilly as a tabletop.

PALM & MAGNOLIA: The wide-open, tree-dotted Magnolia measures 5,232 yards from the front tees, 6,642 from the middle, and 7,190 from the back. The Palm is tighter, with more wooded fairways and nine water hazards; it measures 5,398 yards from the front, 6,461 from the middle, and 6,957 from the back. And the Palm has been ranked among the nation's top 75 resort courses by *Golf Digest* magazine. Together with the Lake Buena Vista course, the pair hosts the Walt Disney World/Oldsmobile Golf Classic every year. The Magnolia and Palm share two driving ranges and two putting greens.

Oak Trail: This nine-hole 2,913-yard layout, a walking course tucked in a corner of the Magnolia, was designed for beginners; but it has some tough holes, including two par 5s.

OSPREY RIDGE & EAGLE PINES: These two par-72 courses play from the Bonnet Creek Golf Club. The Tom Fazio–designed Osprey Ridge measures 5,402 yards from the front tees, 6,680 from the middle, and 7,101 from the back. It escorts guests through some remote areas of WDW property as it winds through the wooded landscape near Fort Wilderness. Dramatic contouring puts some tees 20 to 25 feet above the basic grade. In contrast, the Pete Dye–designed Eagle Pines is a low-profile layout. It plays 4,838 yards from the front tees, 6,309 from the middle, and 6,772 from the pro tees. Many of the fairways are bordered by scrub and pine needles; water comes into play as well. Osprey Ridge and Eagle Pines share a driving range and a putting green.

LAKE BUENA VISTA COURSE: This Joe Lee design measures 5,176 yards from the front tees, 6,268 from the middle, and 6,829 from the rearmost markers. Among the shortest of the 18-hole, par-72 courses, it has a fair amount of water, and its tree-lined fairways are the World's narrowest. This course is well suited for beginners but also equipped to challenge more experienced players. A driving range and putting green are available. Note that this course is the location for the Disney Institute's extensive golf programs.

Essentials

WHEN TO GO: January through April is peak golfing season. To beat the crowds, play on a Monday or Tuesday, tee off in late afternoon, or take advantage of low summer rates. From May 31 through December 31, season badges ($50) net steep discounts.

RESERVATIONS: Call WDW-GOLF (939-4653) to confirm current rates and to secure tee-off times. From January through April, morning and early afternoon tee times should be reserved well in advance; starting times after 3 P.M. are often available at the last minute. Those buying a golf package can reserve tee times up to 90 days prior to their check-in date. Those with confirmed reservations at a WDW resort or Hotel Plaza property can reserve 60 days ahead. Others can book tee times 30 days ahead with a credit card, 7 days in advance without a credit card.

FEES: At the 18-hole courses, greens fees (including the required cart) vary with the course and the season. Rates range from $85 to $105 for WDW resort and Hotel Plaza guests, and from $95 to $120 for day visitors. Twilight rates, usually in effect beginning at 3 P.M., are $40 to $50. Cost for adults to play Oak Trail is $24 for 9 holes, $32 for 18 holes; juniors (under 17) pay $11 for 9 holes, $16 for 18 holes. Prices are subject to change.

INSTRUCTION: Private lessons on any WDW course cost $50 per half hour for adults; $30 for juniors under 17. At the Walt Disney World Golf Studio, based at the Palm and the Magnolia, PGA pros offer 90-minute sessions, complete with video analysis; cost is $75. Nine-hole playing lessons in which a pro gives instruction in club selection, strategy, and more, cost $150 for adults or $75 for juniors under 17. Reservations are necessary for all lessons; call 939-4653. Note, too, that the Disney Institute offers a first-rate golf instruction program—developed by Gary Player—at the Lake Buena Vista course (see page 181 for details on the Institute).

DRESS: Proper golf attire is required. Shirts must have collars and any shorts must be Bermuda length.

EQUIPMENT RENTAL: The pro shops rent graphite clubs ($30), Titleist clubs ($22), range balls ($5 a bucket), and shoes ($6).

Tournaments

The Walt Disney World/Oldsmobile Golf Classic is among the biggest spectator events on WDW's sports calendar. It features most of the pro tour's top players, and usually takes place in mid-October. Guests who plan to golf during their WDW vacation are advised not to visit during tournament week. You can, however, play alongside the pros if you are willing to pay for it: Members of the Classic Club, whose annual dues start at about $5,150, count this privilege among their perks.

The LPGA HealthSouth Inaugural, a relative newcomer to Disney turf, is contested in January. It's exciting to behold, but, again, be advised that tee times can be rather hard to come by. For details on the Classic, Classic Club, or LPGA event, call WDW-GOLF (939-4653). Private tournaments may be arranged at no charge beyond the normal greens fees by calling the same number.

TENNIS EVERYONE

No one comes to Walt Disney World strictly for a tennis vacation; it just doesn't exude the country-club ambience of a tennis resort where everyone is totally immersed in the game. But the facilities and instruction program here are extensive enough that such holidays are certainly possible. And Disney's Sports Complex, with its 11 clay courts and full-blown tennis stadium, promises to expand the WDW tennis scene considerably (see page 207 for details on this new facility). Certainly, a couple of sets of tennis on one of the World's 25 resort courts is a good way to unwind after a mad morning in the parks.

With six courts and a pro shop, Disney's Racquet Club at the Contemporary resort is Walt Disney World's major tennis facility. Located just beyond the hotel's north wing, the club features state-of-the-art hydrogrid clay courts. Elsewhere on property, The Villas at the Disney Institute merits attention, though its four hydrogrid clay courts are available almost exclusively to guests participating in the Institute's tennis programs. The Grand Floridian and BoardWalk each boast a pair of clay courts. All other WDW tennis is played on hard courts. Fort Wilderness has two, the Yacht Club and Beach Club share a pair, Old Key West has three, and the Swan and Dolphin have a four-court facility.

Essentials

WHEN TO GO: Courts are generally open from 8 A.M. to 8 P.M. daily (hours may vary during winter); lighted courts are available at each of the above-mentioned resorts. In February, March, April, June, and July the courts endure fairly heavy use, but there is usually a lull between noon and 3 P.M., and again from dinnertime until 9 P.M. January, October, and November are considered prime months for tennis enthusiasts.

RESERVATIONS: Courts may be reserved up to 30 days in advance for play at Disney's Racquet Club at the Contemporary (call 824-3578) and for Grand Floridian courts (824-2694), and as far ahead as desired for courts at the Swan and Dolphin (934-4396). All other courts are available on a first-come, first-served basis. Solo players seeking partners can find them through the "Tennis Anyone?" program at Disney's Racquet Club. The amount of time a single group of players can occupy a court is restricted only during very busy periods—to two hours on any morning, afternoon, or evening.

FEES: Play is $12 per hour at the Contemporary ($40 per family for length of stay); $12 per hour at the Grand Floridian or Swan and Dolphin. Courts at the Institute are tough to get, but available with a $15 one-day health club pass. All other courts are free.

INSTRUCTION: The tennis program at the Contemporary resort offers clinics ranging in price from $35 to $50; a special clinic for families costs $75. Nobody will try to change your game radically; the idea is to help you play better with what you have. Private lessons with a United States Tennis Association–certified professional run $40 per hour or $20 per half hour; one-hour "Beat the Pro" playing sessions cost $35; win two out of three sets and the match is free. For an extra $10, video analysis can be included in hour-long lessons. For information or reservations, call 824-3578. Lessons at the Grand Floridian are $40 per 45-minute session. For reservations, call 824-2694. Consider, too, that the Disney Institute has an extensive tennis program (for details on the Institute, see page 181).

TOURNAMENTS: Private tourneys may be arranged by calling 824-3578 ($50 per hour).

DRESS: Tennis whites are appropriate, but not required, for play on Disney's courts.

EQUIPMENT RENTAL: Ball machine rental is $10 per half hour; good-quality (adult or child) racquets may be rented for $4. New balls sell for about $5 per can, and used balls are rented for $4 per basket.

LOCKERS: Locker facilities are available at the Contemporary and the Grand Floridian.

WATERS OF THE WORLD

Boating

Walt Disney World is the home of the country's largest fleet of pleasure boats. Cruising on Bay Lake and the adjoining Seven Seas Lagoon can be excellent sport, and a variety of boats are available for rent at WDW resort marinas. Bay Lake excursions originate from the Contemporary, on the lake's western shore; Wilderness Lodge, on the southern shore; and Fort Wilderness, which occupies the lake's southeastern shore. The Polynesian and Grand Floridian resorts send boaters out from their marinas on the southern shore of Seven Seas Lagoon. The Caribbean Beach resort leases watercraft for use on its own 45-acre Barefoot Bay. The Yacht Club, Beach Club, Swan, and Dolphin share a boating haven in 25-acre Crescent Lake. And marinas at Dixie Landings, Port Orleans, Old Key West, and the Disney Village Marketplace set guests up to cruise the waterways adjoining the 35-acre Buena Vista Lagoon.

To rent, day visitors and resort guests alike must show a resort ID, a driver's license, or a valid passport. Rental of certain craft may carry other special requirements (described below). Note that no privately owned boats are permitted on any of the WDW waters. Also, all prices are subject to change.

CANOEING: A long paddle down the glass-smooth, wooded Fort Wilderness canals is such a tranquil way to pass a misty morning that it's hard to remember that the bustle of the Magic Kingdom is just a launch ride away. Canoes are available for rent at the Bike Barn at Fort Wilderness ($4 per hour, $10 per day). Most trips last one to three hours; those who take fishing gear can easily stay out longer. Canoes may also be rented at the Caribbean Beach, Port Orleans, The Villas at the Disney Institute, and Dixie Landings marinas.

CANOPY BOATS: These 16-foot, V-hulled motorized boats with canopies are a good choice for slow, relaxing cruises. They accommodate up to eight adults, and can be rented for about $19 per half hour at the Disney Village Marketplace, Polynesian, Contemporary, Grand Floridian, Wilderness Lodge, Yacht Club and Beach Club, Old Key West, Port Orleans, Caribbean Beach, and Dixie Landings marinas.

PARASAILING: Excursions are offered at the Contemporary marina, where the man who invented the high-flying adventure sport supervises seven- to ten-minute flights over Bay Lake. Cost is $60 per person or $35 to ride along; reservations are necessary (call 824-1000, ext. 3586).

PEDAL BOATS: These craft rent for $5.50 per half hour or $8 per hour at most WDW resort marinas. They're also available for rent (to resort guests only) at the Caribbean Beach, Port Orleans, Dixie Landings, Coronado Springs, and Yacht Club and Beach Club marinas, and at the Fort Wilderness Bike Barn. For pedaling of a different sort, Hydro Bikes (boats resembling upright bicycles affixed to pontoons) may be rented at the marina between the Dolphin and Swan when it's not too windy; single-bike units cost $8 per half hour, doubles, $13 per half hour.

PONTOON BOATS: Flotebotes—motorized, canopied platforms on pontoons—are perfect for families, for inexperienced sailors, and for visitors more interested in serenity than in thrills. Available at most resort marinas, the 20-foot craft hold up to ten adults and cost about $22 per half hour.

SAILBOATS: The running room and usually reliable winds of Bay Lake and the adjoining Seven Seas Lagoon make for good sailing, and the Grand Floridian, Polynesian, Contemporary, Wilderness Lodge, and Fort Wilderness resort marinas rent a variety of craft so that guests might get a little wind in their sails on the 650-acre expanse. Various types of sailboats are available; models accommodate two to six people and rent for $11 to $19 per hour. Experience is required for rental of catamarans, available at the Contemporary, Polynesian, and Grand Floridian.

Sailing conditions are usually best in March and April, and before the inevitable late-afternoon thundershowers in the summer—and that's when demand is greatest. So don't tarry. Head for the marina as soon as the urge to sail strikes.

SPEEDBOATS: Particularly when the weather is warm, there are always dozens of small boats zipping back and forth across Bay Lake, Seven Seas Lagoon, and the lakes at the Disney Village Marketplace and the Caribbean Beach resort. These are called Water Sprites, and they are just as much fun as they look. Though they don't go very fast, they're so small that a rider feels every bit of speed, and they zip around quickly enough so that a lot of watery terrain can be covered in a half-hour rental period (about $16.50).

Water Sprites can be rented at the Grand Floridian, Polynesian, Wilderness Lodge, Contemporary, Yacht Club and Beach Club, Fort Wilderness, Caribbean Beach, and Disney Village Marketplace marinas. When the weather is warm, lines usually form at about 11 A.M. and remain fairly constant until about 4 P.M. The minimum rental age is 12, except at the Marketplace, where the minimum age is 14. Children under the minimum age are not allowed to drive.

At the Contemporary marina, even zippier little boats called Seariders may be rented for

$30 per hour. Accommodating up to three people, Seariders can attain speeds up to 30 miles per hour; riders must be 18 to drive.

WATERSKIING: Ski boats with driver and equipment ($82 an hour, with a minimum of two guests and a maximum of five) are available for rent at the Contemporary, Polynesian, Grand Floridian, Wilderness Lodge, and Fort Wilderness resort marinas. Reservations must be made at least 48 hours in advance; call 824-2621 up to two weeks ahead.

Fishing

The 70,000 bass with which Bay Lake was stocked in the mid-1960s have grown and multiplied as a result of WDW's restrictive fishing policy. (All fishing is strictly catch-and-release.) No angling is permitted on Bay Lake or the Seven Seas Lagoon, except on the guided two-hour Fort Wilderness fishing expeditions. Largemouth bass weighing two to eight pounds are the most common catch. The excursions depart the campground marina at around 8 A.M., 11:30 A.M., and 3 P.M. every day; five people can be accommodated on each trip. The fee per boatload is $137 for two hours ($50 for each additional hour) and includes guide, gear, and refreshments (coffee and pastries in the morning, soft drinks in the afternoon). Reservations must be made at least 24 hours in advance and may be secured up to two weeks ahead; call 824-2621. Guides will pick up guests at the Contemporary, Polynesian, and Grand Floridian resort marinas.

Other trips depart from the Disney Village Marketplace marina at 7 A.M., 9 A.M., and 11 A.M. for fishing on Buena Vista Lagoon and adjoining waterways. Reservations must be made at least 24 hours in advance and can be made up to two weeks ahead; call 828-2204 or 828-2461. Cost for up to five people, including guide, gear, and refreshments, is $137 for two hours ($50 for each additional hour).

At Dixie Landings, a two-hour fishing adventure takes guests on the Sassagoula River and the Buena Vista Lagoon. The daily 6:30 A.M. trip accommodates up to five people; includes guide, gear, artificial bait, and soft drinks; and costs $35 per person. Reservations must be made 24 hours in advance and can be made up to two weeks ahead by calling 934-5409. Children under ten must be accompanied by an adult.

Anglers might also consider the two-hour trips that leave the Yacht Club and Beach Club marina at 7 A.M., 10 A.M., and 1 P.M. daily for fishing on Crescent Lake and the adjoining waterways. The cost for up to five people, including guide, gear, and refreshments, is $130. Reservations must be made 24 hours in advance and can be made as far ahead as 30 days; call 934-3256. Comparable trips are offered from the BoardWalk; call 939-5100.

Fishing on your own—again, strictly catch-and-release—is permitted off the dock at the Disney Village Marketplace; in the canals near The Villas at the Disney Institute, Fort Wilderness, and BoardWalk; and at the stocked fishing hole at Dixie Landings. Fort Wilderness guests may toss in lines from any campground shore. Licenses are not required. Canoes, rods and reels, and cane poles are available for rent at the Fort Wilderness Bike Barn. Poles may also be rented at Dixie Landings, BoardWalk, and the Disney Village Marketplace.

Swimming

Between Bay Lake and the Seven Seas Lagoon, Walt Disney World resort guests have five miles of powdery white sand beach at their disposal. And that doesn't include the many swimming pools that come in all shapes and sizes. River Country, Typhoon Lagoon, and Blizzard Beach (see *Everything Else in the World*) only add to the fun.

BEACHES: When Walt Disney World was under construction during the mid-1960s, Bay Lake had an eight-foot layer of muck on its bottom. It was drained and cleaned, and below the muck, engineers unearthed the pure, white sand that now edges WDW resort shorefronts, most notably at the Contemporary, Grand Floridian, Caribbean Beach, and Fort Wilderness. These four sections of beach, plus the ones at the Polynesian, Wilderness Lodge, Yacht Club and Beach Club, Coronado Springs, and Dolphin and Swan make up WDW's sandy areas. They aren't walk-forever strands, but they are long enough that most people don't bother to go to the end. Note that all WDW resort beaches are open only to guests staying at the respective hotels.

POOLS: With the exception of the sister resorts (Yacht Club and Beach Club, Dixie Landings and Port Orleans, All-Star Sports and All-Star Music, and Dolphin and Swan), which share some of their recreational facilities, WDW hotel pools are open only to guests staying at those resorts. This policy was initiated to prevent overcrowding.

Featuring one pool apiece are the Grand Floridian, Wilderness Lodge, and Port Orleans. The Contemporary, Polynesian, Fort Wilderness, All-Star Sports, and All-Star Music resorts have two pools each. BoardWalk features three pools; Coronado Springs and Old Key West both have four swimming holes, Dixie Landings and The Villas at the Disney Institute have six apiece, and Caribbean Beach has seven. The Yacht Club and Beach Club resorts have between them two quiet pools plus a miniature water park called Stormalong Bay that features slides, jets, and a sand-bottomed

Disney's Sports Complex

Arguably the biggest thing to hit the area sports scene since the Orlando Magic, Disney's multimillion-dollar Sports Complex is slated to open in May 1997 near the junction of I-4 and U.S. 192. The enormous state-of-the-art facility will host all manner of sporting events, from amateur to professional. It will also serve as a training site for amateur and professional teams (the Atlanta Braves plan to come here in spring 1998). Designed as a modern vision of old-time Floridian building styles, its architecture harks back to the days when sports facilities were created as extensions of their neighborhoods; to this end, it even has a town commons.

For up-to-the-minute information about Disney's Sports Complex and specifics about events that will be happening there during 1997, call 824-4321. For now, note the following highlights of this palatial sports campus.

On tap is a 7,500-seat baseball stadium, not to mention ten practice fields suitable for Major League baseball, Little League baseball, and softball. A franchise of the Official All Star Café will carry the sports banner into the restaurant realm. A 5,000-seat field house will accommodate basketball, wrestling, and volleyball, and sport a world-class weight room. There will also be a track-and-field complex; 11 state-of-the-art clay tennis courts, including a stadium court; four multipurpose fields fit for football, soccer, lacrosse, and more; and five sand volleyball courts. Given the possibilities, sports-loving spectators will have a world of choices on their hands—beyond the realm of fireworks in the theme parks.

wading area. The Dolphin and Swan share a themed grotto pool with slide, a huge rectangular pool, and a third smaller pool. For descriptions of the delightfully themed pools at WDW resorts, consult hotel listings in *Transportation & Accommodations*.

There are no diving boards at any of the pools; to practice cannonballs, head for River Country, Blizzard Beach, or Typhoon Lagoon. Lifeguards are on duty during most daylight hours. In addition, each of the seven hotels that make up Disney Village Hotel Plaza has its own pool.

MORE FUN STUFF

BIKING: Pedaling along the rustic pathways and lightly trafficked roads at Fort Wilderness and The Villas at the Disney Institute can be a pleasant way to spend a couple of hours. Both areas are sufficiently spread out that bicycles are a practical means of getting around. Bikes are available for rent at Fort Wilderness, Old Key West, Wilderness Lodge, Port Orleans, Caribbean Beach, Dixie Landings, BoardWalk, The Villas at the Disney Institute, and Coronado Springs. The cost is about $3 an hour or $10 per day; tandem bicycles are offered at some locations.

HEALTH CLUBS: While some of the fitness centers located within WDW hotels are reserved for guests staying at the resort that houses them, several have open-door policies. Olympiad at the Contemporary, Grand Floridian Spa & Health Club, Muscles & Bustles at BoardWalk, and the Sports & Fitness Center at The Villas at the Disney Institute are accessible to all WDW resort guests; Body By Jake at the Dolphin is open to anyone.

The basic facility at the Swan is free to the hotel's guests. Olympiad at the Contemporary features Nautilus, a variety of cardiovascular machines, a sauna, and massage; rates are $8.50 per day or $20 per family for length of stay. Directly comparable to the Olympiad are R.E.S.T. at Old Key West (free to guests), Muscles & Bustles at BoardWalk ($7 per day, $20 per family for length of stay for resort guests; otherwise $10 per day, $35 per family for length of stay), and the club at Coronado Springs (call 939-1000 for rates). Ship Shape at the Yacht Club and Beach Club ($7.50 per day or $21.50 per family for length of stay) has more extensive equipment, a whirlpool, a steamroom, and personal trainers. The Grand Floridian Spa & Health Club ($6 per day, $12 per length of stay) has all that, plus

a luxurious ambience. The Dolphin's first-rate Body By Jake ($8 per day or $16 for length of stay), offers aerobics. The huge Sports & Fitness Center at The Villas at the Disney Institute (free to Institute guests; otherwise $15 per day, $35 for length of stay) has aerobics, a gymnasium, and a state-of-the-art facility with the best lineup of Cybex machines anywhere.

HORSEBACK RIDING: Trail rides into pine woods and scrubby palmetto country set off from the front of Fort Wilderness four times daily. This is not for gallopers—you can't ride off on your own. The horses have been culled for gentleness, so the trips are suitable for novices. Cost is $17 per person. No children under nine are permitted to ride, and there is a weight limit of 250 pounds. Reservations are necessary, and can be made up to two weeks ahead by calling 824-2621.

JOGGING: Except from late fall to early spring, the weather is usually too steamy in Central Florida for comfortable jogging. If you run early in the morning in warm seasons, the heat is somewhat less daunting. The 1.4-mile promenade around the Caribbean Beach resort's lake is ideal for jogging. Fort Wilderness and the Wilderness Lodge share a three-quarter-mile path with exercise stations. Dixie Landings and Old Key West also have scenic routes. Maps are available from each WDW resort's Guest Services desk; courses range from one mile to about three.

MINIATURE GOLF: The Fantasia Gardens mini-golf complex, located near the Dolphin, Swan, and BoardWalk resorts, offers players two 18-hole courses themed to the classic Disney film. Fantasia Fairways offers a challenging layout sure to tantalize serious golfers. Fantasia Gardens is all in fun, with clever things (a dancing hippo, xylophone stairs, brooms dumping buckets of water) at every hole. A round on either course costs about $8 for adults, $7 for children ages 3 to 9. Typical playing time is about an hour. Hours are generally 10 A.M. to midnight, but vary seasonally.

VOLLEYBALL & BASKETBALL: Except for the volleyball courts at River Country and Typhoon Lagoon, all courts are reserved for WDW resort guests. The Grand Floridian, Contemporary, Yacht Club and Beach Club, Fort Wilderness, Swan and Dolphin, Coronado Springs, and The Villas at the Disney Institute have volleyball courts. Fort Wilderness and Old Key West have basketball hoops.

GoodMeals, Great Times

Although fast food is in great supply, it is hardly the entire Walt Disney World dining story. Epcot adds international flavors to the WDW menu. Tempting options at the Disney-MGM Studios, BoardWalk, Disney Village Marketplace, and Pleasure Island—not to mention new dining frontiers in the ever-growing brood of WDW resorts—make deciding where to eat a mouthwatering dilemma. And Disney's ongoing effort to expand its culinary horizons has been quite successful, producing prominent palate pleasers such as California Grill and Artist Point.

Because the number and variety of eateries around the World is so large, this chapter presents dining information in three formats. First, to help guests find a specific eating spot or watering hole, we've provided an alphabetized directory of all restaurants and lounges on the property with their exact locations. Second, we've included an area-by-area rundown—a comprehensive section whose precise descriptions of food purveyors, including sample menu options, will prove most helpful to guests who are getting hungry in a particular part of the World. Third, we've set forth a meal-by-meal primer that highlights restaurants by breakfast, lunch, and dinner specialties. We've even indicated entrées for which we think it's worth going a bit out of your way.

Finally, in the chapter's last section, we offer a guide to the varied lounges of Walt Disney World, along with a briefing on special nighttime entertainment options in the World—and assurance that great times are destined to follow.

 Unless otherwise noted, all phone numbers are in area code 407.

WDW RESTAURANT & LOUNGE INDEX

The list below includes the names and locations of all restaurants, lounges, and snack spots currently operating in Walt Disney World—not only at the theme parks, but also at the hotels, Fort Wilderness, the Disney Village Marketplace, and Pleasure Island. In the sections following this listing, the restaurants and lounges are described in detail.

Note: The Walt Disney World landscape is continually evolving, and while this inventory was complete and correct at press time, changes will inevitably occur. We advise guests to call WDW Information (824-4321) or WDW-DINE (939-3463) shortly before their visit to confirm restaurant information.

Akershus: Epcot; in the Norway pavilion in World Showcase

Ale and Compass: Yacht Club resort; in the lobby

Aloha Isle: Magic Kingdom; in Adventureland, near the Swiss Family Treehouse

Ariel's: Beach Club resort; on the first floor

Artist Point: Wilderness Lodge resort; in the main lodge building

Atlantic Dance: BoardWalk resort; on the farthest end of the boardwalk (to the left)

Aunt Polly's Landing: Magic Kingdom; in Frontierland, on Tom Sawyer Island

Auntie Gravity's Galactic Goodies: Magic Kingdom; near Merchant of Venus in Tomorrowland

Au Petit Café: Epcot; along the promenade in the France pavilion in World Showcase

Avalunch: Blizzard Beach; near Ski Patrol Training Camp

Backlot Express: Disney-MGM Studios; near the Epic Stunt Theater

Banana Cabana: Caribbean Beach resort; near the pool

Barefoot Bar: Polynesian resort; near the Swimming Pool Lagoon

Beaches & Cream Soda Shop: Yacht Club and Beach Club resorts; in the central area between the two hotels

Belle Vue Room: BoardWalk resort; in the lobby

Biergarten: Epcot; to the rear of the St. Georgsplatz in the Germany pavilion in World Showcase

Big River Grille & Brewing Works: BoardWalk resort; on the boardwalk's left side near Jellyrolls

Bistro de Paris: Epcot; upstairs at the France pavilion in World Showcase

BoardWalk Bakery: BoardWalk resort; on the boardwalk

Boatwright's Dining Hall: Dixie Landings resort; adjacent to the Cotton Co-Op lounge

Bonfamille's Café: Port Orleans resort; off the main lobby, across from the front desk

Boulangerie Pâtisserie: Epcot; France pavilion, around the corner from Chefs de France, in World Showcase

Bridgetown Broiler: Caribbean Beach resort; at Old Port Royale food court

Cabana Bar & Grill: Dolphin resort; at the pool

California Grill: Contemporary resort; on the 15th floor

California Grill Lounge: Contemporary resort; on the 15th floor

Cantina de San Angel: Epcot; on the promenade opposite the Mexico pavilion's pyramid in World Showcase

Cape May Café: Beach Club resort; adjacent to the lobby

Cap'n Jack's Oyster Bar: Disney Village Marketplace; on the edge of Buena Vista Lagoon

Captain Cook's Snack & Ice Cream Company: Polynesian resort; on the lobby level of the Great Ceremonial House

Captain's Tavern: Caribbean Beach resort; at Old Port Royale

Casey's Corner: Magic Kingdom; on the west side of Main Street

Catwalk Bar: Disney-MGM Studios; above the Soundstage restaurant

Chef Mickey's: Contemporary resort; on the fourth floor

Chefs de France: Epcot; in the France pavilion in World Showcase

Cinnamon Bay Bakery: Caribbean Beach resort; at Old Port Royale food court

Columbia Harbour House: Magic Kingdom; in Liberty Square, near the entrance to Fantasyland

Commissary: Disney-MGM Studios; near The Great Movie Ride

Concourse Steakhouse: Contemporary resort; on the fourth-floor concourse

Copa Banana: Dolphin resort; lobby level

Coral Café: Dolphin resort; lower level

Coral Isle Café: Polynesian resort; on the second floor of the Great Ceremonial House, around the corner from 'Ohana

Coral Reef: Epcot; in Future World's The Living Seas

Cosmic Ray's Starlight Café: Magic Kingdom; at the Fantasyland edge of Tomorrowland, across from the Tomorrowland Speedway

Cotton Co-Op: Dixie Landings resort; in the main reception area

Crew's Cup: Yacht Club resort; next to the Yachtsman Steakhouse

Crockett's Tavern: Fort Wilderness campground; in Pioneer Hall

Crystal Palace: Magic Kingdom; near the Adventureland bridge at the north end of Main Street

Diamond Horseshoe Saloon Revue: Magic Kingdom; in Frontierland at the edge of Liberty Square

Dinosaur Gertie's: Disney-MGM Studios; on Echo Lake

Dolphin Fountain: Dolphin resort; on the lower level

Donald's Dairy Dip: Disney Village Marketplace; near World of Disney

D-Zertz: Pleasure Island; near Propeller Heads

Egg Roll Wagon: Magic Kingdom; in Adventureland, near the Swiss Family Treehouse

Electric Umbrella: Epcot; in Future World's Innoventions Plaza

El Pirata y el Perico: Magic Kingdom; in Adventureland, opposite Pirates of the Caribbean

Enchanted Grove: Magic Kingdom; on the east side of Fantasyland, opposite Cosmic Ray's Starlight Café

End Zone: All-Star Sports resort; in Stadium Hall

ESPN Club: BoardWalk resort; on the farthest end of the boardwalk (to the right)

Fantasyland Pretzel Wagon: Magic Kingdom; between Pinocchio Village Haus and Cinderella's Golden Carrousel

50's Prime Time Café: Disney-MGM Studios; on the south side of Echo Lake

Fireworks Factory: Pleasure Island; near Portobello Yacht Club restaurant

Flagler's: Grand Floridian resort; on the second floor of the main building

Flying Fish Café: BoardWalk resort; on the boardwalk, near the transportation dock

Food and Fun Center: Contemporary resort; first floor

Fountain View Espresso & Bakery: Epcot; next to Innoventions

Fulton's Crab House: Between Pleasure Island and the Disney Village Marketplace

Garden Grill: Epcot; on the second floor of The Land in Future World

Garden Grove Café: Swan resort; on the first floor

Garden View: Grand Floridian resort; on the Windsor Level

Gasparilla Grill & Games: Grand Floridian resort; first floor of the main building

Good's Food to Go: Old Key West resort; on the boardwalk

Goofy's Grill: Disney Village Marketplace; near Crystal Arts

Gourmet Pantry: Disney Village Marketplace; near Team Mickey's Athletic Club

Grand Floridian Café: Grand Floridian resort; first floor of the main building

Gurgling Suitcase: Old Key West resort; on the boardwalk

Harry's Safari Bar & Grille: Dolphin resort; on the third floor

Hollywood & Vine: Disney-MGM Studios; on Hollywood Boulevard

Hollywood Brown Derby: Disney-MGM Studios; on Hollywood Boulevard

Hook's Tavern: Magic Kingdom; in Fantasyland, next to Peter Pan's Flight

Hot Dog Wagon: Disney-MGM Studios; near The Great Movie Ride

Hot Dog Wagon: Epcot; near The American Adventure in World Showcase

Hurricane Hanna's Grill: Yacht Club and Beach Club resorts; near Stormalong Bay

Intermission: All-Star Music resort; in Melody Hall

Jellyrolls: BoardWalk resort; on the left side of the boardwalk near Atlantic Dance

Juan & Only's: Dolphin resort; lower level

Kimono's: Swan resort; on the first floor

King Stefan's Banquet Hall: Magic Kingdom; in Cinderella Castle

Kingston Pasta Shop: Caribbean Beach resort; at Old Port Royale food court

Kringla Bakeri og Kafé: Epcot; in the Norway pavilion in World Showcase

Leaning Palms: Typhoon Lagoon; near the main entrance

Leaping Horse Libations: BoardWalk resort; near the Luna Park pool

Liberty Inn: Epcot; alongside The American Adventure pavilion in World Showcase

Liberty Square Market: Magic Kingdom; in Liberty Square

Liberty Square Potato Wagon: Magic Kingdom; in Liberty Square

Liberty Tree Tavern: Magic Kingdom; in Liberty Square

Little Big Top: Magic Kingdom; in Fantasyland, near Legend of The Lion King

Lobby Court: Swan resort; in the lobby

L'Originale Alfredo di Roma Ristorante: Epcot; on the east side of the piazza in the Italy pavilion, in World Showcase

Lottawatta Lodge: Blizzard Beach; near the main entrance

Lotus Blossom Café: Epcot; in the China pavilion in World Showcase

Lumière's Kitchen: Magic Kingdom; in Fantasyland, near Dumbo, the Flying Elephant

Lunching Pad at Rockettower Plaza: Magic Kingdom; at the base of the Astro Orbiter in the center of Tomorrowland

Main Street Bake Shop: Magic Kingdom; on the east side of Main Street, halfway between the Hub and Town Square

Mama Melrose's Ristorante Italiano: Disney-MGM Studios; on New York Street

Mardi Grogs: Port Orleans resort; near the pool

Marrakesh: Epcot; in the Morocco pavilion in World Showcase

Martha's Vineyard: Beach Club resort; near Ariel's

Matsu No Ma: Epcot; in the Mitsukoshi building in World Showcase's Japan pavilion

Meadow Trading Post: Fort Wilderness; near the playing fields

Mickey's Tropical Revue: Polynesian resort; Luau Cove

Min & Bill's Dockside Diner: Disney-MGM Studios; on Echo Lake

Minnie Mia's Italian Eatery: Disney Village Marketplace; near the Gourmet Pantry

Missing Link Sausage Co.: Pleasure Island; near 8Trax

Mitsukoshi: Epcot; in the Japan pavilion in World Showcase

Mizner's: Grand Floridian resort; on the second floor of the main building

Montego's Deli: Caribbean Beach resort; at Old Port Royale food court

Mrs. Potts' Cupboard: Magic Kingdom; in Fantasyland near Cinderella's Golden Carrousel

Muddy Rivers: Dixie Landings resort; near Ol' Man Island

Narcoossee's: Grand Floridian resort; at the end of the dock near the marina

Nine Dragons: Epcot; in the China pavilion in World Showcase

1900 Park Fare: Grand Floridian resort; on the first floor of the main building

Oasis: Magic Kingdom; in Adventureland, near the Jungle Cruise

'Ohana: Polynesian resort; second floor of the Great Ceremonial House

Olivia's Café: Old Key West resort; on the boardwalk

Only's Bar & Jail: Dolphin resort; adjacent to Juan & Only's

Outer Rim: Contemporary resort; on the fourth floor

Palio: Swan resort; on the first floor

Pasta Piazza Ristorante: Epcot; in Future World's Innoventions Plaza

Pecos Bill Café: Magic Kingdom; near the Walt Disney World Railroad Frontierland depot

Pepper Market: Coronado Springs resort; in the main building

Pinocchio Village Haus: Magic Kingdom; in Fantasyland, adjoining It's A Small World

Planet Hollywood: Pleasure Island; near the AMC Theatres

Plaza: Magic Kingdom; on Main Street around the corner from Plaza Ice Cream Parlor

Plaza Ice Cream Parlor: Magic Kingdom; on the east side of Main Street

Plaza Pavilion Terrace Dining: Magic Kingdom; east of the Plaza restaurant, on the edge of Tomorrowland

Pop's Place: Fort Wilderness; inside River Country

Portobello Yacht Club: Pleasure Island; near Fulton's Crab House

Port Royale Hamburger Shop: Caribbean Beach resort; at Old Port Royale food court

Potato Wagon: Epcot; in the United Kingdom pavilion in World Showcace

Pretzel Wagon: Epcot; in the Germany pavilion in World Showcase

Pure & Simple: Epcot; in Future World's Wonders of Life pavilion

Rainforest Café: Disney Village Marketplace; near Cap'n Jack's Oyster Bar

Refreshment Outpost: Epcot; between the China and Germany pavilions in World Showcase

Refreshment Port: Epcot; next to the Canada pavilion in World Showcase

Rip Tide: Beach Club resort; in the lobby

Roaring Fork: Wilderness Lodge resort; in the main lodge building

Rose & Crown Pub and Dining Room: Epcot; in the United Kingdom pavilion in World Showcase

Royale Pizza Shop: Caribbean Beach resort; at Old Port Royale food court

San Angel Inn: Epcot; inside the Mexico pavilion's pyramid, in World Showcase

Sand Bar: Contemporary resort; right near the beach

Sand Trap Bar & Grill: Bonnet Creek Golf Club; Osprey Ridge and Eagle Pines

Sassagoula Floatworks & Food Factory: Port Orleans resort; off the main lobby

Scat Cat's Club: Port Orleans resort; next to Bonfamille's Café

Sci-Fi Dine-In Theater: Disney-MGM Studios; near Star Tours

Seashore Sweets': BoardWalk resort; near the transportation dock on the boardwalk

Seasons Dining Room: The Villas at the Disney Institute; next to the Welcome Center

Seasons Lounge: The Villas at the Disney Institute; adjacent to the Welcome Center

Settlement Trading Post: Fort Wilderness; near the marina

Singing Spirits: All-Star Music resort; near the pool and the Intermission food court

Sleepy Hollow: Magic Kingdom; in Liberty Square, near the Liberty Square bridge

Sommerfest: Epcot; in the Germany pavilion in World Showcase

Soundstage: Disney-MGM Studios; near the Animation Building

Splash Grill: Swan resort; near the pool

Spoodles: BoardWalk resort; on the right side of the boardwalk near the bakery

Starring Rolls Bakery: Disney-MGM Studios; on Hollywood Boulevard

Studio Catering Co.: Disney-MGM Studios; near The Loony Bin

Sum Chows: Dolphin resort; on the lower level

Summerhouse: Grand Floridian resort; near the beach

Sunset Ranch Market: Disney-MGM Studios; on Sunset Boulevard

Sunshine Season Food Fair: Epcot; on the first floor of Future World's The Land

Sunshine Tree Terrace: Magic Kingdom; in Adventureland, adjoining Tropical Serenade

Tambu: Polynesian resort; on the second floor of the Great Ceremonial House

Team Spirits: All-Star Music resort; near the pool and the End Zone food court

Tempura Kiku: Epcot; on the second floor of the Mitsukoshi building in World Showcase's Japan pavilion

Teppanyaki Dining Rooms: Epcot; on the second floor of the Mitsukoshi building in World Showcase's Japan pavilion

Territory: Wilderness Lodge resort; in the main lodge building

Tony's Town Square: Magic Kingdom; east side of Town Square

Toy Story Pizza Planet: Disney-MGM Studios; in the arcade near Muppet*Vision 3-D

Trail's End Buffet: Fort Wilderness resort; in Pioneer Hall

Trout Pass: Wilderness Lodge resort; near the beach and the pool

Tubbi's: Dolphin resort; on the lower level

Tune-In Lounge: Disney-MGM Studios; adjacent to the 50's Prime Time Café

Turkey Leg Wagon: Magic Kingdom; in Frontierland, near Pecos Bill Café

Turtle Shack: Old Key West resort; near Turtle Pond Road

Typhoon Tilly's Galley & Grog: Typhoon Lagoon; near Shark Reef

Victoria & Albert's: Grand Floridian resort; on the second floor of the main building

Warming Hut: Blizzard Beach; near Summit Plummet

Westward Ho: Magic Kingdom; in Frontierland, near Pecos Bill Café

Whispering Canyon Café: Wilderness Lodge resort; in the main lodge building

Yacht Club Galley: Yacht Club resort; off the lobby

Yachtsman Steakhouse: Yacht Club resort; overlooking Stormalong Bay

Yakitori House: Epcot; on the east side of the Japan pavilion in World Showcase

Special Requests

Full-service eateries can accommodate special dietary needs, providing kosher, low-sodium, lactose-free, and other selections with 24 hours' notice. Make your request when booking your table by calling WDW-DINE (939-3463).

RESTAURANTS OF WDW
In the Magic Kingdom

The lion's share of eateries here in Walt Disney World's first theme park are fast-food spots. These establishments' colorful facades and costumed servers are natural extensions of the fantasy surrounding the park's seven distinct lands. The healthy variety of food available on the fly is a testament to Magic Kingdom visitors' typical preference for a quick bite with no need for firm plans. For those who prefer an all-out meal, the park's small handful of full-service restaurants offer fine mealtime escapes in magical settings that only Disney could create. Visitors interested in character meals have breakfast, lunch, and dinner options here (see page 244 for details).

First Things First

- As Disney chefs tweak their menus to keep abreast of trends and new concepts are unveiled, the inventory of dining options changes. We advise guests to call WDW-DINE (939-3463) to confirm restaurant information.

- The letters that conclude each entry are a key to meals served there: breakfast (B), lunch (L), dinner (D), or snacks (S).

- As an indication of what you should expect to spend for a meal, we've classified restaurants, based on dinner prices, as very expensive ($30 and up); expensive ($18 to $30); moderate ($8 to $18); or inexpensive (under $8). These prices are based on a typical meal for one adult, not including drinks, tax, or tips. Note that lunch generally costs less.

- All Walt Disney World restaurants and fast-food spots (except those with outside seating or at the Swan and Dolphin resorts) are nonsmoking only.

- Priority seating arrangements for most full-service restaurants should be made in advance by calling WDW-DINE (939-3463). For complete details, see page 246 of this chapter.

Adventureland
FAST FOOD & SNACKS

Aloha Isle: This refreshment stand near the Swiss Family Treehouse often sells pineapple spears and juice along with other tropical offerings including Dole Whip soft serve. Inexpensive. S.

Egg Roll Wagon: Located just outside the Swiss Family Treehouse, this wagon features an assortment of egg rolls. Inexpensive. S.

El Pirata y el Perico: The Spanish name of this snack stand, directly across from Pirates of the Caribbean, means "The Pirate and the Parrot." The offerings feature Mexican items such as tacos, taco salads, and nachos. Open during busy seasons. Inexpensive. L, S.

Oasis: Tucked away near the Jungle Cruise, this is the perfect spot for a soft drink. Inexpensive. S.

Sunshine Tree Terrace: So close to Tropical Serenade that you can hear the Audio-Animatronics parrot José squawking his spiel. Offerings here are some of the tastiest in the Kingdom: orange slushes, nonfat frozen yogurt shakes, frozen yogurt, and the citrus swirl—soft-serve nonfat frozen yogurt swirled through with frozen orange-juice concentrate. Cappuccino, espresso, and soft drinks are also available. Inexpensive. S.

Fantasyland
FULL SERVICE

King Stefan's Banquet Hall: Hostesses at this establishment (named for Sleeping Beauty's father) wear 13th-century-style French headdresses and long medieval gowns. The hall itself is high-ceilinged and as majestic as the old mead hall it is designed to represent. The delightful salads and roast-beef sandwiches on the midday menu make lunch here pleasant indeed. Dinner includes prime rib, seafood, and chicken. There's also a children's menu, and Cinderella is usually on hand to entertain kids and grownups alike.

The "Once Upon A Time" character breakfast is held here every morning. This all-you-can-eat breakfast is $14.95 for adults and $7.95 for children ages three to nine. Priority seating necessary. Expensive. B, L, D.

FAST FOOD & SNACKS

Enchanted Grove: A small stand that's the perfect spot for a lemonade, lemonade slush, or soft-serve swirl. Inexpensive. S.

Hook's Tavern: Soft drinks and chips are available at this small refreshment stand just west of Cinderella's Golden Carrousel. Inexpensive. S.

Little Big Top: Soft drinks, milk shakes, and chips are the draw here. Open seasonally. Inexpensive. S.

Lumière's Kitchen: Located near Dumbo, the Flying Elephant, this spot caters to kids with a variety of selections, including chicken tenders and grilled cheese, to please even finicky eaters. Adult menus are available. Inexpensive. L, D, S.

Mrs. Potts' Cupboard: Ice cream gets top billing at this restaurant just west of the Mad Tea Party. There are soft-serve cones in chocolate, vanilla, and chocolate-vanilla swirl; hot fudge sundaes; and root beer floats. Inexpensive. S.

Pinocchio Village Haus: Located near It's A Small World, this is another of those Magic Kingdom restaurants that seems a lot smaller from the outside than it really is, thanks to a labyrinthine arrangement of a half-dozen rooms decorated with antique cuckoo clocks, European tile-fronted ovens, oak peasant chairs, and murals depicting characters from Pinocchio's story—Figaro the Cat, Cleo the Goldfish, Monstro the Whale, and Geppetto, the puppet's creator. The menu offers hot dogs, cheeseburgers, hamburgers, turkey burgers, cold sandwiches, and pasta salad. Inexpensive. L, D, S.

Frontierland

FAST FOOD & SNACKS

Aunt Polly's Landing: The much-trumpeted sense of getting away from it all that islands always convey can also be found out on Frontierland's Tom Sawyer Island. Though only a couple of minutes' ride across the Rivers of America via the Tom Sawyer Island rafts, this landfall manages to seem remote even when there are dozens of youngsters clambering through its caves, over its hills, and across its rickety barrel bridges. Therein lies the charm of Aunt Polly's. While the adults in a party get some well-needed R&R sipping lemonade in the shade of the old-fashioned porch and watching the gleaming white riverboats docking or chugging by, the kids can go out exploring. And, at nearby Fort Sam Clemens, kids can ping the toy rifles perched on the gunholes as if there were no tomorrow.

It doesn't even matter that Aunt Polly's offers a selection barely wider than the fare that the lady might have served her youthful

nephew—peanut-butter-and-jelly and ham-and-cheese sandwiches, cold fried chicken, apple pie, soft-serve ice cream, cookies, iced tea, lemonade, and soda. Inexpensive. L, S.

Diamond Horseshoe Saloon Revue: From about 10 A.M. until early evening, a troupe of singers and dancers presents a sometimes corny, occasionally sidesplitting, always entertaining show in this Wild West dance-hall saloon. Stop by anytime for sandwiches, potato chips, and cookies. Inexpensive. L, S.

Pecos Bill Café: This is not one of those Magic Kingdom eateries so tucked away that only those who hunt will find it. Sooner or later, almost every guest passing from Adventureland into Frontierland—ambling by the Frontierland depot of the Walt Disney World Railroad on their way to Splash Mountain—walks by Pecos Bill. And as a sidewalk café, this establishment—fitted out with leather-seated chairs, ceilings made of twigs, and red-tile floors—has few peers. There are tables indoors (in air-conditioned rooms) and outdoors under umbrellas and in an open courtyard. Burgers, barbecued-chicken sandwiches, salads, and hot dogs are the staples. Inside, three shaggy animal heads hang on the walls in keeping with the Wild West theme. Guests who stand around long enough will see one animal turn to another and wink, for these are Audio-Animatronics figures, just like the ones on the walls at the Country Bear Jamboree. Inexpensive. L, D, S.

Turkey Leg Wagon: Located just outside Pecos Bill Café, this stand features extra-large smoked turkey legs. Inexpensive. L, D, S.

Westward Ho: Soft drinks, cookies, pretzels, and potato chips are available at this stand across from Pecos Bill Café. Inexpensive. S.

Liberty Square

FULL SERVICE

Liberty Tree Tavern: At this pillared and porticoed eatery opposite the riverboat landing, the floors are wide oak planks, the wallpaper looks as if it might have come from Williamsburg, the curtains hang from cloth loops, and the venetian blinds are made of wood. The rooms reflect mementoes that might have been found in the homes of Thomas Jefferson, George Washington, and Ben Franklin. The window glass was made using 18th-century casting methods, but most of the tables and chairs were mass-produced (for sturdiness' sake). So the Liberty Tree Tavern's charm is not of a random type.

Dinner, served family style, is hosted by Disney characters; menu items include fresh fish, shrimp, prime rib, chicken, and lobster. Oysters and New England clam chowder are served at both meals. The character dinner costs $19.50 for adults and $9.95 for children ages three to nine. Priority seating suggested. Expensive. L, D.

FAST FOOD & SNACKS

Columbia Harbour House: A fast-food fish house with some class. Fresh fish, clam chowder, salads, assorted sandwiches, and chicken are available. There are enough antiques and other knickknacks decking the halls to raise this place, located near the Liberty Square entrance to Fantasyland, above the ordinary. Model ships, copper measures, harpoons, nautical instruments, little tie-back curtains,

small-print wallpaper, and low-beamed ceilings give the place a cozy air. Operates seasonally. Inexpensive. L, D, S.

Liberty Square Market: Bananas, apples, juices, pickles, and sliced melon on ice are among the offerings at this refreshing open-air spot. Inexpensive. S.

Liberty Square Potato Wagon: Baked potatoes and sweet potatoes with a variety of toppings are the fare here. Inexpensive. S.

Sleepy Hollow: Sandwiches made with whole-wheat pita or potato bread, vegetarian chili served in a bread bowl, and a special Legendary Punch (fruity and not half bad) are for sale at this snack stand located beside The Hall of Presidents, near the Liberty Square bridge. Eat on the secluded brick patio outside. Inexpensive. L, D, S.

Healthier Options

Health-conscious folks need not abandon all restraint for want of suitable foodstuffs. Most restaurants offer low-fat, low-cholesterol, low-salt, and vegetarian entrées. Most restaurants, including fast-food stands, are now featuring fresh salads, grilled-chicken sandwiches, fresh fruit, turkey burgers, and non-fat frozen yogurt.

Main Street

FULL SERVICE

Crystal Palace: One of the Magic Kingdom's landmarks, this restaurant takes its architectural cues from a similar structure that once stood in New York, and from San Francisco's Conservatory of Flowers, which still graces Golden Gate Park. The place is huge but not overwhelming, because the tables are scattered among a host of nooks and crannies. Guests dine amid a Victorian-style garden, complete with fresh flowers and hanging greenery. Tables in the front look out on flower beds, while those at the east end have views of a secluded courtyard. The restaurant is located on a pathway at the end of Main Street, heading west toward Adventureland.

Three dried-flower topiaries—Winnie the Pooh, Tigger, and Eeyore—greet guests at the entrance, an indication of the new character presence here. After decades as a cafeteria, the restaurant is now offering all-day buffet dining, with none other than Winnie the Pooh personally stopping at every table.

Menu items vary according to season and available produce. The buffet features a full variety of traditional breakfast items every morning; a salad bar, deli bar, pasta dishes, chicken, and fish for lunch; and Cornish game hen, barbecued beef, chicken, shrimp, and carved meats for dinner. Kids particularly like the sundae bar offered at lunch and dinner. Expensive. B, L, D.

Plaza: This airy, many-windowed establishment, around the corner from the Plaza Ice Cream Parlor, is done up in mirrors with sinuous Art Nouveau frames. The menu offers fresh salads, hamburgers, turkey burgers, and hot and cold sandwiches—plus milk shakes, ice cream, floats, and the biggest sundaes in the Magic Kingdom. Café mocha, which combines chocolate and coffee, is another specialty. Moderate. L, D, S.

Tony's Town Square: One of the best bets for Magic Kingdom meals. The decor comes straight out of Walt Disney's film *Lady and the Tramp*. It is genteelly Victorian, with plenty of polished brass and curlicued, beautifully painted woodwork. The terrazzo-style patio offers a fine view of Town Square.

Breakfast options include eggs, *Lady and the Tramp* character waffles, cold cereals (with low-fat milk on request), and freshly baked pull-apart sweet rolls. The lunch menu offers Italian specialties, steaks, and seafood. Pizzas with selected toppings are perennial favorites. Other specialties include Caesar salad, sandwiches, pasta salads, and a fresh-fruit plate. At dinner select from grilled fish, New York strip steaks, and spaghetti with meatballs, along with a variety of daily specials. For dessert, Italian pastries and spumoni complement a cup of freshly brewed espresso or cappuccino. Children's menus are available. Priority seating suggested. Expensive. B, L, D.

FAST FOOD & SNACKS

Casey's Corner: The small, round tables at this spacious, old-fashioned, red-and-white stop on the west side of Main Street (located adjacent to the Crystal Palace) spill out onto the sidewalk. Except when the weather is terrifically hot, it's a delightful spot for fast food—hot dogs in jumbo sizes, french fries, brownies, soft drinks, and coffee. During busy periods a pianist plinks away on the restaurant's white upright. Inexpensive. L, D, S.

East Center Street Market: Fresh fruit is plentiful at this open-air stand. Inexpensive. S.

Main Street Bake Shop: This genteel little tearoom, with its prim white tables and cane chairs, is an very pleasant place for a light breakfast, midmorning coffee break, or

Magic Kingdom Mealtime Tips

- The hours from 11 A.M. to 2 P.M., and again from about 5 P.M. to 7 P.M., are the mealtime rush hours in Magic Kingdom restaurants. Try to eat earlier or later whenever possible.
- When a restaurant has more than one food-service window, don't just amble into the nearest queue. Instead, inspect them all, because the one farthest from a doorway occasionally will be almost wait-free.
- Sit-down restaurants offering full-scale meals are usually less crowded at lunch than they are at dinner.
- To avoid queues, eat lunch or dinner at a restaurant that offers priority seating—Tony's Town Square, Crystal Palace, or the Plaza restaurant on Main Street; Liberty Tree Tavern in Liberty Square; or King Stefan's in Cinderella Castle. Priority seating arrangements can be made in advance by calling WDW-DINE (939-3463). Check for same-day seating at the individual restaurant or City Hall. Refer to page 246 for further details.
- Consider taking the monorail to the Contemporary, Polynesian, or Grand Floridian to have lunch or dinner in a resort restaurant, and then return to the Magic Kingdom later. (Remember to have your hand stamped and keep your ticket for reentry to the park.)

midafternoon rest stop. Assorted pastries, cakes, and pies are the main temptations. Also offered are delicious cookies: chocolate chunk, oatmeal raisin, Snickerdoodle, sugar, and Nestlé's Original Toll House recipe. Cinnamon rolls are baked fresh on the premises. Inexpensive. B, S.

Plaza Ice Cream Parlor: Ice cream lovers from all over the country converge on this corner of the Kingdom, which boasts the Magic Kingdom's largest variety of ice cream flavors. Inexpensive. S.

Tomorrowland

FAST FOOD & SNACKS

Auntie Gravity's Galactic Goodies: This small spot located across from the Tomorrowland Speedway (between Merchant of Venus and Mickey's Star Traders) serves natural foods, fruit smoothies, soft-serve frozen yogurt, soft drinks, and fresh fruit. Inexpensive. S.

Cosmic Ray's Starlight Café: The largest fast-food spot in the Magic Kingdom, located directly across from the Tomorrowland Speedway. Three distinctive menus are offered. Cosmic Chicken serves rotisserie chicken dinners and drummettes; Blast-off Burgers has cheeseburgers (single and double) and vegetarian burgers; and Starlight Soup, Salad, Sandwich offers soups, Caesar salad, chef's salad, grilled-chicken sandwiches, and cheese steak sandwiches. In addition, a child's menu and soft drinks are available. Inexpensive. L, D, S.

Lunching Pad at Rockettower Plaza: Located at the base of the Astro Orbiter in the center of Tomorrowland's vast concrete plaza, this small spot offers smoked turkey legs, potato chips, assorted desserts, and soft drinks. Inexpensive. S.

Plaza Pavilion Terrace Dining: Just east of the Plaza restaurant on Main Street, this sleek spot on the edge of Tomorrowland serves pan pizzas, fried chicken strips, and Italian specialty sandwiches. Some particularly pleasant tables look past the graceful willow trees nearby, toward the Hub Waterways and an impressive topiary sea serpent. Inexpensive. L, D, S.

A Word to the Wise

Be sure to ride Space Mountain before eating, not afterward. The speed of this attraction can uncomfortably jostle even the strongest stomach.

In Epcot

The two worlds that make up Epcot offer a spectrum of eating options that extends from the usual burgers and fries to mouth-watering international specialties. Future World counts a please-all food court among its fast-food spots, plus two full-service restaurants whose menus and atmosphere innovatively reflect the themes of the pavilions they inhabit. World Showcase, on the other hand, is characterized by international flavors. Here, the cuisine of each country is served in settings that strive to transport visitors, if just for the duration of their meal. While the abundance of appealing full-service restaurants makes World Showcase a popular dining destination, the promenade is also ringed with fast-food spots, most of which feature international fare. Priority seating is an important part of the Epcot dining equation (for complete details, turn to page 246). Character meals are options for breakfast, lunch, and dinner in Future World (for specifics, see page 244).

Future World

FULL SERVICE

Coral Reef: Decorated in cool greens and blues to complement its surroundings, this restaurant in The Living Seas offers diners a panoramic view of the coral reef through

large windows. The acrylic windows are eight feet high and more than eight inches thick. The dining room is constructed on several tiers, so all guests have an unobstructed view. The menu features fresh fish and shellfish, including marinated red snapper; clams; Mediterranean shrimp baked with tomatoes; leeks, and onions; and Maine lobster with crabmeat stuffing. Landlubber selections are also available. The menu varies seasonally. Priority seating suggested. Expensive. L, D.

Garden Grill: Sleek upholstered wood-trimmed booths illuminated with handsome brass lamps help to make this an exceptionally attractive eatery. The restaurant itself revolves, past a mural of giant sunflowers and above scenes of the thunderstorm, sandstorm, prairie, and rain forest featured in the Living with the Land boat ride below. The scenes were designed with diners in mind, and provide them with a peek into a farmhouse window that's out of viewing range of the waterborne passengers.

Mickey and Minnie join Chip 'n' Dale to host three character meals here each day. The all-you-can eat country breakfast is $14.95 for adults and $7.95 for children ages three to nine. Lunch and dinner menus feature rotisserie chicken, hickory-smoked steaks, and fish, with a separate menu for children. The character lunch and dinner both cost $16.95 for adults and $9.95 for children ages three to nine. Priority seating suggested. Moderate to expensive. B, L, D.

FAST FOOD & SNACKS

Electric Umbrella: This large fast-food establishment, located in Innoventions, is decorated in shades of blue, mauve, and magenta. It's a particularly good bet when the weather is temperate enough to allow dining at the tables on the terrace outside—or when bound for World Showcase with finicky eaters in tow. Offerings include chicken sandwiches, grilled ham-and-cheese sandwiches, grilled vegetable pita sandwiches, hot dogs, burgers, fruit salad, and chef's salad. Inexpensive. L, D, S.

Fountain View Espresso & Bakery: Delicious baked goods and desserts—croissants, cheesecake, tiramisù, and éclairs—can be found at this spot located in Innoventions Plaza, across fromt the Fountain of Nations. Espresso, cappuccino, wine, and beer are among the assorted beverages available here. Inexpensive. B, S.

Dining After Hours

Pasta Piazza Ristorante: Pizza, pasta, and antipasto salad are the specialties at this eatery located in Innoventions, located opposite the Electric Umbrella restaurant. The decor is traditional Italian, accented by some unusual neon lights. Inexpensive. B, L, D, S.

Pure & Simple: Located in the Wonders of Life pavilion, this snack spot offers a variety of healthy treats including salads, oat bran waffles with fruit toppings, sandwiches, frozen yogurt, yogurt shakes, muffins, fruit juices, and more. Inexpensive. B, L, S.

Sunshine Season Food Fair: One of the most interesting of the Epcot eateries, and a wrinkle on the Walt Disney World fast-food scene, this handful of diverse counter-service stands is located on the lower level of The Land pavilion. Each of these stands boasts a unique menu. Soup & Salad offers Florida seafood chowder, fruit salad, and rotini pasta salad. The Bakery Shop's morning offerings include fresh fruit, bagels with cream cheese, jumbo cinnamon rolls, Danish

pastries, apricot crumb cake, and muffins. After 11 A.M., apple pies appear, along with cheesecake and chocolate cake, strawberry shortcake, rich double-chocolate brownies, hermit cookies with cinnamon—plus chocolate chip cookies baked on the premises. (The latter are so delicious that some Disney employees make special trips to The Land just to nibble on them.)

The Barbecue stand sells barbecued chicken and ribs smoked on the premises; barbecued beef, pork, or chicken-breast sandwiches; and sides of beans, corn-on-the-cob, and cornbread muffins. The Cheese and Pasta stand offers baked macaroni with ham and cheese, tortellini or fettuccine with meat sauce, noodles with Asian-style chicken, and vegetable lasagne. A Sandwich Shop regales the hungry with several types of hefty combinations, including the Disney Handwich, while an ice cream stand tempts guests with cooling cones and cups, frozen yogurt, and sundaes. The Potato Store serves steaming baked potatoes stuffed with oriental-style chicken and vegetables, cheddar cheese and bacon, and other fillings. Even the Beverage House here proffers

something special—not just an array of soft drinks, beer, and wine, but also alcoholic and nonalcoholic frozen drinks.

Each stand has a farm-style facade done in bright colors, not unlike those that might be found in agricultural exhibit buildings at a Midwestern state fair. With bright, umbrella-topped tables nearby, the effect is cheery. Because of the wide variety of foods available here, this is one of the best bets in Epcot for a family that can't agree on what to eat. It's also a good spot for weight watchers. Inexpensive. B, L, D, S.

World Showcase

FULL SERVICE

Akershus (Norway): The Norwegian castle of Akershus dominates Oslo's harbor, and is the most impressive of Norway's medieval fortresses. It is actually half fortress and half palace, and many of its grand halls continue to be used for elaborate state banquets. At Epcot's castle-like Akershus, guests are treated to an authentic royal Norwegian buffet called the *koldtbord*, literally "cold table." The diverse mix of offerings includes both hot and cold meats and seafood, and a selection of salads, cheeses, and breads. Traditional Norwegian desserts are also served, as are cocktails and Norwegian beer. Hosts and hostesses are on hand to answer any questions about the menu that guests may have. Priority seating suggested. Moderate to expensive. L, D.

Au Petit Café (France): Located prominently at the forefront of the France pavilion, along the World Showcase Promenade, this sidewalk café is a delightful place to stop for a snack or light meal. Under a large canopy with small round tables and black-jacketed waiters, it's as pleasant as it can be, and it can't be beat as a people-watching headquarters. Priority seating is not available, and long lines can develop. So don't stop if you're tired or ravenous. Moderate. L, D, S.

Biergarten (Germany): Located at the rear of the St. Georgsplatz in the Germany pavilion, this huge, tiered restaurant is set in a courtyard rimmed with geranium-studded balconies and punctuated by an old mill. It's every bit as jolly as Alfredo's restaurant in the Italy pavilion. This is partly because of the long tables that encourage a certain togetherness among guests—and partly because Beck's beer is served in 33-ounce steins. But equal credit for the *gemütlich* atmosphere must go to the restaurant's lively entertainment. A German trio performs during lunch. At dinner, yodelers, dancers, and other traditional Bavarian musicians—each appropriately clad in lederhosen or dirndl—play accordions, cowbells, a musical saw, and a harplike stringed instrument known as the "wooden laughter." The exceptionally entertaining dinner shows take place every hour on the half hour. Diners are usually invited to join the fun on stage.

The food is hearty and exquisitely presented on an all-you-can-eat buffet, featuring assorted sausages (grilled bratwurst, *Debrizinger*, *Bauernwurst*), frankfurters, rotisserie chicken, homemade spaetzle, assorted cold dishes, potato salad, cucumber salad, and many more German specialties. Because entertainment is intermittent, there's plenty of time to enjoy the pleasant setting, with the big mill waterwheel slowly

turning and the sound of water splashing into the millstream blending with the rousing oompah music. Priority seating suggested, particularly during peak seasons. Moderate to expensive. L, D.

Bistro de Paris (France): One flight above Chefs de France, this restaurant evokes early 20th-century Paris. Peach and green curlicues decorate the ceiling above brass light fixtures and sconces, large mirrors, colored leaded glass, and simple wood chairs. A traditional bistro menu (created by the same trio of French chefs responsible for the fare at Chefs de France) features roast red snapper topped with potato scales and red wine–lobster sauce; seafood casserole with garlic sauce; roasted rack of lamb; and sautéed breast of duck. The heartiness of the fare makes it an especially good dining choice in cool weather. Priority seating suggested. Expensive. L, D.

Chefs de France (France): Multiple-star restaurants are rare even in France, so it's a notable coup that WDW has somehow managed to lure three of France's finest chefs to run this rather remarkable restaurant. In France, Paul Bocuse and Roger Vergé operate three- and two-star restaurants respectively (Bocuse's is outside Lyons, Vergé's just north of the French Riviera). Together with Gaston Lenôtre (widely recognized as France's premier preparer of pastries and other delicious dessert delicacies), they form a most unusual, and absolutely formidable gastronomic trio. Bocuse, Vergé, and Lenôtre have designed a menu that features fresh ingredients readily available from Florida purveyors. The French chefs make regular visits to WDW to supervise and adjust certain items on the menu, though there has been very little need to tinker.

As you might expect, the fare here is fiercely French, but the foundation of the menu is nouvelle cuisine, which involves lighter sauces using much less cream and butter than in classic French cooking. At dinner, appetizers include chilled potato, leek, and Lyons-style onion soups; salmon soufflé served with lobster sauce; hot pâté of chicken and duck en croûte; and a casserole of escargots in herb butter with garlic. Diners choose from entrées such as fillet of snapper and spinach baked in puff pastry with sautéed scallops and crab dumplings; braised half duck in red wine sauce; or marinated chicken breast baked in puff pastry with port wine cream sauce. At lunch, the menu offers soups, salads, cheeses, and pâtés. Hot dishes such as fillet of orange roughy with hazelnut butter, brochette of prawns, salmon tartare, and a beef filet with bordelaise sauce are also served at lunch. A beef stew redolent of wine and a rich onion soup are available at lunch and dinner, as are an array of absolutely fabulous pastries and desserts (including some wonderful Lenôtre specialties). The atmosphere is as much a delight as the food. Tablecloths are of crisp linen, and decorative touches of brass and etched glass abound. A modest wine list accompanies both lunch and dinner menus. Note that this can be one of the most expensive of all World Showcase restaurants. (There's a separate menu "for the little gourmet"—kids under 12—that features reduced prices.) Priority seating suggested. Expensive. L, D.

L'Originale Alfredo di Roma Ristorante (Italy): This restaurant's trompe l'oeil ("trick the eye") perspective paintings make diners believe they're seeing real scenes rather than mere murals, and lend character to the decor of this popular establishment. As in the famous Roman restaurant of the same name, the house specialty is fettuccine Alfredo—wide, flat noodles tossed in a sauce made of butter and imported Parmesan cheese. But many other sizes and shapes of pasta, all of it made right on the premises, are also available; they are significantly enhanced by tomato, meat, pesto (basil, garlic, and Parmesan), or carbonara (egg, bacon, cream, and pecorino cheese) sauces. There are also a number of less familiar Italian preparations involving chicken, eggplant, seafood, sausage, and veal, all of which are very good. For dessert, choose from a number of specialties such as ricotta cheesecake, spumoni, tortoni, or gelato. Even if you don't eat here, it's fun to stop and just peer through the glass kitchen windows to watch the cooks cranking out the rigatoni, ziti, linguine, lasagne, fettuccine, and spaghetti (which, the eminently readable menu reminds guests, were brought from Europe to America by Thomas Jefferson in 1786). Priority seating suggested. Expensive. L, D.

Marrakesh (Morocco): The most savory part of the Morocco pavilion features a variety of examples of traditional and modern Moroccan cuisine. Waiters are dressed in traditional Moroccan costumes. Menu specialties include roast lamb, chicken brochette, and couscous (steamed semolina served with your choice of lamb, chicken, or vegetables). Sampler platters are also available. The beautiful tilework was done by Moroccan craftsmen. Belly dancers and musicians entertain diners at both lunch and dinner. A children's menu is available. Priority seating suggested. Expensive. L, D.

Mitsukoshi (Japan): This complex of dining and drinking spots, all operated by the Japanese firm for which it is named, occupies the second level of the large structure on the west side of the Japan pavilion. There are two options. *Tempura Kiku* occupies a small corner of the Mitsukoshi restaurant that's devoted to the batter-dipped, deep-fried chicken, beef, seafood, and fresh vegetables that are collectively known as tempura. The individual tidbits are crisp and delicious. Priority seating not available. Expensive. L, D. *Teppanyaki Dining Rooms* is composed of five rooms not unlike those popularized by the Benihana chain all around America.

Guests sit counter style around large flat grills while white-hatted chefs chop vegetables, meat, and fish at lightning speed and then stir-fry it all just as quickly. Whether the chopping and cooking accompanies a mildly comic routine depends on the chef's sense of humor, but in any case the establishment is quite convivial. The seating arrangements make it quite natural to strike up a conversation with fellow diners; in fact, it's almost impossible to keep to yourself. Priority seating suggested. Expensive. L, D.

Nine Dragons (China): This stop on Epcot's varied international restaurant tour offers meals prepared in provincial Chinese cooking styles, including Mandarin, Cantonese, Hunan, Szechuan, and Kiangche. Entrées include braised duck (served Cantonese style), Kang Bao chicken (stir-fried chicken, peanuts, and dried hot peppers), and beef and jade tree (sliced steak and Chinese broccoli). Appetizers range from Chinese pickled cabbage to pan-fried dumplings and hot-and-sour soup. A selection of Chinese teas, beers, and wines is available. The varied dessert menu

features red-bean ice cream, toffee apples, and assorted Chinese pastries. Priority seating suggested. Moderate to expensive. L, D.

Rose & Crown Pub and Dining Room (United Kingdom): The fare here runs to pub grub—that is, fish and chips, steak-and-kidney pie, and chicken-and-leek pie. For lunch, however, it's possible to order hot roast beef with gravy and mashed potatoes, roast lamb, and a truly delicious fresh vegetable platter served with Stilton cheese and walnut dressing. At dinner the standard offerings are supplemented by roast prime rib with horseradish sauce. For dessert there's traditional sherry trifle, a confection of layered whipped cream, custard, strawberries, and sherry wine; and raspberry fool, strictly raspberry purée and whipped cream. Bass India Pale Ale from England, Tennent's lager beer from Scotland, and Harp lager beer and Guinness stout, both from Ireland, are on tap. (They're served cold, in the American fashion, not at room temperature, as Britons prefer.)

The decor is beautiful, mainly polished woods, etched glass, and brass accents. In fine weather it's pleasant to lunch under the sunny yellow umbrellas on the terrace outside and watch the sleek *FriendShip* ferries chugging across World Showcase Lagoon. On the little island just to the east, the wind ruffles the leaves of the Lombardy poplars, a species of tree that is found along roadsides all over Europe.

Horticulturally speaking, it's interesting to note the vines on the pub's northwest wall. These Virginia creepers grow amazingly fast and, when Epcot opened, showed only a few tentative tendrils close to the ground. The spreading tree nearby is a laurel oak, distinguished from the southern live oaks more widely seen at Epcot by its upright growth and its leaves, which are shiny on both sides instead of just one.

As for the pub's architecture, it incorporates three distinct styles. The wall facing the World Showcase Promenade is reminiscent of

urban establishments popular in Britain since the 1890s, while that on the south side evokes London's 17th-century Cheshire Cheese pub, with its brick-walled flagstone terrace, slate roof, and half-timbered exterior. The canal facade, with its stone wall and clay-tile roof, reminds visitors of the charming pubs so common in the English countryside.

The pub section of the Rose & Crown serves such snacks as Stilton cheese and fresh fruit platters, and mini chicken-and-leek pies—along with all the brews noted above and traditional British mixed drinks such as shandies (Bass ale and ginger beer), lager beer with lime juice, black velvets (Guinness stout and champagne), and black and tans (Bass ale and Guinness stout). This drinking and snacking spot is quite popular, so it's often necessary to queue up at the door. But the wait is seldom very long since few guests linger over their drinks. Priority seating is not available in the pub area, but suggested for the adjacent dining room. Moderate to expensive. L, D, S.

San Angel Inn (Mexico): A corporate cousin of the famous Mexico City restaurant of the same name, the food at this establishment, located to the rear of the plaza inside the Mexico pyramid, may come as a surprise to most visitors. Although the tacos and tortillas and other specialties that usually fall under the broad umbrella of Mexican food are available, the menu also offers a wide variety of more subtly flavored fish, poultry, and meat dishes. To start, there's *queso fundido* for two (melted cheese and Mexican pork sausage with corn or flour tortillas). As entrées, the menu offers *sopes de pollo* (fried corn dough shells topped with refried beans, chicken with green tomatillo sauce, and

cheese); grilled tenderloin of beef served with a chicken enchilada, guacamole, and refried beans; *mole poblano* (chicken simmered with spices and a bit of chocolate); *huachinango à la Veracruzana* (fresh fillet of red snapper poached in wine with onions, tomatoes, and peppers); and much more that is good and tasty. Mexican desserts are largely unfamiliar to North Americans, with the possible exceptions of the custard known as flan, and *arroz con leche*, best known in the United States as rice pudding. Still, such desserts as chocolate Kahlua mousse pie and *helado con cajeta* (vanilla ice cream with milk-caramel topping) are well worth trying. Dos Equis brand beer, tart lemon-flavored water, and delicious margaritas make good accompaniments. Priority seating suggested. Expensive. L, D.

CAFETERIA SERVICE

Le Cellier (Canada): Tucked away on the lowest level of the pavilion near Victoria Gardens, this low-ceilinged, stone-walled establishment looks a little like the ancient wine cellars for which it is named. It offers a full menu of Canadian foods, with hearty sandwiches also available for lunch, and roast prime rib added to the offerings at dinner. The savory, Quebec-born pork-and-potato-filled pie known as *tourtière* is dished out in enormous slices, each one fully three inches high and covered with a tempting golden crust. Tangy Canadian cheddar cheese serves as the base of a rich soup and adds zip to some appetizing fruit platters. Chicken and meatball stew, poached fresh salmon in spinach velouté sauce, and carved Canadian bacon—all served with choice of potatoes or rice, and vegetables—round out the selection of entrées. For dessert there's maple-syrup pie, a sweet cousin to pecan pie. Canada's own Molson and Labatt's beers are served in bottles. Children's selections include macaroni and cheese. This tempting combination makes Le Cellier a prime destination for those who haven't been able to book a table at one of the full-service World Showcase restaurants but still want something more substantial than what the fast-food eateries are offering. Operates seasonally. Inexpensive to moderate. L, D, S.

FAST FOOD & SNACKS

Boulangerie Pâtisserie (France): This bakery and pastry shop in the France pavilion is not hard to find: Just follow the wonderful aroma, then watch the crowds line up to consume the establishment's flaky croissants and brioches, éclairs, fruit tarts, and chocolate mousse. The treats are served by women wearing black pinafores with ruffled white blouses, under the management of the stellar trio of chefs who operate the popular Chefs de France

restaurant not far away—Paul Bocuse, Roger Vergé, and Gaston Lenôtre. Hint for those who hate to wait: This has become a favorite snacking stop among Epcot veterans; your best bet is to stop here as soon as World Showcase opens or half an hour before park closing. Inexpensive. S.

Cantina de San Angel (Mexico): Located along the World Showcase Promenade, just outside the entrance to Mexico's pyramid, this fast-food stand serves beef-filled soft tortillas; *tacos al carbon*, flour tortillas filled with grilled chicken breast strips, onions, and peppers and served with refried beans and salsa; and *churros*, a sort of fried dough rolled in cinnamon and sugar. The Cantina is first rate for a tasty rest stop, and even more so for its outdoor lagoonside seating. Dos Equis beer, margaritas, and watermelon juice are available, and the establishment's plant-edged terrace makes a fine grandstand for people-watching. Inexpensive. L, D, S.

Kringla Bakeri og Kafé (Norway): Tucked between the Norway pavilion's wooden church and a cluster of shops, this eating spot serves *kringles*, sweet candied pretzels eaten on special occasions in Norway; *vaflers*, heart-shaped waffles topped with powdered sugar and jam; *kransekake*, almond-pastry rings; and *smörbrods*, open-face sandwiches of smoked salmon, roast beef, or turkey. Ringnes Beer, brewed in Norway, is also available. There is also a shaded outdoor eating area. Inexpensive. L, S.

Liberty Inn (The American Adventure): To many foreigners, American food means hamburgers, hot dogs, and french fries, and these are the staples at the Liberty Inn, located alongside the entrance to The American Adventure show on the far end of the World

Showcase Lagoon. Salads, grilled-chicken sandwiches, ice cream, apple pastries, and chocolate chip cookies round out the selections. As a result, the place is a delight for small children, and also quite a pleasant spot for their parents. There is veranda seating, a fountain, and an array of antique-looking decoys and chests. Inexpensive. L, D, S.

Lotus Blossom Café (China): Adjacent to Yong Feng Shangdian shopping gallery in the China pavilion, this fast-food counter

offers sweet-and-sour pork, egg rolls, and soup. There is a covered outdoor seating area nearby. Inexpensive. L, D.

Refreshment Outpost (between Germany and China): This is a perfect spot for a refreshing cold drink. Frozen yogurt and ice cream are also served. Inexpensive. S.

Refreshment Port (Canada): Another good spot for a quick thirst quencher, next to the Canada pavilion. Canadian beer and wine are served. Fresh fruit, frozen yogurt, and cookies are also available. Inexpensive. S.

Sommerfest (Germany): Bratwurst sandwiches, soft pretzels, Black Forest cake, apple strudel, Beck's beer, and wine are offered at this outdoor establishment, located at the rear of the Germany pavilion; seating is nearby. Inexpensive. L, D, S.

Yakitori House (Japan): The nature of the food offered at this small but comfortable establishment on a hillock in the Japan pavilion is representative of the pace of life in that country. The average Japanese spends about seven minutes consuming his or her *guydon*, a stewlike concoction flavored with soy sauce, spices, and the Japanese rice wine known as sake—all served over rice. That staple, together with skewered chicken known as *yakitori* (which is basted with soy sauce and sesame oil as it broils), teriyaki sandwiches, and Japanese sweets and beverages, typifies the offerings here. Located in the Japanese gardens to the left of the plaza, the restaurant occupies a scaled-down version of the 16th-century Katsura Imperial Summer Palace in Kyoto; sliding screens, lanterns, and kimono-clad hostesses add to the atmosphere. Inexpensive. L, D, S.

Epcot Mealtime Tips

• The international restaurants of World Showcase offer some of the best dining on the property. Since many of them are very popular, it's smart to arrange advance priority seating for any full-service restaurants by calling WDW-DINE (939-3463) long before arriving. However, many tables are left available for same-day seating. To make arrangements, head straight for a WorldKey Information Service terminal or Guest Relations first thing in the morning. Lunch can also be booked at the individual restaurants. Refer to page 246 for more details.

• If you aren't able to secure priority seating for dinner, don't despair. France offers the full-service eatery known as Au Petit Café (though there are sometimes queues). Stop in Canada at the cafeteria-style Le Cellier for a quick but hearty meal. Japan has Tempura Kiku, a full-service spot with batter-dipped, deep fried meats and vegetables, and Yakitori House, good for skewered bits of barbecued beef and chicken. Sample Mexican specialties at Cantina de San Angel (whose lagoonside tables provide a fine view of the sun setting behind Epcot). Also try the open-face sandwiches at Kringla Bakeri og Kafé in Norway, or the sweet-and-sour pork at China's Lotus Blossom Café.

• Cravings for more conventional fast foods will be satisfied at the Electric Umbrella in Innoventions; and at the Liberty Inn in The American Adventure. The Pasta Piazza Ristorante in Innoventions serves Italian fare. The Sunshine Season Food Fair in The Land pavilion offers a little bit of everything.

• Each of the restaurants has something special about it, and there's always a good menu selection even for unadventurous eaters—even in the more exotic restaurants of World Showcase. If you're undecided, ask at Guest Relations to see a book of menus.

• Don't arbitrarily dismiss the idea of an early seating if you can get it: If you have lunch at 11 A.M., a 5 P.M. dinner will not only be welcome, but more important, it will provide the opportunity to spend the most pleasant and uncrowded evening hours enjoying the Epcot attractions.

• Lunch provides guests with another chance to enjoy the most popular Epcot restaurants. It also has another important appeal: With a priority seating for 1 P.M., it's possible to spend some of the most crowded hours in the park consuming a pleasant meal while less fortunate visitors are waiting in some of the longest lines of the day.

In the Disney-MGM Studios

The eateries at the Disney-MGM Studios are a breed apart. Some feature decor that returns guests to a bygone era; others recapture memorable moments from the big or small screen. All reprise a beloved part of Hollywood's star-studded heritage. The Studios has five full-service restaurants, whose atmospheres and menus are so distinct they sate altogether different moods and whims. Priority seating is available for these dining rooms (for details, turn to page 246). Soundstage restaurant offers all-day character meals (see page 244 for specifics). A solid—and fairly diverse—ensemble of fast-food places hits the spot for eaters on the move.

FULL SERVICE

50's Prime Time Café: The setting is straight out of your favorite sitcoms of the 1950s. Each of the plastic-laminate kitchen tables is set under a pull-down lamp, evoking a suburban kitchenette. Video screens all around the room broadcast black-and-white clips (all related to food) from favorite '50s TV comedies; these nostalgic bits are visible from each of the 226 seats. The placemats pose television trivia questions, and meals are served on either Fiesta Ware plates or TV dinner–style three-compartment trays. The waitresses play "Mom" with considerable enthusiasm, making recommendations and encouraging guests to clean their plates (*or no dessert!*).

The menu is packed with "comfort foods." For openers there's a choice of alphabet soup, chili, or the French Fry Feast, served either plain or with chili and cheese. Specialties of the house include Magnificent Meat Loaf, served with mashed potatoes and mushroom gravy; broiled chicken and spuds; chicken pot pie; and Granny's Pot Roast. There are also hamburgers with various toppings, turkey burgers, hot roast beef sandwiches, club sandwiches, and Aunt Selma's Chicken Salad. Milk shakes, ice cream sodas, and root beer floats are filling accompaniments. And when you've finished everything on your plate, "Mom" will ask if you'd like dessert. Standouts include s'mores, a graham cracker topped with chocolate and toasted marshmallows (you'll feel like you're back at summer camp); sundaes; banana splits; and

apple pie à la mode. Beer and wine are served. Kids love this place, and a children's menu is available. Priority seating suggested. Moderate. L, D, S.

Hollywood Brown Derby: The home of the famous Cobb Salad is alive and well. This re-creation of the former Vine Street mainstay is quite faithful, right down to the caricatures (lovingly reproduced from the original Derby collection) that cover the walls. Arch rivals Louella Parsons and Hedda Hopper (portrayed by convincing actresses) still reign over the restaurant from reserved tables, just as they did when the real Brown Derby was in its heyday.

The 235-seat restaurant is decorated predominantly in teak and mahogany, and the elegant chandeliers and perimeter lamps (shaped like miniature derbies) are reminiscent of those in the original eatery. The china is embossed with the Brown Derby logo. The only nonauthentic element in the atmosphere is the theme park clientele who show up in shorts and tennis shoes.

The menu features the famed Cobb Salad, created by owner Bob Cobb in the 1930s. It's a mixture of finely chopped fresh salad greens, tomato, bacon, turkey, egg, bleu cheese, and avocado. It's tossed tableside and served with old-fashioned French dressing. A modern incarnation of the salad is also available with shrimp or lobster. Other menu selections of note include Fettuccine Derby, pasta in a Parmesan cheese sauce with chicken and red and green peppers, and fillet of grouper. The dessert tray is tempting—particularly the grapefruit cake, a Brown Derby institution. A children's menu is available, although the slightly formal atmosphere is not likely to enchant most youngsters. Priority seating suggested. Expensive. L, D.

Mama Melrose's Ristorante Italiano: A pizzeria has opened in a warehouse that has been converted into a dining room. Pizzas are prepared in a wood-burning oven; fresh fish and steaks are grilled over a hardwood charbroiler. Other menu items include lasagne, chicken, veal chops, and pasta with a variety of toppings. Priority seating suggested. Moderate to expensive. L, D (during busy seasons).

Sci-Fi Dine-In Theater: This 250-seat eatery recreates a 1950s drive-in theater. The tables are actually flashy, 1950s-era cars, complete with fins and whitewalls. Fiber-optic stars twinkle overhead in the "night sky," and real drive-in theater speakers are mounted beside each car. All the tables face a large screen, where a 45-minute compilation of the best (and worst) of science fiction trailers and cartoons plays in a continuous loop. Popcorn is served before meals, which include the Monster Mash—actually roast turkey with dressing and mashed potatoes. Tossed in Space is a (rather huge) chef's salad and Towering Terror is a platter of barbecued pork ribs with corn-on-the-cob

and coleslaw. There are also hot and cold sandwiches and a unique slate of tempting desserts, including the Cheesecake That Ate New York; Twin Terrors, a banana-split cake; Science Gone Mad, Dutch apple pie served warm; and The Black Hole, a chocolate layer cake. There is also a children's menu. Priority seating suggested. Moderate to expensive. L, D.

Soundstage: This cavernous restaurant located in the Animation Courtyard has been transformed into an all-day character buffet, featuring stars from animated clas-

sics. Characters from such hits as *Beauty and the Beast*, *Aladdin*, *The Hunchback of Notre Dame*, and *Pocahontas* gather at this restaurant all day long. Music from the films plays in the background. The buffet offers a salad bar, pasta, herb-baked chicken, beef stew, baked fish, roast pork, and various accompaniments. A kid's buffet includes chicken tenders, macaroni and cheese, and Mexican hot dogs. Priority seating suggested. Moderate to expensive. B, L, D.

CAFETERIA SERVICE

Hollywood & Vine: The distinctive Art Deco facade ushers guests into a contemporary version of a 1950s diner—all stainless steel with pink accents. An elaborate 42- by 8-foot wall mural depicts notable Hollywood landmarks, including the Disney Studios, Columbia Ranch, and Warner Brothers (back when they were the only studios in the San Fernando Valley). At the center of the mural is the Carthay Circle Theatre, where *Snow White* premiered in 1937.

The 368-seat cafeteria presents a varied menu. At breakfast, there's the Hollywood Scramble, two eggs served with bacon or

sausage and a choice of potatoes or grits and a breakfast biscuit; french toast; pancakes; omelettes; assorted hot and cold cereals; and fresh fruit. Muffins, Danish pastries, and croissants are also served. Lunch features a variety of salads. Baby-back ribs, roast chicken, and spaghetti and meatballs are offered. Pies head the dessert list. Beer and wine are available, and a children's menu is posted. Inexpensive to moderate. B, L, D.

FAST FOOD & SNACKS

Backlot Express: This counter-service restaurant looks like the old crafts shops on a studio backlot. There's a paint shop, a stunt hall, a sculpture shop, and a model shop. The paint shop has paint-speckled floors, chairs, and tables; the prop shop is decked out in` car engines, bumpers, and fan belts. There is outdoor seating amid stored streetlights, plants, and trees. Menu offerings include burgers, hot dogs, chef's salad, and chili. For dessert, there's chocolate-chip cheesecake, apple pie, and fresh fruit. Beer and wine are available. Inexpensive. L, D, S.

Commissary: Fast food with a healthy twist is the bill of fare at this streamlined moderne eatery. The 550-seat restaurant is located between the Chinese Theatre and SuperStar Television. Chicken-breast sandwiches and fresh salads are the norm. There is a children's menu. Inexpensive. L, D.

Dinosaur Gertie's: "Ice Cream of Extinction," claims the sign at this lifesize dinosaur set on Echo Lake. And, indeed, ice cream has in fact been replaced with frozen slush drinks in a variety of flavors. Inexpensive. S.

Min & Bill's Dockside Diner: "There's good eats in our galley," proclaims the welcoming sign posted on the *S.S. Down the Hatch*, a bit of "California crazy" 1950s architecture. The little tramp steamer, complete with a cartoonlike smokestack, mast, and booms, doesn't sail. Min & Bill's offerings include the Portside Sandwich (turkey ham and turkey salami, lettuce, and tomato rolled in a soft tortilla). Soft-serve ice cream is available in cups or cones with a variety of toppings. Inexpensive. L, D, S.

Starring Rolls Bakery: Freshly baked rolls (not roles), pastries, muffins, and croissants are sold at this sweet-smelling shop. Coffee, tea, and soft drinks are also served, making this a good place for an eat-and-run breakfast. For lunch, ready-made croissant sandwiches with ham and cheese or tuna salad are available. Inexpensive. B, L, S.

Studio Catering Co.: Guests on the Studio Backlot Tour come across this spot at the end of the tram ride. Situated just behind The Loony Bin, the eatery offers desserts and snacks. Beer is available. Inexpensive. S.

Sunset Ranch Market: Three food stands on Sunset Boulevard offer good snacking opportunities. Rosie's Red Hot Dogs specializes in the obvious, serving a curious assortment of hot dogs, including foot-long options. Catalina Eddie's offers frozen yogurt and fruit drinks. Popcorn, fresh fruit and vegetables, fruit juices, and soft drinks are also available. Inexpensive. L, D, S.

Toy Story Pizza Planet: This arcade looks as if it were plucked right out of the animated hit *Toy Story*. The eye-catching centerpiece: a Space Crane, complete with aliens and mechanical grabber. A limited menu includes individual pizzas, salad, pasta salad, Italian ices, and juice boxes. Inexpensive. L, D, S.

Studios Mealtime Tips

- To avert mealtime traffic jams at fast-food spots, consider eating lunch or dinner at one of the restaurants that offers priority seating—Hollywood Brown Derby, 50's Prime Time Café, Sci-Fi Dine-In Theater, Soundstage, or Mama Melrose's Ristorante Italiano. To arrange for priority seating in advance, call WDW-DINE (939-3463). To obtain same-day seating, go to the kiosk at Hollywood Junction (on the corner of Hollywood and Sunset, before 1 P.M.) or to the restaurant itself. Refer to page 246 for details.

- The many indoor and outdoor nooks within Backlot Express' seating area are nicely removed from the beaten path; relative quiet can frequently be enjoyed here even during prime mealtimes.

- Characters now appear at the Soundstage restaurant all day long, so it's perhaps the best place at the Disney-MGM Studios to meet them.

In the Resorts

Among the more pleasant surprises at Walt Disney World is the delightful theming of the Disney hotels. Each resort sports a fanciful setting quite foreign to Central Florida, reminiscent of such places as the Pacific Northwest; the more regional-minded offer a tasty sampling of the native cuisine to complete the picture. Whereas the deluxe properties provide a variety of dining options including at least one full-service restaurant, moderate resorts feature a sprawling food court plus an informal dining room, and the value-oriented All-Star resorts keep guests' appetites in check with huge food courts.

Suffice it to say that the possibilities range from hearty dinners served family style on lazy susans to innovative cuisine you might not expect from Disney, served in settings worthy of special occasions. Priority seating is an important part of the resorts' full-service dining circuit (for complete details turn to page 246). Character meals are an option for breakfast, Sunday brunch, and dinner (for specifics see page 244).

All-Star Sports & All-Star Music

Each of these resorts features a themed central food court. The **End Zone** food court in Stadium Hall at the All-Star Sports resort and the **Intermission** food court in Melody Hall at the All-Star Music resort have similar food stands. The selections include pasta, hand-tossed pizza, chicken, ribs, burgers, hot dogs, sandwiches, salads, frozen yogurt, and a wide variety of baked goods. Inexpensive. B, L, D, S.

Beach Club

Ariel's: The Beach Club's signature restaurant, named for the star of *The Little Mermaid*, features a 2,500-gallon saltwater aquarium. The menu is strong in fresh seafood (not straight from the tank, though), and lobster is a specialty. Paintings of underwater scenes, school-of-fish chandeliers, and seaworthy china accent the theme. Priority seating suggested. Expensive. D.

Beaches & Cream Soda Shop: This restaurant straddles the Yacht Club and the Beach Club. Patterned after a turn-of-the-century ice cream parlor, it features oversize sundaes, cones, floats, shakes, and sodas, as well as the Fenway Park Burger—which can be ordered as a single, double, triple, or home-run. Breakfast items are available as well. Inexpensive to moderate. B, L, D, S.

Cape May Café: An all-you-can-eat New England clambake is held every evening. A cooking pit used for steaming is in full view of diners, and menu items include clams, mussels, chicken, shrimp, corn, red-skin potatoes, and chowder. Lobster is available for an extra charge. There is a character breakfast buffet each morning. Priority seating suggested. Moderate to expensive. B, D.

Hurricane Hanna's Grill: Located in the Stormalong Bay area shared by the Yacht Club and Beach Club. Hot dogs, hamburgers, sandwiches, french fries, and ice cream are on the menu. There is also a full bar. Inexpensive. L, S.

BoardWalk

BoardWalk Bakery: The aromas wafting from Spoodles' next-door neighbor on the boardwalk reveal the fresh-baked goods therein. Display windows allow guests to watch bakers at work. "Bun rises" are held each morning. Inexpensive. B, S.

Flying Fish Café: This upbeat boardwalk eatery beside Seashore Sweets' delivers creative seasonal menus with an emphasis on seafood and healthy options. As an example of the entrées created in the open kitchen, consider Dungeness crab cakes with spicy remoulade. Steaks are also served. Tasting menus are available. Expensive. D.

Seashore Sweets': Located next to the Flying Fish Café, this old-fashioned spot sates sweet tooths with cookies, candies, saltwater taffy, and hand-dipped gelato. Specialty coffees are also offered. Inexpensive. S.

Spoodles: This family-oriented restaurant with butcher-block tables and Mediterranean tastes is on the boardwalk between Seashore Sweets' and the BoardWalk Bakery. The lunch and dinner menus highlight specialties from Greece, Spain, Northern Africa, and

Italy, and encourage diners to share dishes and try new foods. Offerings range from pizzas baked in wood-burning ovens to such creations as yogurt-marinated chicken kebabs served with corn risotto. Breakfast items are more traditional. Outdoor seating is available, and a take-out window allows passersby to buy pizza by the slice. Priority seating suggested. Moderate to expensive. B, L, D.

Caribbean Beach

Captain's Tavern: Prime rib, chicken, and crab legs are on the menu at this cozy 200-seat restaurant located within Old Port Royale. Tropical drinks, beer, wine, and cocktails are also served. Moderate. D, S.

Old Port Royale: The food court in Old Port Royale features a 500-seat dining area and the following counter-service eateries. *Bridgetown Broiler* offers spit-roasted chicken and homestyle meals. *Cinnamon Bay Bakery* serves croissants, freshly baked rolls, pastries, ice cream, and other caloric treats. Italian specialties are the order at *Kingston Pasta Shop*. Soups, salads, and hot and cold sandwiches make up the selections at *Montego's Deli*. Burgers and grilled-chicken sandwiches are among the offerings at *Port Royale Hamburger Shop*. And pizza is available by the slice or the pie at *Royale Pizza Shop*. Inexpensive. B, L, D, S.

Contemporary

California Grill: Perched on the hotel's 15th floor with terrific views of sunsets and Magic Kingdom fireworks. This acclaimed restaurant offers the best in West Coast cuisine in a stylish, relaxing atmosphere. The ever-changing menu is defined by sophisticated use of fresh produce. Wood-fired California pizzas, alderwood-smoked salmon, sushi, spit-roasted chicken, and jumbo soufflés are made

to order in an open kitchen. Maui onion and artichoke soup, and oak-fired quail with zinfandel risotto suggest the culinary prowess. The excellent wine list is updated daily. Priority seating suggested. Expensive. D.

Chef Mickey's: This recently transplanted restaurant has assumed a new identity here at the Contemporary. As Chef Mickey and pals cook up a buffet-style feast, a glass window affords views of the passing monorail. Colorful lifesize illustrations of characters decorate the room. The changing menu takes advantage of seasonal offerings; a sundae bar provides a sweet finish. Priority seating suggested. Moderate to expensive. B, D.

Concourse Steakhouse: On the fourth-floor concourse, this spot offers omelettes, pancakes, and fresh fruit for breakfast. At lunch there are salads, soups, burgers, sandwiches, and individual pizzas. Dinner adds prime rib and steaks to the menu. Priority seating suggested. Moderate to expensive. B, L, D.

Food and Fun Center: On the first floor adjacent to the arcade, this casual spot serves light fare from 6 A.M. to midnight. Inexpensive. B, L, D, S.

Disney's Coronado Springs

This new resort, due to open in late summer 1997, offers two dining options. The hotel's full-service restaurant features a show grill and a menu emphasizing southwestern dishes. **Pepper Market** food court, modeled after an open-air market, has a large seating area and lots of stands where vendors sell pizza, sandwiches, salads, burgers, regional specialties, margaritas, and more.

Disney's Old Key West

Good's Food to Go: Burgers, grilled-chicken sandwiches, ice cream, and frozen yogurt are among the offerings. Inexpensive. L, D, S.

Olivia's Café: An assortment of Key West favorites, including Key lime pie and conch fritters, is featured alongside more traditional items like Florida paella and crab cakes. The menu changes seasonally. A Winnie the Pooh character breakfast is held Wednesday and Sunday. Priority seating suggested. Moderate. B, L, D.

Dixie Landings

Boatwright's Dining Hall: Be sure to notice the boat that's being built in this 200-seat, full-service eatery. The specialties of the house include Cajun dishes as well as American homestyle favorites. Priority seating available for dinner. Moderate. B, D.

Colonel's Cotton Mill: This high-ceilinged food court styled in the image of a working cotton mill offers half a dozen different counters and a sprawling seating area. Collectively, the stands offer pizza; pasta; fried, grilled, and spit-roasted chicken; burgers; barbecued ribs; salads; sandwiches; and fresh baked goods, including pies and sticky cinnamon buns. For guests on the go, the food court's deli doubles as a convenience store, stocking sandwiches, beer, wine, snack items, and prepared salads. Inexpensive. B, L, D, S.

Dolphin

Cabana Bar & Grill: Burgers, grilled-chicken sandwiches, fresh fruit, and yogurt are offered at this full-service poolside eatery. Inexpensive. L, S.

Coral Café: Buffets are offered for breakfast and dinner in this bright and casual restaurant. An à la carte menu is also available, offering turkey burgers, chicken, club sandwiches, pasta, and cheese steaks. Moderate. B, L, D, S.

Dolphin Fountain: Homemade ice cream is the highlight here. Flavors include dark chocolate, cappuccino, and mint chocolate chip. Oreo and Heath Bar mixes are available in waffle cones, cups, or as part of super sundaes. Burgers, shakes, and malts are also available. The old-time 1950s atmosphere is enhanced by an energetic staff that breaks into song and dance several times a day. Inexpensive to moderate. L, D, S.

Harry's Safari Bar & Grille: Grilled steaks, seafood, and chicken seasoned with herbs bought by "Harry" during his world travels mark the adventuresome menu. On Sunday there is a character brunch. Reservations suggested for dinner, necessary for brunch. Expensive. D, Sunday brunch.

Juan & Only's: This festive restaurant features authentic Mexican food. Specialties include fresh *pico de gallo* served with blue corn and spicy red chips; grilled beef, chicken, shrimp, and a special meatless fajita from the fajita bar; chimichangas; burritos; taco salads; and other Mexican fare. Reservations suggested. Moderate to expensive. D.

Sum Chows: A broad spectrum of Asian dishes with creative culinary flair are served in this elegant dining room. Favorites such as Firecracker Snapper and Tangerine Peel Chicken are among the many flavorful entrées supplementing the restaurant's full sushi menu. The flash-fried spinach is a highlight, and the relaxed, yet stylish setting sets the tone for a pleasant meal. On request, the chef can create a special menu for a truly unique dining experience. Reservations suggested. Expensive. D.

Tubbi's: Checkerboard decor and a jukebox raise this cafeteria above the norm. The food, including meatball subs and pizza, is fresh, and the lines are seldom long. The adjoining convenience store (open 24 hours) stocks snacks, sundries, and lots of baby items. Inexpensive. B, L, D, S.

Fort Wilderness

Most people cook their own meals here; ample supplies are available at both the Meadow Trading Post and the Settlement Trading Post (open from 8 A.M. to 10 P.M. in winter, to 11 P.M. in summer).

Crockett's Tavern: Appetizers, steaks, ribs, and chicken are available in this Pioneer Hall eatery. A children's menu is offered. Cocktails are served. Moderate. D.

Trail's End Buffet: This informal, log-walled restaurant offers standard breakfasts, plus grits, biscuits, gravy, and a seven-inch "breakfast pizza" that vaguely resembles an omelette. Hearty lunches and dinners feature barbecued chicken, fish, chicken pot pie, and spare ribs. There are sandwiches and a taco bar at lunch. Specially priced children's portions are available. Pizza is served every night from 9:30 P.M. until 11 P.M. (until midnight on weekends). Beer and wine are served by the glass or by the pitcher. Inexpensive to moderate. B, L, D, S.

Grand Floridian

Flagler's: Italian influences predominate in the hotel's largest restaurant. Pasta, seafood, veal, and steaks are served. Dessert offerings include homemade gelato. There are strolling musicians, and the restaurant offers a lovely view of the Seven Seas Lagoon. Priority seating suggested. Expensive. D.

Gasparilla Grill & Games: Grilled chicken, hamburgers, pizza, hot dogs, and soft-serve ice cream are the mainstays at this 24-hour take-out, self-service restaurant near the pool. Continental breakfast is also available. Inexpensive. B, L, D, S.

Grand Floridian Café: Southern cooking is the specialty at this picturesque spot. Selections include honey-dipped fried chicken and a sandwich of turkey, ham, tomatoes, bacon, cheddar cheese, and crispy onions. There are also salads and an assortment of more traditional entrées. Priority seating available. Moderate. B, L, D.

Narcoossee's: The open kitchen is the focal point at this casual, airy, octagonal restaurant on the shore of the Grand Floridian beach. Specialties include grilled swordfish marinated in garlic, olive oil, and basil; grilled steaks; double lamb chops; veal chops; and grilled chicken. The Seven Seas, Seven Scoops Spectacular is a 48-ounce snifter filled with berries, seven scoops of ice cream, and topped with whipped cream and a touch of amaretto. Priority seating suggested. Expensive. L, D.

menu. At the completion of the meal, women receive a long-stemmed rose. Jackets are required. One oddity of note: Every host and hostess at the restaurant is named Victoria or Albert. Priority seating necessary. Very expensive. D.

Polynesian

Captain Cook's Snack & Ice Cream Company: A good spot for continental breakfast, hamburgers, hot dogs, fruit salad, soft-serve ice cream, and snacks; cans of beer are also available. Open 24 hours. Inexpensive. B, L, D, S.

Coral Isle Café: Located on the second floor of the Great Ceremonial House, just around the corner from 'Ohana. This standard coffee shop with a faintly South Seas decor serves the usual assortment of eggs every morning, plus granola and other cereals, and wonderful banana-stuffed french toast, one of the many unique Walt Disney World dishes. At lunch, the house does a booming business in burgers and a variety of sandwiches. At dinnertime, 20-ounce New York strip steaks, ribs, and tempting desserts are among the offerings. All things considered, it's a good choice when you want a no-fuss meal. Priority seating available. Moderate. B, L, D, S.

1900 Park Fare: The all-American menu takes a backseat to the decor in this 248-seat buffet restaurant. Big Bertha, a band organ built in Paris nearly a century ago, sits 15 feet above the floor in a proscenium. The bellows-powered instrument simultaneously plays pipes, drums, bells, cymbals, and xylophone. Mary Poppins joins other Disney characters here during breakfast. The dinner buffet features seafood, salads, vegetables, breads, and prime rib. Mickey and Minnie entertain at dinner. The offerings change weekly. Priority seating suggested. Expensive. B, D.

Victoria & Albert's: The premier restaurant of not only the Grand Floridian, but probably the entire Walt Disney World complex. The intimate dining room seats only 65, and elegant touches include Royal Doulton china, Sambonet silver, and Schott-Zweisel crystal. There is no formal, printed menu. Each night there are fish, fowl, red meat, veal, and lamb selections, which depend on the best ingredients in the market and are described in detail by your waiter. The chef may even make a personal appearance to accommodate special requests from patrons, or guests may choose to dine at the chef's table in the kitchen. There are also choices of two soups, two salads, and desserts, including the specialty soufflés of fresh berries, chocolate, or Grand Marnier. There is an extensive wine list, and wine pairings are available with each course.

Once guests have made their selections, they are presented a handwritten souvenir

'Ohana: On the second floor of the Great Ceremonial House, this restaurant features a 16-foot-long open fire pit. Dinner choices in the all-you-can-eat feast include shrimp, poultry, pork, and beef, all roasted on skewers up to three feet long. Meats are marinated in original combinations of soy, ginger, lemon grass, or garlic, and are served family style with an assortment of fresh vegetables, salads, and homemade bread. The dessert offerings include passion fruit crème

brûlée. The room itself is large and open and offers fine views across the Seven Seas Lagoon all the way to Cinderella Castle. Minnie's Menehune character breakfast is held daily. Polynesian singers and dancers entertain at dinner. Priority seating suggested. Expensive. B, D.

Port Orleans

Bonfamilles Café: The name of this full-service restaurant derives from the Disney movie *The Aristocats*. Steaks, seafood, and Creole cooking highlight the menu. Breakfast is also served. Priority seating available for dinner. Moderate. B, D.

Sassagoula Floatworks & Food Factory: The stands at this festive food court feature pizza, pasta, gumbo, burgers, sandwiches, soups, salads, spit-roasted chicken, barbecued ribs, ice cream, and a full selection of fresh bakery products, including beignets. Inexpensive. B, L, D, S.

Swan

Garden Grove Café: Situated in a five-story greenhouse, this dining spot offers a full breakfast menu, and fresh fish and shellfish at lunch. At dinner, the restaurant is transformed into Gulliver's Grill, where you can order Blushklooshen (red snapper) and drink Caff Dupooshpoosh (double espresso) from oversize cups. Desserts are baked fresh daily in an open pastry kitchen. As you approach the restaurant, take a look through the glass windows to see the chefs at work. Character breakfasts and dinners are held here on certain days. Reservations suggested for dinner. Expensive. B, L, D, S.

Kimono's: This spot, attractively decorated in Japanese style, offers sushi, a variety of oriental specialties, and a full bar. Reservations accepted. Moderate to expensive. D, S.

Palio: This Italian bistro gets high marks for its bruschetta, foccacia, pasta, and pizza. Other specialties include veal and fish dishes. A strolling musician adds to the ambience. Reservations suggested. Expensive. D.

Splash Grill: Burgers and other grilled fare join ice cream and frozen yogurt on the menu at this poolside spot. Beer and frozen drinks are served. Prepackaged snacks are also on hand. Inexpensive. B, L, S.

Par for the Course

The pleasant **Sand Trap Bar & Grill** in the Bonnet Creek Golf Club is a convenient dining option for golfers playing the adjacent Eagle Pines and Osprey Ridge courses. It's also close to the Magic Kingdom resorts. In addition to a variety of appetizers, burgers, Reuben sandwiches, barbecued pork, and grilled-chicken sandwiches are served. There is a full bar; ice cream and milk shakes are also available. Moderate. L, D, S.

Wilderness Lodge

Artist Point: Decorated with artwork representing the painters who first chronicled the Northwest landscape, this fine dining spot offers a creative menu that incorporates

wild game as well as more traditional items such as steaks, salmon, and other Pacific seafood. The solid wine list spotlights wines from the Pacific Northwest. A character breakfast hosted by Pocahontas and friends is served every morning. Priority seating suggested. Expensive. B, D.

Roaring Fork: Light snacks, salads, and yogurt are available 24 hours a day at this simple nook adjacent to the hotel's arcade. Inexpensive. B, L, D, S.

Whispering Canyon Café: A traditional family-style restaurant that's open for all-day dining. Hearty fare includes warm apple cakes and biscuits for breakfast, barbecued beef brisket for lunch, and apple-rosemary rotisserie chicken for dinner. Priority seating suggested. Moderate. B, L, D.

The Villas at the Disney Institute

Seasons Dining Room: Even the setup of this restaurant is seasonally driven. Four dining rooms are decorated to reflect the distinct seasons. At breakfast, seasonal fruit syrups are offered with the pancakes. Lunch options range from club sandwiches to shrimp couscous salad. For dinner (served family style or à la carte), a different cuisine is highlighted each night of the week: Mediterranean, Californian, Best of Institute Garden, South Seas, New Orleans, Key West, and Pacific Northwest. Family-style dinners include appetizers, entrées, drinks, and desserts, all corresponding to the evening's theme. Priority seating suggested. Expensive. B, L, D.

Yacht Club

Beaches & Cream Soda Shop: This ice cream parlor is located between the Yacht Club and the Beach Club. For a full description, see the Beach Club listing.

Hurricane Hanna's Grill: This fast-food spot is in the Stormalong Bay pool area shared by the Yacht Club and Beach Club. See the Beach Club listing for a description.

Yacht Club Galley: Vivid ceramic-tile tabletops help emphasize the yachting theme. Breakfast features a buffet and a full menu; lunch and dinner are à la carte only. Priority seating suggested. Moderate. B, L, D.

Yachtsman Steakhouse: As its name implies, aged beef is the specialty of the house. Guests can see the butcher choosing cuts of meat in the glassed-in shop, and watch meals being prepared in the display kitchen. Fresh seafood and chicken are available. Priority seating suggested. Expensive. D.

Pleasure Island

The six acres of Pleasure Island bustle with activity mostly during evening hours, but the restaurants are open for both lunch and dinner and offer several tempting dining options for WDW guests. While an admission fee applies after 7 P.M. for club-goers, there is no charge simply to dine at any of Pleasure Island's full-service restaurants. The restaurants generally operate from 11:30 A.M. to midnight; most of the snack spots are open from 11 A.M. to 2 A.M. For up-to-the-minute details on hours call 824-4321.

D-Zertz: Pastries, chocolates, candy, frozen yogurt, and other such sweet treats are the mouth-watering fare available here. Coffee and cappuccino are also served, making it a pleasant spot for a quick snack. Inexpensive. S.

Fireworks Factory: One of three Pleasure Island eateries operated by the Levy Restaurants. The 400-seat dining spot features high ceilings juxtaposed with antique brick walls, metal stairs, and a floor stained with black gunpowder. Some of the props around the restaurant are on loan from the Gruccis, the famous fireworks family of New York. There are two dining rooms and a bar.

Upon entering, guests are invited into a casual atmosphere where they sit at bench tables topped with yellow tablecloths. Ribs are the specialty of the house: baby back and Texas beef. They are seasoned with a blend of spices, smoked slowly over an applewood grill, and then doused in the Fireworks Factory's own barbecue sauce.

But ribs aren't the only thing on the innovative menu. If all the appetizers sound good, try the appetizer sampler of quesadilla, spicy hot chicken wings, rock shrimp, and applewood-smoked baby-back ribs. Chicken, steaks, and pork chops are among the grilled entrées. Dessert selections include Atomic Chocolate Cake, topped and filled with chocolate mousse and coated with chocolate chips; turtle pie; Key lime pie; Edy's ice cream; and the Tollhouse Cookie Sundae, a large, warm cookie served in a cast-iron skillet and topped with vanilla ice cream and hot fudge.

A children's menu is available, as is a selection of T-shirts, sweatshirts, hats, and other items bearing the Fireworks Factory logo. Fireworks' special barbecue sauce is sold in souvenir jars. Reservations accepted. Moderate to expensive. L, D.

Fulton's Crab House: This traditional seafood house, also operated by Levy Restaurants, occupies the three-deck riverboat formerly known as the *Empress Lilly*. Permanently docked on the western edge of Buena Vista Lagoon, it is a tribute to Robert Fulton, who invented the steamboat. The place is so serious about seafood that it has hooked up with fishermen worldwide to ensure that the truckloads of fish and shellfish arriving daily at Fulton's back door are at their freshest.

The menu changes each day to reflect new arrivals, but is always brimming with several types of crabs, oysters, and fish, plus

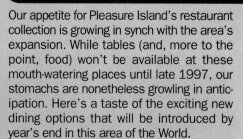

Pleasure Island's New Brood

Our appetite for Pleasure Island's restaurant collection is growing in synch with the area's expansion. While tables (and, more to the point, food) won't be available at these mouth-watering places until late 1997, our stomachs are nonetheless growling in anticipation. Here's a taste of the exciting new dining options that will be introduced by year's end in this area of the World.

Wolfgang Puck's Café: Even local chefs are chomping at the bit to pull up a chair at this offspring of L.A.'s famed culinary wizard. Wolfgang Puck's choice of Walt Disney World for his Florida debut is sure to spur a surge in cravings for his trademark California cuisine. But make no mistake, the restaurant will be no elegant elitist. It'll be as casual as they come, with a menu that's equal parts sophisticated and straightforward—and ever so fresh.

Lario's: While predominantly a dance club, this sizzling creation of Gloria Estefan and her husband will spice up the Pleasure Island dining repertoire with a menu driven by Cuban and Latin American flavors. Like its big sister in Miami Beach, the spot is destined to tantalize taste buds with its slate of traditional and nouvelle Cuban dishes.

House of Blues: The nightclub that Blues Brother Dan Aykroyd helped launch will double as a Mississippi Delta–inspired dining spot. With the opening of this music-focused establishment, Pleasure Island gets a culinary boost from the bayou—namely homestyle Cajun and Creole cooking. Finally, the island will have a haven for diners desperately seeking to have their fill of such savory things as jambalaya, étouffé, and homemade bread pudding.

Planet Hollywood: This branch of the international chain is a standout for its spherical silhouette. Co-owned by Arnold Schwarzenegger, Sylvester Stallone, Bruce Willis, and Demi Moore, this globe is built on three levels. Movie and television memorabilia abound. The wide-ranging menu features

lobster, steaks, roast chicken, grilled vegetables, and combination platters. Signature Fulton's dishes include cioppino, a savory San Francisco–style seafood stew with a tomato broth base. Accompaniments extend to corn-whipped potatoes and sugar snap peas. Desserts, coffee, and specialty drinks are also served. The children's menu runs from fish and chips to spaghetti.

Fulton's handsome polished-wood interior is awash in nautical knickknacks and nostalgia. Seating on the deck is sometimes available. The adjoining Stone Crab lounge has a mouthwatering raw bar. A grand character breakfast with Captain Mickey and friends is held twice daily (seatings are at 8 A.M. and 10 A.M.). The meal features scrambled eggs, chicken-apple sausage, hash browns, apple pastry, fruit, and mini muffins. Priority seating suggested for breakfast and dinner. Expensive. B, L, D, S.

Missing Link Sausage Co.: Hot dogs, bratwurst, kielbasa, and sausages (including a chicken-apple variety, and both mild and hot Italian links) dominate the menu of this snack spot across from 8Trax. Cheese steaks are also available. Inexpensive. L, D, S.

first-rate salads, sandwiches, pasta dishes, burgers, appetizer pizzas, fajitas, and dessert specialties. Moderate. L, D, S.

Portobello Yacht Club: The elegant Bermuda-style house combines high gables and beamed ceilings, bright Mediterranean colors and earthy tones. This was the first dining spot opened by the Levy Restaurants of Chicago, and is one of our favorites on the WDW property. The 326-seat establishment is divided into several informal dining rooms, each of which displays an impressive collection of maritime memorabilia.

But food is the highlight of the Portobello Yacht Club. The bustling open kitchen turns out grilled meat and fish and absolutely delicious small gourmet pizzas baked in the wood-burning oven. Try the *quattro formaggi*, a four-cheese pie that's a true taste treat, and a great appetizer or snack. Pasta offerings include *spaghettini alla Portobello*—pasta with shrimp, scallops, clams, mussels, crab legs, tomatoes, garlic, olive oil, wine, and herbs—and *bucatini all'amatriciana*, long pasta tubes with plum tomatoes, Italian bacon, garlic, and fresh basil. Be sure to save some room for desserts such as *crema brucciata*, Italian custard with a caramelized sugar glaze or *cioccolato paradiso*, a rich layer cake with chocolate ganache frosting, chocolate toffee crunch filling, and warm caramel sauce. A children's menu is available. No reservations are accepted. Expensive. L, D, S.

Disney Village Marketplace

A couple of the World's more popular dining spots are located in this waterside shopping enclave on the southeastern edge of the property. It's worth noting that while the restaurants here really hop at dinnertime, none is terribly crowded at lunch, except on Saturday and Sunday, when Orlando and Kissimmee residents make the trip to the Disney Village Marketplace for a day of shopping. And several restaurants have the advantage of being just a couple of hundred yards' dash from the marina, so kids can go hire a pedal boat or a Water Sprite (during lunchtime and in late afternoon) while parents linger over coffee or drinks.

Cap'n Jack's Oyster Bar: This pier house juts right out over Buena Vista Lagoon, providing diners with water views. The menu is so full of good things—seafood marinara, shrimp, ceviche, crab claws, Maryland crab cakes, and baked garlic clams—that it's as good for a light lunch or dinner as it is for a snack, even though the place is nominally a lounge. Cap'n Jack's is a terrific place to be, especially in late afternoon, as the sun streams through the narrow-slatted blinds and glints on the polished tables and the copper above the bar. And the house's special frozen strawberry margaritas—made with fresh fruit, strawberry tequila, and a couple of other potent ingredients—are as tasty as they are beautiful. They're served in big balloon-shaped goblets, with a slice of lime astraddle the rim: tart, fruity, and altogether delightful. Moderate. L, D, S.

Donald's Dairy Dip: This is a perfect spot for ice cream. Milk shakes and hot-fudge sundaes are only a couple of the many tasty creations here. Assorted hard ice cream flavors, chocolate and vanilla soft-serve ice cream, and frozen yogurt are available. Inexpensive. S.

Goofy's Grill: The shopping area's main fast-food spot offers both indoor and outdoor seating. It's a good place to grab a hot breakfast on the quick. Lunch and dinner options include hamburgers and french fries, plus soft drinks, thick milk shakes, and beer. Inexpensive. B, L, D, S.

Gourmet Pantry: Though it's technically a shop, this food-oriented establishment is positively brimming with sweet and savory possibilities. Among the delectables standing by for snackers and impromptu picnickers are specialty salads and sandwiches, heros sold by the inch, fresh baked cookies and desserts, chocolates, nuts, beer, wine, spirits, and gourmet coffees. Seating is available right outside and also along the waterfront. Inexpensive. B, L, D, S.

Minnie Mia's Italian Eatery: Pizza, pasta, and pasta salads are on the menu at this fast-food restaurant. Beer and soft drinks are also available. Inexpensive. L, D, S.

Rainforest Café: There's no mistaking the environmental orientation of this Amazon-emulating new eatery near Cap'n Jack's Oyster Bar. The incredible dining environs transport guests to a makeshift rain forest complete with banyan trees, tropical fish, gushing waterfalls, and a friendly population of hand-raised parrots. A talking tree offers a constant stream of ecological insights, and animal experts are on hand to field questions. Sophisticated special effects envelop guests in tropical storms, complete with lightning and thunder. Menu items include Planet Earth Pasta and Island Hopper Chicken. The eatery, part of a national chain, is equally environment-conscious behind the scenes: All paper and plastic goods are recycled after use. No net-caught fish are served. Leftover food is donated to pig farmers. And proceeds from the restaurant's wishing well are donated to selected environmental groups. A merchandise shop stocks logo clothing. Moderate to expensive. L, D, S.

Crossroads of Lake Buena Vista

WDW visitors also have several restaurants from which to choose at the Crossroads of Lake Buena Vista shopping center, adjacent to the Disney Village Hotel Plaza. These include Pebbles (the best bet here), T.G.I. Friday's, Red Lobster, McDonald's, Taco Bell, Jungle Jim's, Johnny Rockets, Pacino's, Chevy's Mexican Restaurant, and Pizzeria Uno.

Disney Village Hotel Plaza

At the seven Disney Village Hotel Plaza properties, you can dine in casual cafés, in an upscale dining room with a Tinker Bell's-eye view or Florida Keys ambience, or in an evocative restaurant with a Down Under or Sherlock Holmes theme. The larger properties offer more dining choices, of course, but even the smaller hotels have a family-style eatery on the premises. And if you go to a late movie or dance way past midnight at Pleasure Island, you can always count on a late-night bite at one of the Hotel Plaza's round-the-clock cafés.

BUENA VISTA PALACE: Arthur's 27 has an international menu, and boasts a dramatic view over Walt Disney World Village. Very expensive. D. The lively **Outback** (not part of the chain of the same name), with Australia-inspired decor and a multilevel waterfall, serves dinner with an accent on steaks and fish. Expensive. D. The garden-like **Watercress Café & Pastry Shop** offers full meals and snacks, as well as a Sunday character breakfast. The bakery section of the café serves pastries, sandwiches, and fruit, and is open 24 hours a day. Moderate. B, L, D, S.

COURTYARD BY MARRIOTT: Courtyard Café & Grille serves an eclectic menu ranging from salads and sandwiches to seafood. There is a breakfast buffet, but guests may also order from an à la carte menu. Moderate. B, L, D. **Village Deli** features muffins, sandwiches, Pizza Hut pizza, and TCBY yogurt. Inexpensive. B, L, D, S. The **2 Go** is a breakfast bar and take-out facility adjacent to an open seating area in the atrium lobby. Inexpensive. B.

DOUBLETREE GUEST SUITES: Streamers offers classic American dishes as well as shrimp tortellini and filet mignon. There is a breakfast buffet. Moderate. B, L, D, S. **Streamers Market** can provide snack items and groceries. Inexpensive. S.

GROSVENOR: This high-rise hotel's casual **Baskervilles** restaurant has a not-so-casual Sherlock Holmes theme. Prime-rib dinner buffets are popular. There is a Mystery Show here on Saturday night. A Wednesday character dinner supplements the character breakfasts, held Tuesday, Thursday, and Saturday. Moderate. B, L, D. **Crumpets** lobby café, open 24 hours, serves continental breakfast and lighter fare. Inexpensive. B, L, S.

HILTON: Finn's Grill specializes in fresh seafood and steaks, served in an old Key West atmosphere. Expensive. D. At the **Benihana** Japanese steak house, chefs put on a tableside show; there's also a sushi bar. Moderate to expensive. D. **County Fair** serves a full breakfast (characters make rounds on Sunday); salads, sandwiches, and pasta are available for lunch and dinner. Moderate. B, L, D. **County Fair Terrace** offers outdoor seating as well as continental breakfast and menu items from the adjacent County Fair restaurant. Inexpensive to moderate. B, L, S. The **Old-Fashioned Soda Shoppe** menu spans from ice cream to pizza. Inexpensive. L, D, S. **John T's Plantation Bar** serves light fare and cocktails. Inexpensive to moderate. L, S. **Rum Largo Pool Bar & Café** serves salads, sandwiches, and burgers alfresco. Inexpensive. L, D, S.

ROYAL PLAZA: Plaza Diner serves full-service, buffet, and family-style meals. Inexpensive to moderate. B, L, D, S. A deli provides yogurt, espresso, and take-out items.

TRAVELODGE: Traders has a buffet and à la carte breakfast; the à la carte dinner focuses on fresh seafood and steaks. Expensive. B, D. **Parakeet Café** offers pizza, baked goods, salads, and snacks. Inexpensive. B, L, D, S.

MEAL BY MEAL

When you're looking for something special in the way of a meal, and you're willing to go a bit out of your way to find it, the descriptions below should provide sufficient suggestions to sate your appetite. What follows are the highlights of WDW breakfasts, lunches, and dinners, as well as some suggestions for avoiding mealtime crowds at the eatery of your choice. This is a selective, not comprehensive, list; for complete information see the preceding listings under "Restaurants of WDW."

Breakfast

Most people opt for eggs and bacon or something similar at their own hotel. But those who decide to venture farther afield will be amazed at the choices available. For instance, the french toast served at the Polynesian resort's Coral Isle Café restaurant is made with thick slices of sourdough bread stuffed with bananas, deep fried, and then rolled in cinnamon and sugar—and is one of the best breakfast concoctions ever.

At most hotel breakfast spots, there are likely to be lines between 8 A.M. and 10 A.M., the morning rush hour. So allow plenty of time at these hours; eat earlier or later, or stop at a snack shop for something light to stave off hunger until it's possible to have a no-wait breakfast (or an early lunch). At many of the Walt Disney World resorts, it's also possible to order breakfast from room service the night before.

The Magic Kingdom has no shortage of options for quick morning meals. During busy seasons, however, even early birds might wait for a table. Most fast-food spots serve coffee and pastries from park opening until about 11 A.M. For a hearty breakfast, try Tony's Town Square or the Crystal Palace.

In Epcot, the Sunshine Season Food Fair in The Land offers bagels and cream cheese, as well as eggs and delicious pastries. Fountain View Espresso & Bakery next to Innoventions has a great selection of pastries and specialty coffees to enjoy in the morning.

At the Disney-MGM Studios, try a home-cooked breakfast at the Hollywood & Vine cafeteria or coffee and a croissant at the Starring Rolls Bakery.

Lunch

Breaking up a day in the theme parks with lunch at one of the resorts can provide the energy needed to keep you going until closing time. A few of the eating spots do get crowded around midday, but the Coral Isle Café at the Polynesian resort tends to be exceptionally peaceful.

Choice lunch spots in the Disney Village Marketplace are Minnie Mia's Italian Eatery and Cap'n Jack's Oyster Bar. At Pleasure Island, the Portobello Yacht Club's terrific individual pizzas hit the spot; ditto the barbecued ribs and chicken at the Fireworks Factory and the seafood chowder at Fulton's Crab House. Burgers, unique salads, pasta, and desserts are good at Planet Hollywood. Or for something lighter, try the frozen yogurt at D-Zertz.

If you can't tear yourself away from the Magic Kingdom for even an hour to go elsewhere for lunch, there's still no lack of selection. Burgers and french fries are for sale at practically every turn, but better yet are the salads, sandwiches, and pizza at Tony's Town Square restaurant; the sandwiches and seafood salads served (seasonally) at Columbia Harbour House in Liberty Square; the clam chowder and oysters served at the Liberty Tree Tavern, also in Liberty Square; the pizza at Plaza Pavilion Terrace Dining in Tomorrowland; and the salads at King Stefan's Banquet Hall in Cinderella Castle.

As at breakfast, crowds can be a problem; the three hours between 11 A.M. and 2 P.M. are the busiest. To avoid the rush, eat a light breakfast and a big early lunch—or have a late breakfast and a late lunch. If necessary, snatch a midmorning snack to tide you over until things get less hectic.

In Epcot, lunch is a prime opportunity to sample the full-service restaurants offering ethnic specialties. Linger over their culinary delights, out of the heat of the midday sun, while hordes of other guests are lining up for attractions. Try not to miss the pub grub at the Rose & Crown, the beef stew and the pastries at Chefs de France, and the *queso fundido* at Mexico's San Angel Inn restaurant. Germany's Biergarten has lively entertainment and a hearty buffet throughout the day. Among full-service eateries, the Garden Grill is special for its family-style rotisserie chicken and hickory-smoked steaks. In World Showcase, meat pies and Epcot's best salad (the fresh vegetable platter) may be found at the Rose & Crown Pub and Dining Room; stir-fried meats and vegetables are the prime fare in the Mitsukoshi restaurants; Moroccan sampler platters are offered at Marrakesh; Chinese specialties are served at the Nine Dragons restaurant; hearty German food is offered in Germany's Biergarten; and fairly authentic Mexican fare constitutes the menu in Mexico's San Angel Inn restaurant. An enormous buffet is served at Akershus in Norway. The delightful Au Petit Café on the World Showcase Promenade in France and Tempura Kiku in Japan are the only full-service restaurants that don't require priority seating. The most elaborate cooking is done at Italy's Alfredo's and at France's Chefs de France.

Ethnic fast food is available at Japan's Yakitori House, China's Lotus Blossom Café, Norway's Kringla Bakeri og Kafé, and Mexico's Cantina de San Angel. But for burgers and other standard fast-food fare, try the Electric Umbrella restaurant in Innoventions or Liberty Inn at The American Adventure. The Sunshine Season Food Fair in The Land offers a cornucopia of choices, from baked potatoes, soups, and salads to barbecued sandwiches and more—and is therefore an ideal place for a family that can't arrive at a consensus. The pizza quiche served at the Cheese Shoppe there is a favorite, and the chocolate chip cookies from the nearby bakery make a good dessert.

At the Disney-MGM Studios, consider the famous Cobb Salad at the Hollywood Brown Derby; a good home-cooked meal served by "Mom" at the 50's Prime Time Café; the character buffet at the Soundstage; salads, ribs,

grilled chicken, and fruit at the Hollywood & Vine cafeteria; chili, charbroiled chicken, and burgers at Backlot Express; salads and healthful fast food at the Commissary; or huge sandwiches and salads, and barbecued pork ribs at the Sci-Fi Dine-In Theater restaurant.

Dinner

There's an awesome choice, from the humblest snack center to Victoria & Albert's. Walt Disney World has never exactly been a bastion of haute cuisine, but that doesn't mean that dinner experiences are anything less than pleasant. In fact, new restaurants popping up all over the World are continually changing the face of the dining scene. Service is almost unfailingly good (slipping just slightly during the busiest seasons), and the best of Walt Disney World's dinners are sure to impress. The fact that the famed L.A. chef Wolfgang Puck plans to open a new restaurant here before year's end is a testament to the World's upwardly mobile culinary consciousness.

Factor this kitchen can-do into the unique only-at-WDW atmosphere, and it's obvious why we like to make time on each trip for a dinner-as-event (when the only point of the evening is to savor a relaxing meal). For a night on the World, good choices abound. Of course, we certainly have our favorites.

The WDW resorts are particularly good places to find an exceptional meal. At the top of the list for special occasions is Victoria & Albert's at the Grand Floridian, one of the more extravagant meals money can buy. Try the wine pairings with each course for an extra treat. Narcoosee's, also at the Grand Floridian, is another favorite. At the Polynesian, 'Ohana delivers a South Seas feast (grilled meats that keep coming until you say when). Ariel's at the Beach Club is a fine choice for an elegant seafood experience; the Yachtsman Steakhouse at the Yacht Club is equally good for a heartier meal. Combine either of these meals with a pre-dinner drink in the adjoining lounge, and you've got yourself some enchanted evening. Artist Point at the Wilderness Lodge is a culinary addition that keeps us coming back for more tastes of the Pacific Northwest (and that heavenly berry cobbler). California Grill at the Contemporary is another find, where the scents from the open kitchen and the panorama of the Magic Kingdom would warrant a visit even if the cuisine (paired with a wide selection of California wines) weren't excellent. Spoodles at the BoardWalk is a good place to try flavorful Mediterranean dishes, while the BoardWalk's Flying Fish Café sates with fresh seafood.

Elsewhere in the world, the Hollywood Brown Derby at the Disney-MGM Studios is the most elegant theme park meal around. And some of our old-time favorites, as well as notable newcomers, are at Pleasure Island.

Combine a meal at one of these restaurants with a night of dancing on the Island, and you just might not make it to the parks the next day. Portobello Yacht Club is an old standby that's worth getting to early (it's first-come seating, and lines develop quickly). We could recommend any number of the Italian specialties on the menu (and we've tried quite a few, including all of the desserts). Fulton's Crab House is the best bet on property for fresh seafood that seems to arrive hourly, served in a knockout setting (the former *Empress Lilly* riverboat has had quite a facelift). And we can't wait to pull up a chair at all the new restaurants that the Pleasure Island expansion will bring (see page 236).

Of course, most of the aforementioned suggestions require a baby-sitter, since not a kid in the world (especially not *this* World) would sit still through such a meal. Refer to the *Getting Ready to Go* chapter's "Traveling with Children" section if that's what you have in mind. On the other hand, there are plenty of great meals to be had with kids in tow. Refer to the box below for our best recommendations, many of which are suitable dinner options for kids and adults alike. Note that nearly all of the restaurants we list have been tested by the kids who help create *Birnbaum's Walt Disney World For Kids, By Kids*.

WDW restaurants outside the Magic Kingdom are busiest in the evening between 7 P.M. and 9 P.M. Those in the Magic Kingdom are busiest between 5 P.M. and 7 P.M.

During busy seasons, guests visiting the Magic Kingdom will do well to eat a late lunch and have dinner after 8 P.M. in order to catch the second, less crowded showing of SpectroMagic. Those traveling with young children should plan to eat their meals on the early side and take in the first show.

Best Bets for Family Fare

Children are welcome at every Walt Disney World restaurant, but the leisurely pace of service at some places can make kids fidget. Still, there are plenty of choices that are well suited to dining *en famille*. Restaurants at the resorts especially good for families are Chef Mickey's at the Contemporary resort, Whispering Canyon Café at the Wilderness Lodge, Boatwright's Dining Hall at Dixie Landings, and Bonfamille's Café at Port Orleans. The buffet-style clambake held at Cape May Café in the Beach Club resort is a hit with kids, (as is any other buffet-style meal where they can serve themselves). The food courts at the Caribbean Beach, Port Orleans, Dixie Landings, All-Star Sports, and All-Star Music resorts are other options for finicky eaters.

Most of the restaurants at the Magic Kingdom cater to kids, but Pecos Bill Café (for burgers and fries) and Tony's Town Square (for pizza) get particularly high marks. The character dinner at Liberty Tree Tavern offers a welcome compromise for kids and parents alike (the meal suits both tastes and characters keep kids entertained).

At Epcot, Pasta Piazza Ristorante and Liberty Inn are top picks for kids who love fast food. Garden Grill in The Land pavilion provides a meal that both kids and adults appreciate: Characters come to each table during the family-style meal, with a separate "bottomless skillet" menu for kids and adults (served all day long). Sunshine Season Food Fair, also in The Land, is a huge food court with myriad choices—a good option for family members with differing tastes.

At the Disney-MGM Studios, kids particularly enjoy the 50's Prime Time Café and the Sci-Fi Dine-In Theater; both have adult appeal as well. The new all-day character buffet at Soundstage is also a top choice. Other options include a quicker meal at Hollywood & Vine, Commissary, or Backlot Express.

One of the best places to dine out with kids is Planet Hollywood at Pleasure Island. The movie memorabilia hanging from the ceiling and the great food are always a hit. Also try the new Rainforest Café at the Disney Village Marketplace, a themed restaurant with environmental (and kid) appeal.

Dinner Shows

The fact that the Disney organization is the king of family entertainment is nowhere more strongly apparent than amid the whooping and hollering troupe of singers and dancers who race toward the stage at Fort Wilderness resort's Pioneer Hall. As guests plow through barbecued ribs, fried chicken, corn-on-the-cob, and strawberry shortcake, these enthusiastic performers sing, dance, and joke up a storm. It's all in the course of an evening at the Hoop-Dee-Doo Musical Revue, presented nightly at 5 P.M., 7:15 P.M., and 9:30 P.M. Cost is $36 per adult and $18 for children (3 through 11).

Mickey's Tropical Luau, presented daily at 4:30 P.M. at the Polynesian resort, is a Polynesian show geared toward the younger set. Disney characters, dressed in traditional costumes, dance alongside the Polynesian performers. A full dinner complete with dessert is served. Cost is $30 for adults and $14 for children.

The Polynesian Luau at the Polynesian resort, presented nightly at 6:45 P.M. and 9:30 P.M., also has its moments. The performers' dancing is some of the most authentic this side of Hawaii. Many of the WDW dancers have studied at the well-respected Polynesian Cultural Center in Hawaii. A full Polynesian-style meal, including honey roasted chicken, spareribs, and a tropical ice cream sundae is served. Cost is $34 for adults and $18 for children.

The Biergarten at Epcot's Germany pavilion entertains diners with a musical trio during lunch and throughout the evening with intermittent shows featuring traditional German musicians, yodelers, and dancers. A hefty buffet is served. Lunch is $9.95 for adults, $3.99 for children; dinner is $14.75 for adults, $3.99 for children.

Plan to arrive 15 minutes or so before starting time, and allow enough time for transportation and parking. (Note that prices, which do not include tax or gratuity, are subject to change.)

Reservations for all these shows (priority seating suggested for Biergarten) can be made by calling WDW-DINE (939-3463). Reservations are required well in advance and are generally hard to come by. Groups of eight or more should call 939-7707.

Dining With Disney Characters

At some sites, food takes second place to Mickey Mouse, Donald Duck, Minnie Mouse, Goofy, and the rest of the Disney gang, who take turns making special appearances at these especially delightful affairs. Options abound, as the characters host meals throughout the day all over the World. Unless otherwise noted, character meals below are offered daily, and priority seating arrangements can generally be made up to 60 days in advance by calling WDW-DINE (939-3463). We strongly suggest making these arrangements prior to your visit, especially during busy seasons. Also, be sure to arrive at least 15 minutes before your seating time. Walk-ins are possible, but highly unlikely for any except the Swan's first-come, first-served character breakfast (held Saturday at the hotel's Garden Grove Café). Bottomless buffets and all-you-can-eat family-style dining are the rule, particularly for breakfast, but specific offerings vary from place to place. Finally, as you make note of the following menu of character affairs—organized by meal—keep in mind that the lineup is subject to change.

Character Restaurants: Meals with the Disney characters have become so popular that there are now several restaurants dedicated to providing them all day long. Winnie the Pooh entertains during the buffet-style meals at Crystal Palace in the Magic Kingdom. Epcot has its family-style Garden Grill restaurant, with homey fare and Chip 'n' Dale appearances. In the Disney-MGM Studios, characters from the most recent animated films preside over buffet-style meals at the Soundstage restaurant. At the Contemporary resort, Chef Mickey and friends cook up a buffet-style breakfast and dinner (at Chef Mickey's restaurant, of course). Breakfast costs $13.95 for adults and $7.95 for children ages 3 to 11. For other meals, cost ranges from $14.95 to $19.95 for adults, and from $7.95 to $9.95 for children.

Breakfast: Fulton's Crab House (between Pleasure Island and the Disney Village Marketplace) is the site of the biggest character shindig around, hosted by Captain Mickey and his crew. There are two seatings every morning. Guests may also have breakfast with characters at 1900 Park Fare in the Grand Floridian resort (Mary Poppins drops in); at Cape May Café in the Beach Club resort (Admiral Goofy runs the show); at Olivia's Café at Old Key West (Winnie the Pooh and friends hold court on Wednesday and Sunday); at Artist Point in the Wilderness Lodge (Pocahontas, John Smith, and Meeko host a rustic affair); and at 'Ohana in the Polynesian resort (where Minnie Menehune carries the South Seas theme). Character breakfasts are also served forth in the theme parks. Among the most popular is the "Once Upon A Time" breakfast at King Stefan's in the Magic Kingdom. Prices are $14.95 for adults, $7.95 for children 3 to 11.

Sunday brunch: Disney favorites host brunch at Harry's Safari Bar & Grille in the Dolphin resort (call 934-4858 in advance for reservations). Prices are about $15.50 for adults and $9.25 for children ages 3 to 11.

Dinners: The Liberty Tree Tavern in the Magic Kingdom hosts a character supper. Character dinners are also held at 1900 Park Fare in the Grand Floridian resort. Gullivers's Grill at Garden Grove in the Swan holds a character dinner each Monday, Thursday, and Friday (on certain nights The Lion King characters pay a visit); call 934-1609 to make reservations. Prices are about $19.50 for adults, $9.95 for children ages 3 to 11; the à la carte meal at the Swan may run higher.

Scoops, Sundaes, & Soft Serve

MAGIC KINGDOM: Plaza Ice Cream Parlor and the Plaza restaurant on Main Street.
DISNEY-MGM STUDIOS: 50's Prime Time Café (hot fudge, caramel, marshmallow, or the works); Sci-Fi Dine-In Theater.
DISNEY VILLAGE MARKETPLACE: Donald's Dairy Dip.
PLEASURE ISLAND: Tollhouse Cookie Sundae at the Fireworks Factory.

SOFT SERVE

HOTELS: Captain Cook's Snack and Ice Cream Company at the Polynesian resort; Food and Fun Center at the Contemporary resort; Gasparilla Grill & Games at the Grand Floridian resort; Trail's End Buffet at Fort Wilderness campground; Colonel's Cotton Mill at Dixie Landings; and Cinnamon Bay Bakery at Caribbean Beach resort.
MAGIC KINGDOM: Mrs. Potts' Cupboard; Enchanted Grove; Aloha Isle; Sunshine Tree Terrace; and Aunt Polly's Landing.
EPCOT: Refreshment Port; Refreshment Outpost; and Electric Umbrella.
DISNEY-MGM STUDIOS: Studio Catering Co.; Min & Bill's Dockside Diner.
DISNEY VILLAGE MARKETPLACE: Donald's Dairy Dip.

BY THE SCOOP

HOTELS: Beaches & Cream Soda Shop at the Yacht Club and Beach Club; Seashore Sweets' at the BoardWalk; Dolphin Fountain at the Dolphin; Splash Grill at the Swan; Sassagoula Floatworks & Food Factory at Port Orleans; Colonel's Cotton Mill at Dixie Landings; and Cinnamon Bay Bakery at the Caribbean Beach.
MAGIC KINGDOM: Liberty Tree Tavern, Tony's Town Square restaurant, Plaza Ice Cream Parlor, Plaza restaurant, and King Stefan's Banquet Hall.
EPCOT: The ice cream stand at Sunshine Season Food Fair in The Land.
DISNEY-MGM STUDIOS: Dinosaur Gertie's.
DISNEY VILLAGE MARKETPLACE: Donald's Dairy Dip.

ASSORTED SUNDAES

HOTELS: Narcoossee's at the Grand Floridian (custard, berries, seven scoops of ice cream, whipped cream, and amaretto); Dolphin Fountain in the Dolphin resort (super sundaes with homemade ice cream); and Coral Isle Café at the Polynesian.

FROZEN YOGURT

HOTELS: Intermission food court at the All-Star Music resort; End Zone food court at the All-Star Sports resort; Splash Grill at the Swan resort.
MAGIC KINGDOM: Auntie Gravity's Galactic Goodies; Sunshine Tree Terrace.
EPCOT: Pure & Simple; Sunshine Season Food Fair; Refreshment Port; and Refreshment Outpost.
DISNEY VILLAGE MARKETPLACE: Donald's Dairy Dip.
PLEASURE ISLAND: D-Zertz.

INTERNATIONAL TREATS

EPCOT: Specialties at L'Originale Alfredo di Roma Ristorante include Italian concoctions like spumoni and tortoni. For a Mexican treat, visit San Angel Inn for *helado con cajeta* (vanilla ice cream with caramel topping).

All About Priority Seating

Priority seating has replaced reservations at almost all WDW full-service restaurants. Disney initiated the new policy to provide the assurance of a reservation without the delays caused by no-shows and late-comers. Ideally, the system ensures that guests are not left waiting if a table is available. Here's how it works: You call ahead to request a priority seating time; then you arrive at the assigned time, check in at the podium, and receive the next available table that can accommodate your party. The priority seating system works very much like reservations, so you will always be seated before any walk-ins.

We strongly recommend making advance arrangements and arriving about 15 minutes early. Priority seating times can be secured up to 60 days ahead by calling WDW-DINE (939-3463). The number of tables available in advance varies. If you are unable to book a table ahead of time, try to make same-day arrangements (for details about how to do this in the theme parks, see the adjacent listing).

While priority seating is the prevalent policy at WDW restaurants, there are several exceptions in which tables may be booked solely via traditional reservations. Most notably, reservations are necessary for certain dinner shows—the Hoop-Dee-Doo Musical Revue, Mickey's Tropical Luau, and the Polynesian Luau; they can be made up to two years ahead through WDW-DINE (939-3463). If you can't get a table for an early performance, try for a later one (usually less heavily booked). Also falling outside the priority seating domain are Fireworks Factory at Pleasure Island (reservations suggested; call 934-8989); Harry's Safari Bar & Grille, Sum Chows, and Juan & Only's at the Dolphin resort (call 934-4858); and Palio and Garden Grove Café at the Swan resort (call 934-1609).

A concise guide to WDW restaurants that offer priority seating is provided below. For at-a-glance advice about the necessity of priority seating arrangements (or reservations) at specific restaurants, consult the chart on pages 22 to 23 of the *Getting Ready to Go* chapter.

Note: Because the dining scene at Walt Disney World is tremendously dynamic and procedures have changed more than a few times over the years, we advise calling WDW-DINE (939-3463) to confirm current policies.

MAGIC KINGDOM: Priority seating is suggested at Tony's Town Square, Plaza, Crystal Palace, and Liberty Tree Tavern; necessary at King Stefan's. For same-day seating, go to the individual restaurant or City Hall.

EPCOT: Advance priority seating arrangements are strongly recommended for nearly all full-service restaurants at Epcot, particularly for dinner. However, on the day of your visit, it is possible to book lunch or dinner tables via WorldKey Information System screens. Look for the screens at Guest Relations (where hosts and hostesses can also assist), on the east side of the pathway between Future World and World Showcase, and in Germany. Same-day lunch tables can also be booked in person at the chosen restaurant. Never bypass an eatery for which you have a sudden appetite; occasionally, you can walk right in. **Note:** Priority seating is not available for Au Petit Café or Tempura Kiku.

DISNEY-MGM STUDIOS: Priority seating is suggested for 50's Prime Time Café, Hollywood Brown Derby, Mama Melrose's Ristorante Italiano, Sci-Fi Dine-In Theater, and Soundstage. Go to Hollywood Junction or the chosen restaurant for same-day seating.

PLEASURE ISLAND: Because of the restaurant's popularity, priority seating is suggested at Fulton's Crab House.

WDW RESORTS: Priority seating is suggested for full-service resort restaurants, with a few exceptions (where it is necessary or offered only for dinner); a complete lineup follows. *Beach Club:* Ariel's, Cape May Café. *Contemporary:* the California Grill, Chef Mickey's, Concourse Steakhouse. *Dixie Landings:* Boatwright's Dining Hall. *Grand Floridian:* Flagler's, Grand Floridian Café, Narcoossee's, 1900 Park Fare, Victoria & Albert's. *Old Key West:* Olivia's Café. *Polynesian:* Coral Isle Café, 'Ohana. *Port Orleans:* Bonfamille's Café. *Wilderness Lodge:* Artist Point, Whispering Canyon Café. *Yacht Club:* Yacht Club Galley, Yachtsman Steakhouse.

DINNER FOR TWO

LOUNGES OF WDW

No one ever said the Magic Kingdom's no-liquor policy means that everyone in the World is a teetotaler. Actually, some of WDW's tastiest offerings are liquid (and decidedly alcoholic), and some of its most entertaining places are its bars and lounges.

Hours vary depending on the locale, but generally watering holes at Epcot and the Disney-MGM Studios shut their doors at park closing. Pool bars at the resorts generally keep daytime pool hours. Last call at lounges in the resorts is anywhere from 10 P.M. to midnight. Spots in the Disney Village Marketplace stay open until the shops close, usually 11 P.M. Pleasure Island clubs keep things going until 2 A.M. Note that soft drinks, juices, and specialty drinks sans alcohol are available at all establishments.

ALL-STAR SPORTS & ALL-STAR MUSIC

Singing Spirits: Beer, wine, and mixed drinks are served by the pool.

Team Spirits: Specialty drinks, wines, and beer are available at this poolside spot.

BEACH CLUB

Hurricane Hanna's Grill: This refreshment spot, located near Stormalong Bay between the Yacht Club and the Beach Club, offers specialty drinks and beer as well as a selection of fast-food items.

Martha's Vineyard: A light and airy atmosphere prevails at this cozy retreat right next to Ariel's. Wines from a real Martha's Vineyard winery, as well as selections from California, Long Island, and European vineyards, are on the extensive list. While wine is the house specialty, this is a full bar. Hors d'oeuvres and desserts are served as well.

Rip Tide: This lobby bar features California wines, wine coolers, and frosty drinks that are consistent with the hotel's beachside theme.

BOARDWALK

Atlantic Dance: This classic dance hall showcases a ten-piece band, hors d'oeuvres, a full bar, and champagne.

Belle Vue Room: Snacks and a full bar accompany old-time tunes from antique radios in this lobby cocktail lounge.

Big River Grille & Brewing Works: Pub grub complements the fresh ales made in this working brew pub.

ESPN Club: The ultimate sports bar provides live radio and television broadcasts along with a menu of ballpark favorites.

Jellyrolls: Dueling pianos and lively sing-alongs are the draw at this unique club, serving snacks and drinks.

Leaping Horse Libations: The pool bar at Luna Park offers fast food and cocktails in a carnival setting.

BONNET CREEK GOLF CLUB

Sand Trap Bar & Grill: Appetizers and sandwiches supplement the myriad libations offered at this fully stocked bar.

CARIBBEAN BEACH

Banana Cabana: All types of drinks and a variety of fast-food items are available at this poolside bar.

Captain's Tavern: Tropical drinks, beer, wine, and cocktails are served at this restaurant lounge in Old Port Royale. Chicken, crab legs, and specialty items from the restaurant are available during dinner hours.

CONTEMPORARY

California Grill Lounge: Prime 15th-story digs eye-level to the Magic Kingdom fireworks. California wines, all manner of other drinks, and appetizers are offered in this atmospheric spot adjoining the California Grill.

Outer Rim: This lounge overlooking Bay Lake serves beer (including a special microbrew called Monorail Ale), wine, cocktails, appetizers and desserts.

Sand Bar: Beer, frozen drinks, and fast-food items are offered poolside. Seasonal.

DISNEY-MGM STUDIOS

Catwalk Bar: Above the Soundstage restaurant sits this 90-seat full-service cocktail lounge designed to resemble a movie prop storage area. Appetizers, specialty drinks, beer, and wine are served.

Tune-In Lounge: A sitcom living room setting, with couches, chairs, and fold-up TV dinner–tray tables, characterizes this lounge adjacent to the 50's Prime Time Café. Waiters in V-neck sweaters play the roles of sitcom "Dads," and old television sets play scenes from beloved sitcoms. Appetizers, mixed drinks, beer, and wine are served.

DISNEY'S OLD KEY WEST

Gurgling Suitcase: This pocket-size lounge on the Turtle Krawl boardwalk serves an assortment of Key West specialties along with traditional cocktails, beer, and wine.

Turtle Shack: Refreshments at this poolside spot include beer, specialty drinks, and fast-food items.

DISNEY VILLAGE MARKETPLACE

Cap'n Jack's Oyster Bar: Agleam with copper and right on the water, this bar's specialty is its delicious strawberry margaritas. The nibbles of baked garlic clams, crab claws, Maryland crab cakes, shrimp, and seafood marinara are great for a snack, but also substantial enough for a light lunch or dinner.

DIXIE LANDINGS

Cotton Co-Op: Situated in a room designed as a cotton exchange, this lounge features specialty drinks as well as some light hors d'oeuvres. There is entertainment here five nights a week.

Muddy Rivers: The poolside bar serves beer, specialty concoctions, and selected fast-food items.

DOLPHIN

Cabana Bar & Grill: Beer, frozen drinks, and fast-food selections are the main offerings at this poolside spot.

Copa Banana: Tabletops designed to resemble slices of fruit, and giant pineapples and palm trees offer a fitting backdrop for tropical libations. There is a large-screen TV, and deejay music and karaoke are featured in the evenings.

Harry's Safari Bar: Join the peripatetic "Harry" for a drink and maybe a story or two in this restaurant bar. Appetizers, a house microbrew, and unique specialty drinks are featured.

Only's Bar & Jail: Rare tequilas, an array of margaritas, sangria, and beers from every region of Mexico join Mexican-style appetizers on the menu here. The small yet atmospheric lounge, adjacent to Juan & Only's restaurant, is decorated to resemble a jail.

EPCOT

All restaurants, including some of the counter-service establishments, offer alcoholic beverages on their menus. Restaurants such as the San Angel Inn have a small lounge at which patrons may wait for tables. Then there are a few other places that specialize in spirituous liquid refreshments:

Matsu No Ma: In addition to exotic sake-based specialty drinks, this Japan pavilion establishment offers a fine panoramic view over the whole of Epcot—including the World Showcase Lagoon with Spaceship Earth as a backdrop—one of the best vistas of the property available. Japanese beer, green tea, and sushi are also served.

Rose & Crown Pub: This watering hole—a veritable symphony of polished woods, brass, and etched glass—adjoins the Rose & Crown Dining Room in the United Kingdom pavilion. British, Irish, and Scottish beers are available, along with a score of specialty drinks and appetizing snacks imported from the other side of the Atlantic. An entertaining pianist plays and sings just about any request well into the evening.

Sommerfest: Just outside the Biergarten restaurant in Germany, there's a small shaded terrace where soft pretzels, bratwurst, Black Forest cake, steins of Beck's beer, and German wine are available.

FORT WILDERNESS

Crockett's Tavern serves cocktails, specialty drinks, beer, wine, appetizers, and full meals. For a change of pace, take a blue-flagged watercraft to the Contemporary resort.

GRAND FLORIDIAN

Garden View: A view of the lushly landscaped pool and garden area makes this lounge a pleasant place to meet for a drink or dessert. Afternoon tea is also served here.

Mizner's: Named after the eccentric architect who defined much of the flavor of southeastern Florida's Gold Coast, this handsome retreat is on the second floor of the main building. Ports, brandies, and appetizers are featured.

Summerhouse: This bar between the pool and the beach stands by with beer, frozen drinks, and fast-food items.

Narcoossee's: An unusual manner of service in this lagoonside bar-within-a-restaurant allows guests to choose from a mug, a half-yard, or a yard of beer. And they mean a yard.

PLEASURE ISLAND

All the clubs have bars that serve specialty drinks (with and without alcohol), beer, wine, and cocktails. The **Stone Crab** lounge at Fulton's Crab House is notable for its waterside seating, fresh Bloody Marys, and raw bar (including stone crab, of course). The Fireworks Factory and Portobello Yacht Club also have pleasant lounges.

POLYNESIAN

Barefoot Bar: This oasis adjoining the swimming pool lagoon serves beer, frozen tropical drinks, and fast-food items. Seasonal.

Tambu: This bar adjoining 'Ohana restaurant offers Polynesian-style appetizers and specialty drinks in a tropical setting.

PORT ORLEANS

Mardi Grogs: Beer, specialty drinks, popcorn, hot dogs, and hot pretzels are among the offerings at this poolside spot.

Scat Cat's Club: Traditional offerings from the bar join New Orleans specialties and hors d'oeuvres at this comfy little lounge. There is musical entertainment here five nights a week.

SWAN

Lobby Court : The winding corridors of the hotel lobby have comfortable couches and chairs, punctuated by pianos where able musicians often perform. Specialty coffees, desserts, and wines by the glass are featured. A special menu with ports, cognacs, and cigars is offered seasonally.

Splash Grill: Beer, frozen drinks, and fast-food items are served at this poolside café.

THE VILLAS AT THE DISNEY INSTITUTE

Seasons Lounge, a comfortable and inviting setting adjoining the Seasons Dining Room, serves specialty drinks, cocktails, beer, and wine. Entertainment is sometimes offered here in the evening.

WILDERNESS LODGE

Territory: Located between Artist Point and the Whispering Canyon Café, this homage to the Old West is a popular pre-dinner retreat. Appetizers, microbrew beer, specialty coffees, and espresso are among the featured offerings. Lunch is also served.

Trout Pass: This poolside bar serves beer, frozen drinks, and fast-food selections.

YACHT CLUB

Ale and Compass: The lobby watering hole proffers a specialty drink menu complete with coffee and ale.

Crew's Cup: Styled after a New England waterfront pub, this lounge has a masculine feel to it. It's right next door to the Yachtsman Steakhouse, has almost 40 beers on hand, and is a choice spot for a drink before dinner.

Hurricane Hanna's Grill: Fast-food items, beer, and frozen drinks are offered at this poolside refreshment station, located near Stormalong Bay between the Yacht Club and the Beach Club.

More Special Nighttime Fun

The Magic Kingdom takes on additional dazzle after dark. SpectroMagic is a procession so spectacular that it alone is worth the trip to Walt Disney World. In honor of the World's 25th anniversary, it is scheduled nightly (along with Fantasy in the Sky fireworks) through the end of 1997. Epcot is particularly lovely at night, when the lights sparkle on the lagoon, Spaceship Earth is all aglow, and IllumiNations 25 lights up the sky. And the Disney-MGM Studios is home to Walt Disney World's terrific Sorcery in the Sky fireworks.

But there are always a dozen or so other special happenings and events going on after dark throughout WDW. Call 824-4321 to find out what's in store during your visit.

CAMPFIRE PROGRAM: This event at Fort Wilderness, held nightly near Meadow Trading Post at the center of the campground, features a fun sing-along, Disney movies, and cartoons. Open only to Walt Disney World resort guests.

ELECTRICAL WATER PAGEANT: Best seen from the nearest beach on Bay Lake, this sparkling show is composed of a 1,000-foot-long string of illuminated floating creatures. Guest Services or City Hall can tell you when and where it can be seen—usually it's visible at 9 P.M. from the Polynesian, 9:20 P.M. from the Grand Floridian, 9:35 P.M. from the Wilderness Lodge, 9:45 P.M. from Fort Wilderness, and 10:05 P.M. from the Contemporary resort.

FANTASY IN THE SKY: Since the Magic Kingdom is open late, it features nightly fireworks. The show lasts five to ten minutes, and outshines displays many times its length.

ILLUMINATIONS 25: This nightly show is an anniversary tribute featuring new music and spectacular effects above and beyond its usual arresting display of laser lights, fireworks, and dancing water fountains. It can be seen from any point on Epcot's World Showcase Promenade, usually at closing time. Check at Guest Relations for the exact time.

SORCERY IN THE SKY: Every night during busy seasons, this ten-minute pyrotechnical production outshines the stars over the Chinese Theatre at the Disney-MGM Studios. It features music from the silver screen and narration by Vincent Price, and stands out as one of Disney's best fireworks shows.

SPECTROMAGIC: The Magic Kingdom's biggest extravaganza, this parade makes its way down Main Street every night throughout 1997, twice each night during busy seasons. The advanced technology incorporates holograms, special lighting techniques, and a state-of-the-art sound system.

TENNIS: Courts at the Contemporary, Grand Floridian, Fort Wilderness, Yacht Club and Beach Club, Old Key West, Board-Walk, and The Villas at the Disney Institute are usually open until 8 P.M. Those at the Dolphin and Swan are open 24 hours a day.

INDEX

Dining at

10% discount off dinner at

- Liberty Inn (at The American Adventure, World Showcase)
- Electric Umbrella (Innoventions Plaza, Future World)

50% off Accommodations at

Vacation Club Resorts

- Buy two nights accommodations at Disney's Vero Beach Resort and get the third night at 50% off.
- Buy three nights accommodations at Disney's Hilton Head Island Resort and get the fourth night at 50% off.

Dining at the

10% discount off dinner at

- Hollywood & Vine
- Commissary

Dining at the

10% discount off dinner at

- Tony's Town Square
- Crystal Palace

28% OFF

Your guide to all that's new, classic, and magic at Disney.

CALL 800-333-8734 and receive 8 issues (2 years) for $16.95—it's like getting 2 issues FREE!

One Car Class Upgrade

We appreciate your business. And invite you to present this certificate at a National rental counter for a one car class upgrade on a Compact through Full-size 2-door up to a Full-size 4-door car. Valid at participating National locations in the U.S.

Reservations recommended. Contact your travel agent or National today at 800-CAR-RENT®.

Subject to terms and conditions on reverse side.

PC# 011502-1

Valid Through: December 31, 1997

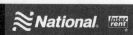

YOU'VE GOT PLACES TO GO. WE'VE GOT THE KEYS.™

©1996 National Car Rental System, Inc.

One Free Bucket of Golf Range Balls (per person) at

- Palm/Magnolia Golf Courses
- Bonnet Creek Golf Club
- Lake Buena Vista Club

Free Half Hour of Tennis Ball Machine Use at

Disney's Racquet Club
(Contemporary Resort)
Purchase one half hour and receive the second half hour free.

Coupon valid:
Disney's Vero Beach Resort: 1/1/97–3/27/97;
4/6/97–5/22/97; 5/26/97–8/28/97; 9/1/97–11/25/97;
11/30/97–12/2/97; 12/7/97–12/26/97.
Disney's Hilton Head Island Resort: 1/1/97–5/22/97;
5/26/97–6/26/97; 8/17/97–12/31/97

Subject to limited availability.
Advance reservations required.
Not available with any other offer.
Photocopies are not accepted.
Be sure to mention this offer
when making reservations.

Expires 12/31/97

Not good for early seating specials
or with any special offer.

Excluding tax and gratuity.

Expires 12/31/97

RETAILER: We will pay you the face value plus 8¢ if all terms are met.

TERMS: RETAILER MAIL TO: Eveready Battery Company, CMS Department 39800, 1 Fawcett Drive, Del Rio, Texas 78840. Good only in U.S.A. on specified Product(s). Limit 1 coupon (any kind) per purchase. Coupon void if a reproduction, transferred before store redemption, prohibited, licensed, taxed or restricted by law, not presented by you or agency authorized by us; you do not show on request Product invoices for all redeemed coupons. Consumer pays sales tax. Cash Value 1/20¢

Excluding 10/7/97–10/20/97
(WDW/Oldsmobile Golf Classic period)
Offer good with paid greens fee.

Expires 12/31/97

Photocopies not accepted.
Subject to availability.

Expires 12/31/97

Not good for early seating specials or
with any other offer.

Excluding tax and gratuity.

Expires 12/31/97

Not good for early seating specials or
with any special offer.

Excluding tax and gratuity.

Expires 12/31/97

Disney Magazine is currently published quarterly
(Spring, Summer, Fall, and Winter)
by Disney Magazine Publishing, Inc.,
publishers of *FamilyFun*, *FamilyPC*,
Disney Adventures, and *Discover* Magazine.

Not valid in combination with any other
discounts. May not be exchanged for cash.
This coupon may not be used for commercial
purpose or resale.

Expires 12/31/97

Terms and Conditions.

Valid for car classes indicated on front at participating National locations in the U.S. (Not Valid in Manhattan, NY.) • Subject to availability and blackout dates. • Local rental, rate parameters and minimum rental day requirements apply. • Cannot be used in multiples or with any other certificate, special discount, or promotion. • Standard rental qualifications apply. • Minimum rental age at most locations is 25.

Where applicable: Optional Loss Damage Waiver, up to $15.99 per day; a per mile charge in excess of mileage allowance; taxes; surcharges; additional charges if car is not returned within prescribed rental period; drop charge and additional driver fee; optional refueling charge; optional insurance benefits are extra.

Rental Agent Instructions:

1. Rental Screen 1:
   • Key Promo Coup #011502-1
2. Rental Screen 3:
   • Charge rate for one car class lower than class of car actually rented.
   • Key applicable rate code in (RATECODE) field.
3. Write RA# and rental date below.
4. Retain certificate at rental. Send certificate to Headquarters, Attn: Travel Industry Billing.

RA#_____ Rental Date_____